Yo, Miss

A GRAPHIC LOOK AT HIGH SCHOOL

LISA WILDE

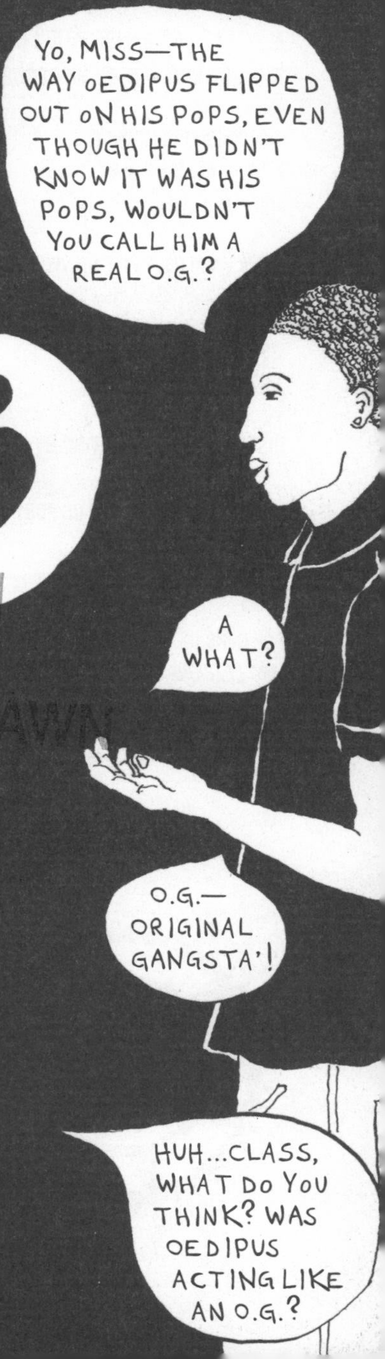
YO, MISS—THE WAY OEDIPUS FLIPPED OUT ON HIS POPS, EVEN THOUGH HE DIDN'T KNOW IT WAS HIS POPS, WOULDN'T YOU CALL HIM A REAL O.G.?
A WHAT?
O.G.— ORIGINAL GANGSTA'!
HUH...CLASS, WHAT DO YOU THINK? WAS OEDIPUS ACTING LIKE AN O.G.?

MICROCOSM PUBLISHING
PORTLAND, OR

YO, MISS
A GRAPHIC LOOK AT HIGH SCHOOL

LISA WILDE

FIRST PRINTING, MARCH 17, 2015

ALL TEXT AND ILLUSTRATION IS © LISA WILDE, 2013, 2014, 2015
THIS EDITION IS © BY MICROCOSM PUBLISHING, 2015

MICROCOSM PUBLISHING
2752 N. WILLIAMS AVE
PORTLAND, OR 97227

FOR A CATALOG, WRITE OR VISIT
MICROCOSMPUBLISHING.COM

ISBN 978-1-62106-219-6
THIS IS MICROCOSM #185

DISTRIBUTED WORLDWIDE BY LEGATO / PERSEUS BOOKS GROUP AND IN THE UK BY TURNAROUND.

THIS BOOK WAS PRINTED ON POST-CONSUMER PAPER BY UNION WORKERS IN THE U.S.

WWW.YOMISS.COM

PORTIONS OF THIS WORK PREVIOUSLY APPEARED IN *SHOW & TELL: A COLLECTION OF COMICS ABOUT TEACHING AND LEARNING, THE WRITING DISORDER: A LITERARY JOURNAL, KUGELMASS: A JOURNAL OF LITERARY HUMOR, ALIVE WITH VIGOR: SURVIVING YOUR ADVENTUROUS LIFESTYLE,* AND EDWIZE.ORG.

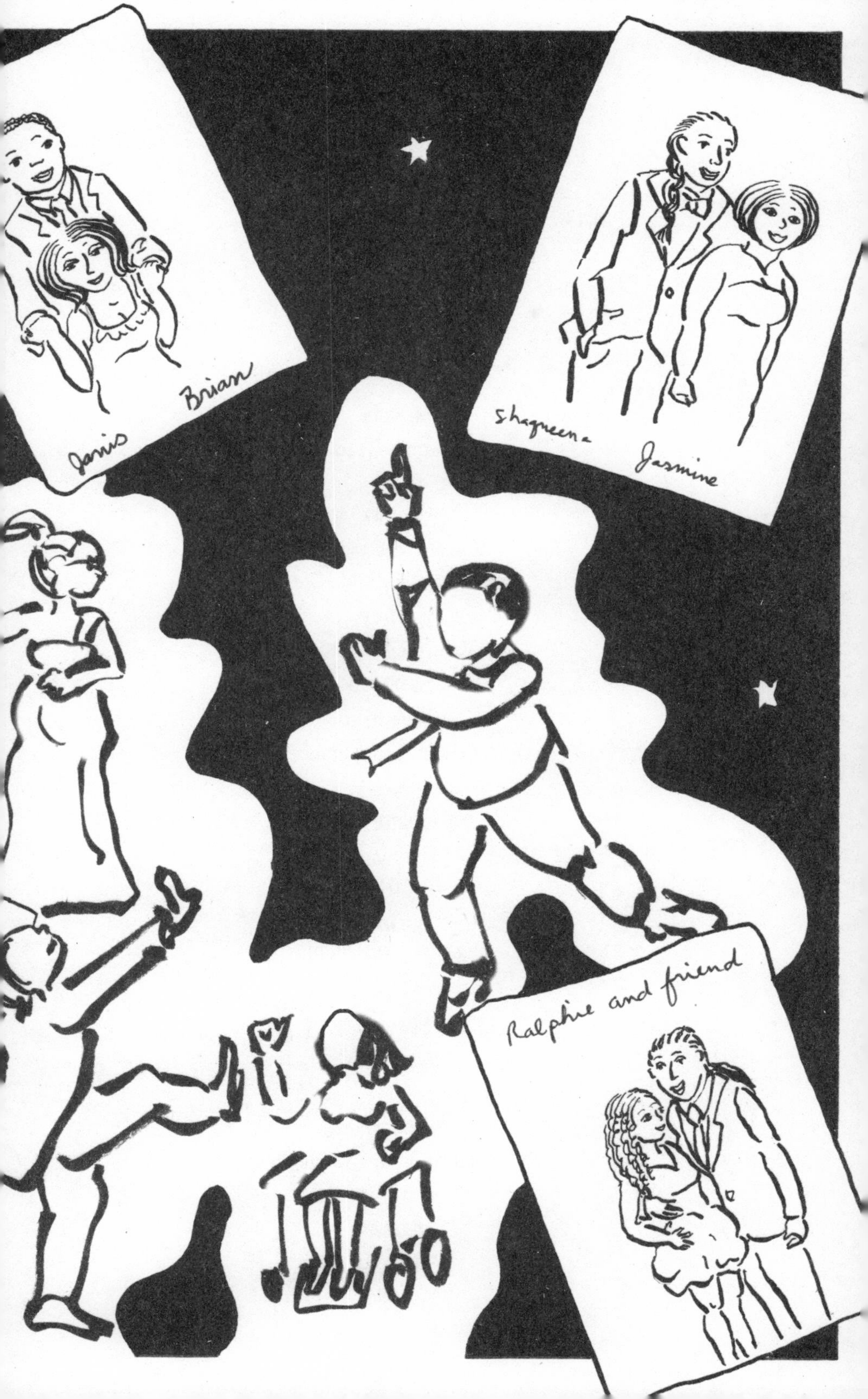
Brian
Janis
Shaqueena
Jasmine
Ralphie and friend

CONTENTS

Dedicated with love
to all Wildcat students—
past, present and future;
and to the memory of
Andrew Green.
Your commanding presence
and joyous laugh
are missed every day,
but your legacy continues
through the lives
of each student
who had the privilege
to know you.

NOTE TO THE READER

Yo, Miss: A Graphic Look at High School is based on my experience teaching at John V. Lindsay Wildcat Academy, a second chance public high school in New York City. The students in the book are fictionalized composites. However, I have tried to be as true as possible to my understanding of who these kids are. That said, ultimately everything expressed is my opinion and not those of the staff, students or administration of J.V. L. Wildcat Academy.

"THE RIGHT ROCK"

KAYCEE ECKHARDT

author of Katrina's Sandcastles: *New Hope From the Ruins of New Orleans Schools*
Louisiana Charter Teacher of the Year 2009

Teaching is not a series of days, or a litany of plans, or even a series of to do's and checklists and tasks, though sometimes it feels that way. Teaching is about the moments of gigantic success and cringing failure, the children who live them, and the teacher who is educator, mentor, friend, and conscience along the way. In these pages, all three are brought to life with humor, calamity, and love.

Teaching is to watch the moments of days bump and scramble together at the bottom of a stream, nicking and smoothing each other, rushing far too quickly. Despite the speed, some stand out. Moments shimmer and wink brilliantly against the moving waves. Others crumble when touched, anticlimactic and intangible. And others should most appropriately float downstream and from memory, more clotted pond scum than pebble, unwelcome.

In *Yo, Miss*, Wilde takes our hand and draws us deep into this rushing current. Through her candid drawings, she provides us a glimpse into a world where nothing, and yet everything, is possible, and the smallest of successes are celebrated as defiant victories over the status quo.

Wilde points out the right rocks to be turning over, uses her pen to suggest the places we may have missed. Look closely. More than storyline, these sketches reveal the details of moments shared in a time that moves by too quickly: a last chance high school for students society has largely written off. Here, horses prance between the spokes of wheelchairs, and a single snowflake prevents disaster. These metaphors should not be lost on us. The brutal realities of her environment and students do not escape scrutiny, yet she is able to draw them with love and the hope of redemption.

Teaching—and Wilde's book—is also about children, both their imperfections and their triumphs. In each of Wilde's students there is reason to both cringe and smile. I find myself laughing at Danny, and aching for Janis, and being furious with Natalie; I shamelessy cheated, flipping to the end to scan the drawings: who will, in the end, make it across the coveted stage, diploma crunched in one proud fist?

In New Orleans, my students forged the same waters and fought the same demons. It is achingly clear that a system has failed these children; they have not failed themselves. Their determination, joy, and hope despite the chaos of their surroundings reminds me of what is valuable, and what is worth sacrifice. They are not damaged, and they are not causalities of a status quo gone wrong. They deserve, and fight for, lives worth living, and here their humanity becomes startlingly clear. In this book are brilliant examples of both the deficiencies of our system, and those who work for its lasting change.

Finally, teaching is about choosing to be a teacher. Poignantly, Wilde uses her pen to expose both the imperfection and genius of her daily work. She exposes herself as flawed and desperately seeking answers. She struggles constantly for balance in the current, in ways to connect her family and art and the kids who need her most.

Rather than whitewashing her challenges and ambiguity, she bares both for us courageously, never failing to wade forward. In her drawings, she smirks and scowls, hair standing on end, a fiercely committed look behind the squints and glasses. I get the sense that Wilde will never give up. She wades in the proverbial waters and yet rises above it, superimposed.

Daily, teachers and students make decisions that have great significance. As an educator, I know too well the exhaustion of these choices, knowing their portents, and owning the mistakes to be made. Wilde doesn't turn away from this reality by making these decisions look easy. But she does make all of it—the struggle, frustration, joy, panic, late nights, graphic organizers, fistfights and torpedoes—look *worthwhile.*

It is the close examination of all of this being worthwhile that is at the heart of this adventure. Whether a failed fishing trip or the comic-agony of Danny—again—Wilde makes these students stand out in stark contrast to their often-bleak realities and situations, lines drawn towards futures rather than dead ends.

Wilde lays bare each moment with compassion, and infuses us, in the end, with the sense that "at some point in life, the world's beauty becomes enough." The stream, for Wilde and her students, keeps rumbling along, its lives and circumstances intersect and bounce apart. And while her students' trajectory is not for the faint of heart, there is more gold here than glitter. These children do, indeed, shine.

CHAPTER ONE

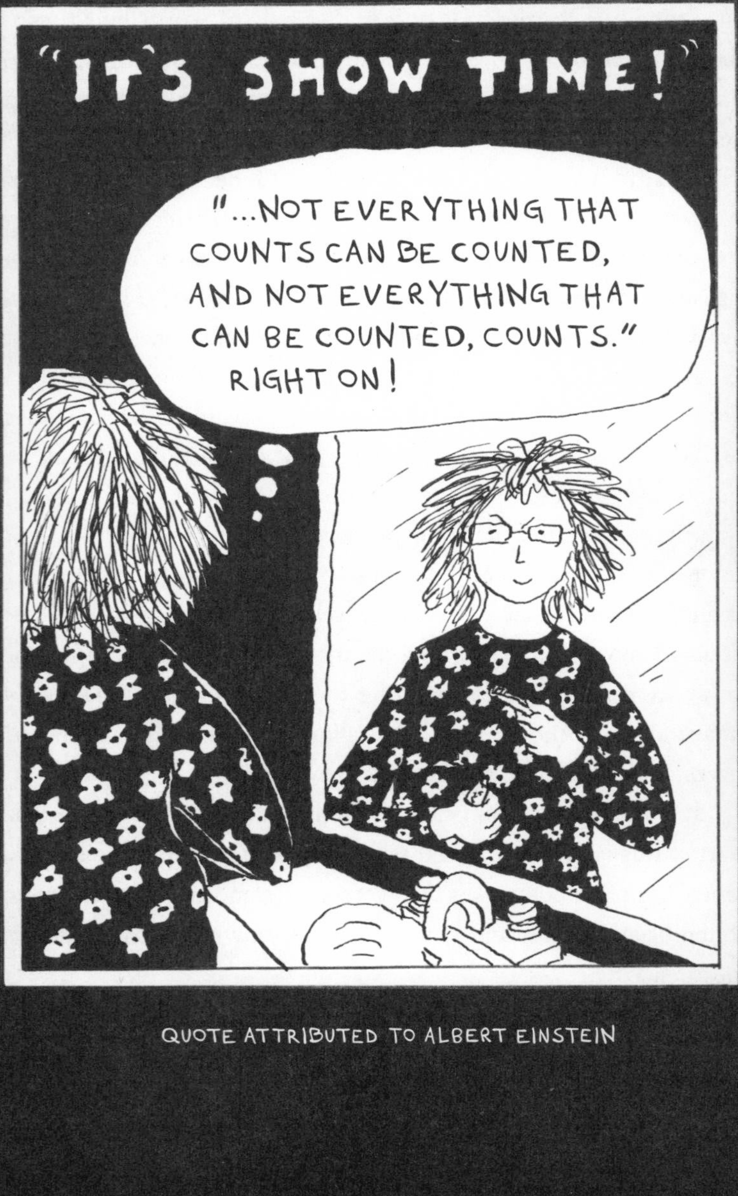
"IT'S SHOW TIME!"
"...NOT EVERYTHING THAT COUNTS CAN BE COUNTED, AND NOT EVERYTHING THAT CAN BE COUNTED, COUNTS." RIGHT ON!

QUOTE ATTRIBUTED TO ALBERT EINSTEIN

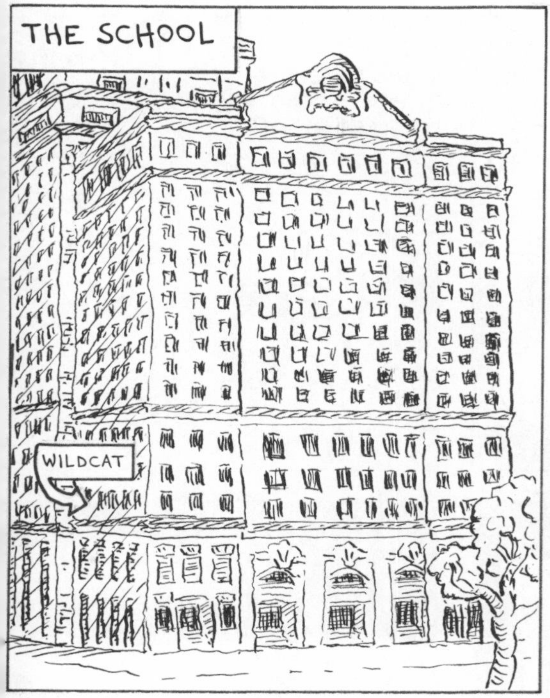
THE SCHOOL
WILDCAT

I TEACH AT JOHN V. LINDSAY WILDCAT ACADEMY, A PUBLIC CHARTER HIGH SCHOOL IN LOWER MANHATTAN, N.Y.C.

IT'S A SECOND CHANCE SCHOOL. THAT MEANS MANY OF OUR STUDENTS HAVE DROPPED OUT, BEEN KICKED OUT, OR FLUNKED OUT OF OTHER HIGH SCHOOLS

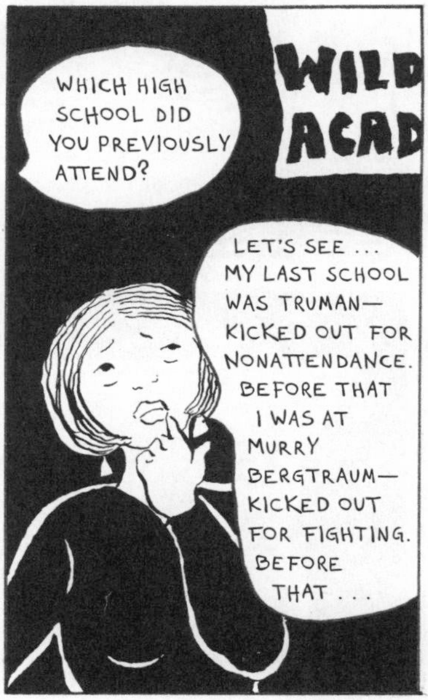
WHICH HIGH SCHOOL DID YOU PREVIOUSLY ATTEND?
LET'S SEE ... MY LAST SCHOOL WAS TRUMAN— KICKED OUT FOR NONATTENDANCE. BEFORE THAT I WAS AT MURRY BERGTRAUM— KICKED OUT FOR FIGHTING. BEFORE THAT ...

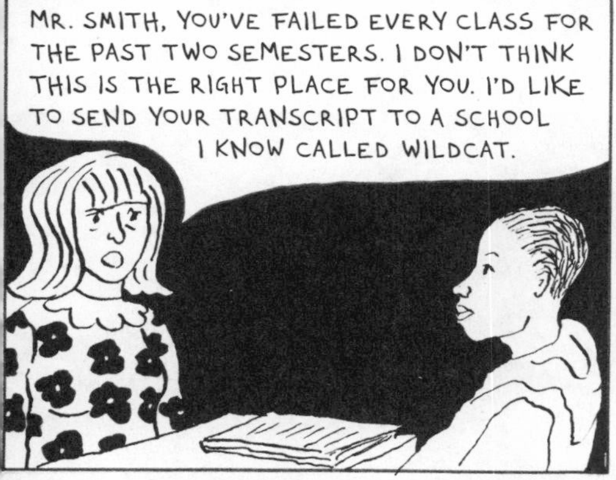
MR. SMITH, YOU'VE FAILED EVERY CLASS FOR THE PAST TWO SEMESTERS. I DON'T THINK THIS IS THE RIGHT PLACE FOR YOU. I'D LIKE TO SEND YOUR TRANSCRIPT TO A SCHOOL I KNOW CALLED WILDCAT.

SOME STUDENTS ARE EVEN "REFERRED" BY THEIR PREVIOUS SCHOOL.

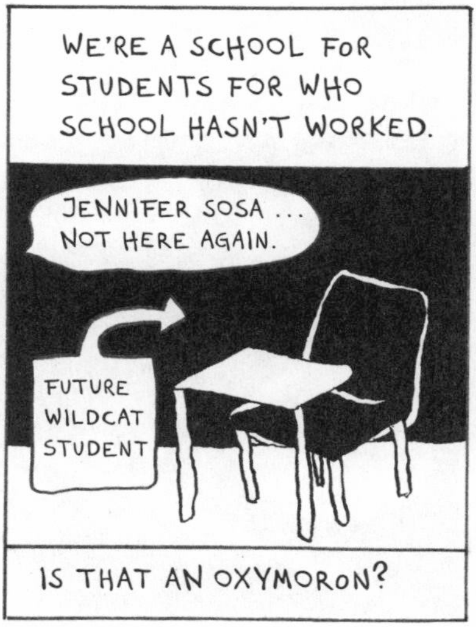
WE'RE A SCHOOL FOR STUDENTS FOR WHO SCHOOL HASN'T WORKED.
JENNIFER SOSA ... NOT HERE AGAIN.
FUTURE WILDCAT STUDENT
IS THAT AN OXYMORON?

THE NIGHT BEFORE THE FIRST DAY OF SCHOOL

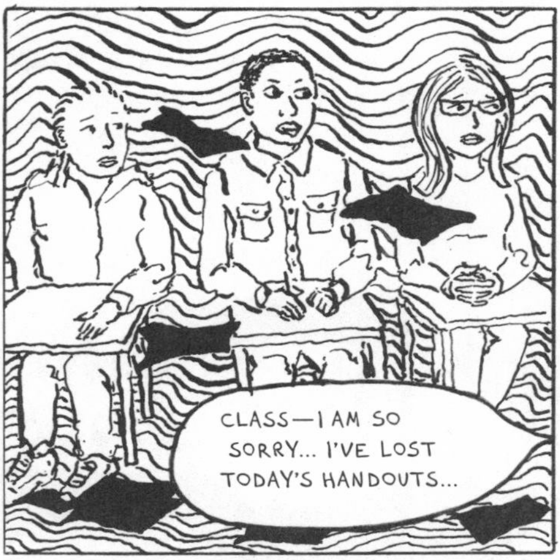
CLASS—I AM SO SORRY... I'VE LOST TODAY'S HANDOUTS...

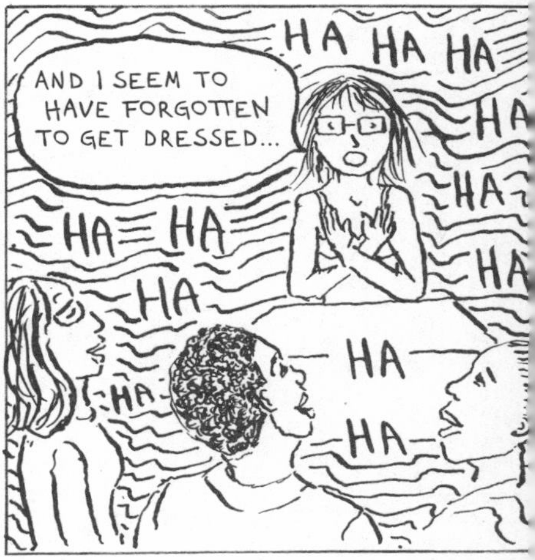
AND I SEEM TO HAVE FORGOTTEN TO GET DRESSED...
HA HA HA
HA
HA
HA
HA HA
HA
HA
HA
HA

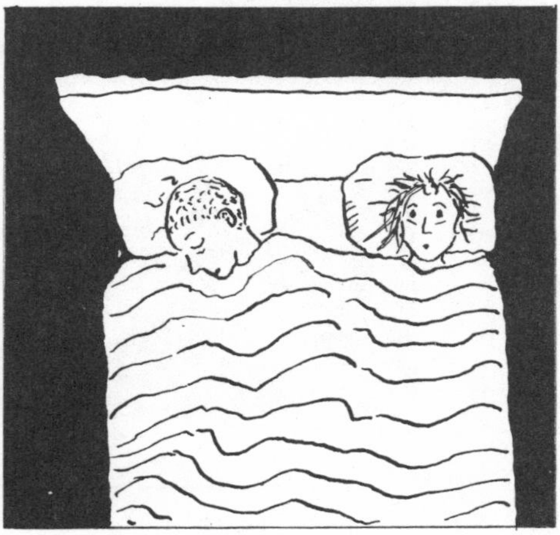

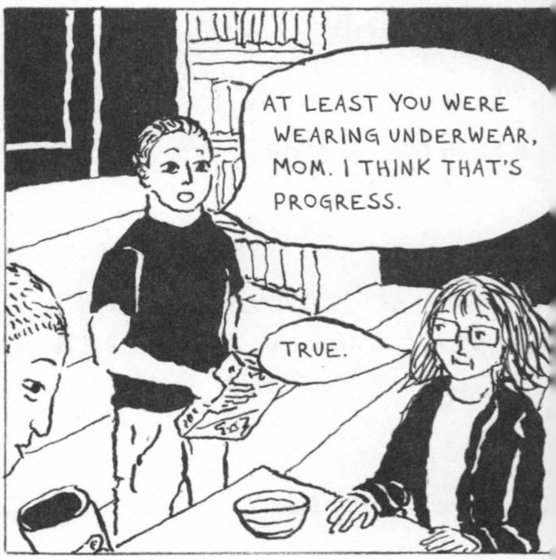
AT LEAST YOU WERE WEARING UNDERWEAR, MOM. I THINK THAT'S PROGRESS.
TRUE.

NIGHTMARES ASIDE, THE FIRST DAY OF SCHOOL IS ALWAYS A PLEASURE

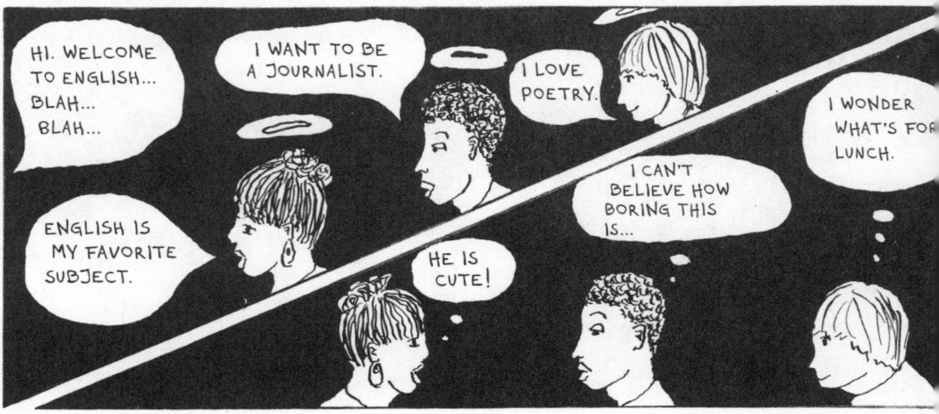
HI. WELCOME TO ENGLISH... BLAH... BLAH...
I WANT TO BE A JOURNALIST.
I LOVE POETRY.
ENGLISH IS MY FAVORITE SUBJECT.
HE IS CUTE!
I CAN'T BELIEVE HOW BORING THIS IS...
I WONDER WHAT'S FOR LUNCH.

REALITY HASN'T YET COMPLICATED THIS ROUND OF SCHOOL. ON THAT FIRST DAY, THERE IS NOTHING THAT WILL STOP THESE KIDS FROM ACHIEVING THE DREAM OF GRADUATION.

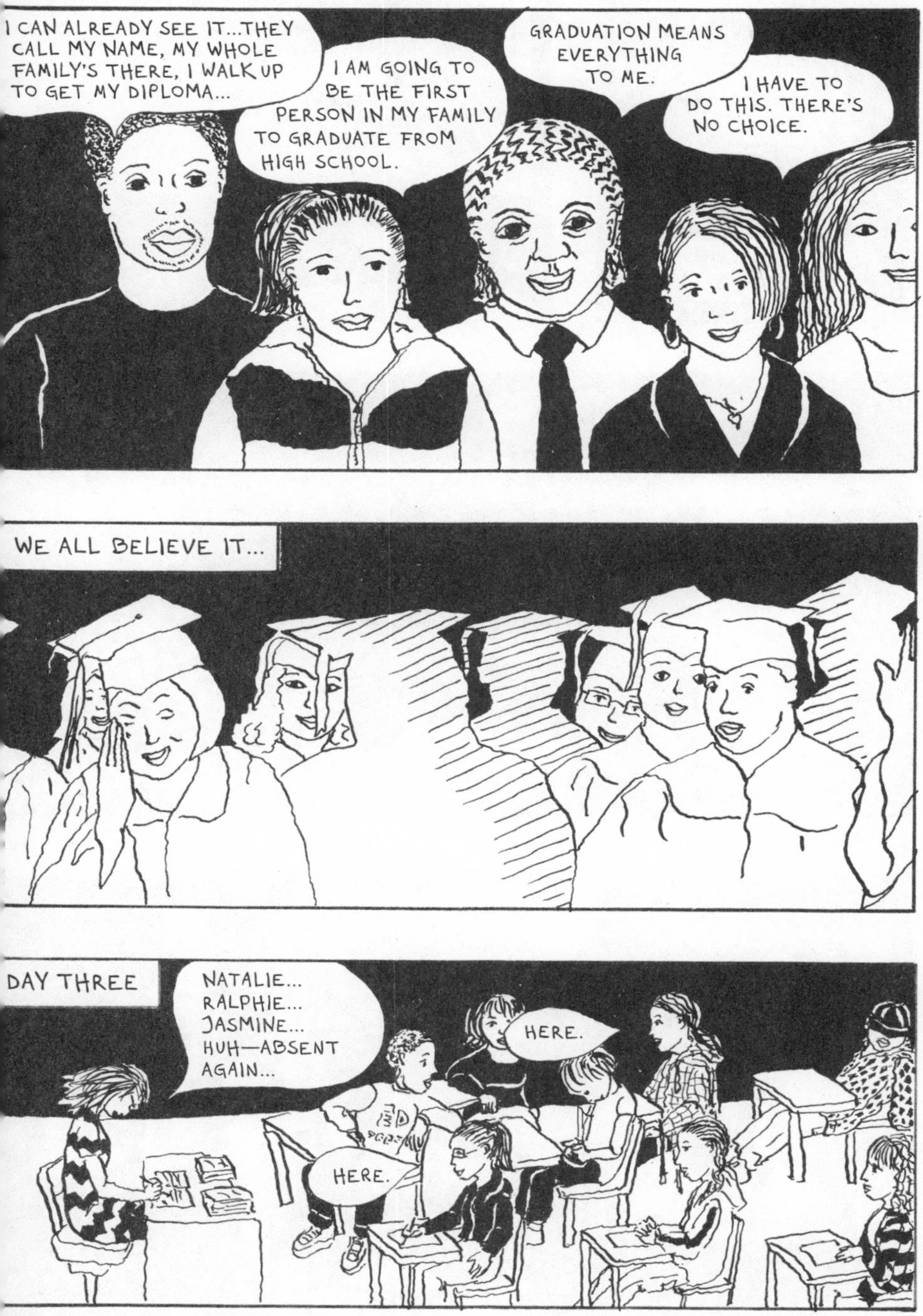

I CAN ALREADY SEE IT...THEY CALL MY NAME, MY WHOLE FAMILY'S THERE, I WALK UP TO GET MY DIPLOMA...
I AM GOING TO BE THE FIRST PERSON IN MY FAMILY TO GRADUATE FROM HIGH SCHOOL.
GRADUATION MEANS EVERYTHING TO ME.
I HAVE TO DO THIS. THERE'S NO CHOICE.
WE ALL BELIEVE IT...
DAY THREE
NATALIE... RALPHIE... JASMINE... HUH—ABSENT AGAIN...
HERE.
HERE.

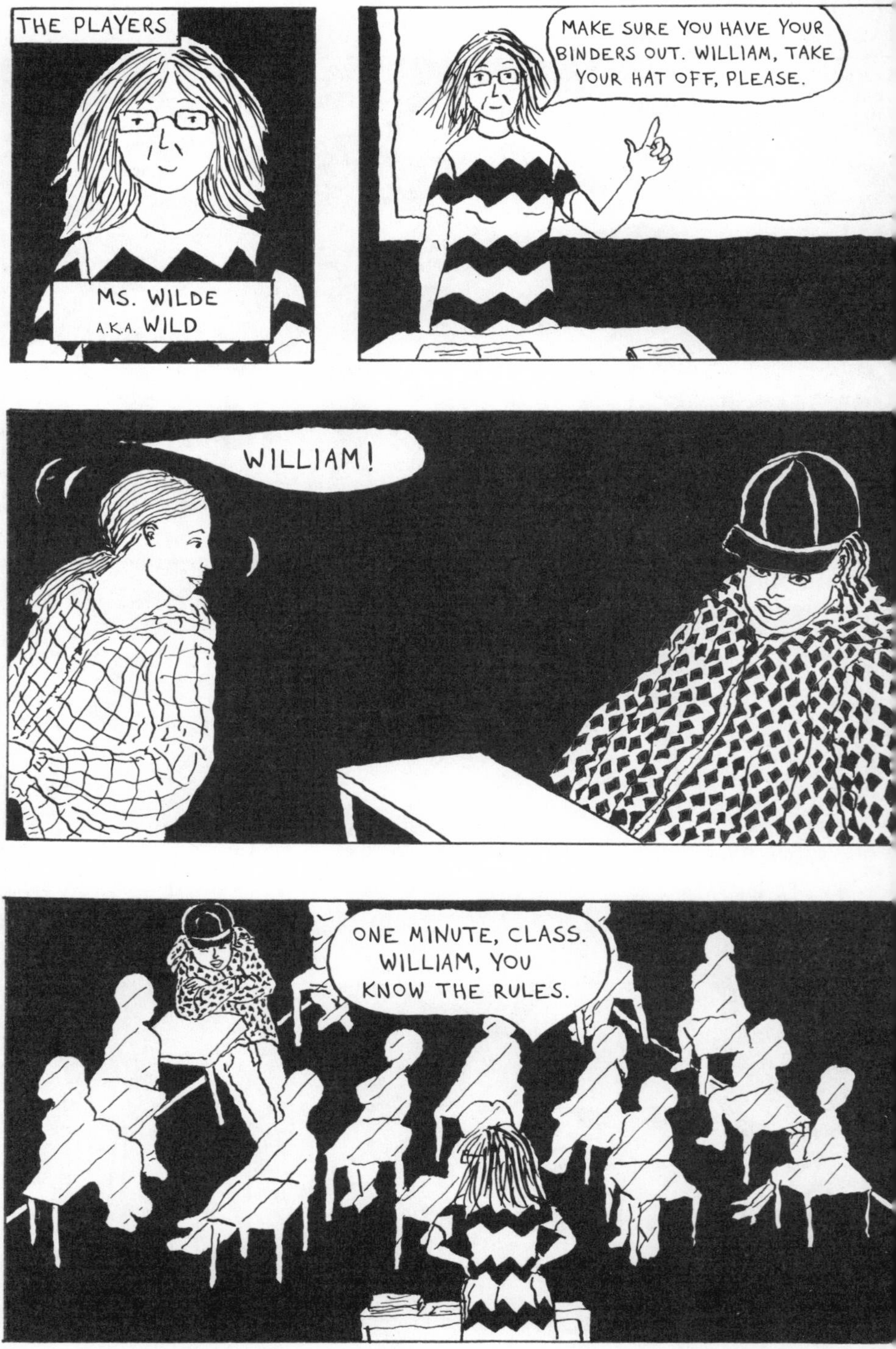
THE PLAYERS
MS. WILDE
A.K.A. WILD
MAKE SURE YOU HAVE YOUR BINDERS OUT. WILLIAM, TAKE YOUR HAT OFF, PLEASE.
WILLIAM!
ONE MINUTE, CLASS. WILLIAM, YOU KNOW THE RULES.

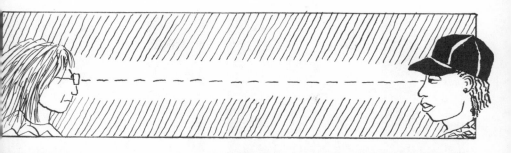

ALL RIGHT, WE CAN'T SPEND ANY MORE TIME ON THIS. LET ME GET MR. GREEN.

"Ode to Broken Thin

THANKS, WILLIAM. SO YESTERDAY WE TALKED ABOUT THE SETTING OF...

"Ode to Broken Thin

Set

THE PLAYERS

WILLIAM
A.K.A. STREETZ

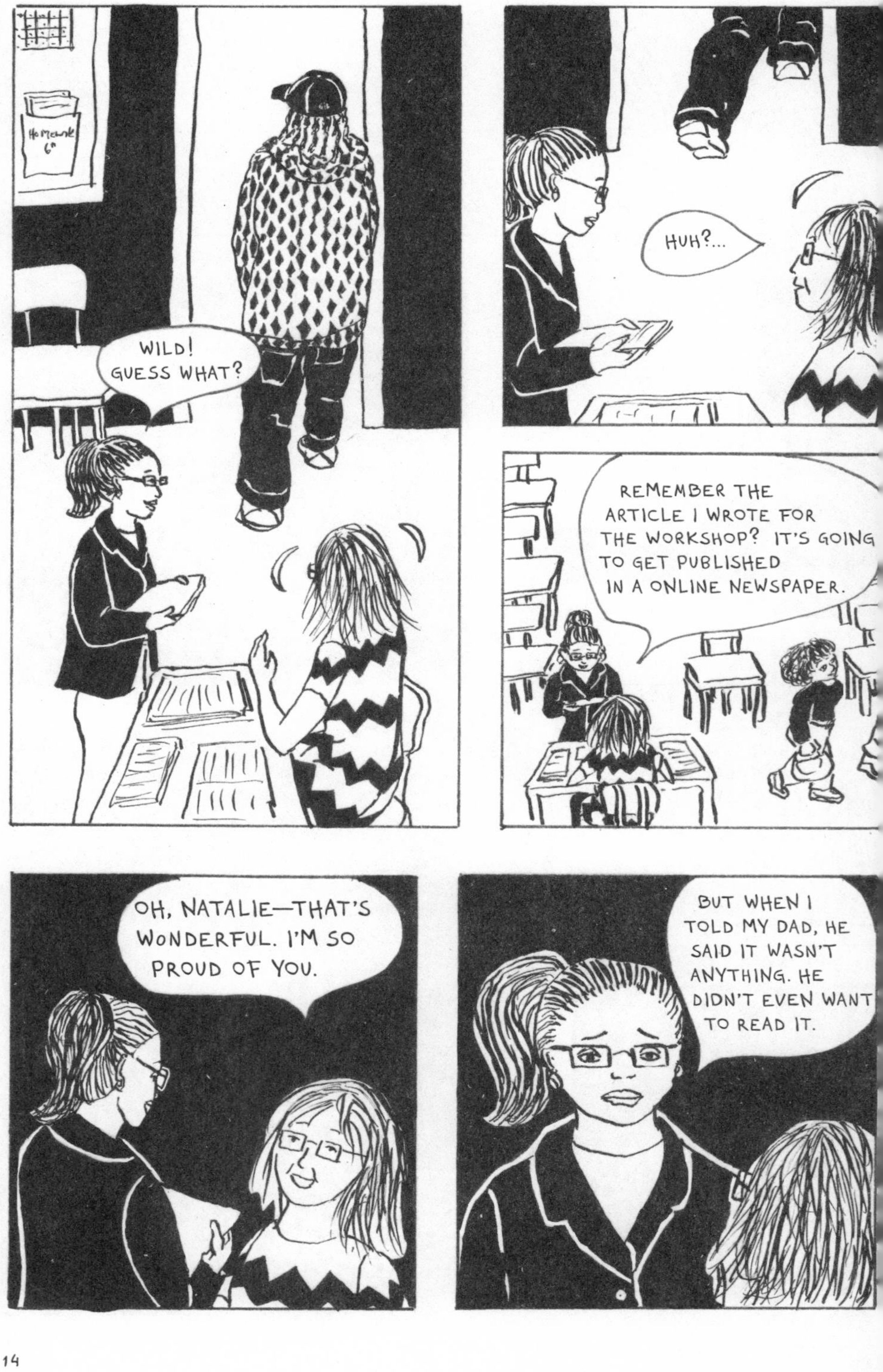
WILD! GUESS WHAT?
HUH?...
REMEMBER THE ARTICLE I WROTE FOR THE WORKSHOP? IT'S GOING TO GET PUBLISHED IN A ONLINE NEWSPAPER.
OH, NATALIE—THAT'S WONDERFUL. I'M SO PROUD OF YOU.
BUT WHEN I TOLD MY DAD, HE SAID IT WASN'T ANYTHING. HE DIDN'T EVEN WANT TO READ IT.

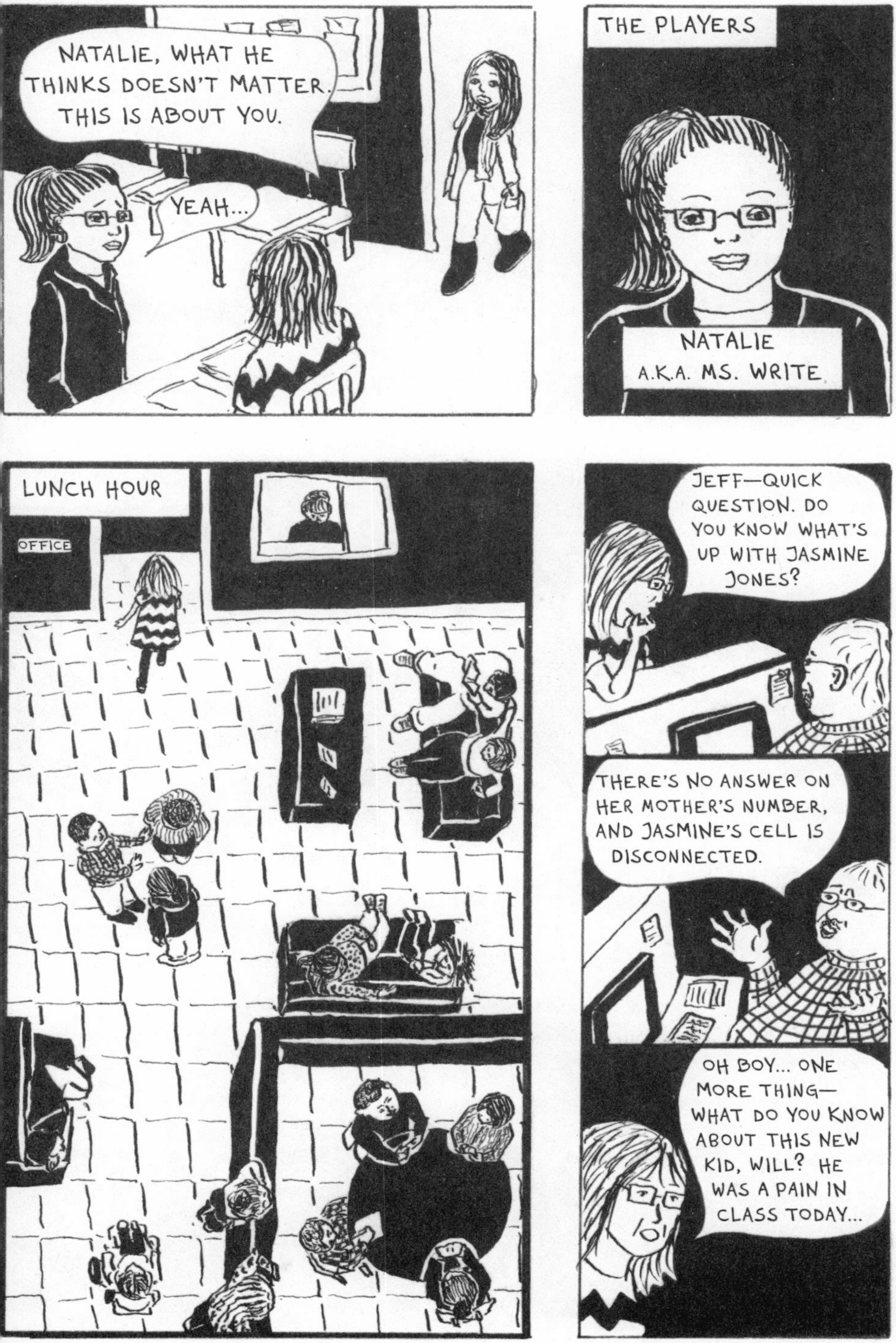
NATALIE, WHAT HE THINKS DOESN'T MATTER. THIS IS ABOUT YOU.
YEAH...
THE PLAYERS
NATALIE
A.K.A. MS. WRITE
LUNCH HOUR
OFFICE
JEFF—QUICK QUESTION. DO YOU KNOW WHAT'S UP WITH JASMINE JONES?
THERE'S NO ANSWER ON HER MOTHER'S NUMBER, AND JASMINE'S CELL IS DISCONNECTED.
OH BOY... ONE MORE THING— WHAT DO YOU KNOW ABOUT THIS NEW KID, WILL? HE WAS A PAIN IN CLASS TODAY...

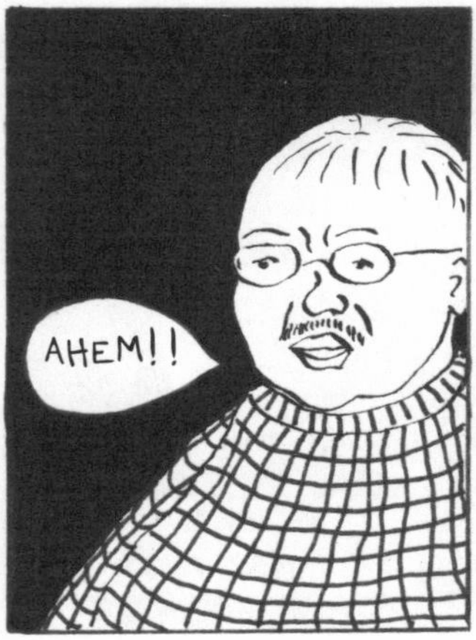
AHEM!!

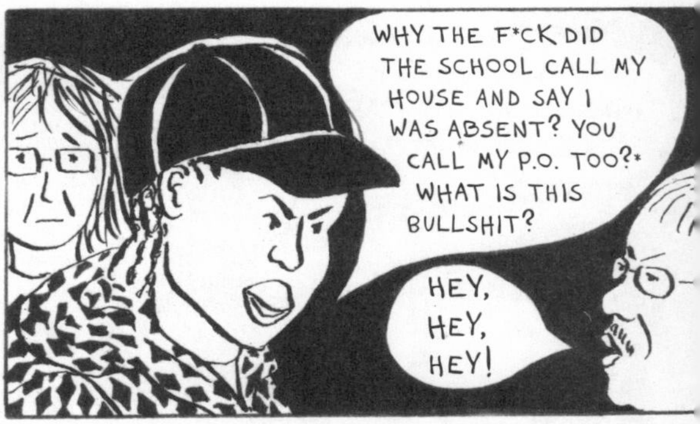
WHY THE F*CK DID THE SCHOOL CALL MY HOUSE AND SAY I WAS ABSENT? YOU CALL MY P.O. TOO?* WHAT IS THIS BULLSHIT?
HEY, HEY, HEY!

*PROBATION OFFICER. ACCORDING TO THE TERMS OF WILL'S PROBATION, HE MUST ATTEND SCHOOL.

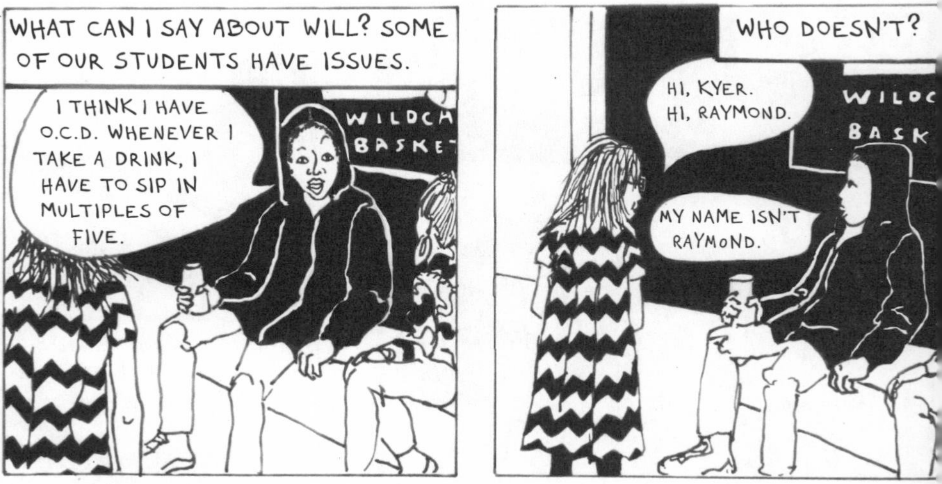
WHAT CAN I SAY ABOUT WILL? SOME OF OUR STUDENTS HAVE ISSUES.
I THINK I HAVE O.C.D. WHENEVER I TAKE A DRINK, I HAVE TO SIP IN MULTIPLES OF FIVE.
WILDCH
BASKET
WHO DOESN'T?
HI, KYER.
HI, RAYMOND.
MY NAME ISN'T RAYMOND.
WILDC
BASK

SPEAKING OF ISSUES,

I TEACH FIVE CLASSES A DAY, WITH THREE DIFFERENT CURRICULA.

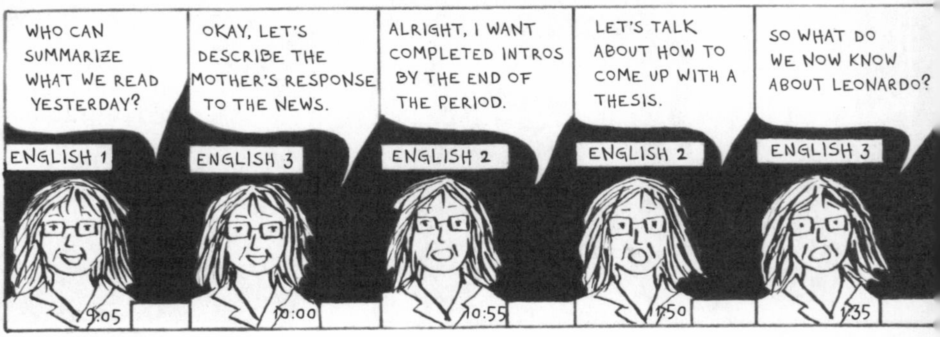
WHO CAN SUMMARIZE WHAT WE READ YESTERDAY?
ENGLISH 1
9:05
OKAY, LET'S DESCRIBE THE MOTHER'S RESPONSE TO THE NEWS.
ENGLISH 3
10:00
ALRIGHT, I WANT COMPLETED INTROS BY THE END OF THE PERIOD.
ENGLISH 2
10:55
LET'S TALK ABOUT HOW TO COME UP WITH A THESIS.
ENGLISH 2
11:50
SO WHAT DO WE NOW KNOW ABOUT LEONARDO?
ENGLISH 3
1:35

EACH CLASS HAS ITS OWN DYNAMIC,

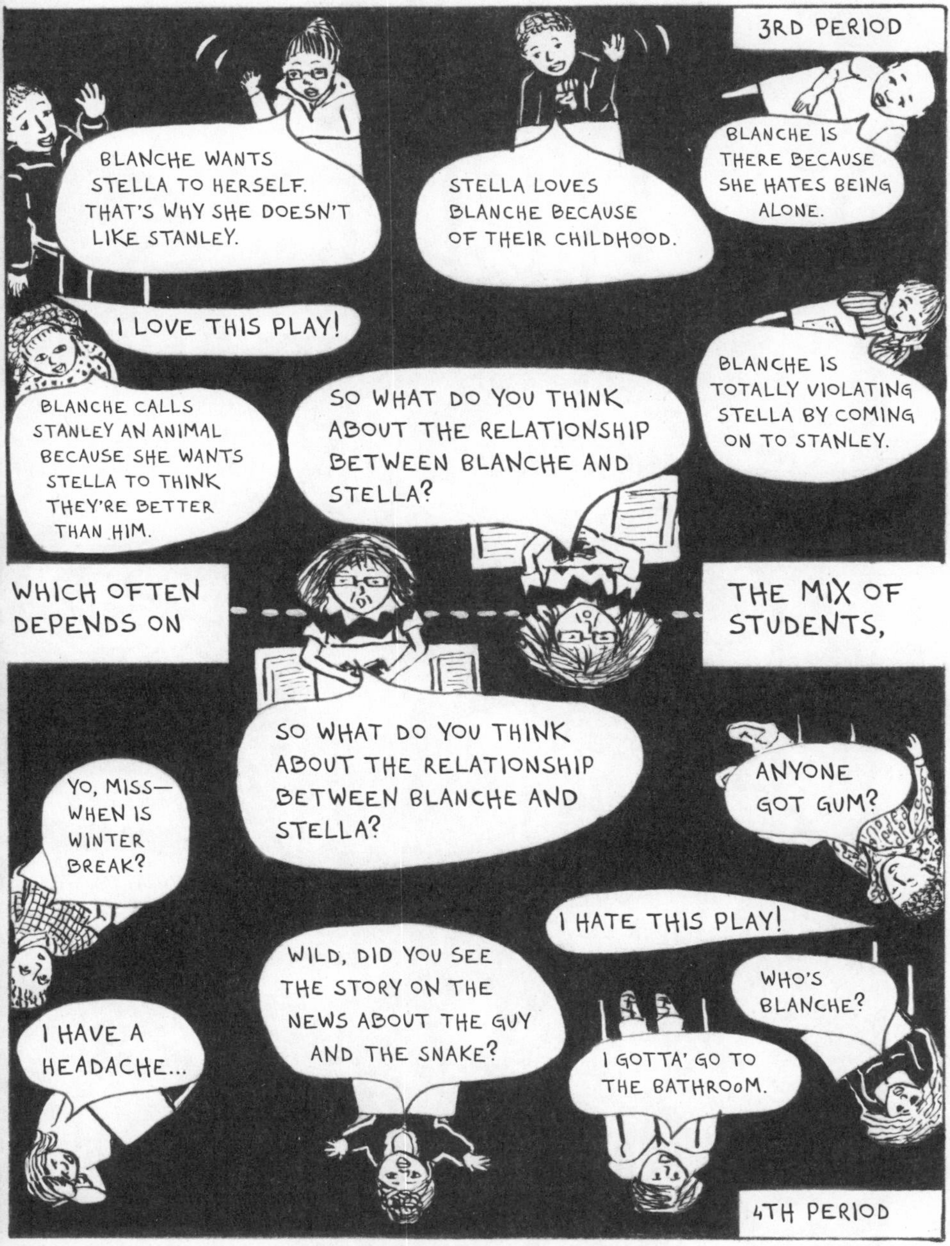
3RD PERIOD
BLANCHE WANTS STELLA TO HERSELF. THAT'S WHY SHE DOESN'T LIKE STANLEY.
STELLA LOVES BLANCHE BECAUSE OF THEIR CHILDHOOD.
BLANCHE IS THERE BECAUSE SHE HATES BEING ALONE.
I LOVE THIS PLAY!
BLANCHE IS TOTALLY VIOLATING STELLA BY COMING ON TO STANLEY.
BLANCHE CALLS STANLEY AN ANIMAL BECAUSE SHE WANTS STELLA TO THINK THEY'RE BETTER THAN HIM.
SO WHAT DO YOU THINK ABOUT THE RELATIONSHIP BETWEEN BLANCHE AND STELLA?
WHICH OFTEN DEPENDS ON
THE MIX OF STUDENTS,
SO WHAT DO YOU THINK ABOUT THE RELATIONSHIP BETWEEN BLANCHE AND STELLA?
ANYONE GOT GUM?
YO, MISS— WHEN IS WINTER BREAK?
I HATE THIS PLAY!
WILD, DID YOU SEE THE STORY ON THE NEWS ABOUT THE GUY AND THE SNAKE?
WHO'S BLANCHE?
I HAVE A HEADACHE...
I GOTTA' GO TO THE BATHROOM.
4TH PERIOD

AND EVERY NOW AND THEN,
YOU GET A MIX THAT MAKES YOU WONDER...

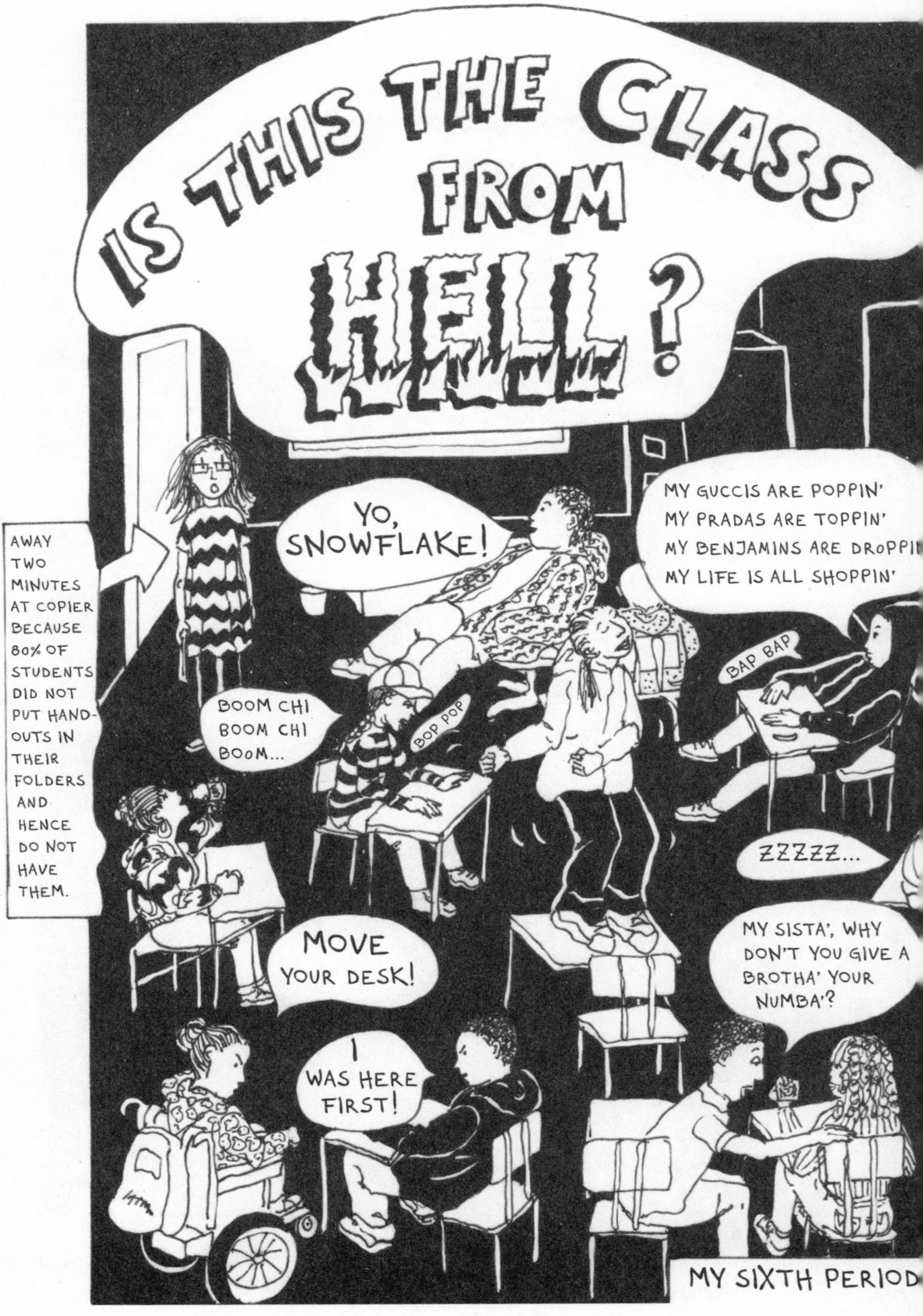
IS THIS THE CLASS FROM HELL?
AWAY TWO MINUTES AT COPIER BECAUSE 80% OF STUDENTS DID NOT PUT HAND-OUTS IN THEIR FOLDERS AND HENCE DO NOT HAVE THEM.
YO, SNOWFLAKE!
MY GUCCIS ARE POPPIN'
MY PRADAS ARE TOPPIN'
MY BENJAMINS ARE DROPPI
MY LIFE IS ALL SHOPPIN'
BAP BAP
BOOM CHI BOOM CHI BOOM...
BOP POP
ZZZZZ...
MOVE YOUR DESK!
MY SISTA', WHY DON'T YOU GIVE A BROTHA' YOUR NUMBA'?
I WAS HERE FIRST!
MY SIXTH PERIOD

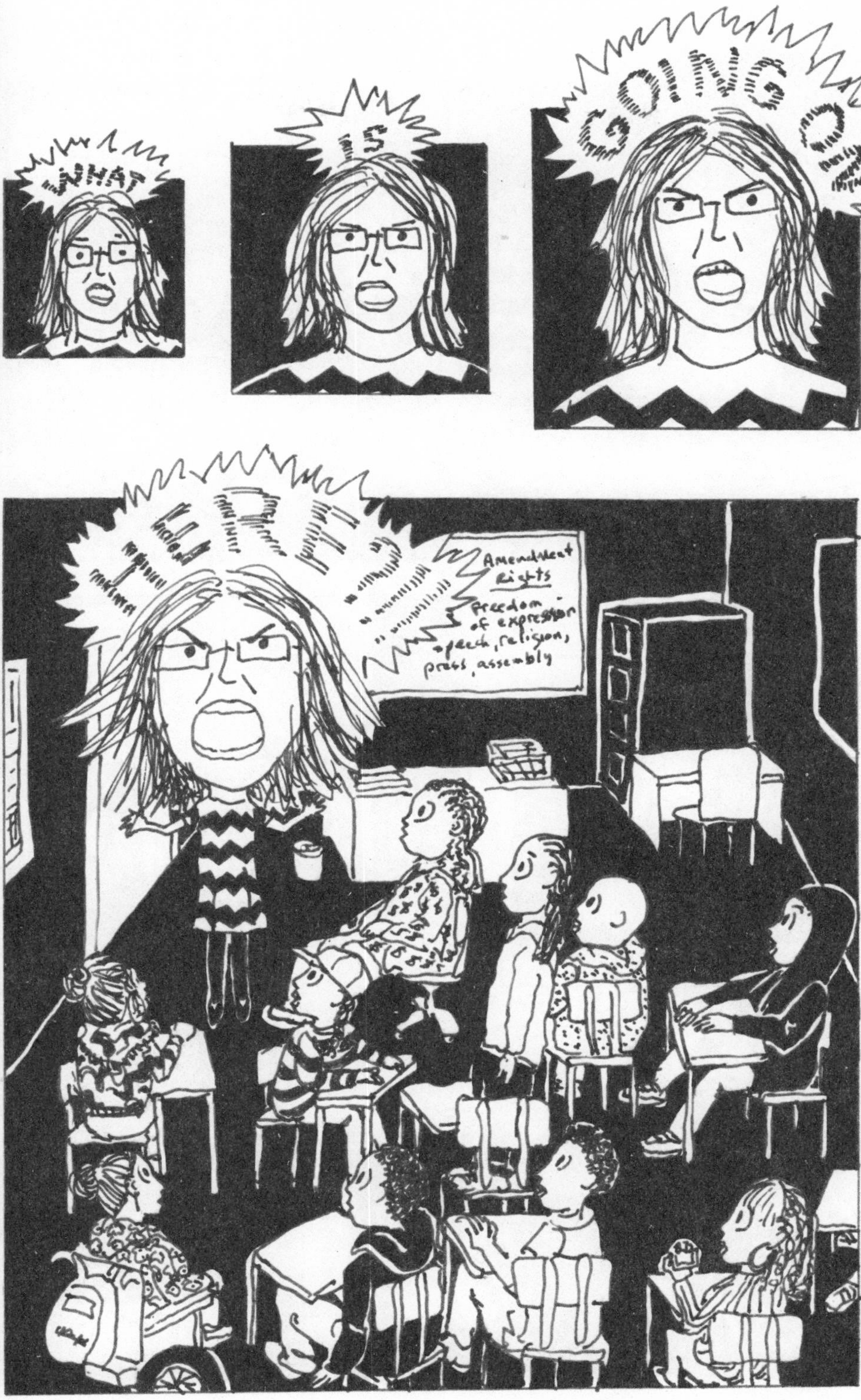
WHAT
IS
GOING ON
IN
HERE?!
Amendment Rights
Freedom of expression
speech, religion, press, assembly

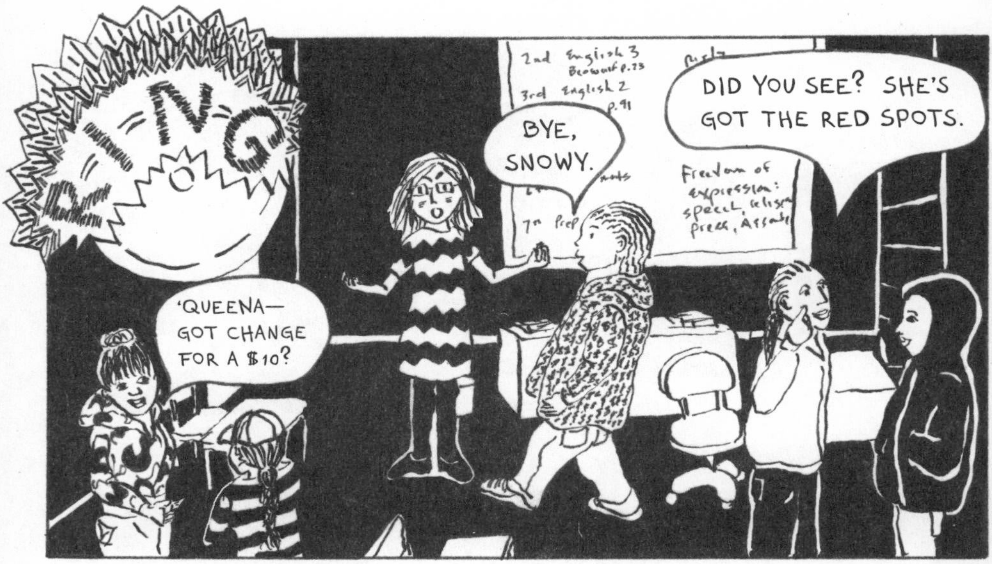
BING
'QUEENA— GOT CHANGE FOR A $10?
BYE, SNOWY.
DID YOU SEE? SHE'S GOT THE RED SPOTS.

END OF THE DAY

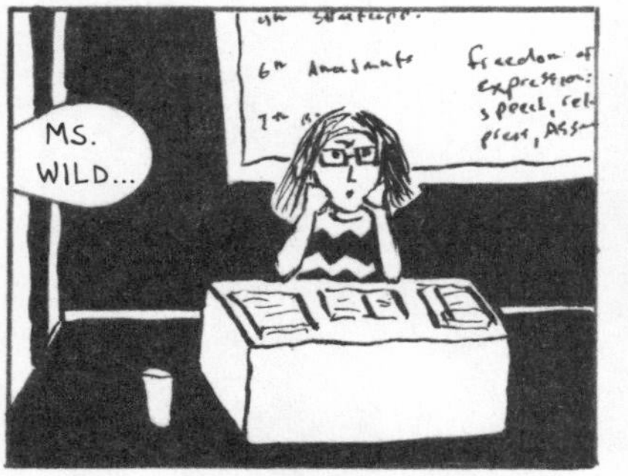
MS. WILD...

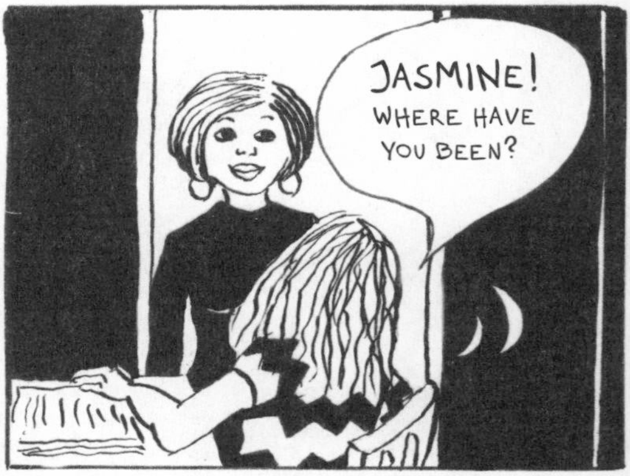
JASMINE! WHERE HAVE YOU BEEN?

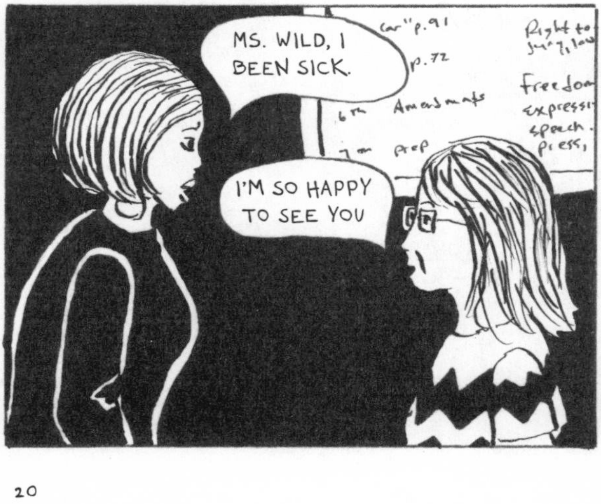
MS. WILD, I BEEN SICK.
I'M SO HAPPY TO SEE YOU

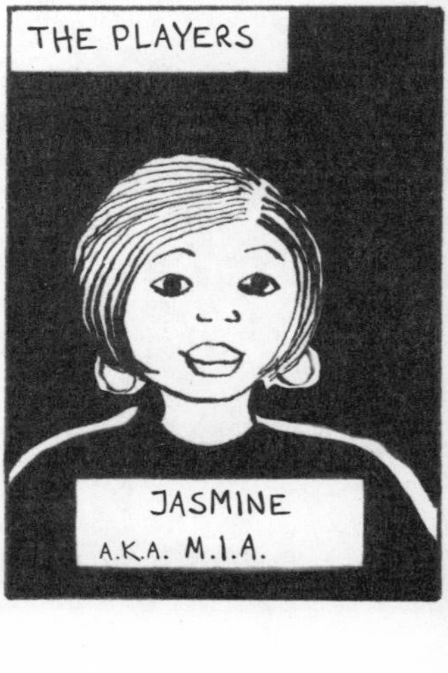
THE PLAYERS
JASMINE
A.K.A. M.I.A.

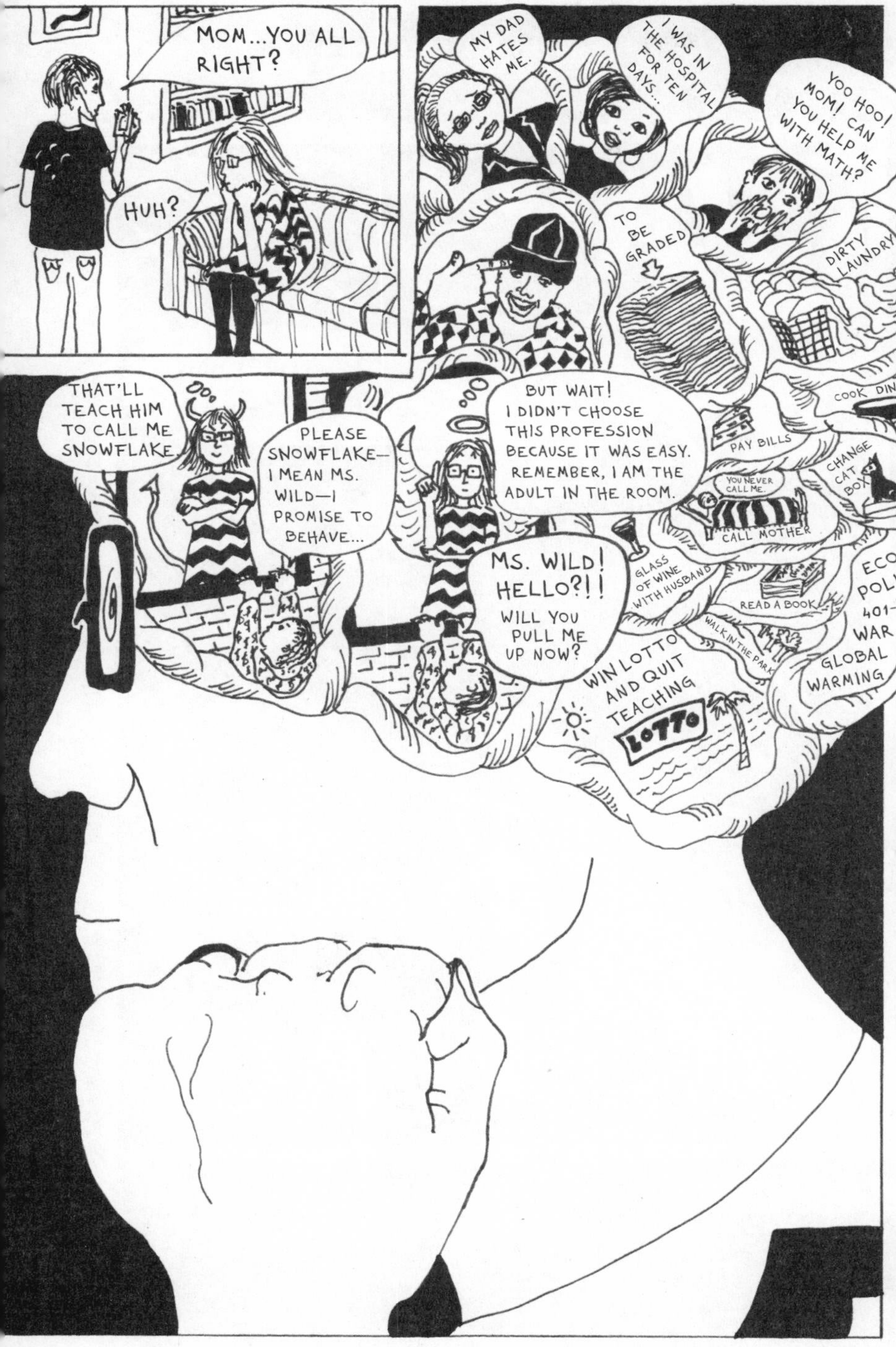
MOM...YOU ALL RIGHT?
HUH?
MY DAD HATES ME.
I WAS IN THE HOSPITAL FOR TEN DAYS...
YOO HOO! MOM! CAN YOU HELP ME WITH MATH?
TO BE GRADED
DIRTY LAUNDRY
COOK DINNER
PAY BILLS
CHANGE CAT BOX
YOU NEVER CALL ME.
CALL MOTHER
THAT'LL TEACH HIM TO CALL ME SNOWFLAKE.
PLEASE SNOWFLAKE—I MEAN MS. WILD—I PROMISE TO BEHAVE...
BUT WAIT! I DIDN'T CHOOSE THIS PROFESSION BECAUSE IT WAS EASY. REMEMBER, I AM THE ADULT IN THE ROOM.
MS. WILD! HELLO?!! WILL YOU PULL ME UP NOW?
GLASS OF WINE WITH HUSBAND
READ A BOOK
WALK IN THE PARK
ECONOMY
POLITICS
401-K
WAR
GLOBAL WARMING
WIN LOTTO AND QUIT TEACHING
LOTTO

CHAPTER TWO

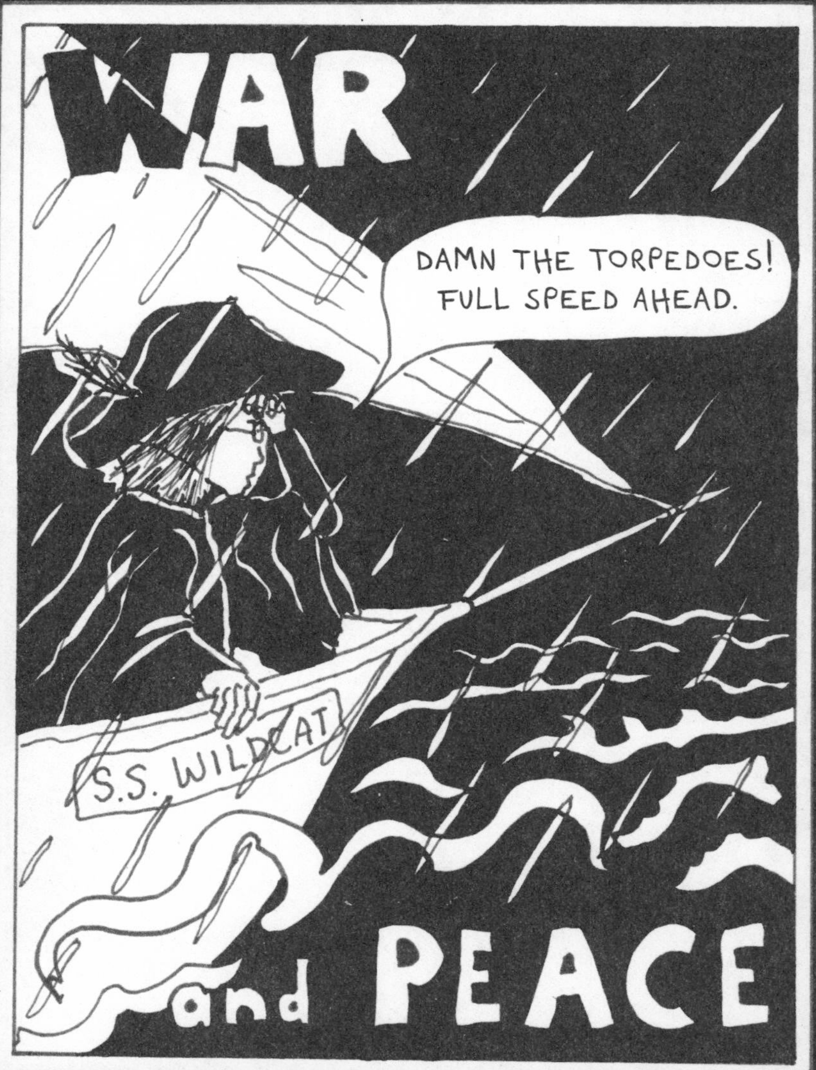
WAR
DAMN THE TORPEDOES! FULL SPEED AHEAD.
S.S. WILDCAT
and PEACE

"WE LOST BECAUSE WE TOLD OURSELVES WE LOST."

LEO TOLSTOY

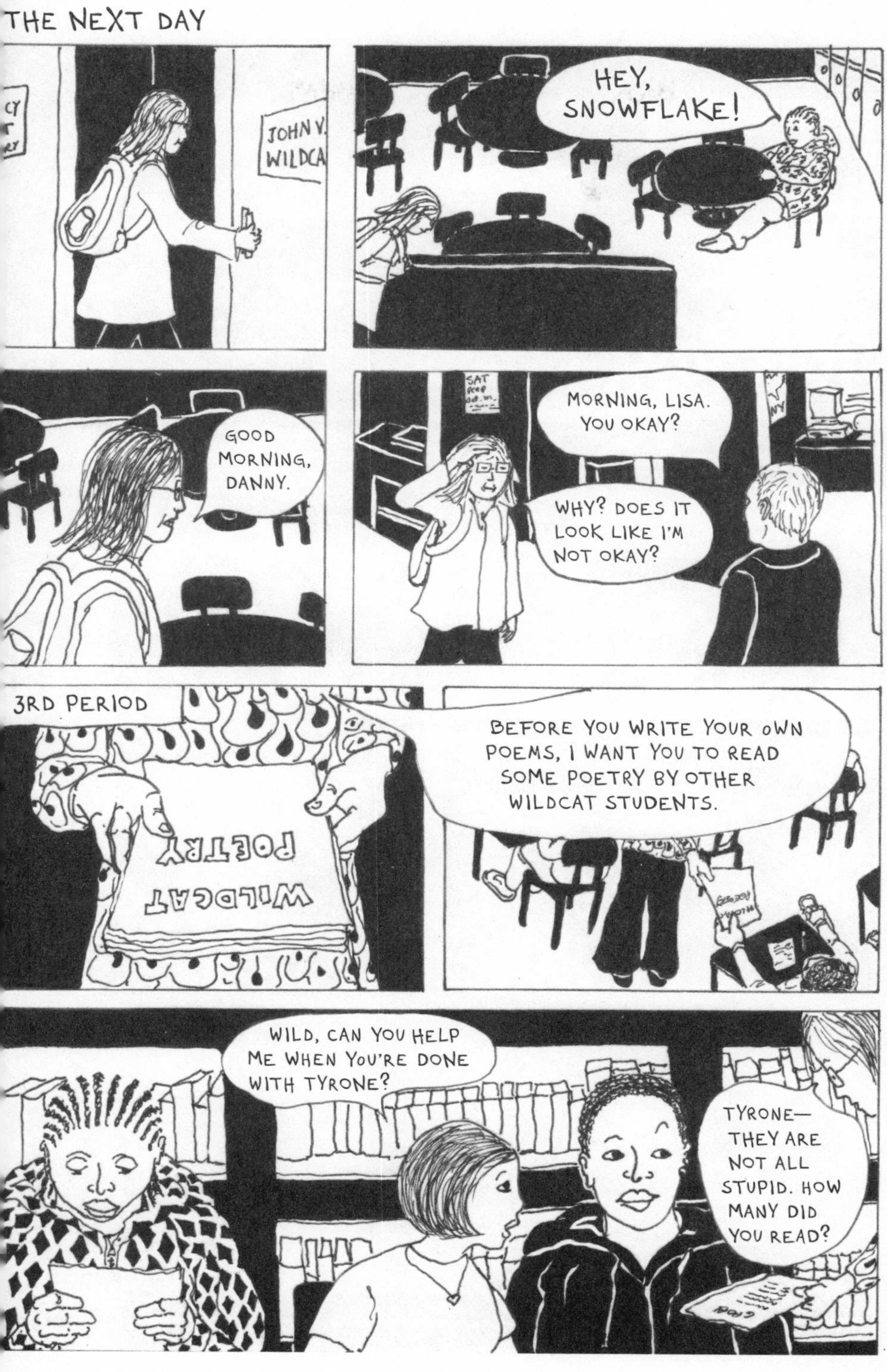
THE NEXT DAY
JOHN V. WILDCA
HEY, SNOWFLAKE!
GOOD MORNING, DANNY.
MORNING, LISA. YOU OKAY?
WHY? DOES IT LOOK LIKE I'M NOT OKAY?
3RD PERIOD
WILDCAT POETRY
BEFORE YOU WRITE YOUR OWN POEMS, I WANT YOU TO READ SOME POETRY BY OTHER WILDCAT STUDENTS.
WILD, CAN YOU HELP ME WHEN YOU'RE DONE WITH TYRONE?
TYRONE— THEY ARE NOT ALL STUPID. HOW MANY DID YOU READ?

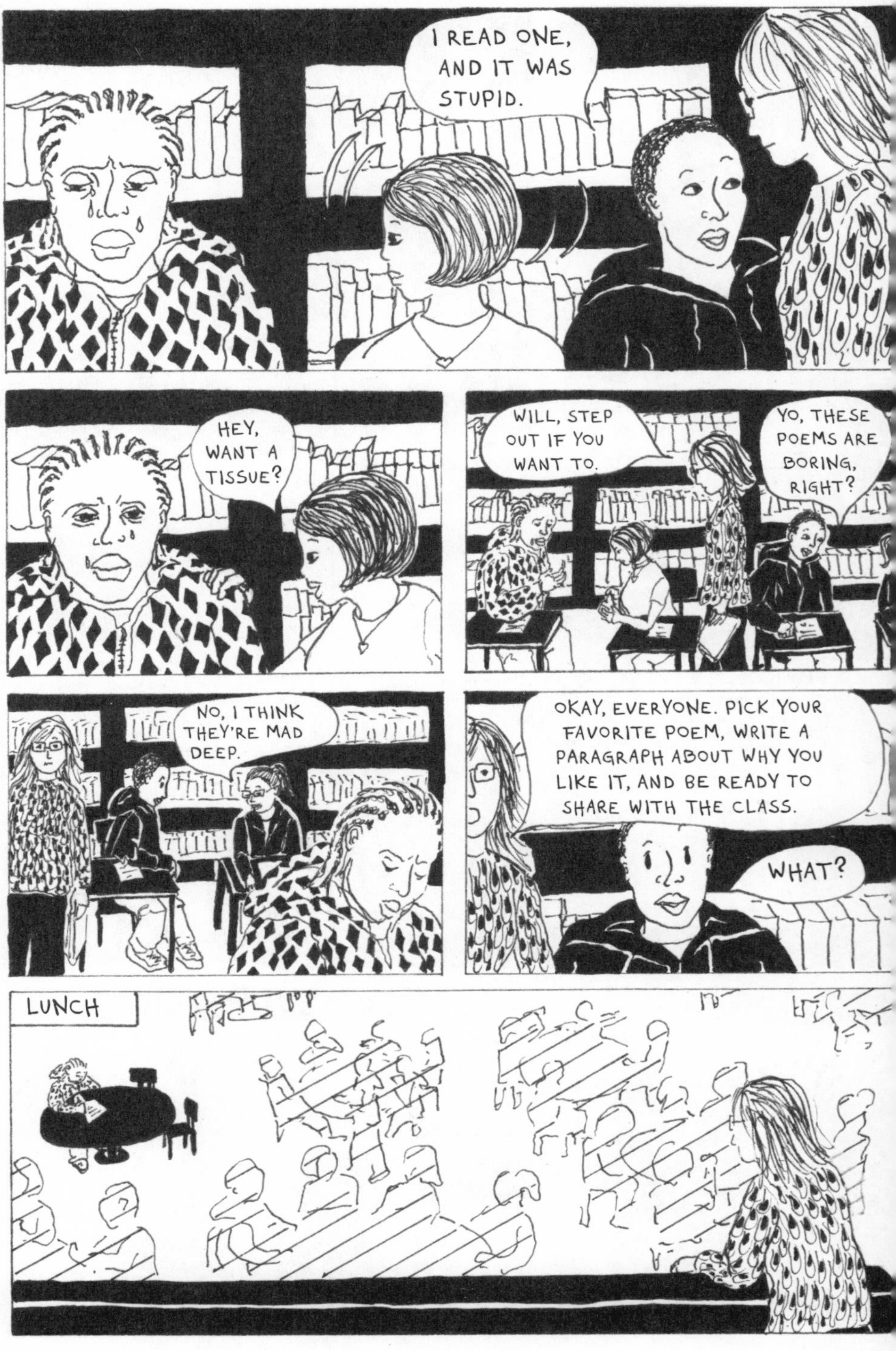
I READ ONE, AND IT WAS STUPID.
HEY, WANT A TISSUE?
WILL, STEP OUT IF YOU WANT TO.
YO, THESE POEMS ARE BORING, RIGHT?
NO, I THINK THEY'RE MAD DEEP.
OKAY, EVERYONE. PICK YOUR FAVORITE POEM, WRITE A PARAGRAPH ABOUT WHY YOU LIKE IT, AND BE READY TO SHARE WITH THE CLASS.
WHAT?
LUNCH

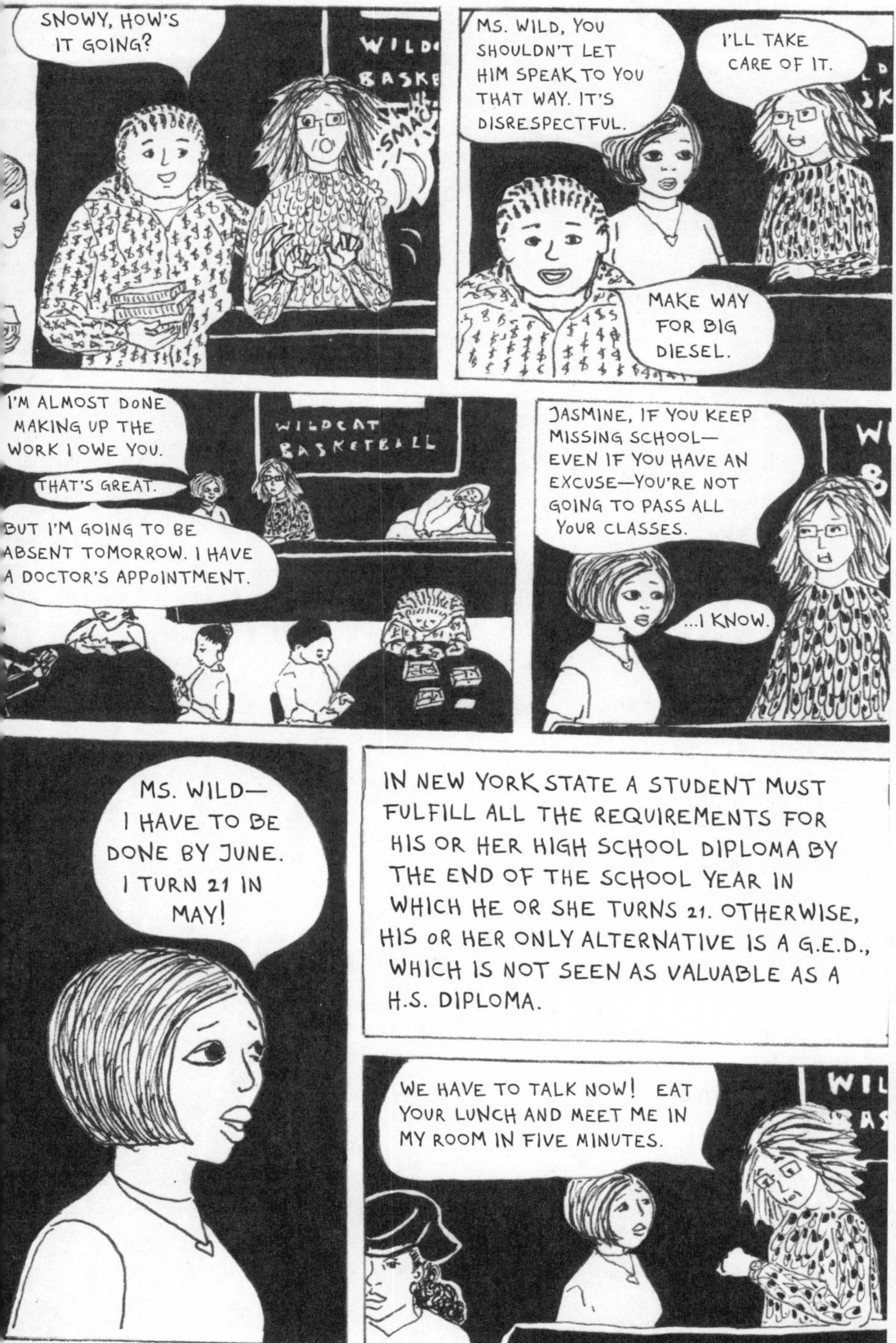
SNOWY, HOW'S IT GOING?
WILD
BASKE
SMACK
MS. WILD, YOU SHOULDN'T LET HIM SPEAK TO YOU THAT WAY. IT'S DISRESPECTFUL.
I'LL TAKE CARE OF IT.
MAKE WAY FOR BIG DIESEL.
I'M ALMOST DONE MAKING UP THE WORK I OWE YOU.
WILDCAT BASKETBALL
THAT'S GREAT.
BUT I'M GOING TO BE ABSENT TOMORROW. I HAVE A DOCTOR'S APPOINTMENT.
JASMINE, IF YOU KEEP MISSING SCHOOL—EVEN IF YOU HAVE AN EXCUSE—YOU'RE NOT GOING TO PASS ALL YOUR CLASSES.
...I KNOW.
MS. WILD— I HAVE TO BE DONE BY JUNE. I TURN 21 IN MAY!
IN NEW YORK STATE A STUDENT MUST FULFILL ALL THE REQUIREMENTS FOR HIS OR HER HIGH SCHOOL DIPLOMA BY THE END OF THE SCHOOL YEAR IN WHICH HE OR SHE TURNS 21. OTHERWISE, HIS OR HER ONLY ALTERNATIVE IS A G.E.D., WHICH IS NOT SEEN AS VALUABLE AS A H.S. DIPLOMA.
WE HAVE TO TALK NOW! EAT YOUR LUNCH AND MEET ME IN MY ROOM IN FIVE MINUTES.

DO YOU WANT TO KNOW JASMINE'S STORY? WHY SHE'S 20 AND STILL IN HIGH SCHOOL?

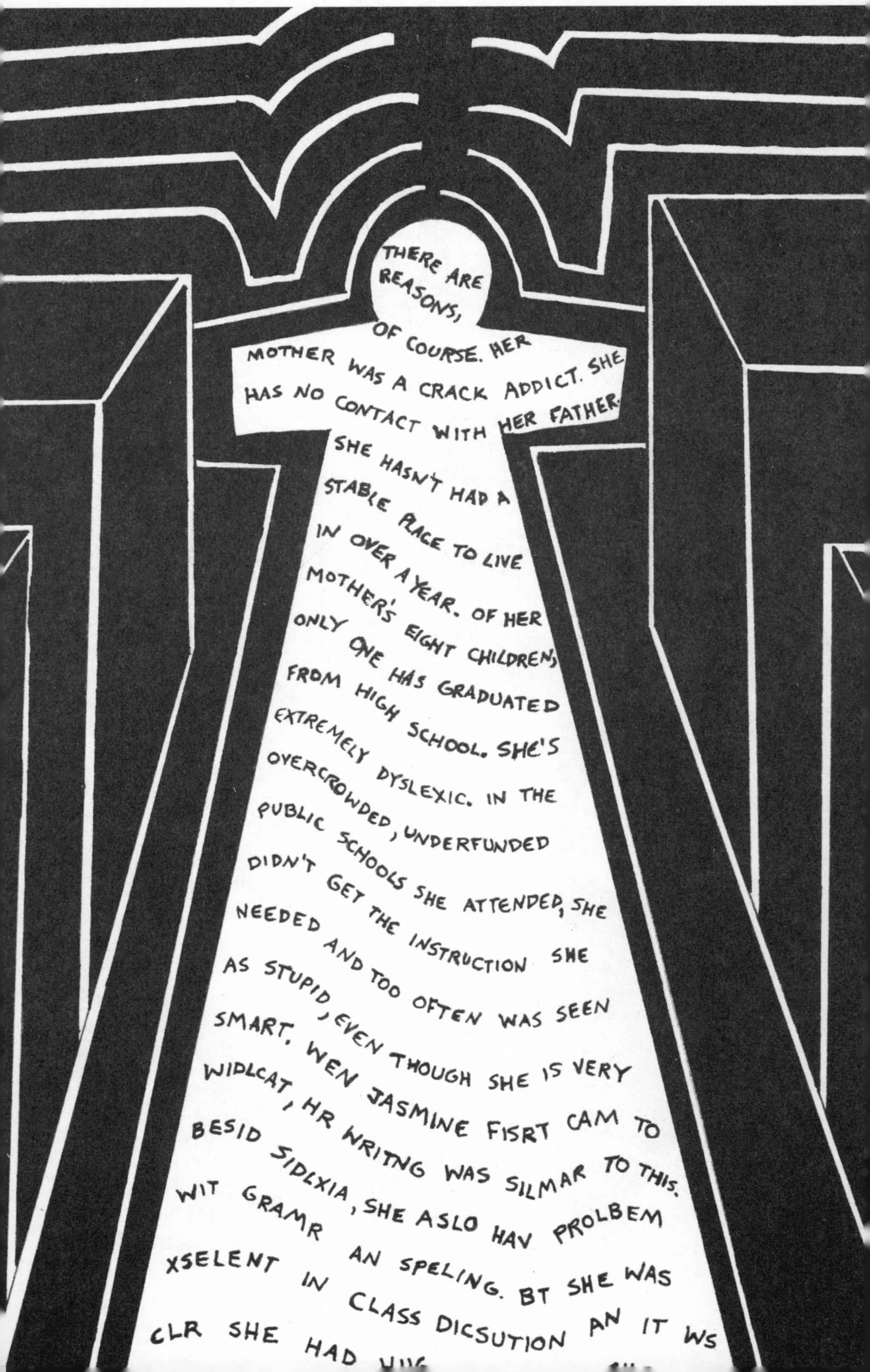
THERE ARE REASONS, OF COURSE. HER MOTHER WAS A CRACK ADDICT. SHE HAS NO CONTACT WITH HER FATHER. SHE HASN'T HAD A STABLE PLACE TO LIVE IN OVER A YEAR. OF HER MOTHER'S EIGHT CHILDREN, ONLY ONE HAS GRADUATED FROM HIGH SCHOOL. SHE'S EXTREMELY DYSLEXIC. IN THE OVERCROWDED, UNDERFUNDED PUBLIC SCHOOLS SHE ATTENDED, SHE DIDN'T GET THE INSTRUCTION SHE NEEDED AND TOO OFTEN WAS SEEN AS STUPID, EVEN THOUGH SHE IS VERY SMART. WEN JASMINE FISRT CAM TO WIDLCAT, HR WRITNG WAS SILMAR TO THIS. BESID SIDLXIA, SHE ASLO HAV PROLBEM WIT GRAMR AN SPELING. BT SHE WAS XSELENT IN CLASS DICSUTION AN IT WS CLR SHE HAD

DO I KNOW THAT SHE WILL REALLY GRADUATE?

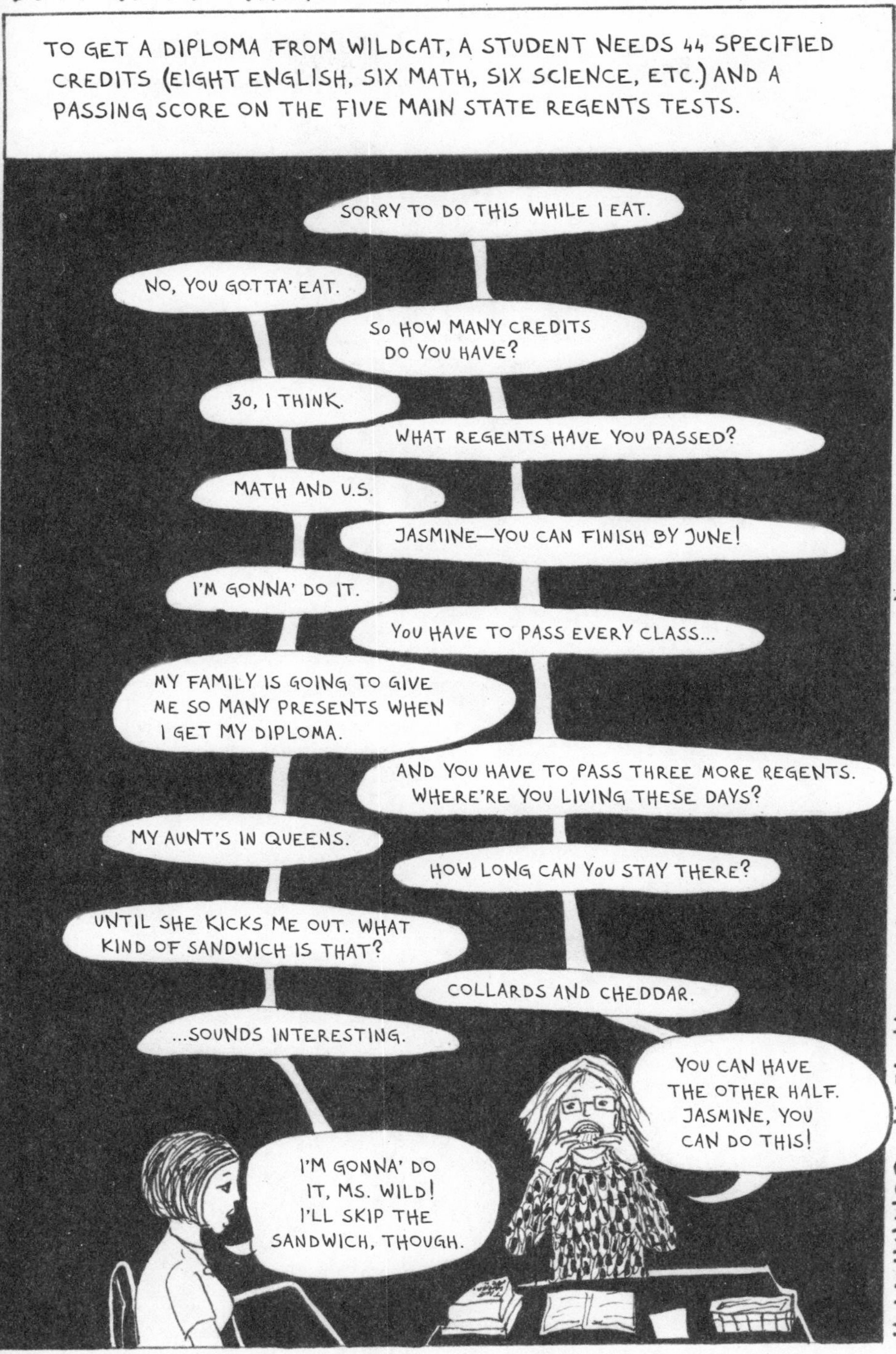

TO GET A DIPLOMA FROM WILDCAT, A STUDENT NEEDS 44 SPECIFIED CREDITS (EIGHT ENGLISH, SIX MATH, SIX SCIENCE, ETC.) AND A PASSING SCORE ON THE FIVE MAIN STATE REGENTS TESTS.
SORRY TO DO THIS WHILE I EAT.
NO, YOU GOTTA' EAT.
SO HOW MANY CREDITS DO YOU HAVE?
30, I THINK.
WHAT REGENTS HAVE YOU PASSED?
MATH AND U.S.
JASMINE—YOU CAN FINISH BY JUNE!
I'M GONNA' DO IT.
YOU HAVE TO PASS EVERY CLASS...
MY FAMILY IS GOING TO GIVE ME SO MANY PRESENTS WHEN I GET MY DIPLOMA.
AND YOU HAVE TO PASS THREE MORE REGENTS. WHERE'RE YOU LIVING THESE DAYS?
MY AUNT'S IN QUEENS.
HOW LONG CAN YOU STAY THERE?
UNTIL SHE KICKS ME OUT. WHAT KIND OF SANDWICH IS THAT?
COLLARDS AND CHEDDAR.
...SOUNDS INTERESTING.
YOU CAN HAVE THE OTHER HALF. JASMINE, YOU CAN DO THIS!
I'M GONNA' DO IT, MS. WILD! I'LL SKIP THE SANDWICH, THOUGH.

NO... BUT FOR BOTH OUR SAKES, I NEED TO ACT AS IF IT IS A CERTAINTY.

JASMINE IS VERY SMART. I WONDER WHERE SHE WOUL

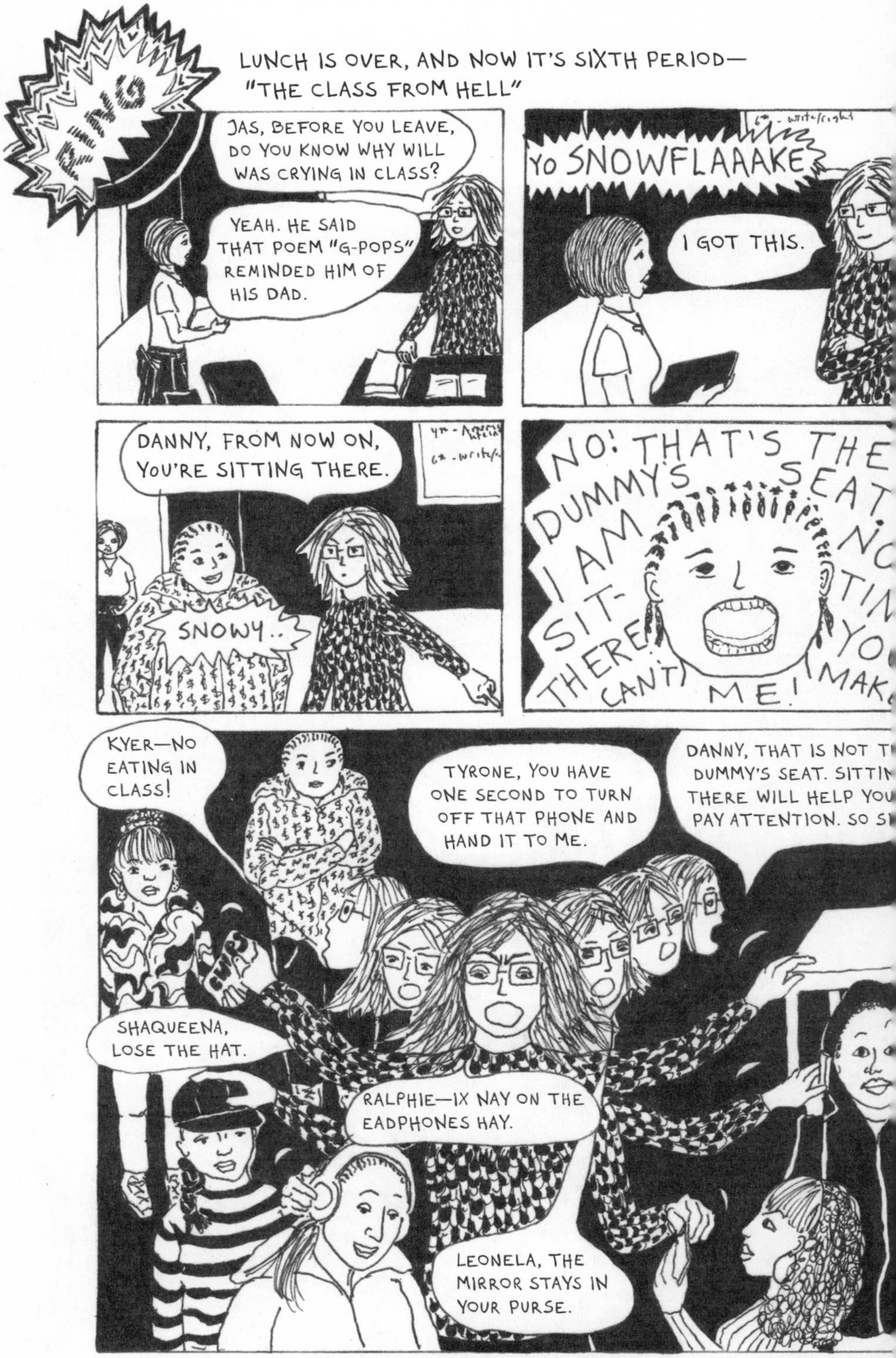
RING
LUNCH IS OVER, AND NOW IT'S SIXTH PERIOD—
"THE CLASS FROM HELL"
JAS, BEFORE YOU LEAVE, DO YOU KNOW WHY WILL WAS CRYING IN CLASS?
YEAH. HE SAID THAT POEM "G-POPS" REMINDED HIM OF HIS DAD.
YO SNOWFLAAAKE
I GOT THIS.
DANNY, FROM NOW ON, YOU'RE SITTING THERE.
SNOWY..
NO! THAT'S THE DUMMY'S SEAT
I AM NO SIT- TIN THERE! YO CAN'T MAK ME!
KYER—NO EATING IN CLASS!
TYRONE, YOU HAVE ONE SECOND TO TURN OFF THAT PHONE AND HAND IT TO ME.
DANNY, THAT IS NOT T DUMMY'S SEAT. SITTI THERE WILL HELP YOU PAY ATTENTION. SO S
SHAQUEENA, LOSE THE HAT.
RALPHIE—IX NAY ON THE EADPHONES HAY.
LEONELA, THE MIRROR STAYS IN YOUR PURSE.

THIS CLASSROOM TECHNIQUE IS INSPIRED BY KALI, A MULTI-ARMED HINDU GODESS, WHO I FRIGHTENING, BUT WITH THE HEART OF A MOTHER.

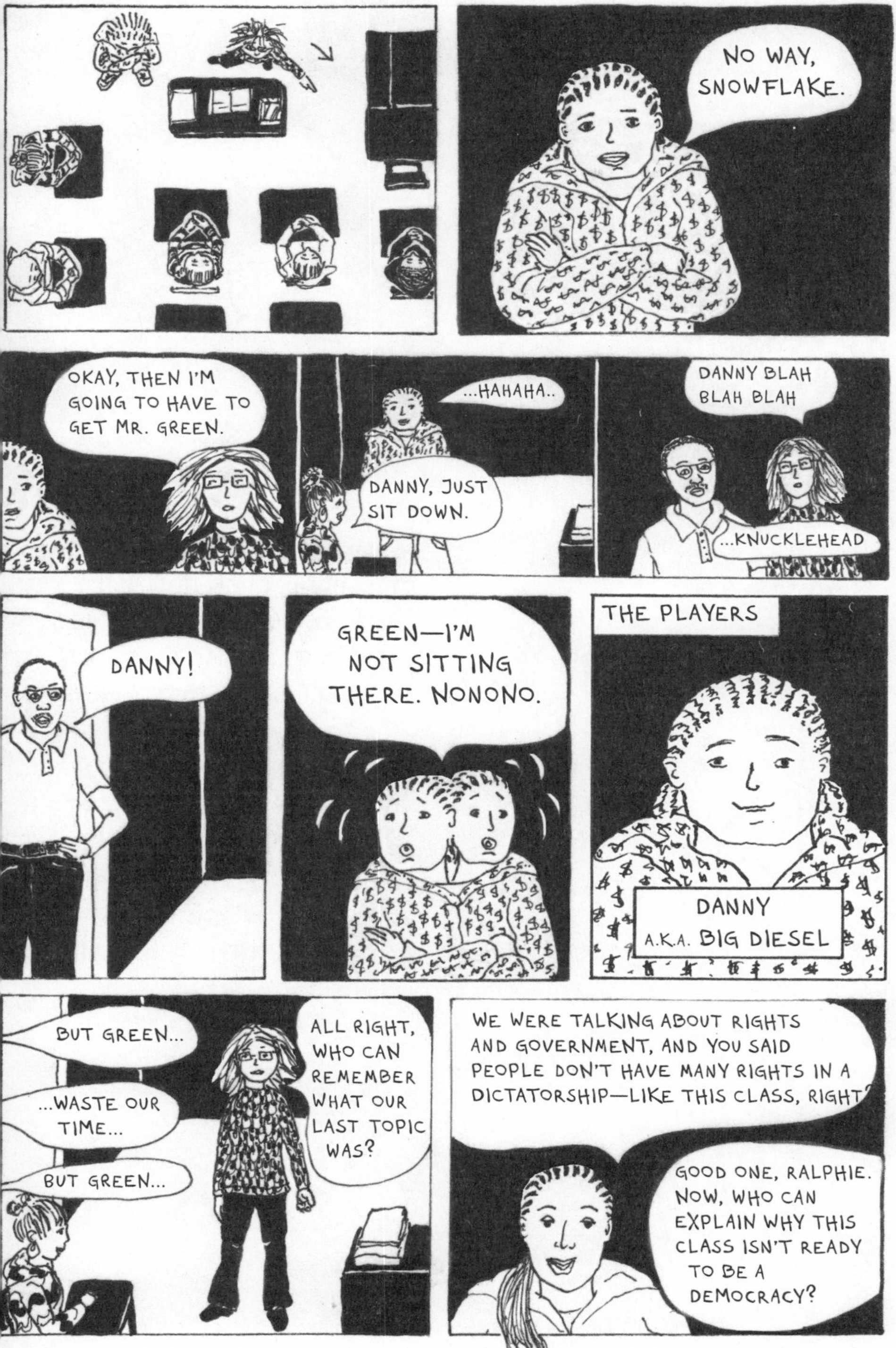
NO WAY, SNOWFLAKE.
OKAY, THEN I'M GOING TO HAVE TO GET MR. GREEN.
...HAHAHA..
DANNY, JUST SIT DOWN.
DANNY BLAH BLAH BLAH
...KNUCKLEHEAD
DANNY!
GREEN—I'M NOT SITTING THERE. NONONO.
THE PLAYERS
DANNY
A.K.A. BIG DIESEL
BUT GREEN...
...WASTE OUR TIME...
BUT GREEN...
ALL RIGHT, WHO CAN REMEMBER WHAT OUR LAST TOPIC WAS?
WE WERE TALKING ABOUT RIGHTS AND GOVERNMENT, AND YOU SAID PEOPLE DON'T HAVE MANY RIGHTS IN A DICTATORSHIP—LIKE THIS CLASS, RIGHT?
GOOD ONE, RALPHIE. NOW, WHO CAN EXPLAIN WHY THIS CLASS ISN'T READY TO BE A DEMOCRACY?

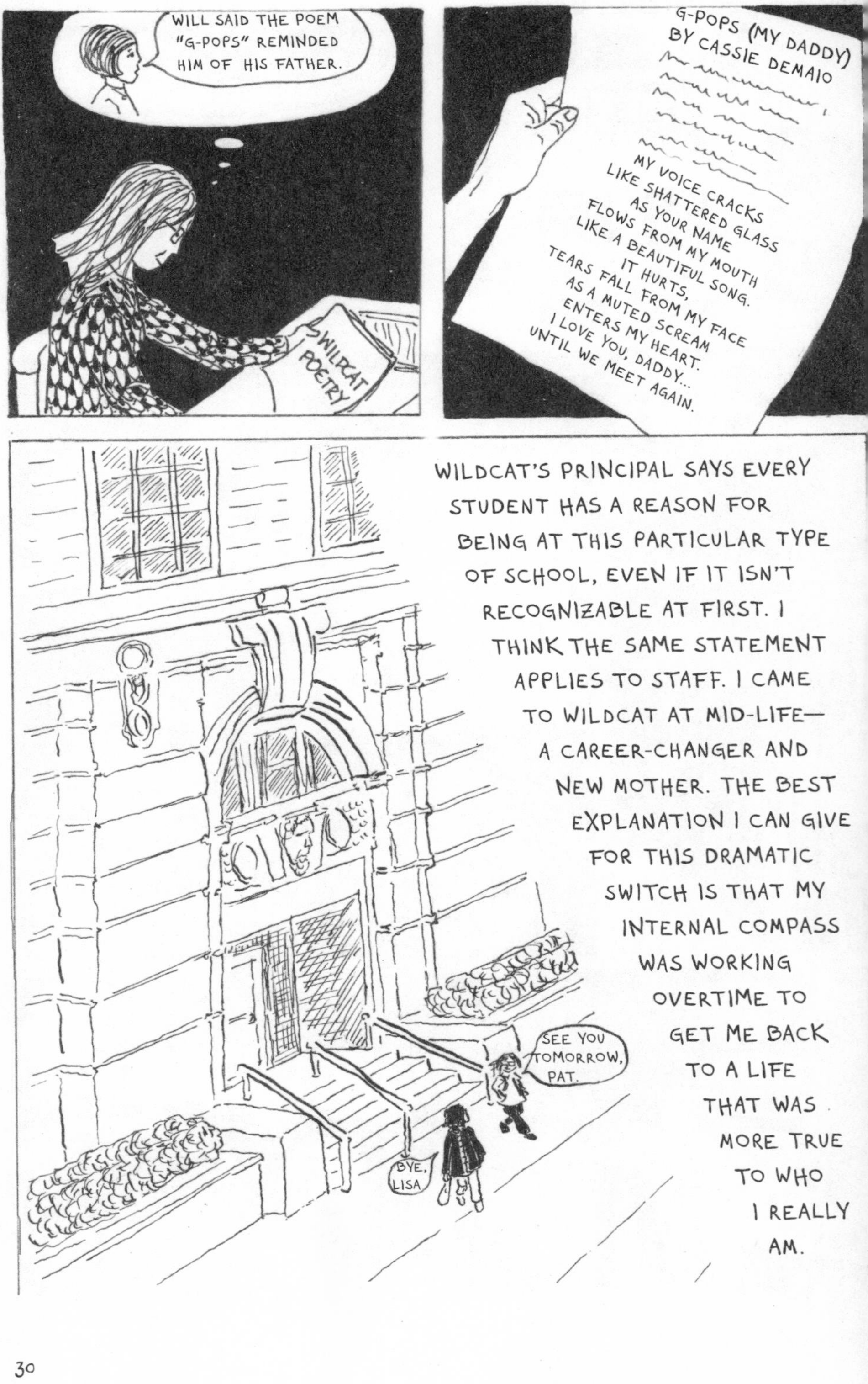
WILL SAID THE POEM "G-POPS" REMINDED HIM OF HIS FATHER.
WILDCAT POETRY
G-POPS (MY DADDY)
BY CASSIE DEMAIO
MY VOICE CRACKS
LIKE SHATTERED GLASS
AS YOUR NAME
FLOWS FROM MY MOUTH
LIKE A BEAUTIFUL SONG.
IT HURTS,
TEARS FALL FROM MY FACE
AS A MUTED SCREAM
ENTERS MY HEART.
I LOVE YOU, DADDY...
UNTIL WE MEET AGAIN.
WILDCAT'S PRINCIPAL SAYS EVERY STUDENT HAS A REASON FOR BEING AT THIS PARTICULAR TYPE OF SCHOOL, EVEN IF IT ISN'T RECOGNIZABLE AT FIRST. I THINK THE SAME STATEMENT APPLIES TO STAFF. I CAME TO WILDCAT AT MID-LIFE— A CAREER-CHANGER AND NEW MOTHER. THE BEST EXPLANATION I CAN GIVE FOR THIS DRAMATIC SWITCH IS THAT MY INTERNAL COMPASS WAS WORKING OVERTIME TO GET ME BACK TO A LIFE THAT WAS MORE TRUE TO WHO I REALLY AM.
SEE YOU TOMORROW, PAT.
BYE, LISA

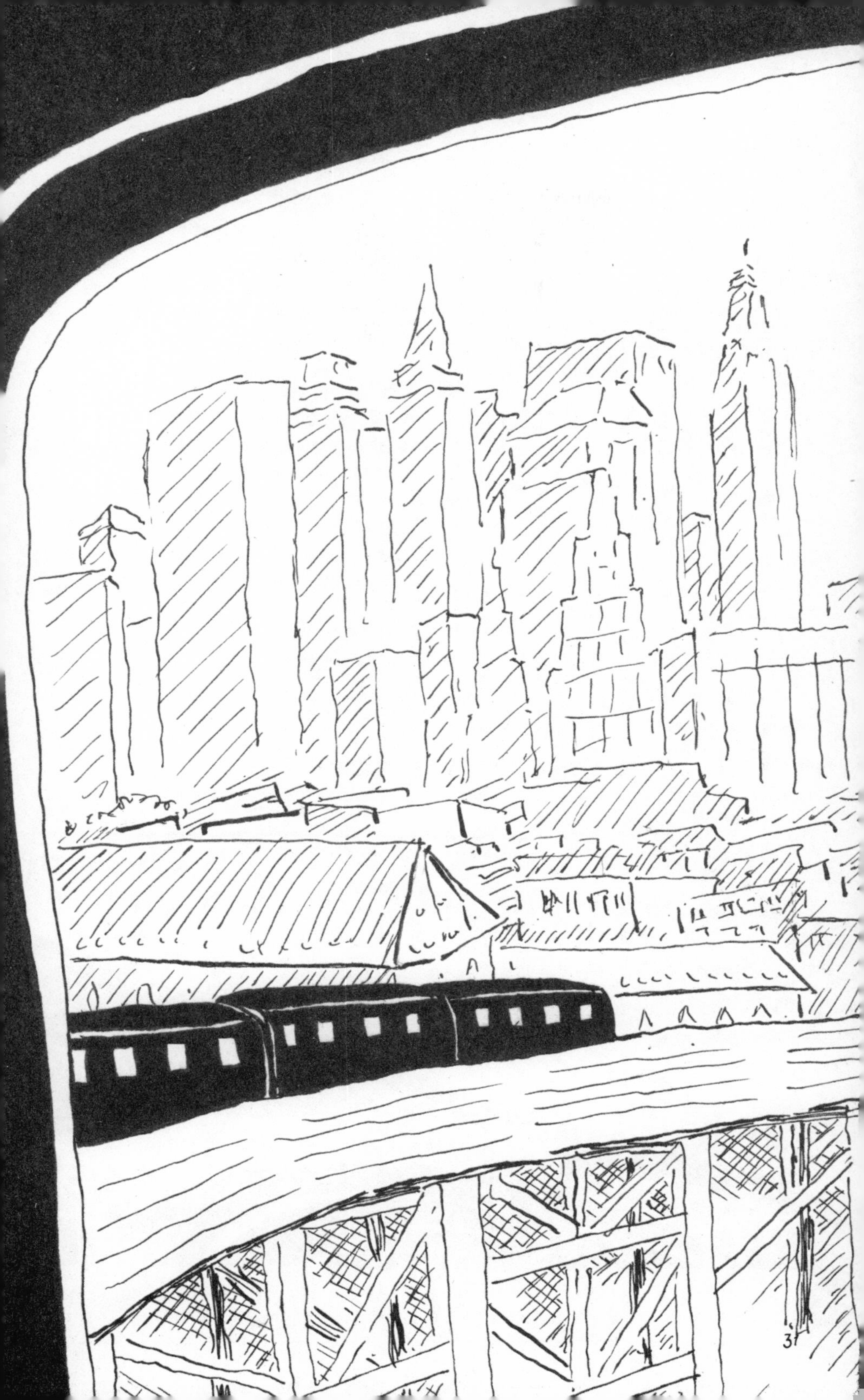

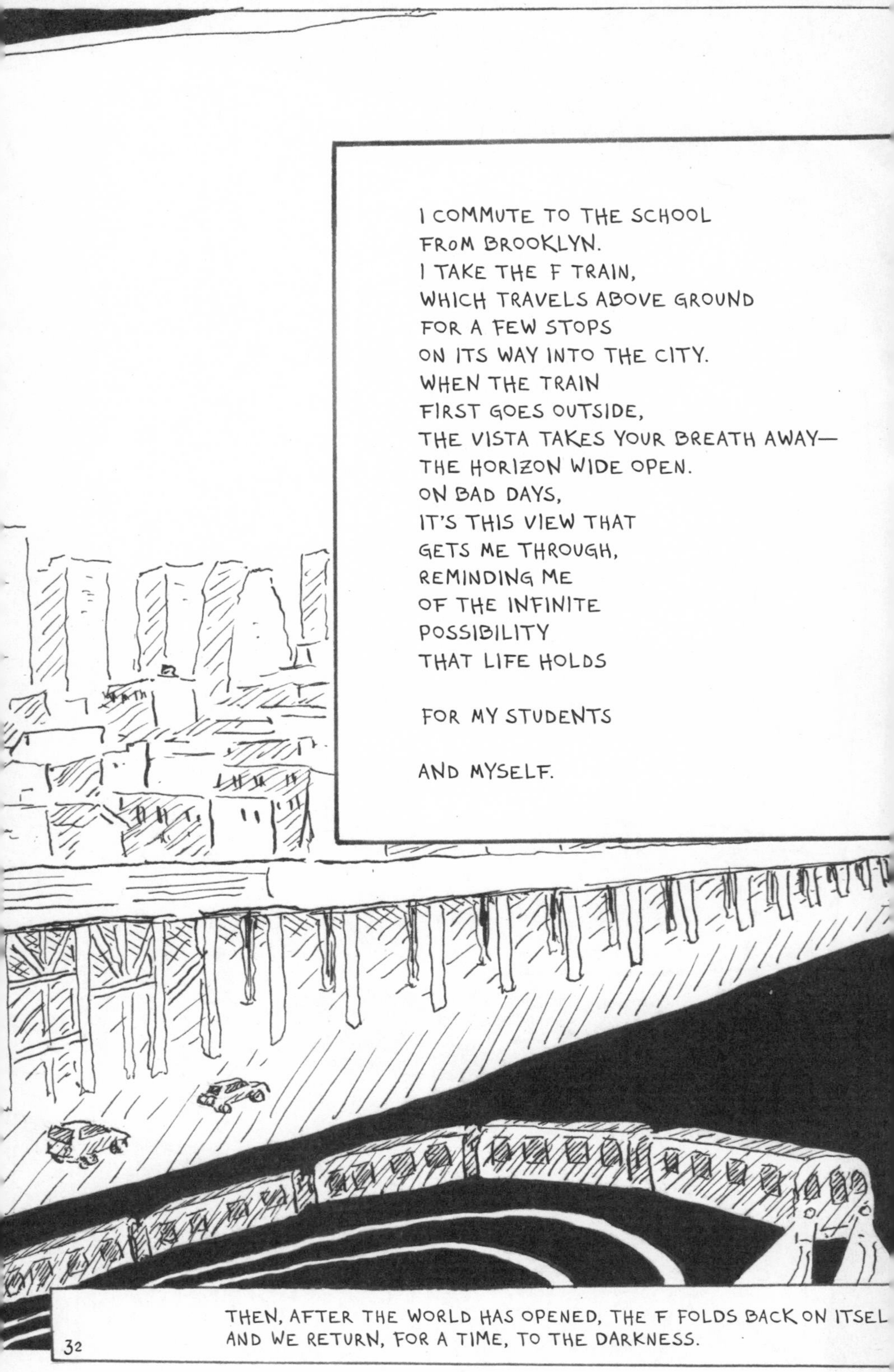
I COMMUTE TO THE SCHOOL
FROM BROOKLYN.
I TAKE THE F TRAIN,
WHICH TRAVELS ABOVE GROUND
FOR A FEW STOPS
ON ITS WAY INTO THE CITY.
WHEN THE TRAIN
FIRST GOES OUTSIDE,
THE VISTA TAKES YOUR BREATH AWAY—
THE HORIZON WIDE OPEN.
ON BAD DAYS,
IT'S THIS VIEW THAT
GETS ME THROUGH,
REMINDING ME
OF THE INFINITE
POSSIBILITY
THAT LIFE HOLDS
FOR MY STUDENTS
AND MYSELF.
THEN, AFTER THE WORLD HAS OPENED, THE F FOLDS BACK ON ITSEL
AND WE RETURN, FOR A TIME, TO THE DARKNESS.

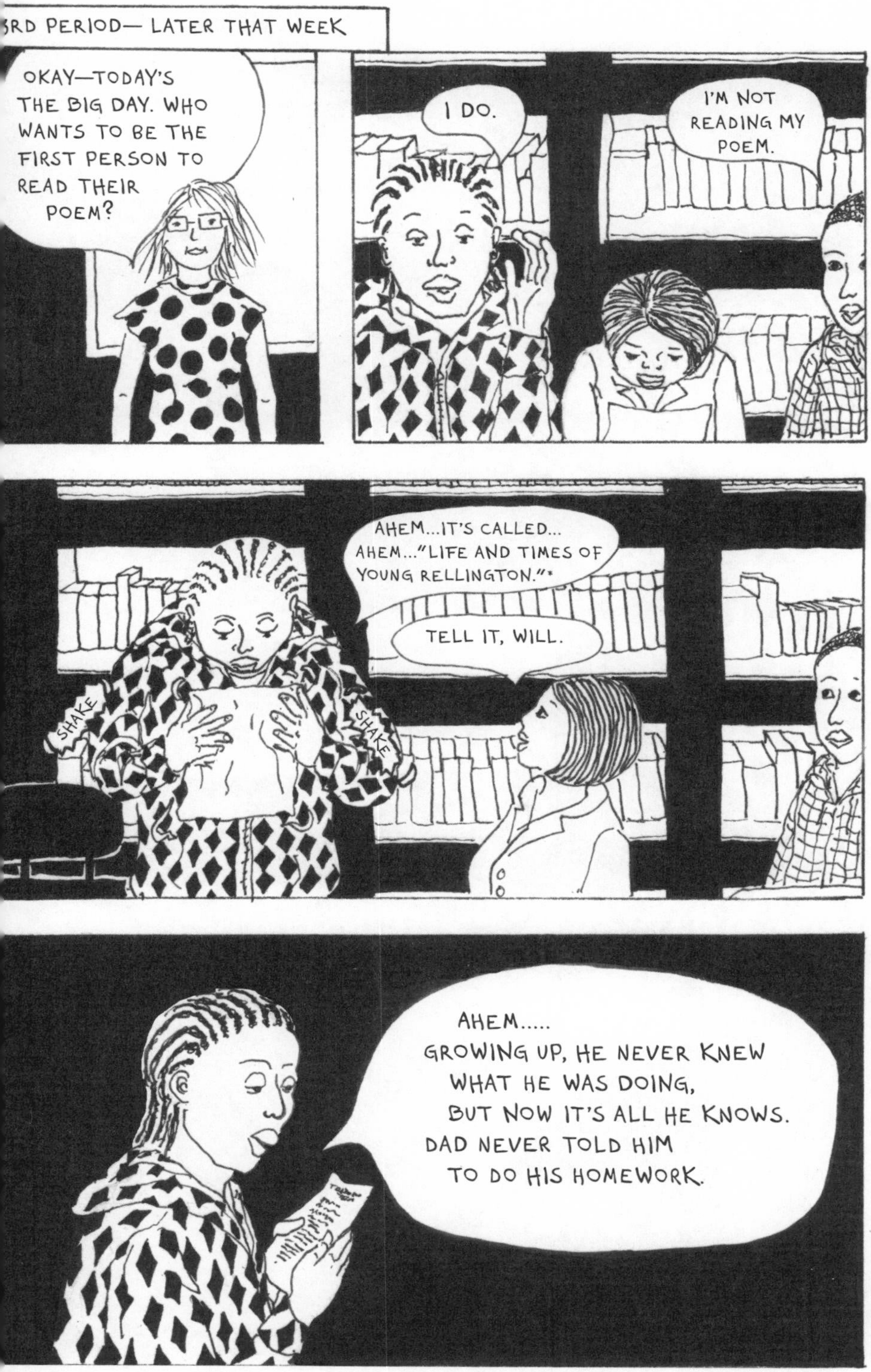
3RD PERIOD— LATER THAT WEEK
OKAY—TODAY'S THE BIG DAY. WHO WANTS TO BE THE FIRST PERSON TO READ THEIR POEM?
I DO.
I'M NOT READING MY POEM.
AHEM...IT'S CALLED... AHEM..."LIFE AND TIMES OF YOUNG RELLINGTON."*
TELL IT, WILL.
SHAKE
SHAKE
AHEM.....
GROWING UP, HE NEVER KNEW
WHAT HE WAS DOING,
BUT NOW IT'S ALL HE KNOWS.
DAD NEVER TOLD HIM
TO DO HIS HOMEWORK.

*POEM WRITTEN BY TYRELL BRAMBLE, WILDCAT GRADUATE. USED WITH PERMISSION.

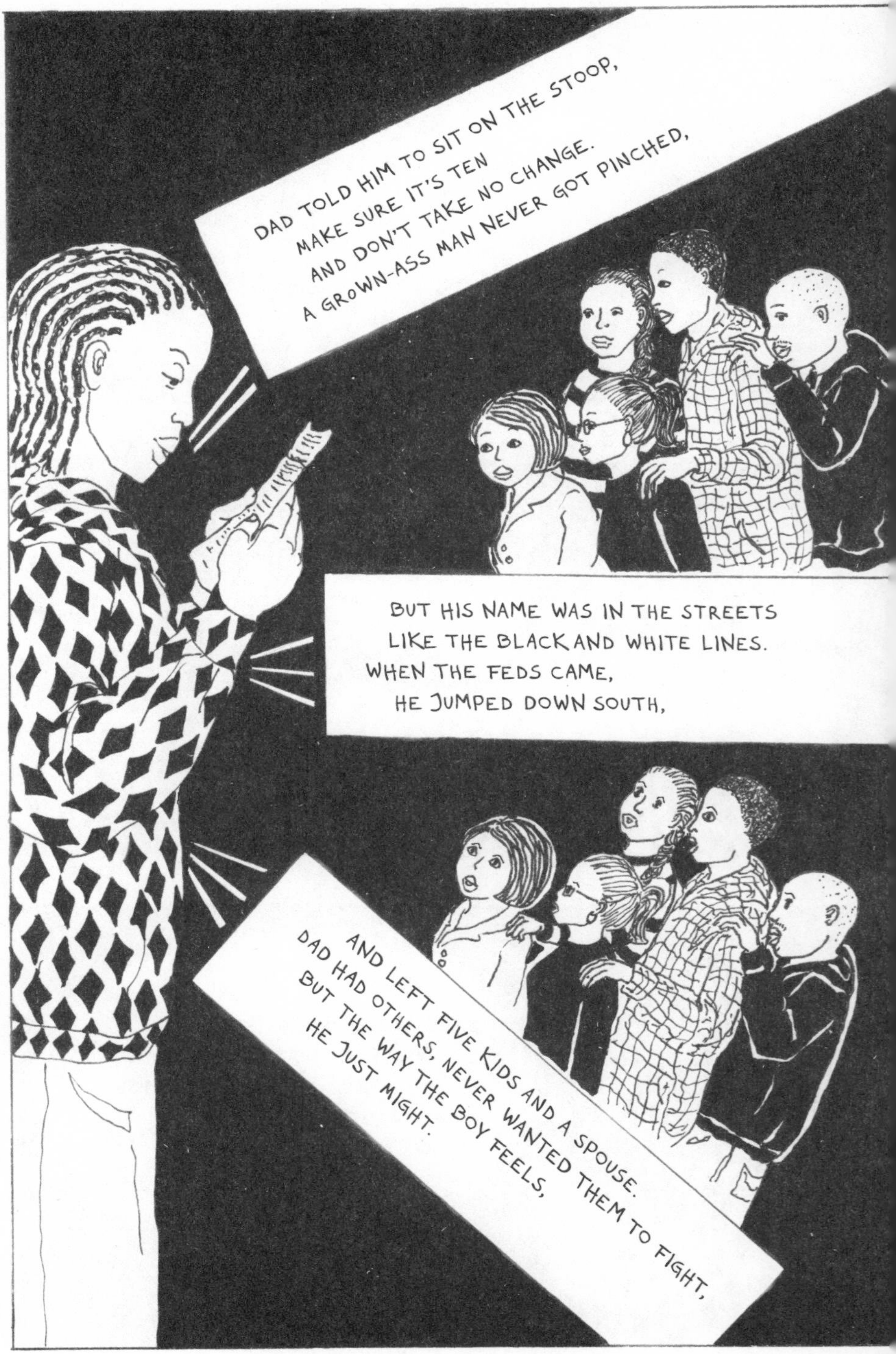
DAD TOLD HIM TO SIT ON THE STOOP,
MAKE SURE IT'S TEN
AND DON'T TAKE NO CHANGE.
A GROWN-ASS MAN NEVER GOT PINCHED,
BUT HIS NAME WAS IN THE STREETS
LIKE THE BLACK AND WHITE LINES.
WHEN THE FEDS CAME,
HE JUMPED DOWN SOUTH,
AND LEFT FIVE KIDS AND A SPOUSE.
DAD HAD OTHERS, NEVER WANTED THEM TO FIGHT,
BUT THE WAY THE BOY FEELS,
HE JUST MIGHT.

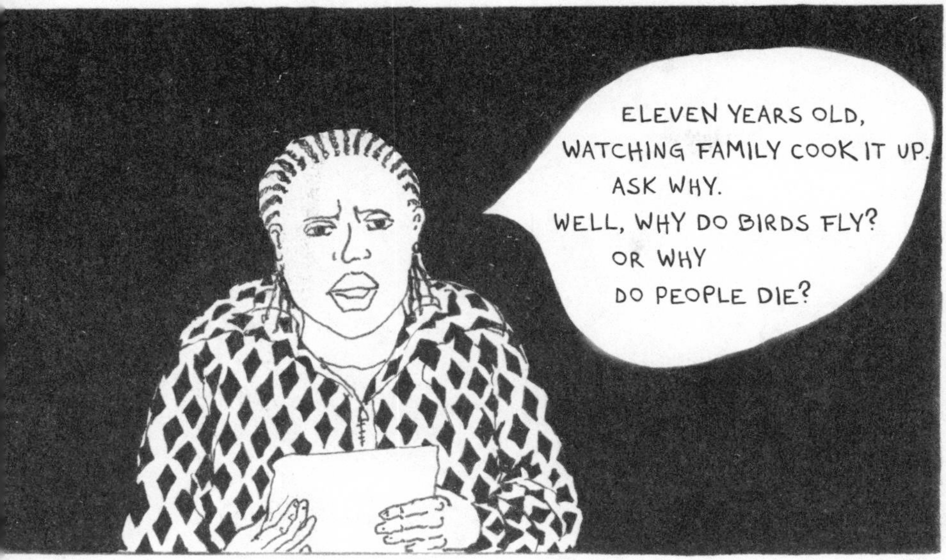
ELEVEN YEARS OLD,
WATCHING FAMILY COOK IT UP.
ASK WHY.
WELL, WHY DO BIRDS FLY?
OR WHY
DO PEOPLE DIE?

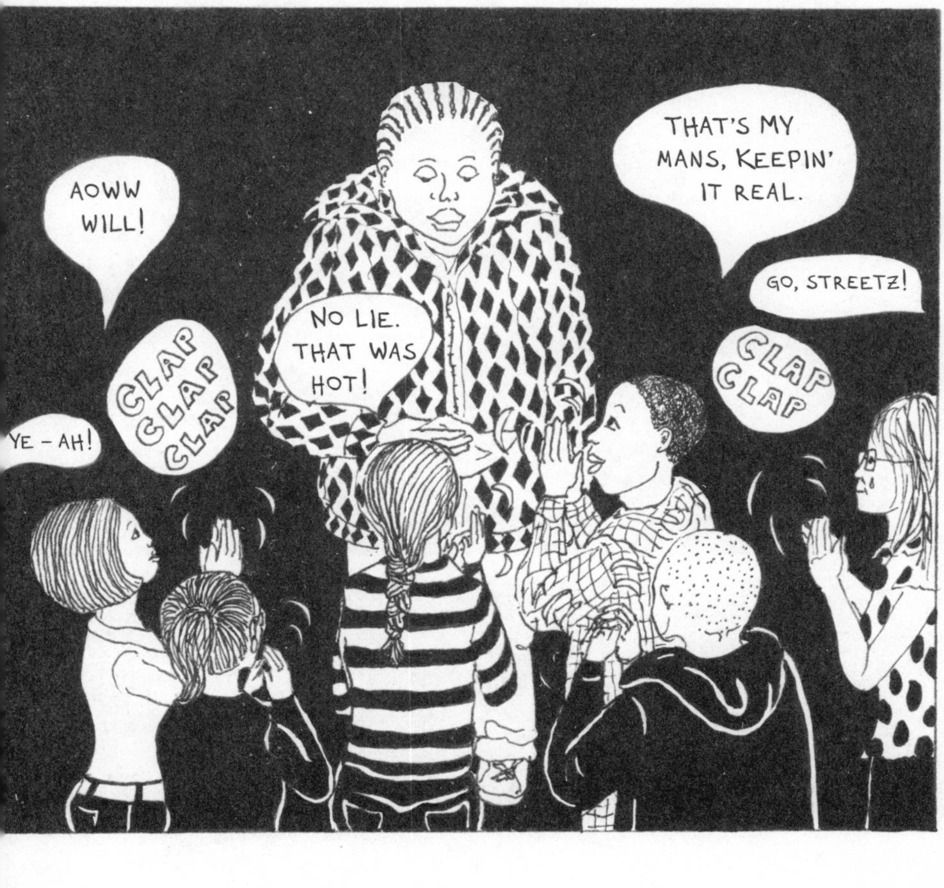
AOWW WILL!
THAT'S MY MANS, KEEPIN' IT REAL.
GO, STREETZ!
NO LIE. THAT WAS HOT!
CLAP CLAP CLAP
CLAP CLAP
YE - AH!

CHAPTER THREE

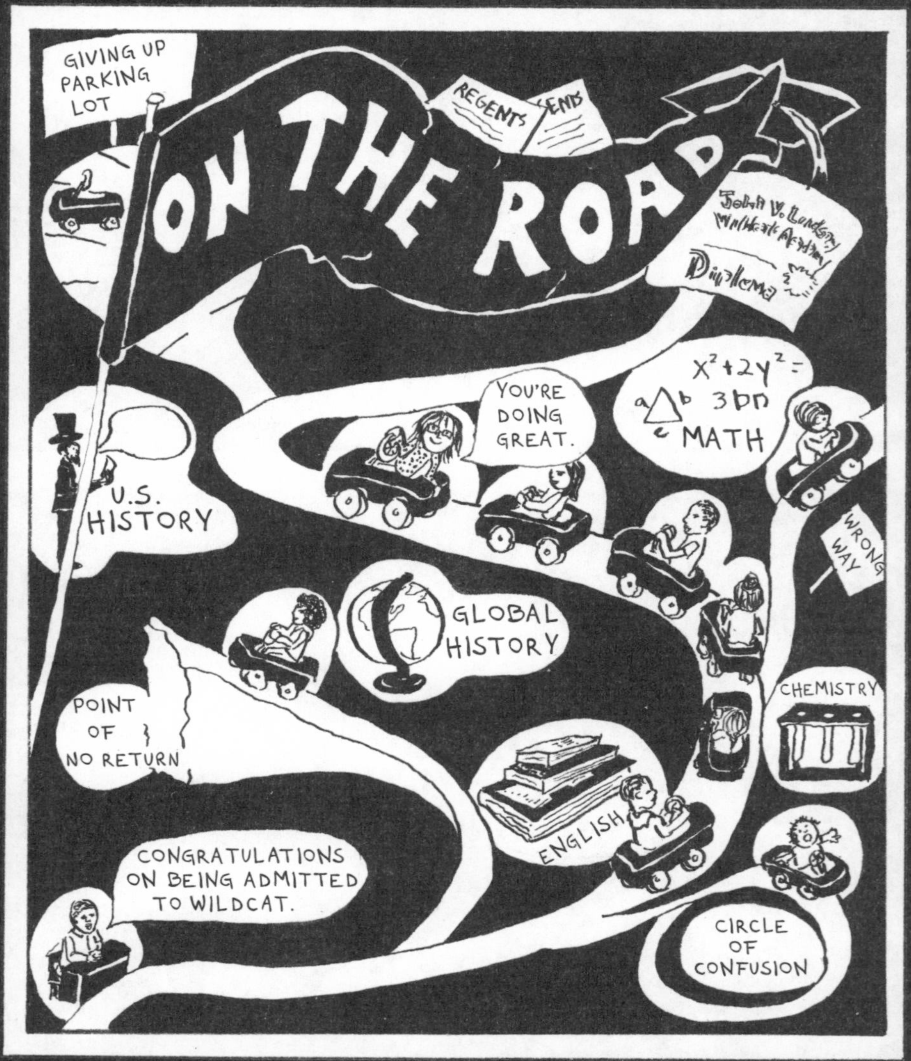

GIVING UP PARKING LOT
ON THE ROAD
REGENTS
YOU'RE DOING GREAT.
MATH
U.S. HISTORY
WRONG WAY
GLOBAL HISTORY
CHEMISTRY
POINT OF NO RETURN
ENGLISH
CONGRATULATIONS ON BEING ADMITTED TO WILDCAT.
CIRCLE OF CONFUSION

"HERE'S TO THE CRAZY ONES, THE MISFITS, THE REBELS, THE TROUBLEMAKERS, THE ROUND PEGS IN THE SQUARE HOLES...THE ONES WHO SEE THINGS DIFFERENTLY— THEY'RE NOT FOND OF RULES."

JACK KEROUAC

A SEMESTER ALWAYS HAS ITS PHASES, THE BEGINNING

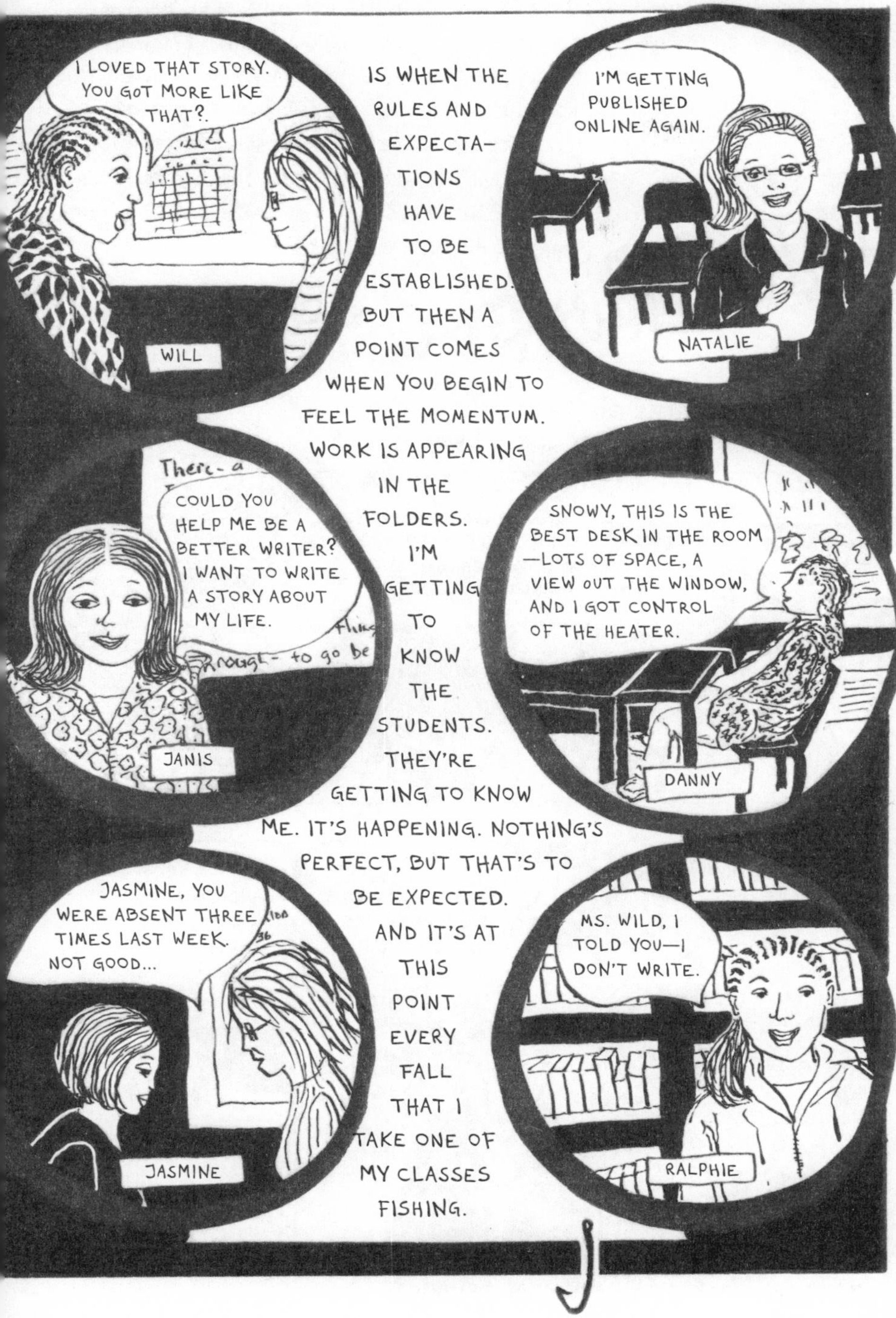
I LOVED THAT STORY. YOU GOT MORE LIKE THAT?.
WILL
IS WHEN THE RULES AND EXPECTATIONS HAVE TO BE ESTABLISHED. BUT THEN A POINT COMES WHEN YOU BEGIN TO FEEL THE MOMENTUM. WORK IS APPEARING IN THE FOLDERS. I'M GETTING TO KNOW THE STUDENTS. THEY'RE GETTING TO KNOW ME. IT'S HAPPENING. NOTHING'S PERFECT, BUT THAT'S TO BE EXPECTED. AND IT'S AT THIS POINT EVERY FALL THAT I TAKE ONE OF MY CLASSES FISHING.
I'M GETTING PUBLISHED ONLINE AGAIN.
NATALIE
COULD YOU HELP ME BE A BETTER WRITER? I WANT TO WRITE A STORY ABOUT MY LIFE.
JANIS
SNOWY, THIS IS THE BEST DESK IN THE ROOM —LOTS OF SPACE, A VIEW OUT THE WINDOW, AND I GOT CONTROL OF THE HEATER.
DANNY
JASMINE, YOU WERE ABSENT THREE TIMES LAST WEEK. NOT GOOD...
JASMINE
MS. WILD, I TOLD YOU—I DON'T WRITE.
RALPHIE

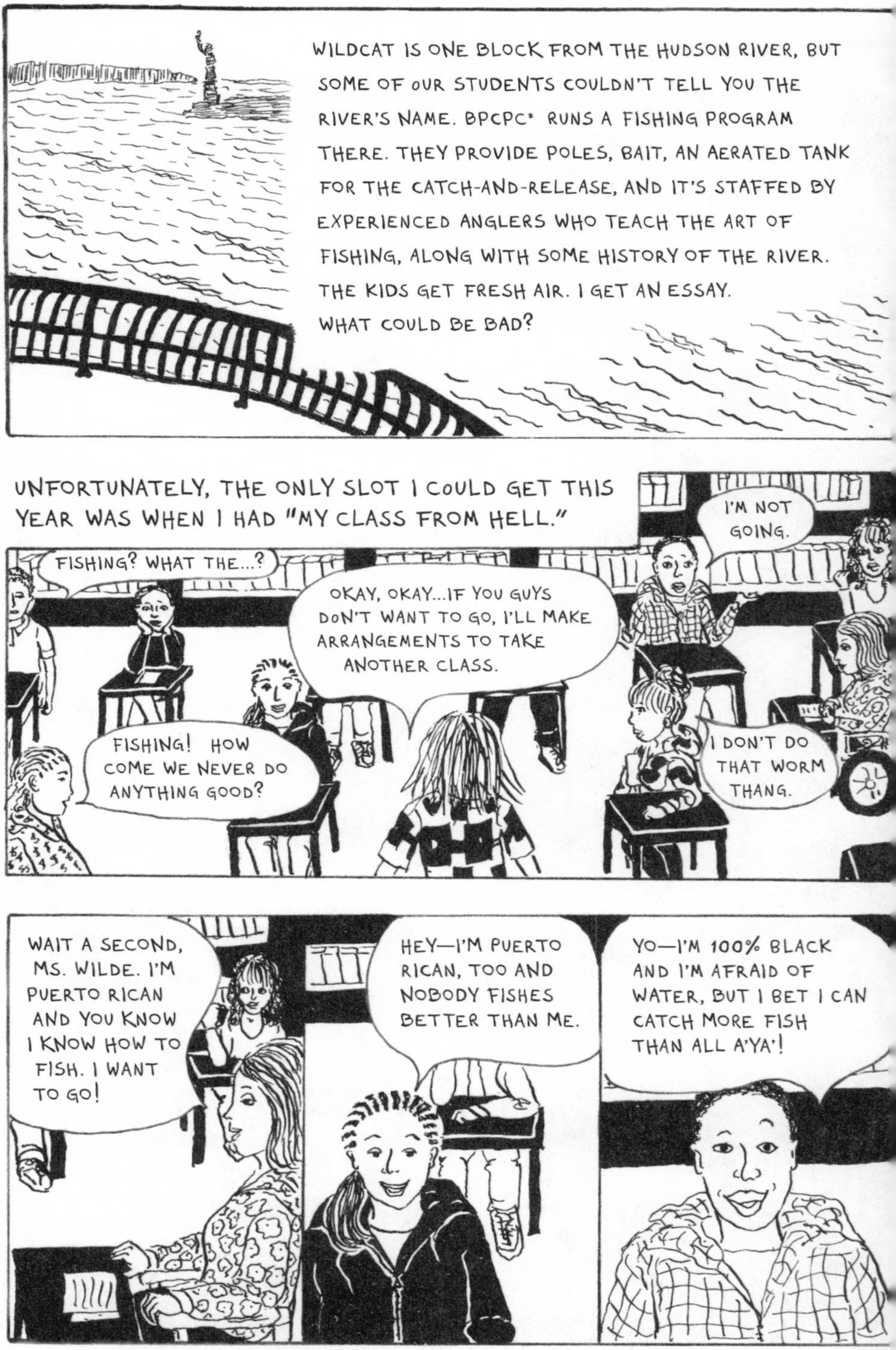
WILDCAT IS ONE BLOCK FROM THE HUDSON RIVER, BUT SOME OF OUR STUDENTS COULDN'T TELL YOU THE RIVER'S NAME. BPCPC* RUNS A FISHING PROGRAM THERE. THEY PROVIDE POLES, BAIT, AN AERATED TANK FOR THE CATCH-AND-RELEASE, AND IT'S STAFFED BY EXPERIENCED ANGLERS WHO TEACH THE ART OF FISHING, ALONG WITH SOME HISTORY OF THE RIVER. THE KIDS GET FRESH AIR. I GET AN ESSAY.
WHAT COULD BE BAD?
UNFORTUNATELY, THE ONLY SLOT I COULD GET THIS YEAR WAS WHEN I HAD "MY CLASS FROM HELL."
FISHING? WHAT THE...?
OKAY, OKAY...IF YOU GUYS DON'T WANT TO GO, I'LL MAKE ARRANGEMENTS TO TAKE ANOTHER CLASS.
I'M NOT GOING.
FISHING! HOW COME WE NEVER DO ANYTHING GOOD?
I DON'T DO THAT WORM THANG.
WAIT A SECOND, MS. WILDE. I'M PUERTO RICAN AND YOU KNOW I KNOW HOW TO FISH. I WANT TO GO!
HEY—I'M PUERTO RICAN, TOO AND NOBODY FISHES BETTER THAN ME.
YO—I'M 100% BLACK AND I'M AFRAID OF WATER, BUT I BET I CAN CATCH MORE FISH THAN ALL A'YA'!

* BATTERY PARK CITY PARK CONSERVANCY

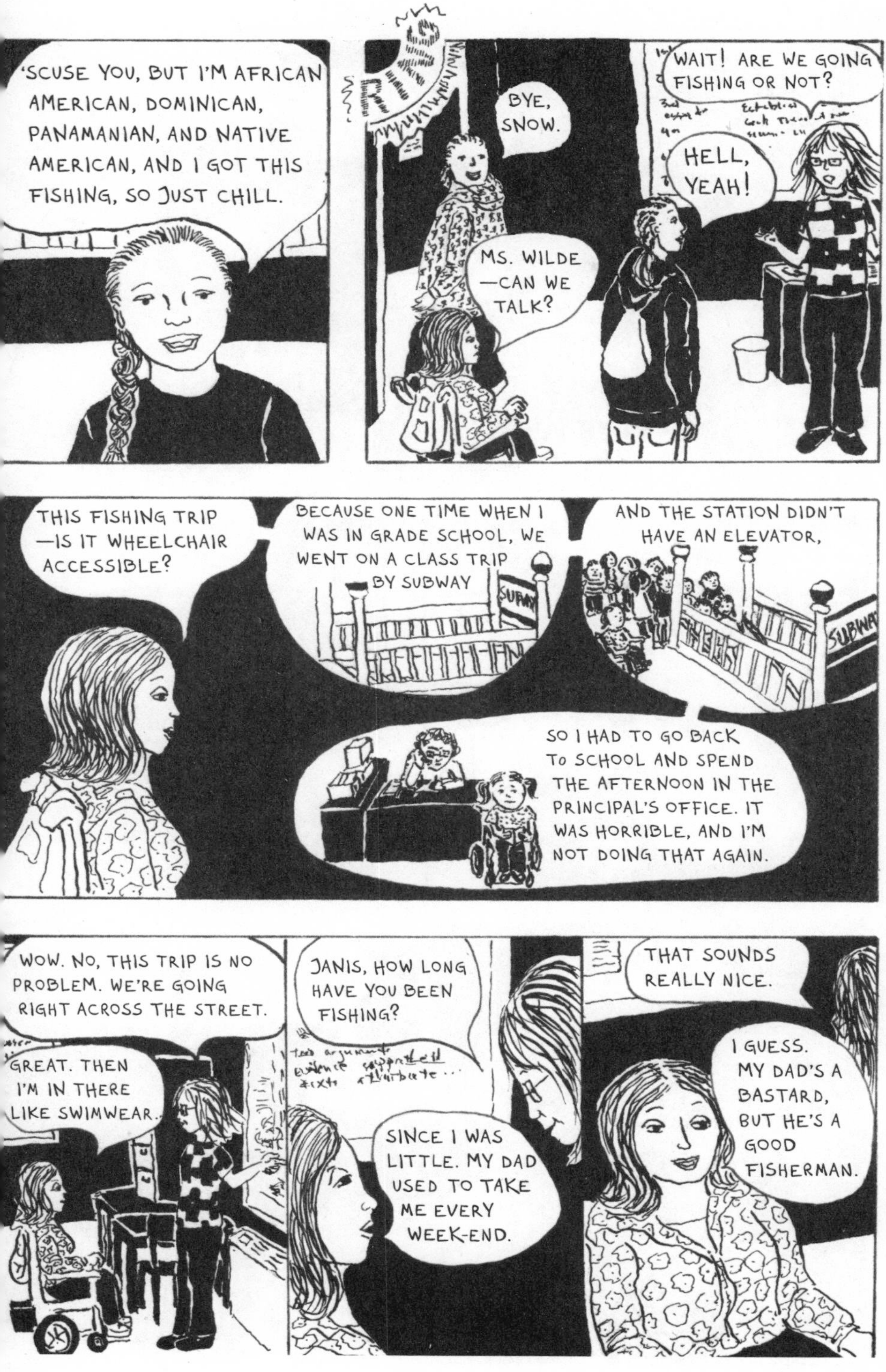
'SCUSE YOU, BUT I'M AFRICAN AMERICAN, DOMINICAN, PANAMANIAN, AND NATIVE AMERICAN, AND I GOT THIS FISHING, SO JUST CHILL.
BYE, SNOW.
MS. WILDE —CAN WE TALK?
WAIT! ARE WE GOING FISHING OR NOT?
HELL, YEAH!
THIS FISHING TRIP —IS IT WHEELCHAIR ACCESSIBLE?
BECAUSE ONE TIME WHEN I WAS IN GRADE SCHOOL, WE WENT ON A CLASS TRIP BY SUBWAY
SUBWAY
AND THE STATION DIDN'T HAVE AN ELEVATOR,
SUBWAY
SO I HAD TO GO BACK TO SCHOOL AND SPEND THE AFTERNOON IN THE PRINCIPAL'S OFFICE. IT WAS HORRIBLE, AND I'M NOT DOING THAT AGAIN.
WOW. NO, THIS TRIP IS NO PROBLEM. WE'RE GOING RIGHT ACROSS THE STREET.
GREAT. THEN I'M IN THERE LIKE SWIMWEAR.
JANIS, HOW LONG HAVE YOU BEEN FISHING?
SINCE I WAS LITTLE. MY DAD USED TO TAKE ME EVERY WEEK-END.
THAT SOUNDS REALLY NICE.
I GUESS. MY DAD'S A BASTARD, BUT HE'S A GOOD FISHERMAN.

DAY OF THE FISHING TRIP

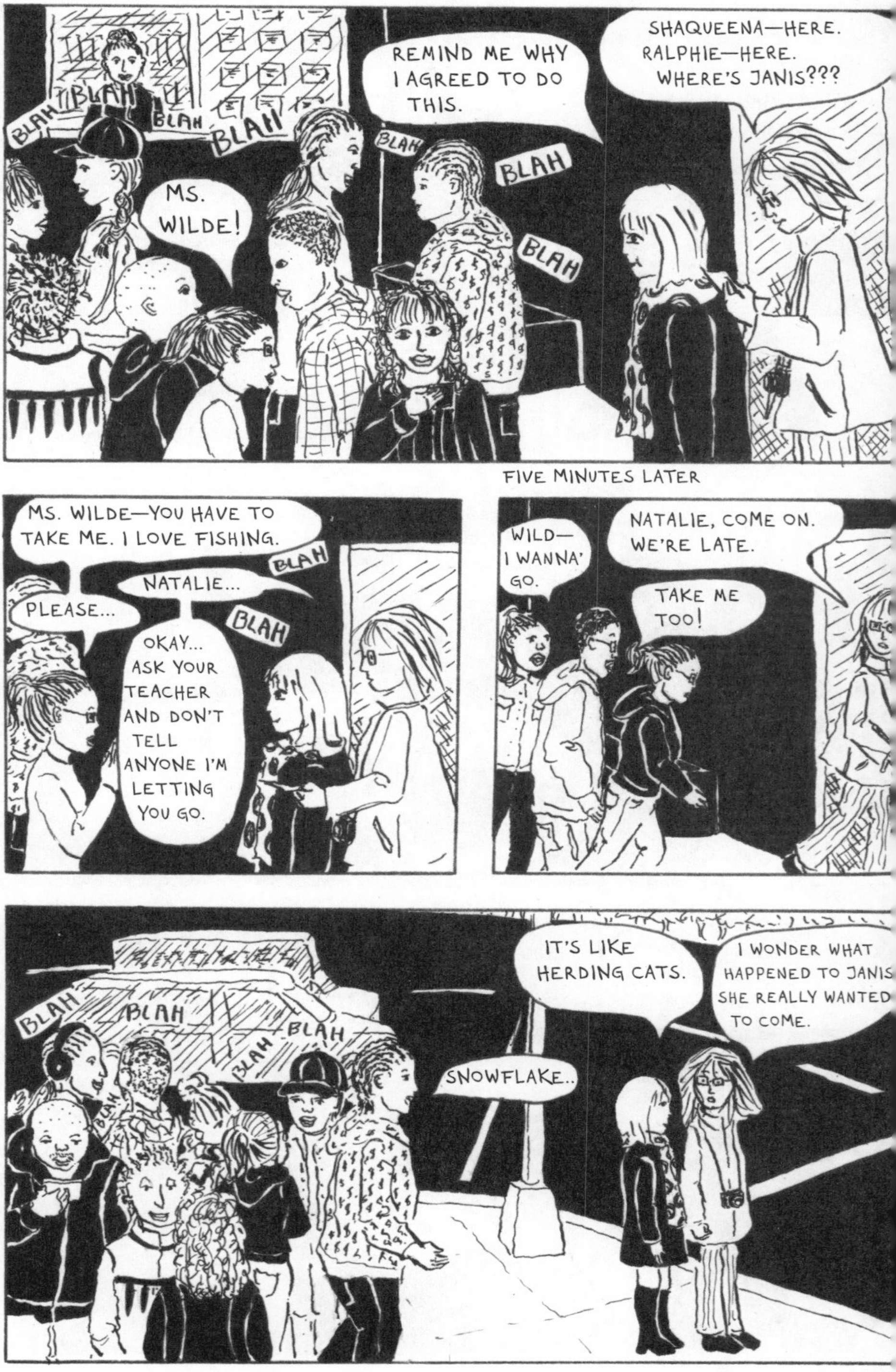
BLAH BLAH BLAH BLAH BLAH
MS. WILDE!
REMIND ME WHY I AGREED TO DO THIS.
BLAH BLAH BLAH
SHAQUEENA—HERE. RALPHIE—HERE. WHERE'S JANIS???
FIVE MINUTES LATER
MS. WILDE—YOU HAVE TO TAKE ME. I LOVE FISHING.
BLAH
PLEASE...
NATALIE...
BLAH
OKAY... ASK YOUR TEACHER AND DON'T TELL ANYONE I'M LETTING YOU GO.
WILD— I WANNA' GO.
NATALIE, COME ON. WE'RE LATE.
TAKE ME TOO!
BLAH BLAH BLAH BLAH BLAH
SNOWFLAKE..
IT'S LIKE HERDING CATS.
I WONDER WHAT HAPPENED TO JANIS SHE REALLY WANTED TO COME.

AT THE RIVER

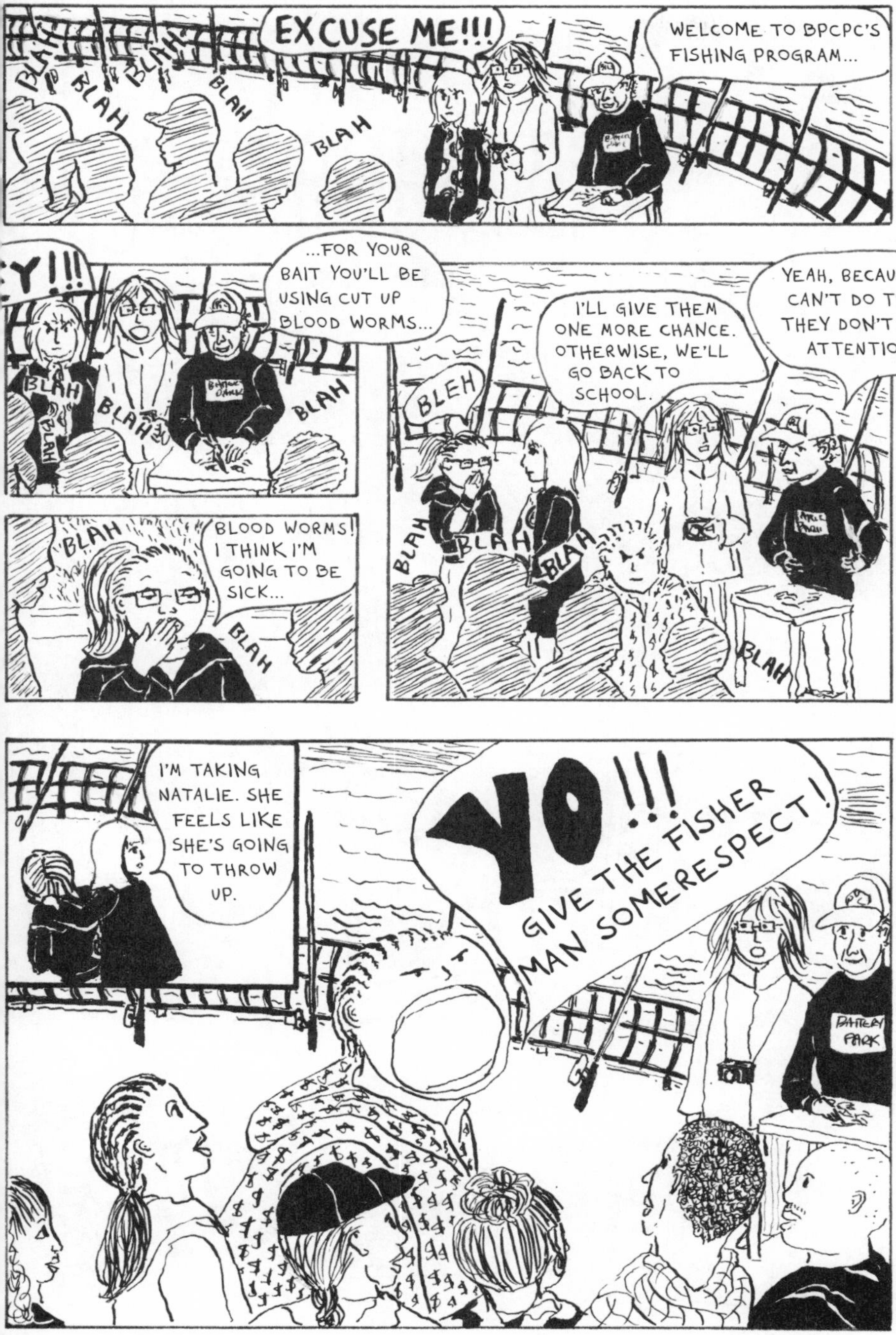
BLAH BLAH BLAH BLAH BLAH BLAH
EXCUSE ME!!!
WELCOME TO BPCPC'S FISHING PROGRAM...
Y!!!
...FOR YOUR BAIT YOU'LL BE USING CUT UP BLOOD WORMS...
BLAH BLAH BLAH BLAH
BLOOD WORMS! I THINK I'M GOING TO BE SICK...
BLAH BLAH
BLEH
I'LL GIVE THEM ONE MORE CHANCE. OTHERWISE, WE'LL GO BACK TO SCHOOL.
YEAH, BECAUSE I CAN'T DO THIS IF THEY DON'T PAY ATTENTION
BLAH BLAH BLAH BLAH
I'M TAKING NATALIE. SHE FEELS LIKE SHE'S GOING TO THROW UP.
YO!!! GIVE THE FISHER MAN SOMERESPECT!
BATTERY PARK

FISHING SNAPS

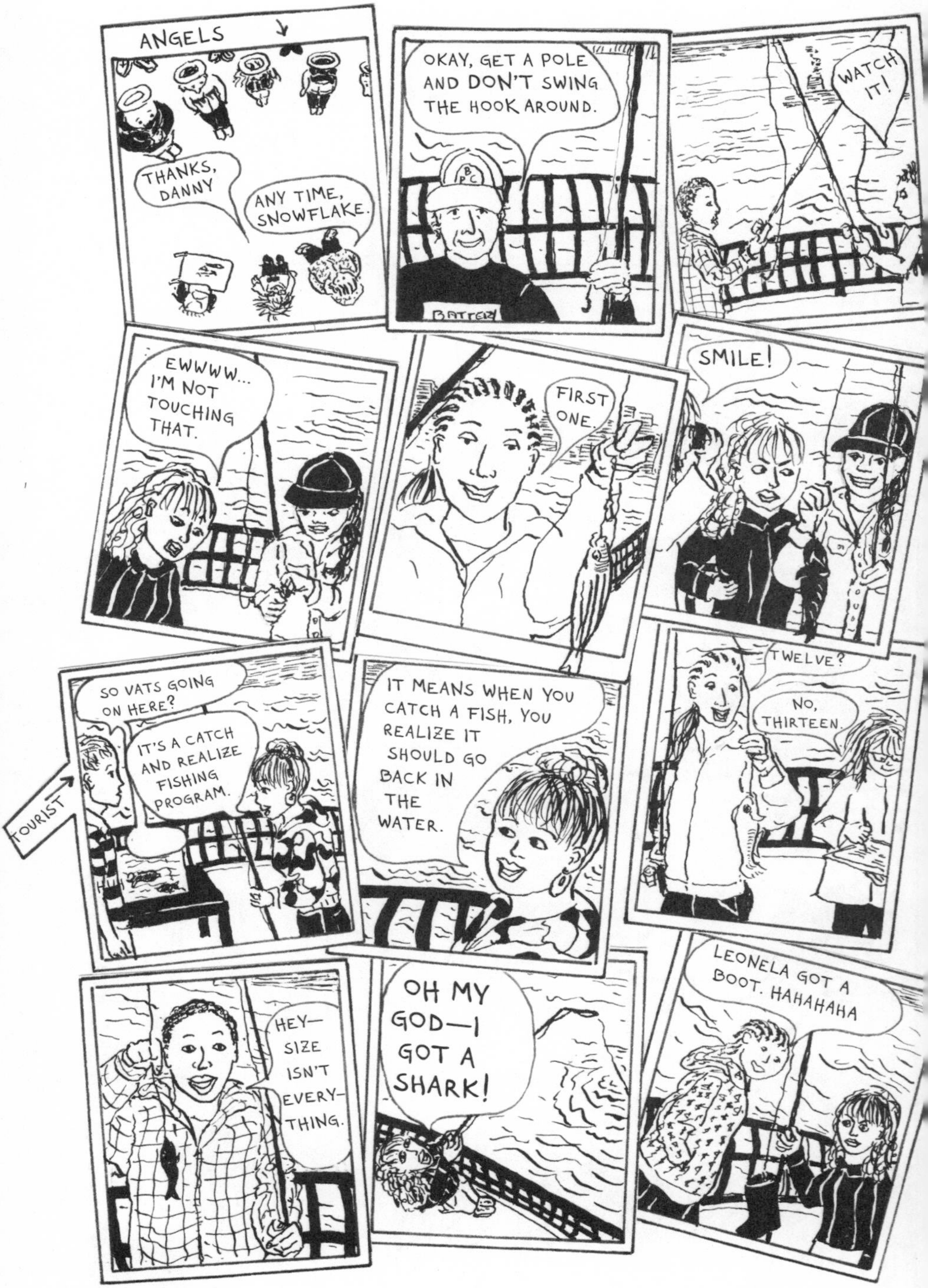
ANGELS
THANKS, DANNY
ANY TIME, SNOWFLAKE.
OKAY, GET A POLE AND DON'T SWING THE HOOK AROUND.
BATTERY
WATCH IT!
EWWWW... I'M NOT TOUCHING THAT.
FIRST ONE.
SMILE!
SO VATS GOING ON HERE?
TOURIST
IT'S A CATCH AND REALIZE FISHING PROGRAM.
IT MEANS WHEN YOU CATCH A FISH, YOU REALIZE IT SHOULD GO BACK IN THE WATER.
TWELVE?
NO, THIRTEEN.
HEY— SIZE ISN'T EVERYTHING.
OH MY GOD—I GOT A SHARK!
LEONELA GOT A BOOT. HAHAHAHA

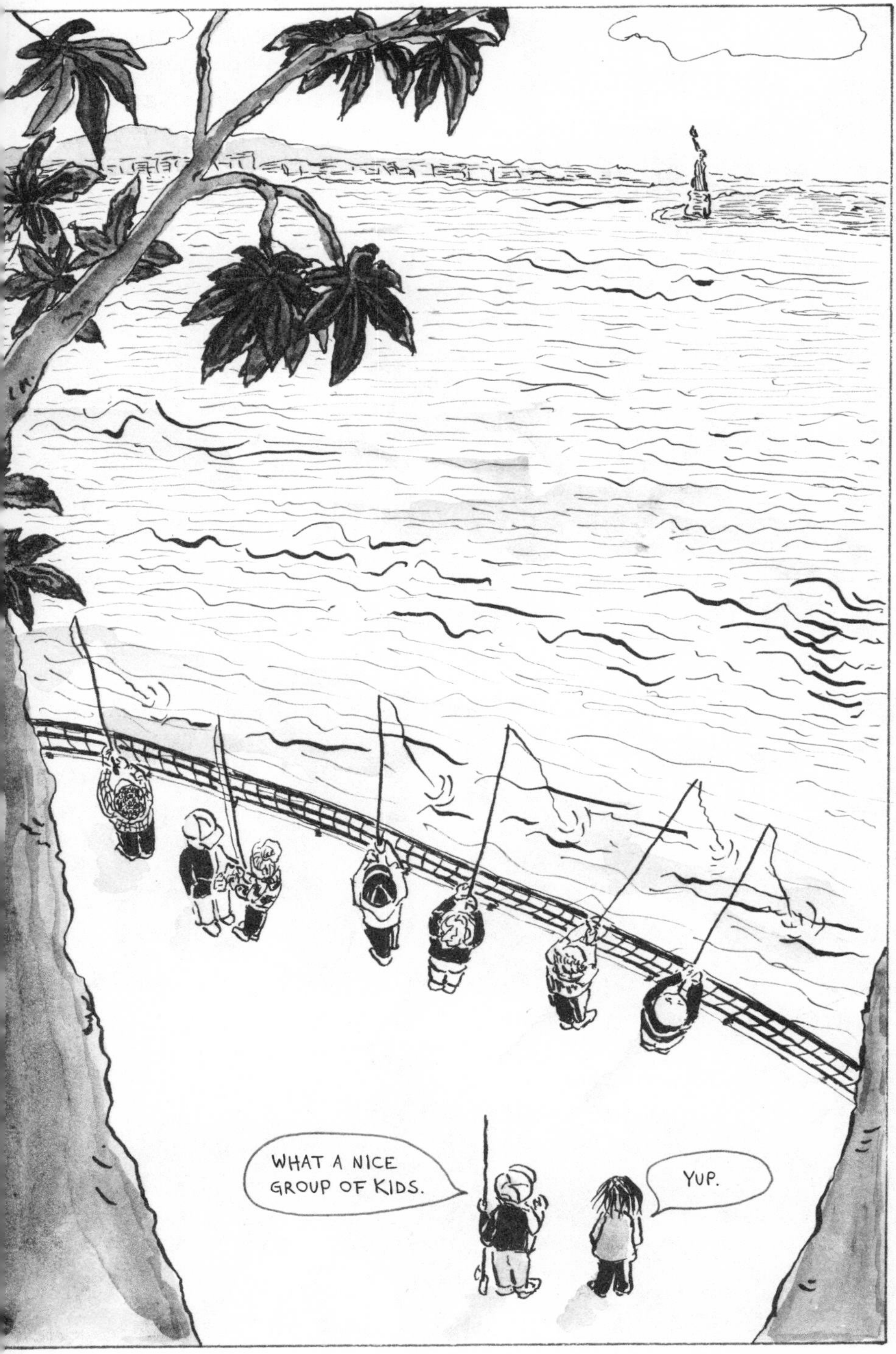
WHAT A NICE GROUP OF KIDS.
YUP.

BACK AT SCHOOL

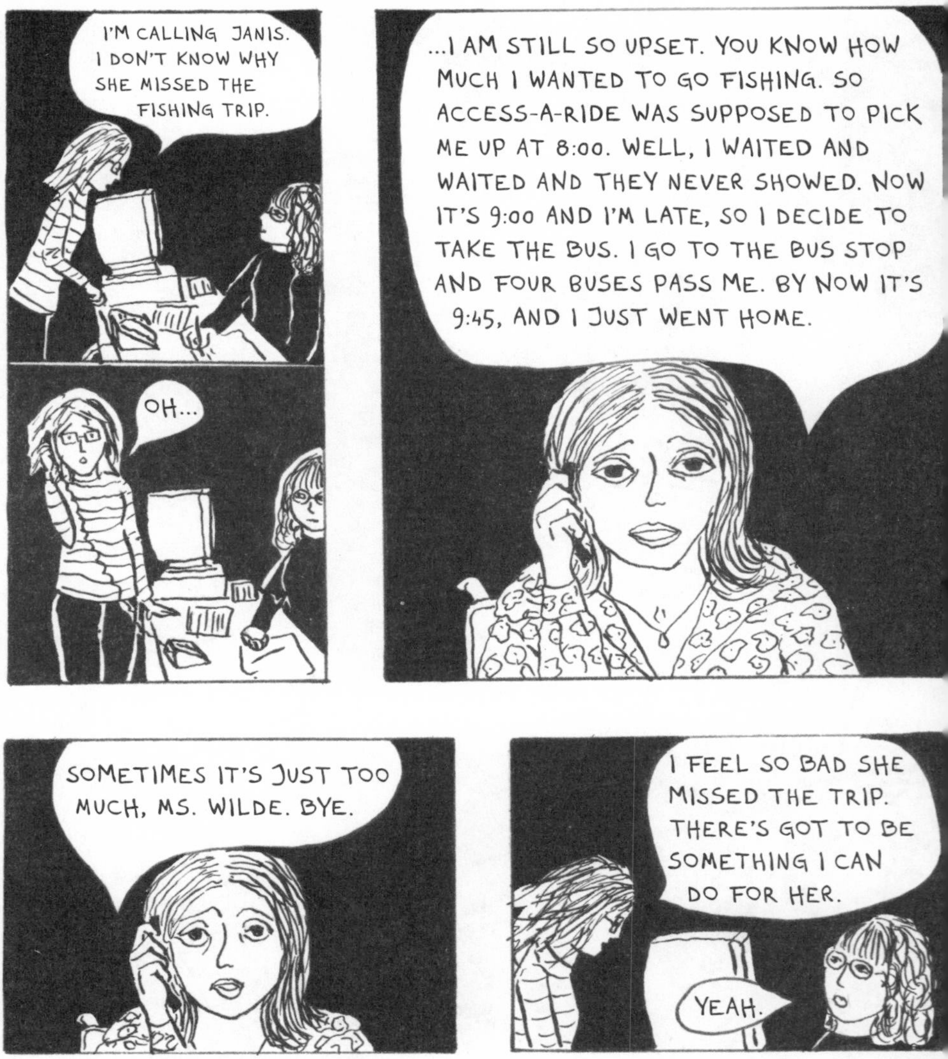
I'M CALLING JANIS. I DON'T KNOW WHY SHE MISSED THE FISHING TRIP.
OH...
...I AM STILL SO UPSET. YOU KNOW HOW MUCH I WANTED TO GO FISHING. SO ACCESS-A-RIDE WAS SUPPOSED TO PICK ME UP AT 8:00. WELL, I WAITED AND WAITED AND THEY NEVER SHOWED. NOW IT'S 9:00 AND I'M LATE, SO I DECIDE TO TAKE THE BUS. I GO TO THE BUS STOP AND FOUR BUSES PASS ME. BY NOW IT'S 9:45, AND I JUST WENT HOME.
SOMETIMES IT'S JUST TOO MUCH, MS. WILDE. BYE.
I FEEL SO BAD SHE MISSED THE TRIP. THERE'S GOT TO BE SOMETHING I CAN DO FOR HER.
YEAH.

AT HOME THAT EVENING

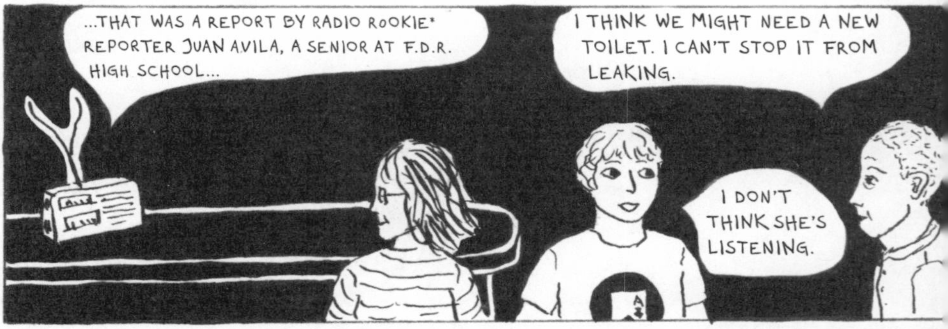
...THAT WAS A REPORT BY RADIO ROOKIE* REPORTER JUAN AVILA, A SENIOR AT F.D.R. HIGH SCHOOL...
I THINK WE MIGHT NEED A NEW TOILET. I CAN'T STOP IT FROM LEAKING.
I DON'T THINK SHE'S LISTENING.

*RADIO ROOKIES IS A PROGRAM SPONSORED BY PUBLIC RADIO THAT GIVES TEENS THE OPPORTUNITY TO CREATE THEIR OWN RADIO STORY.

THE NEXT DAY

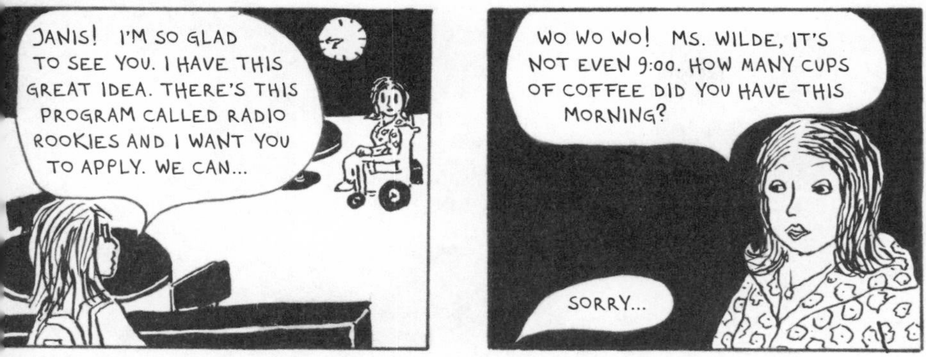
JANIS! I'M SO GLAD TO SEE YOU. I HAVE THIS GREAT IDEA. THERE'S THIS PROGRAM CALLED RADIO ROOKIES AND I WANT YOU TO APPLY. WE CAN...
WO WO WO! MS. WILDE, IT'S NOT EVEN 9:00. HOW MANY CUPS OF COFFEE DID YOU HAVE THIS MORNING?
SORRY...

6TH PERIOD

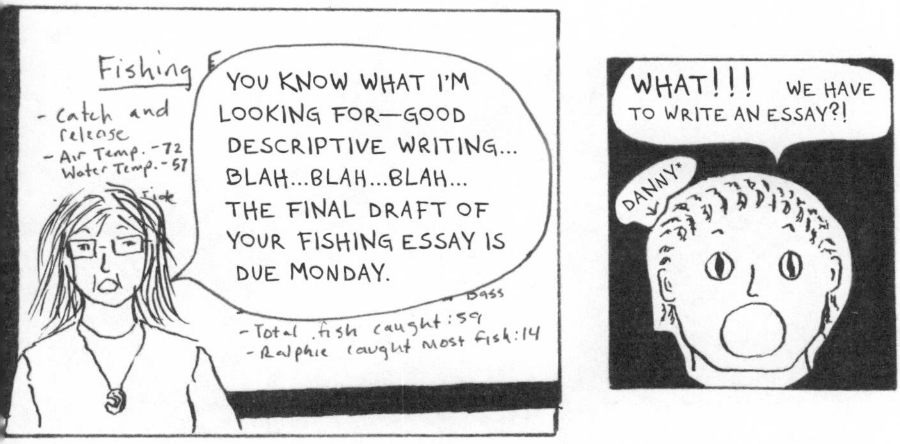
Fishing
- Catch and release
- Air Temp. - 72
Water Temp. - 57
YOU KNOW WHAT I'M LOOKING FOR—GOOD DESCRIPTIVE WRITING... BLAH...BLAH...BLAH... THE FINAL DRAFT OF YOUR FISHING ESSAY IS DUE MONDAY.
- Total fish caught: 59
- Ralphie caught most fish: 14
WHAT!!! WE HAVE TO WRITE AN ESSAY?!
DANNY*

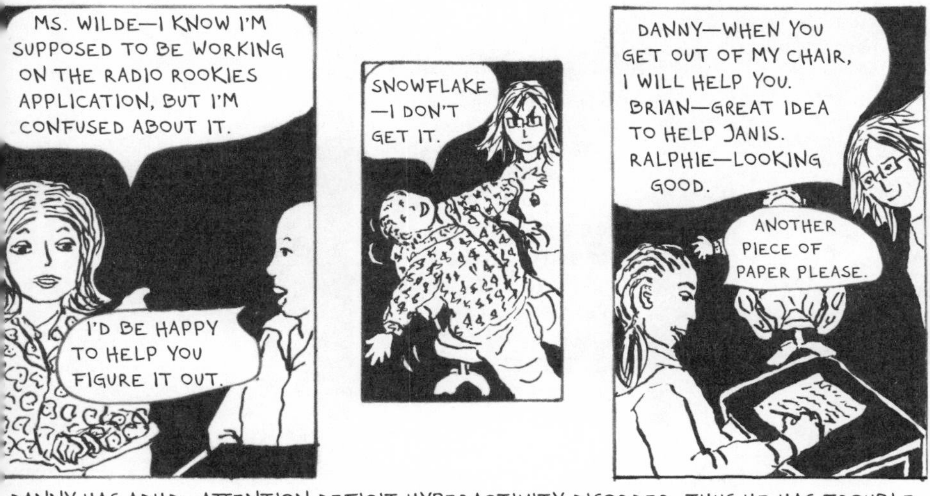
MS. WILDE—I KNOW I'M SUPPOSED TO BE WORKING ON THE RADIO ROOKIES APPLICATION, BUT I'M CONFUSED ABOUT IT.
I'D BE HAPPY TO HELP YOU FIGURE IT OUT.
SNOWFLAKE—I DON'T GET IT.
DANNY—WHEN YOU GET OUT OF MY CHAIR, I WILL HELP YOU. BRIAN—GREAT IDEA TO HELP JANIS. RALPHIE—LOOKING GOOD.
ANOTHER PIECE OF PAPER PLEASE.

*DANNY HAS ADHD—ATTENTION DEFICIT HYPERACTIVITY DISORDER, THUS HE HAS TROUBLE STAYING FOCUSED AND HE GETS HYPER EASILY.

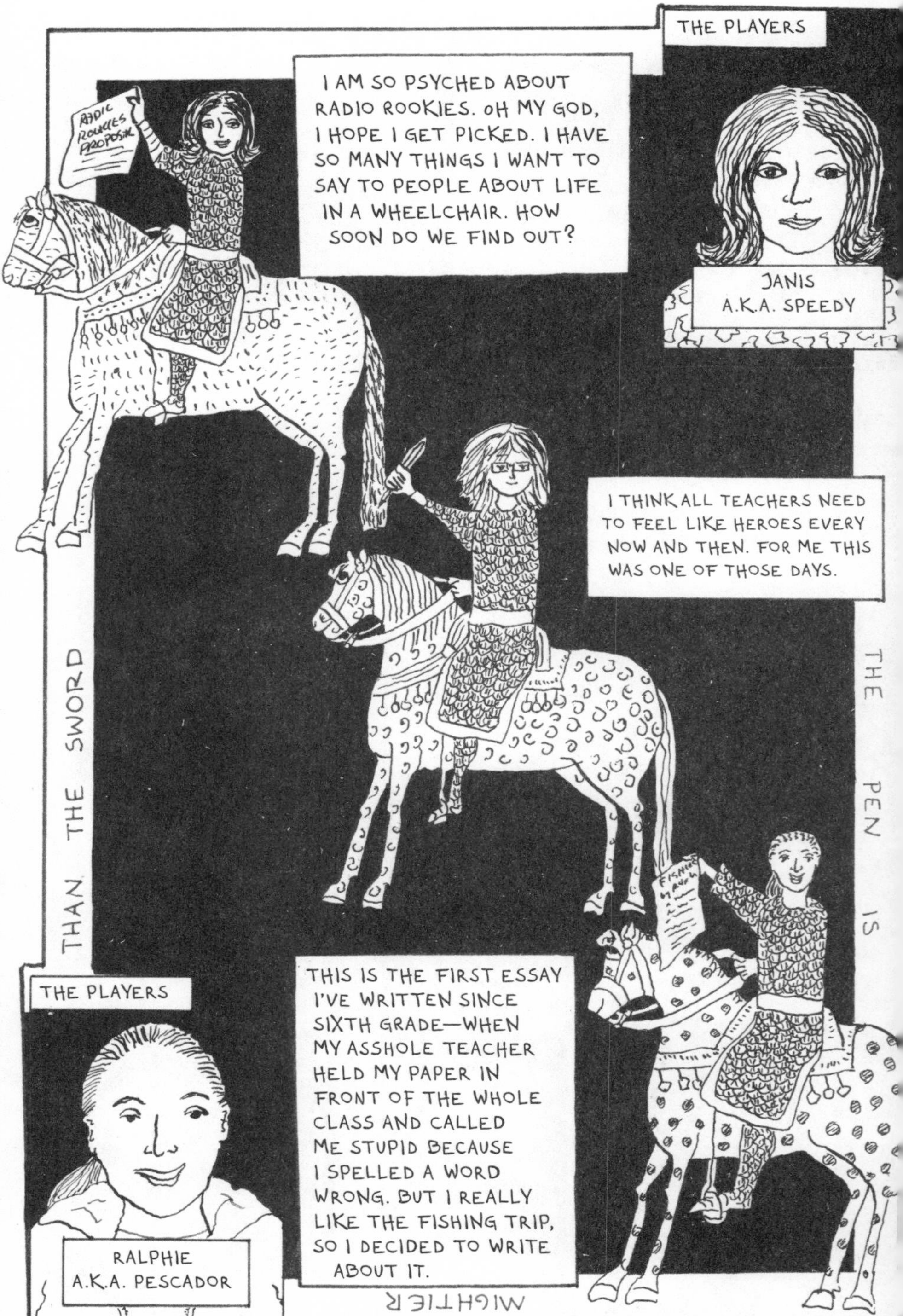
THE PLAYERS
I AM SO PSYCHED ABOUT RADIO ROOKIES. OH MY GOD, I HOPE I GET PICKED. I HAVE SO MANY THINGS I WANT TO SAY TO PEOPLE ABOUT LIFE IN A WHEELCHAIR. HOW SOON DO WE FIND OUT?
JANIS
A.K.A. SPEEDY
I THINK ALL TEACHERS NEED TO FEEL LIKE HEROES EVERY NOW AND THEN. FOR ME THIS WAS ONE OF THOSE DAYS.
THE PEN IS MIGHTIER THAN THE SWORD
THE PLAYERS
RALPHIE
A.K.A. PESCADOR
THIS IS THE FIRST ESSAY I'VE WRITTEN SINCE SIXTH GRADE—WHEN MY ASSHOLE TEACHER HELD MY PAPER IN FRONT OF THE WHOLE CLASS AND CALLED ME STUPID BECAUSE I SPELLED A WORD WRONG. BUT I REALLY LIKE THE FISHING TRIP, SO I DECIDED TO WRITE ABOUT IT.

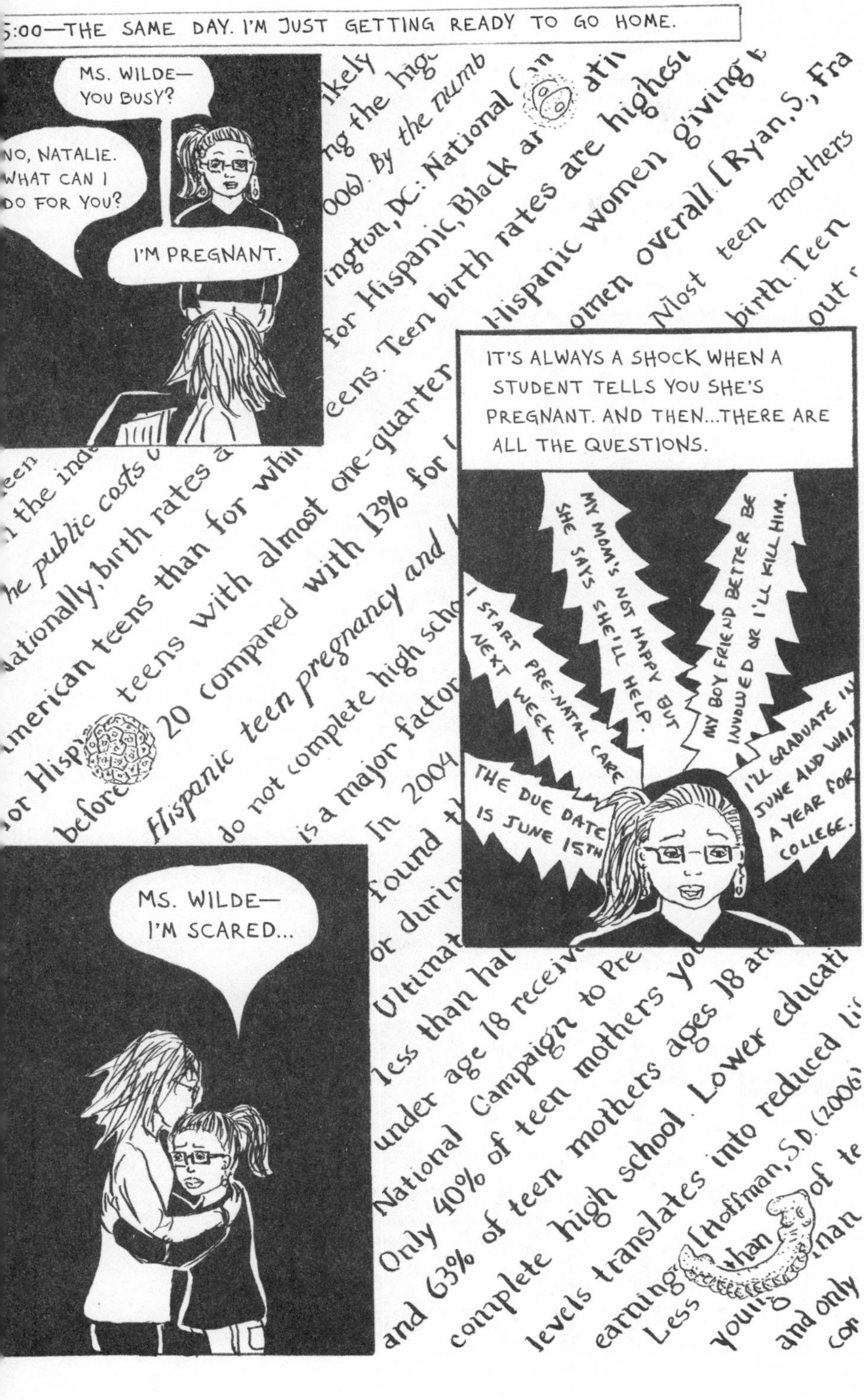
5:00—THE SAME DAY. I'M JUST GETTING READY TO GO HOME.
MS. WILDE— YOU BUSY?
NO, NATALIE. WHAT CAN I DO FOR YOU?
I'M PREGNANT.
IT'S ALWAYS A SHOCK WHEN A STUDENT TELLS YOU SHE'S PREGNANT. AND THEN...THERE ARE ALL THE QUESTIONS.
MY MOM'S NOT HAPPY BUT SHE SAYS SHE'LL HELP.
MY BOY FRIEND BETTER BE INVOLVED OR I'LL KILL HIM.
I START PRE-NATAL CARE NEXT WEEK.
THE DUE DATE IS JUNE 15TH
I'LL GRADUATE IN JUNE AND WAIT A YEAR FOR COLLEGE.
MS. WILDE— I'M SCARED...

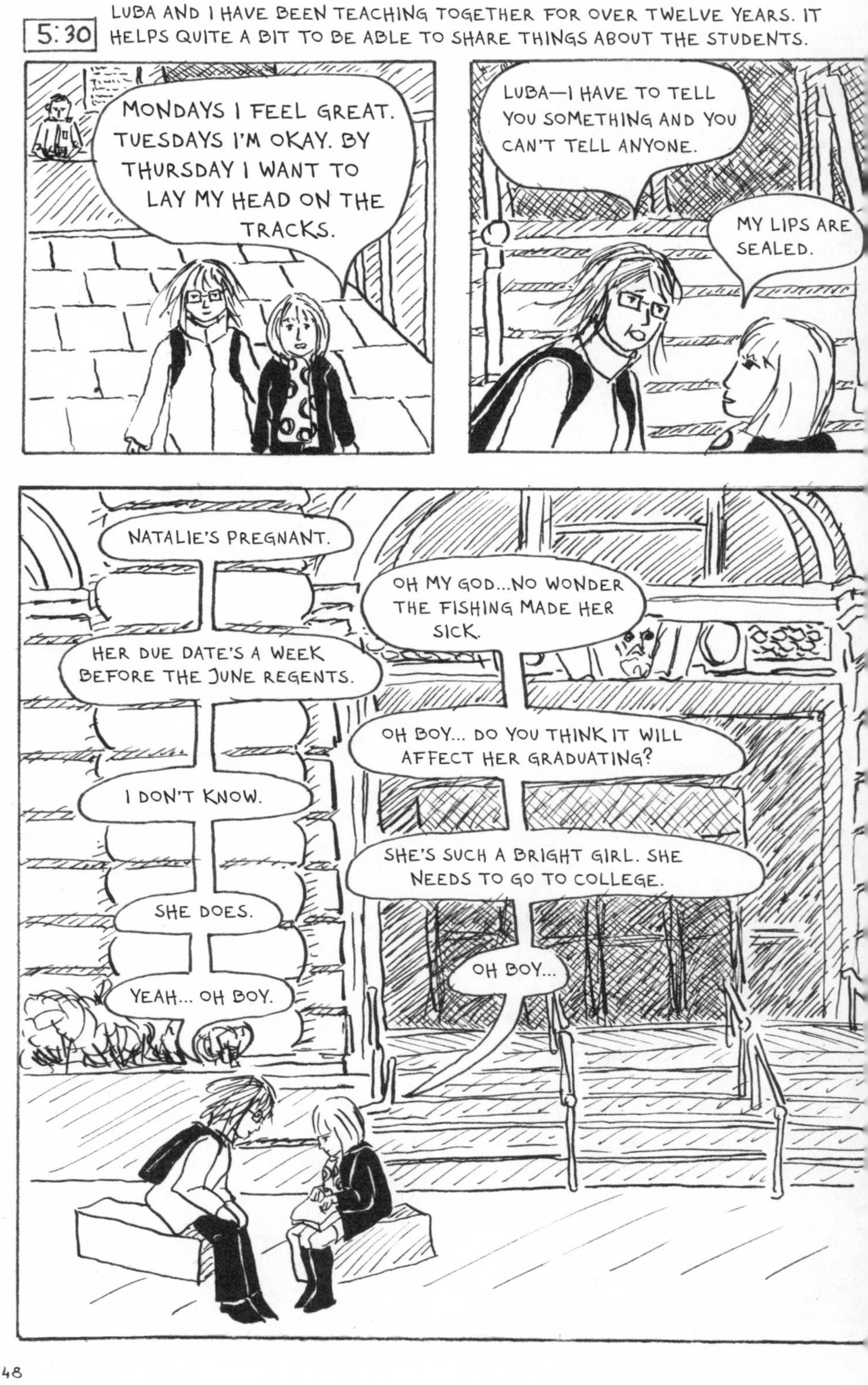
5:30
LUBA AND I HAVE BEEN TEACHING TOGETHER FOR OVER TWELVE YEARS. IT HELPS QUITE A BIT TO BE ABLE TO SHARE THINGS ABOUT THE STUDENTS.
MONDAYS I FEEL GREAT. TUESDAYS I'M OKAY. BY THURSDAY I WANT TO LAY MY HEAD ON THE TRACKS.
LUBA—I HAVE TO TELL YOU SOMETHING AND YOU CAN'T TELL ANYONE.
MY LIPS ARE SEALED.
NATALIE'S PREGNANT.
OH MY GOD...NO WONDER THE FISHING MADE HER SICK.
HER DUE DATE'S A WEEK BEFORE THE JUNE REGENTS.
OH BOY... DO YOU THINK IT WILL AFFECT HER GRADUATING?
I DON'T KNOW.
SHE'S SUCH A BRIGHT GIRL. SHE NEEDS TO GO TO COLLEGE.
SHE DOES.
OH BOY...
YEAH... OH BOY.

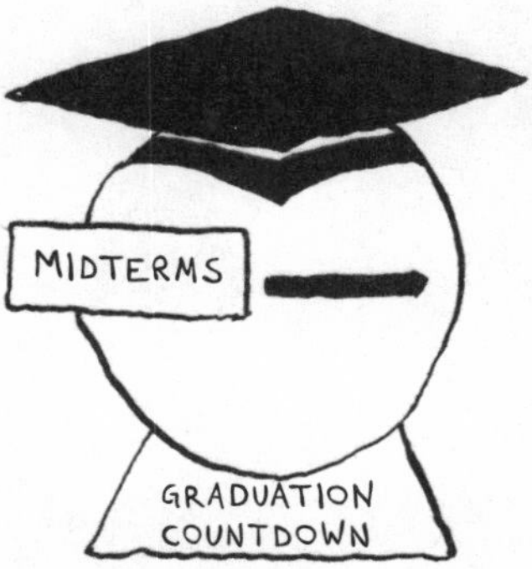
MIDTERMS
GRADUATION
COUNTDOWN

CHAPTER FOUR

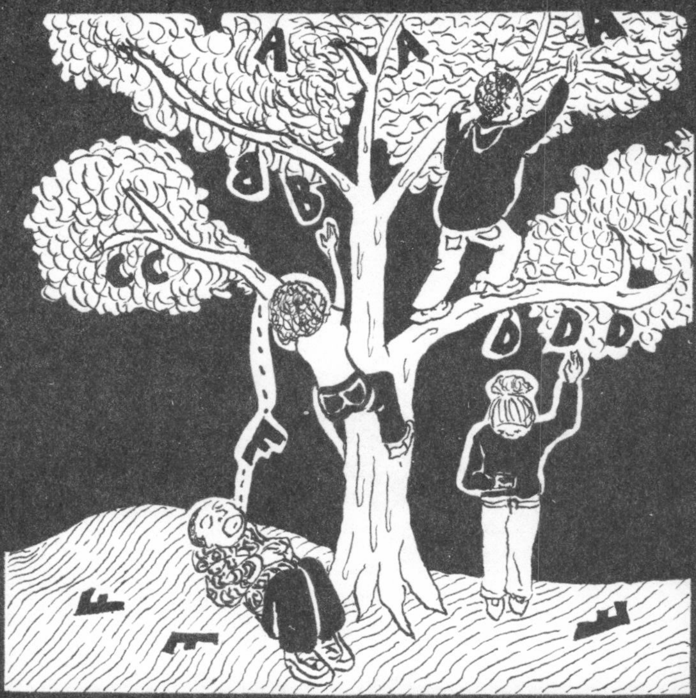

GREAT EXPECTATIONS

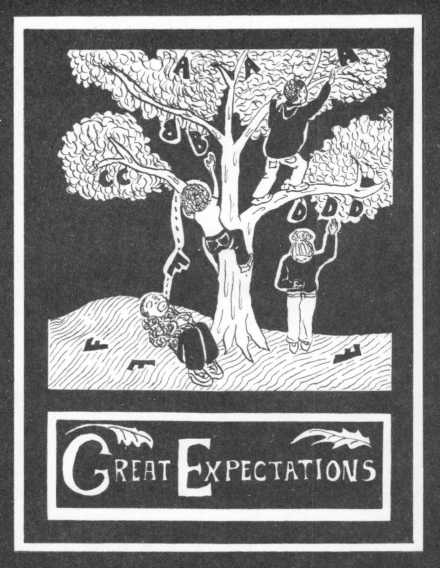

"THERE IS NOTHING SO STRONG OR SAFE IN AN EMERGENCY OF LIFE AS THE SIMPLE TRUTH."

CHARLES DICKENS

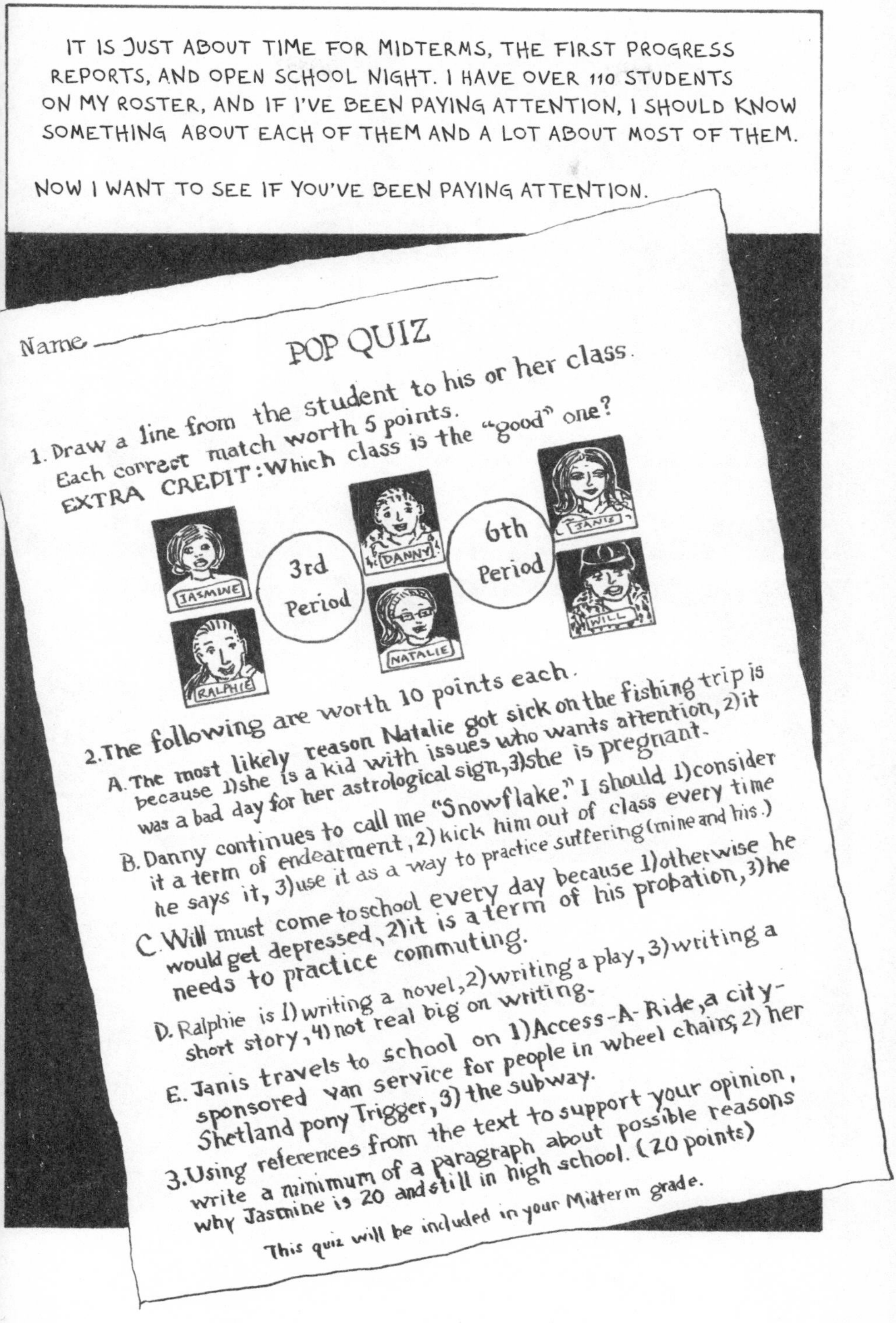
IT IS JUST ABOUT TIME FOR MIDTERMS, THE FIRST PROGRESS REPORTS, AND OPEN SCHOOL NIGHT. I HAVE OVER 110 STUDENTS ON MY ROSTER, AND IF I'VE BEEN PAYING ATTENTION, I SHOULD KNOW SOMETHING ABOUT EACH OF THEM AND A LOT ABOUT MOST OF THEM.
NOW I WANT TO SEE IF YOU'VE BEEN PAYING ATTENTION.
Name
POP QUIZ
1. Draw a line from the student to his or her class. Each correct match worth 5 points. EXTRA CREDIT: Which class is the "good" one?
JASMINE
RALPHIE
3rd Period
DANNY
NATALIE
6th Period
JANIS
WILL
2. The following are worth 10 points each.
A. The most likely reason Natalie got sick on the fishing trip is because 1) she is a kid with issues who wants attention, 2) it was a bad day for her astrological sign, 3) she is pregnant.
B. Danny continues to call me "Snowflake." I should 1) consider it a term of endearment, 2) kick him out of class every time he says it, 3) use it as a way to practice suffering (mine and his.)
C. Will must come to school every day because 1) otherwise he would get depressed, 2) it is a term of his probation, 3) he needs to practice commuting.
D. Ralphie is 1) writing a novel, 2) writing a play, 3) writing a short story, 4) not real big on writing.
E. Janis travels to school on 1) Access-A-Ride, a city-sponsored van service for people in wheel chairs, 2) her Shetland pony Trigger, 3) the subway.
3. Using references from the text to support your opinion, write a minimum of a paragraph about possible reasons why Jasmine is 20 and still in high school. (20 points)
This quiz will be included in your Midterm grade.

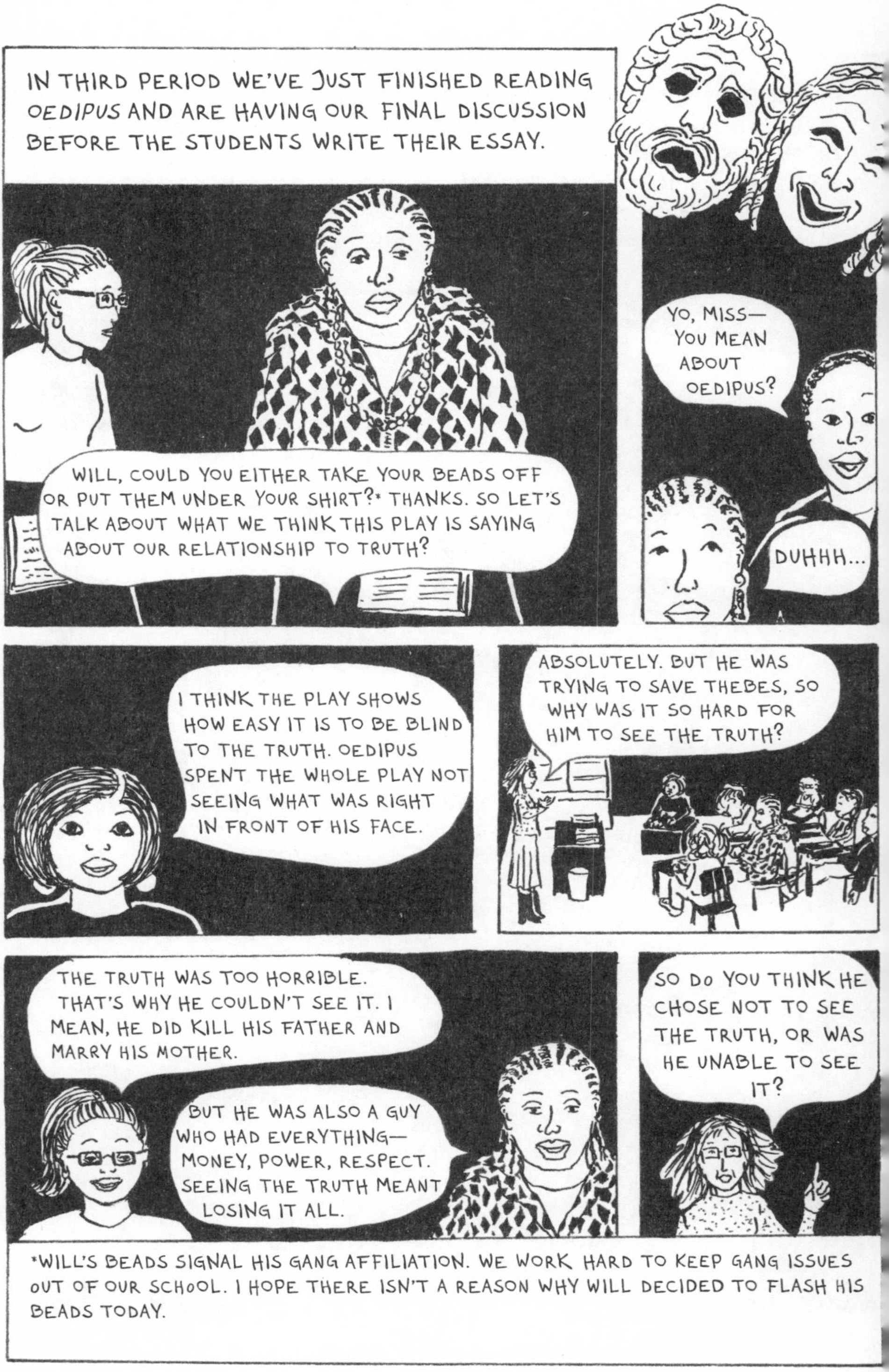
IN THIRD PERIOD WE'VE JUST FINISHED READING OEDIPUS AND ARE HAVING OUR FINAL DISCUSSION BEFORE THE STUDENTS WRITE THEIR ESSAY.
WILL, COULD YOU EITHER TAKE YOUR BEADS OFF OR PUT THEM UNDER YOUR SHIRT?* THANKS. SO LET'S TALK ABOUT WHAT WE THINK THIS PLAY IS SAYING ABOUT OUR RELATIONSHIP TO TRUTH?
YO, MISS— YOU MEAN ABOUT OEDIPUS?
DUHHH...
I THINK THE PLAY SHOWS HOW EASY IT IS TO BE BLIND TO THE TRUTH. OEDIPUS SPENT THE WHOLE PLAY NOT SEEING WHAT WAS RIGHT IN FRONT OF HIS FACE.
ABSOLUTELY. BUT HE WAS TRYING TO SAVE THEBES, SO WHY WAS IT SO HARD FOR HIM TO SEE THE TRUTH?
THE TRUTH WAS TOO HORRIBLE. THAT'S WHY HE COULDN'T SEE IT. I MEAN, HE DID KILL HIS FATHER AND MARRY HIS MOTHER.
BUT HE WAS ALSO A GUY WHO HAD EVERYTHING— MONEY, POWER, RESPECT. SEEING THE TRUTH MEANT LOSING IT ALL.
SO DO YOU THINK HE CHOSE NOT TO SEE THE TRUTH, OR WAS HE UNABLE TO SEE IT?
*WILL'S BEADS SIGNAL HIS GANG AFFILIATION. WE WORK HARD TO KEEP GANG ISSUES OUT OF OUR SCHOOL. I HOPE THERE ISN'T A REASON WHY WILL DECIDED TO FLASH HIS BEADS TODAY.

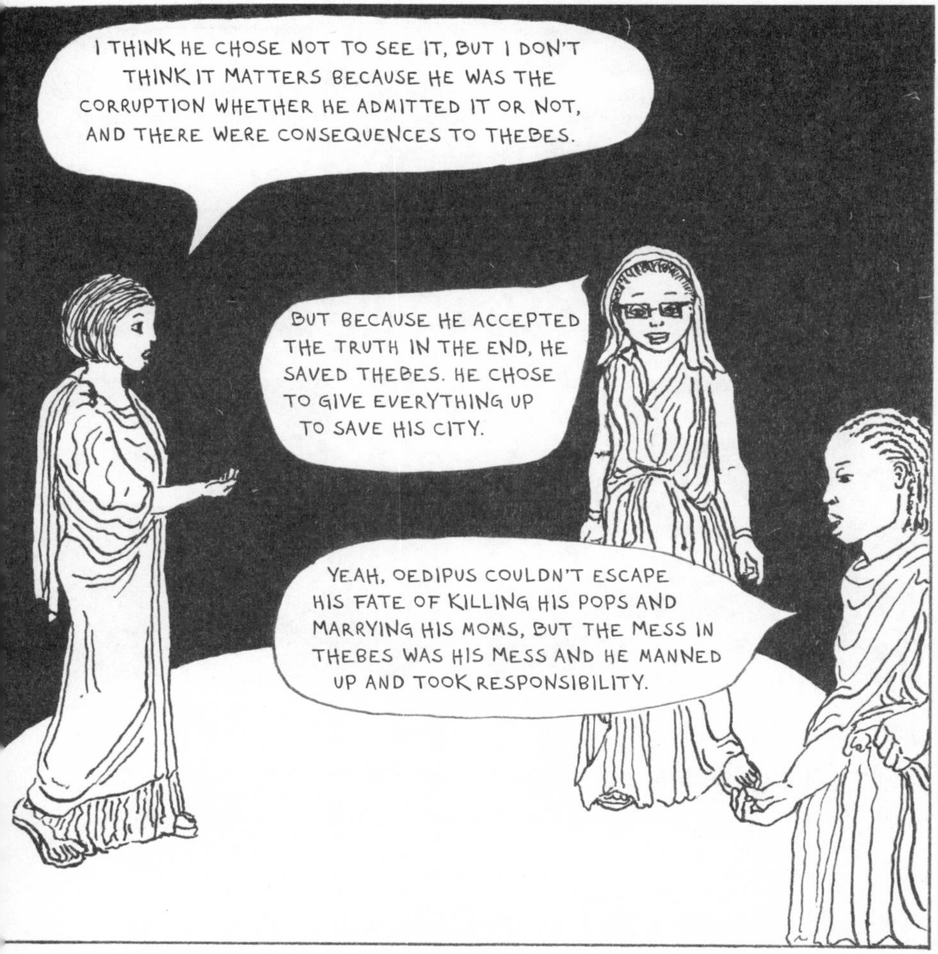
I THINK HE CHOSE NOT TO SEE IT, BUT I DON'T THINK IT MATTERS BECAUSE HE WAS THE CORRUPTION WHETHER HE ADMITTED IT OR NOT, AND THERE WERE CONSEQUENCES TO THEBES.
BUT BECAUSE HE ACCEPTED THE TRUTH IN THE END, HE SAVED THEBES. HE CHOSE TO GIVE EVERYTHING UP TO SAVE HIS CITY.
YEAH, OEDIPUS COULDN'T ESCAPE HIS FATE OF KILLING HIS POPS AND MARRYING HIS MOMS, BUT THE MESS IN THEBES WAS HIS MESS AND HE MANNED UP AND TOOK RESPONSIBILITY.

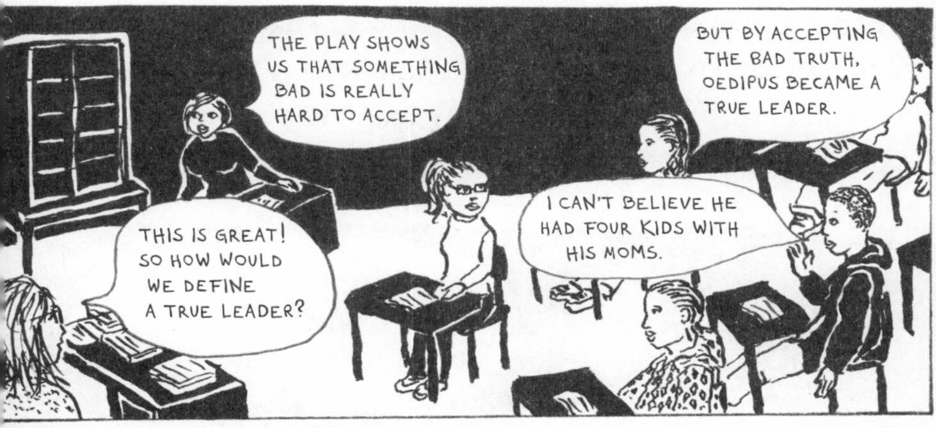
THE PLAY SHOWS US THAT SOMETHING BAD IS REALLY HARD TO ACCEPT.
BUT BY ACCEPTING THE BAD TRUTH, OEDIPUS BECAME A TRUE LEADER.
THIS IS GREAT! SO HOW WOULD WE DEFINE A TRUE LEADER?
I CAN'T BELIEVE HE HAD FOUR KIDS WITH HIS MOMS.

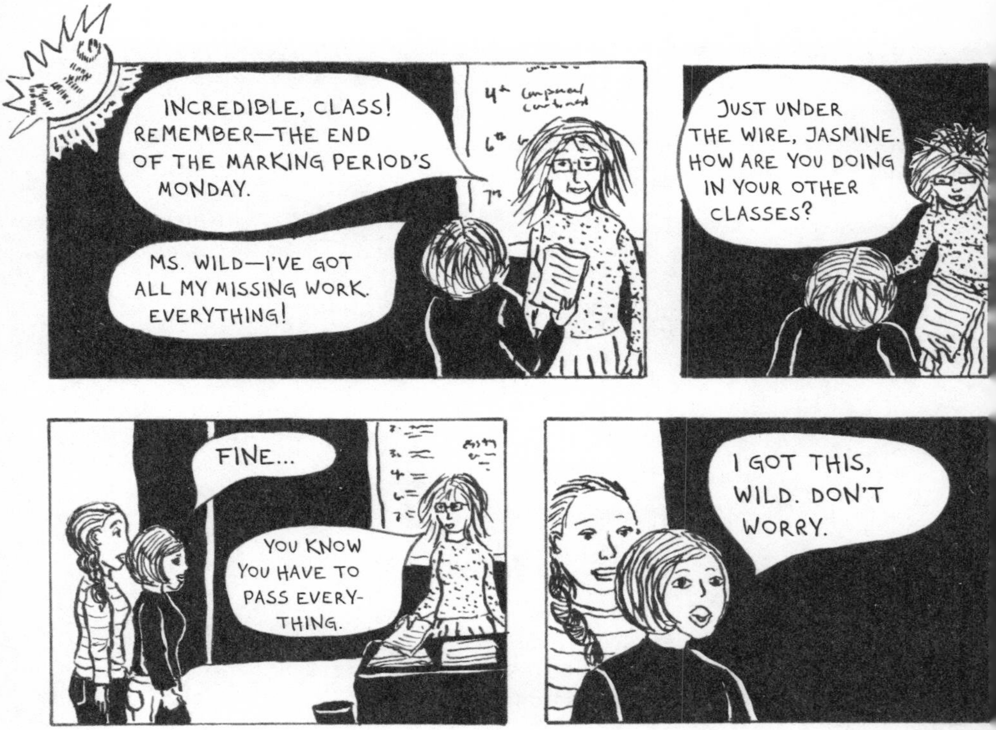
INCREDIBLE, CLASS! REMEMBER—THE END OF THE MARKING PERIOD'S MONDAY.
MS. WILD—I'VE GOT ALL MY MISSING WORK. EVERYTHING!
JUST UNDER THE WIRE, JASMINE. HOW ARE YOU DOING IN YOUR OTHER CLASSES?
FINE...
YOU KNOW YOU HAVE TO PASS EVERY-THING.
I GOT THIS, WILD. DON'T WORRY.

SIXTH PERIOD IS ALSO FINISHING WORK BEFORE MIDTERMS. THIS CLASS HAS A DIFFERENT FOCUS FROM THIRD PERIOD. STUDENTS ARE PLACED HERE BECAUSE THEY NEED SKILL BUILDING. BECAUSE WE'RE A SECOND CHANCE SCHOOL, THIS ISN'T SURPRISING. MANY OF OUR STUDENTS HAVE A HISTORY OF ABSENTEEISM AND/OR ACADEMIC FAILURE; FOR SOME, THIS TRANSLATES INTO READING COMPREHENSION OR WRITING SKILLS THAT ARE BELOW GRADE LEVEL. MY BRIEF IS TO MOVE THEM AS CLOSE AS POSSIBLE TO HIGH SCHOOL LEVEL SKILLS.

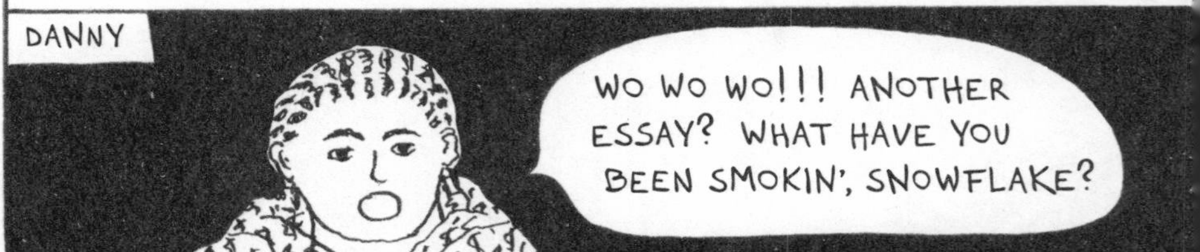
DANNY
WO WO WO!!! ANOTHER ESSAY? WHAT HAVE YOU BEEN SMOKIN', SNOWFLAKE?

BUILDING THE SKILLS OF THE STUDENTS IN SIXTH PERIOD
MEANS USING DIFFERENT TEXTS FROM THIRD PERIOD,
AS WELL AS DIFFERENT METHODS, INCLUDING EXTRA

SCAFFOLDING,

CREATING

INTERIM
STEPS

THAT BREAK
THE

LEARNING
INTO MORE

MANAGEABLE
PIECES.

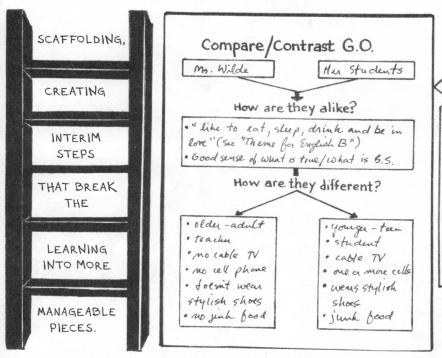

EXAMPLE OF A GRAPHIC ORGANIZER

Compare/Contrast G.O.

Ms. Wilde — Her Students

How are they alike?
- "like to eat, sleep, drink and be in love" (see "Theme for English B")
- Good sense of what is true / what is B.S.

How are they different?

(Ms. Wilde)	(Her Students)
• older – adult	• younger – teen
• teacher	• student
• no cable TV	• cable TV
• no cell phone	• one or more cells
• doesn't wear stylish shoes	• wears stylish shoes
• no junk food	• junk food

SIXTH PERIOD IS WORKING ON ONE OF THOSE INTERIM STEPS
RIGHT NOW. THEY'RE USING A GRAPHIC ORGANIZER TO HELP GET
THEIR IDEAS TOGETHER FOR AN ESSAY COMPARING AND CONTRASTING
THEMSELVES WITH DAVE, THE MAIN CHARACTER IN RICHARD
WRIGHT'S STORY, "THE MAN WHO WAS ALMOST A MAN."

XTH PERIOD: WORKING ON THEIR GRAPHIC ORGANIZERS

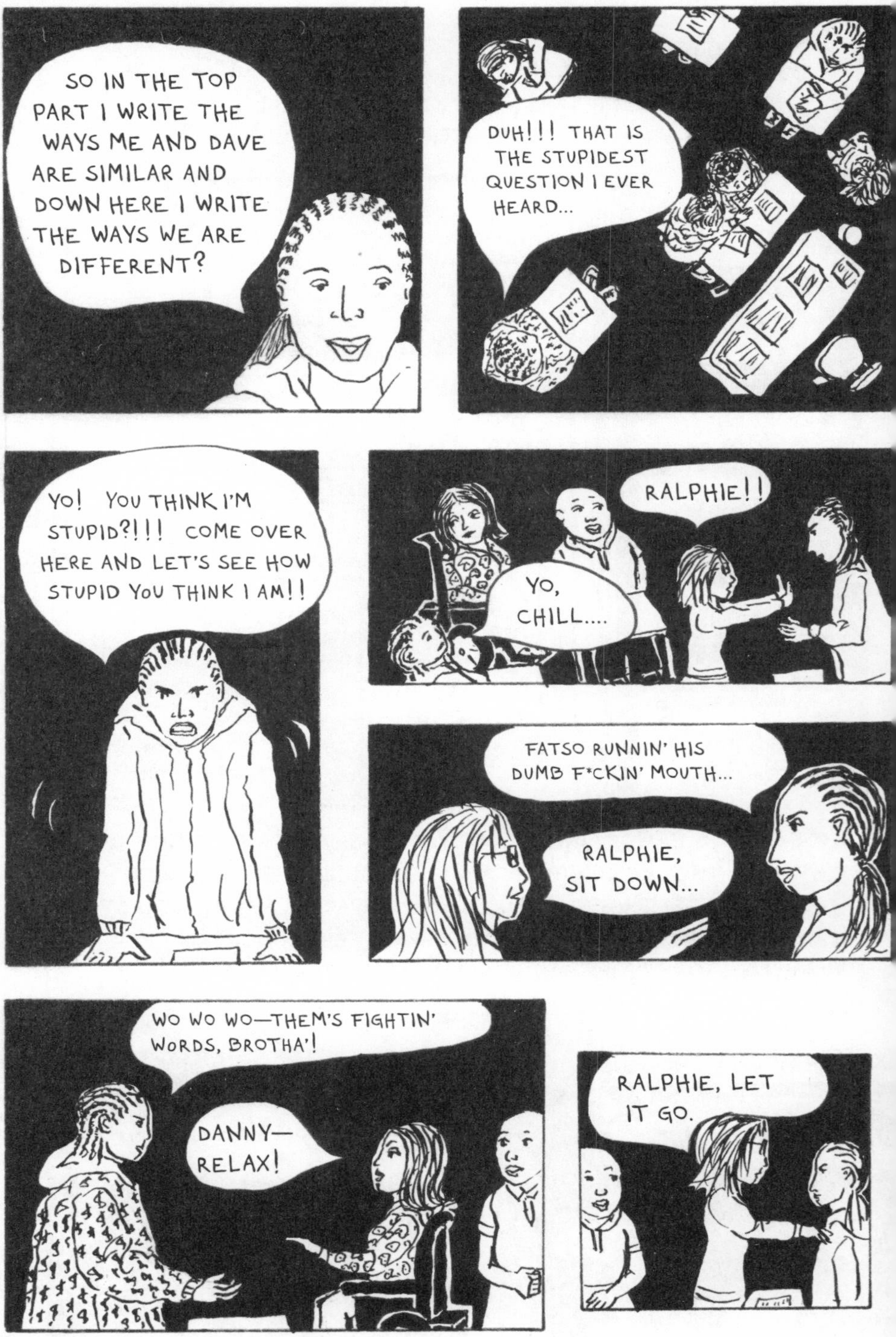
SO IN THE TOP PART I WRITE THE WAYS ME AND DAVE ARE SIMILAR AND DOWN HERE I WRITE THE WAYS WE ARE DIFFERENT?
DUH!!! THAT IS THE STUPIDEST QUESTION I EVER HEARD...
YO! YOU THINK I'M STUPID?!!! COME OVER HERE AND LET'S SEE HOW STUPID YOU THINK I AM!!
RALPHIE!!
YO, CHILL....
FATSO RUNNIN' HIS DUMB F*CKIN' MOUTH...
RALPHIE, SIT DOWN...
WO WO WO—THEM'S FIGHTIN' WORDS, BROTHA'!
DANNY— RELAX!
RALPHIE, LET IT GO.

TEACHING OFTEN INVOLVES MULTI-TASKING

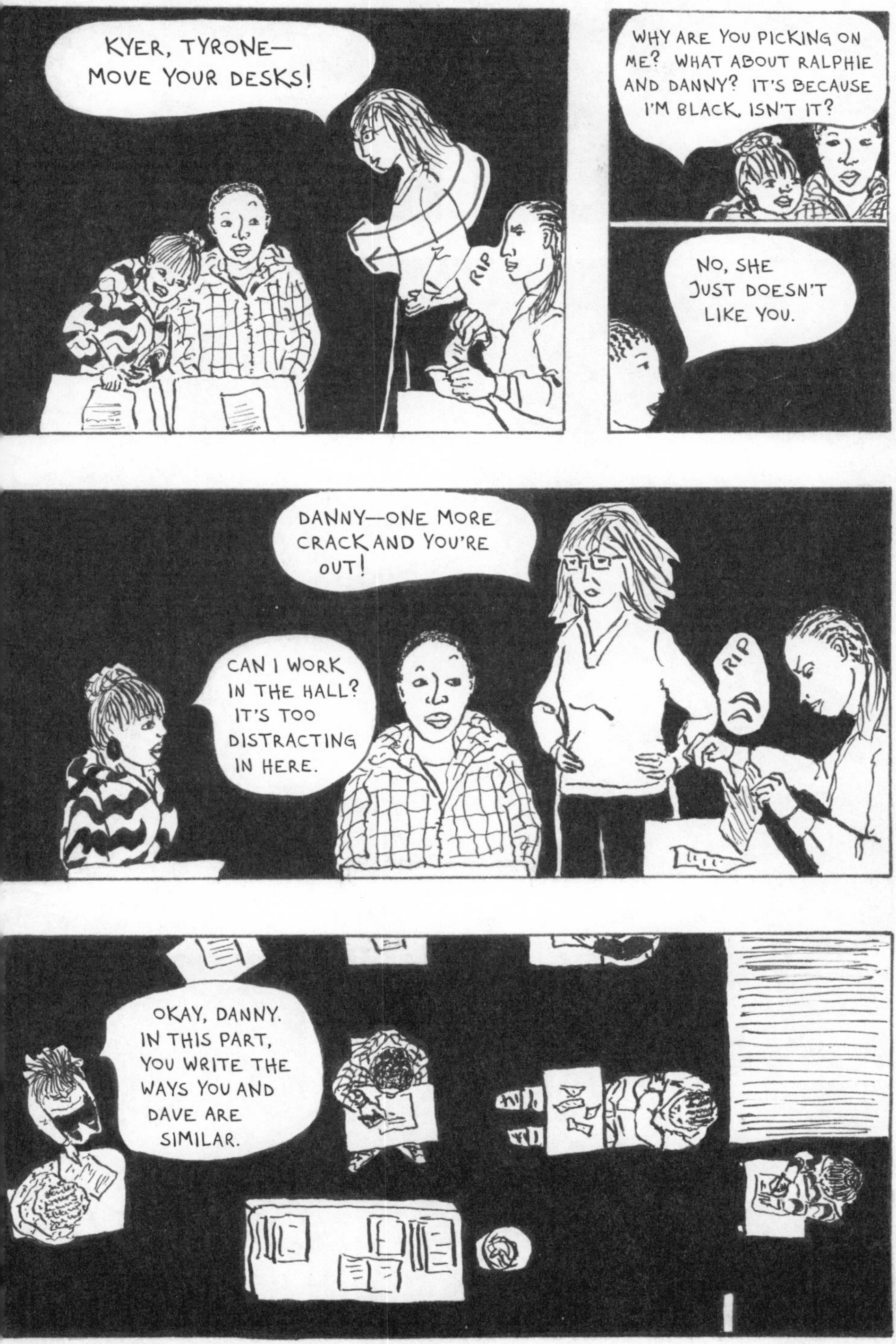
KYER, TYRONE— MOVE YOUR DESKS!
RIP
WHY ARE YOU PICKING ON ME? WHAT ABOUT RALPHIE AND DANNY? IT'S BECAUSE I'M BLACK, ISN'T IT?
NO, SHE JUST DOESN'T LIKE YOU.
DANNY—ONE MORE CRACK AND YOU'RE OUT!
CAN I WORK IN THE HALL? IT'S TOO DISTRACTING IN HERE.
RIP
OKAY, DANNY. IN THIS PART, YOU WRITE THE WAYS YOU AND DAVE ARE SIMILAR.

THIRTY MINUTES LATER

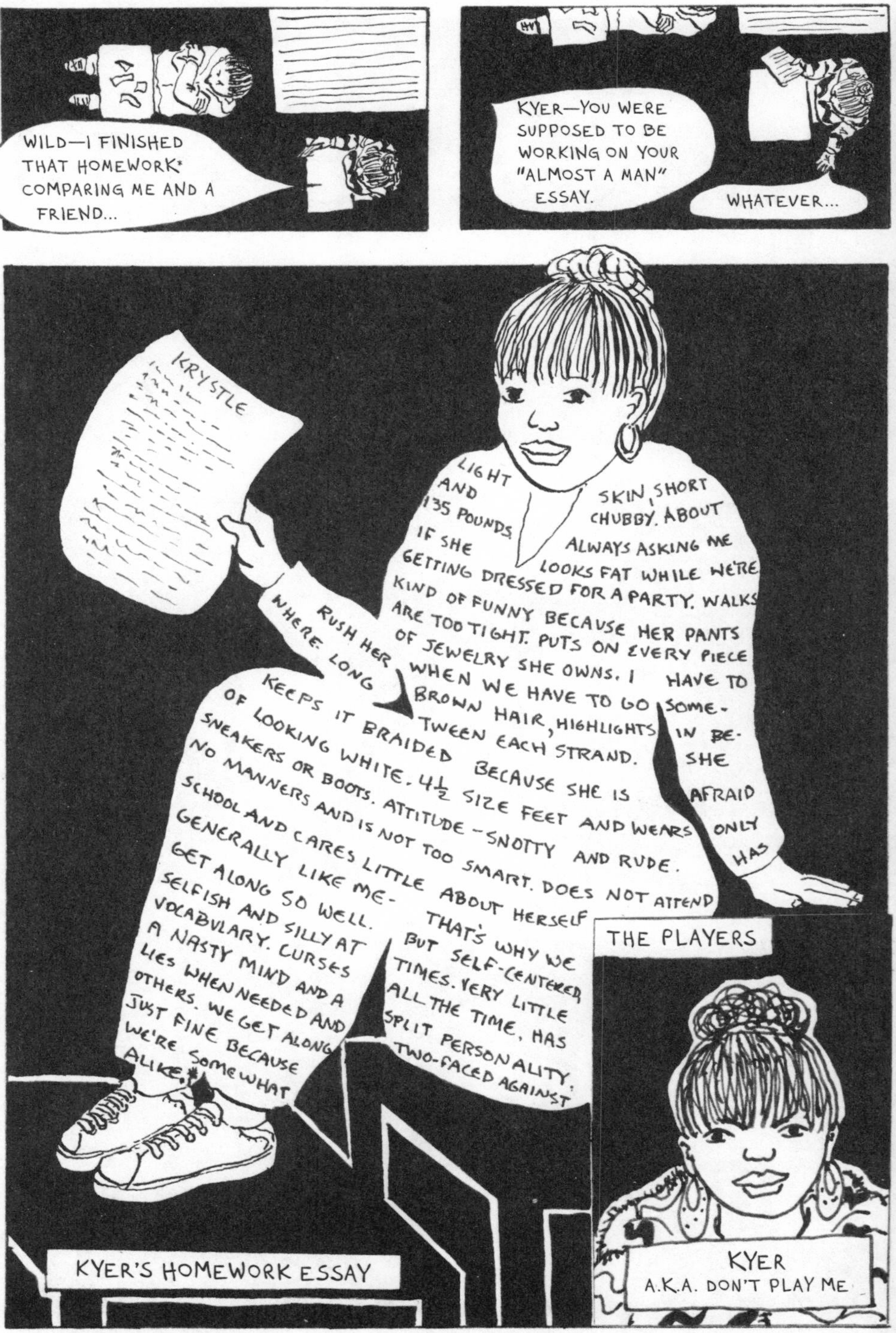

WILD—I FINISHED THAT HOMEWORK* COMPARING ME AND A FRIEND...
KYER—YOU WERE SUPPOSED TO BE WORKING ON YOUR "ALMOST A MAN" ESSAY.
WHATEVER...
KRYSTLE
LIGHT SKIN, SHORT AND CHUBBY. ABOUT 135 POUNDS. ALWAYS ASKING ME IF SHE LOOKS FAT WHILE WE'RE GETTING DRESSED FOR A PARTY. WALKS KIND OF FUNNY BECAUSE HER PANTS ARE TOO TIGHT. PUTS ON EVERY PIECE OF JEWELRY SHE OWNS. I HAVE TO RUSH HER WHEN WE HAVE TO GO SOME-WHERE. LONG BROWN HAIR, HIGHLIGHTS IN BE-TWEEN EACH STRAND. SHE KEEPS IT BRAIDED BECAUSE SHE IS AFRAID OF LOOKING WHITE. 4½ SIZE FEET AND WEARS ONLY SNEAKERS OR BOOTS. ATTITUDE - SNOTTY AND RUDE. HAS NO MANNERS AND IS NOT TOO SMART. DOES NOT ATTEND SCHOOL AND CARES LITTLE ABOUT HERSELF GENERALLY LIKE ME - THAT'S WHY WE GET ALONG SO WELL. BUT SELF-CENTERED SELFISH AND SILLY AT TIMES. VERY LITTLE VOCABULARY. CURSES ALL THE TIME. HAS A NASTY MIND AND A SPLIT PERSONALITY. LIES WHEN NEEDED AND TWO-FACED AGAINST OTHERS. WE GET ALONG JUST FINE BECAUSE WE'RE SOMEWHAT ALIKE.*
THE PLAYERS
KYER
A.K.A. DON'T PLAY ME
KYER'S HOMEWORK ESSAY

* ESSAY BY TANICA DAVIS

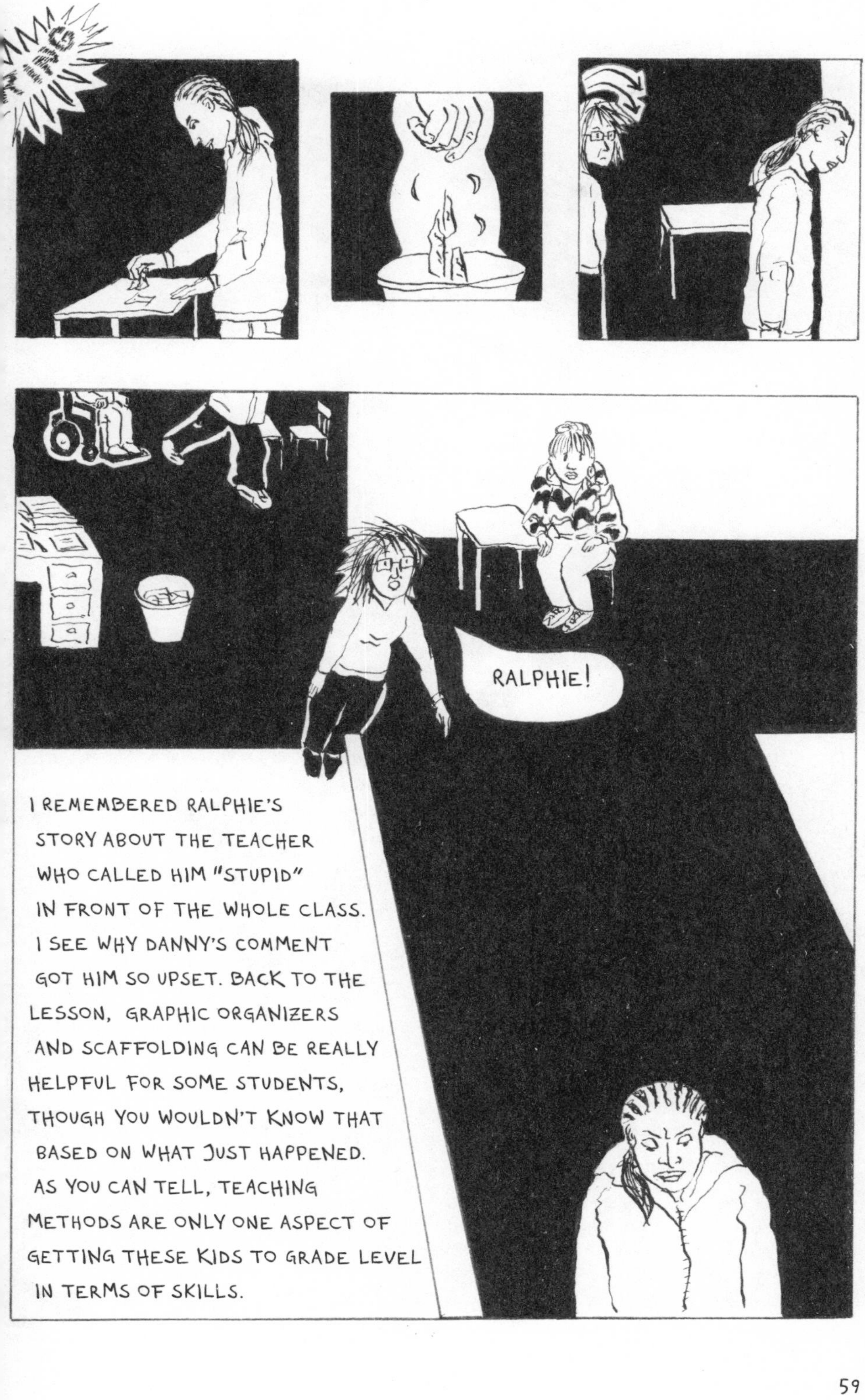
RALPHIE!
I REMEMBERED RALPHIE'S STORY ABOUT THE TEACHER WHO CALLED HIM "STUPID" IN FRONT OF THE WHOLE CLASS. I SEE WHY DANNY'S COMMENT GOT HIM SO UPSET. BACK TO THE LESSON, GRAPHIC ORGANIZERS AND SCAFFOLDING CAN BE REALLY HELPFUL FOR SOME STUDENTS, THOUGH YOU WOULDN'T KNOW THAT BASED ON WHAT JUST HAPPENED. AS YOU CAN TELL, TEACHING METHODS ARE ONLY ONE ASPECT OF GETTING THESE KIDS TO GRADE LEVEL IN TERMS OF SKILLS.

NOW THE MARATHON BEGINS—MIDTERMS...

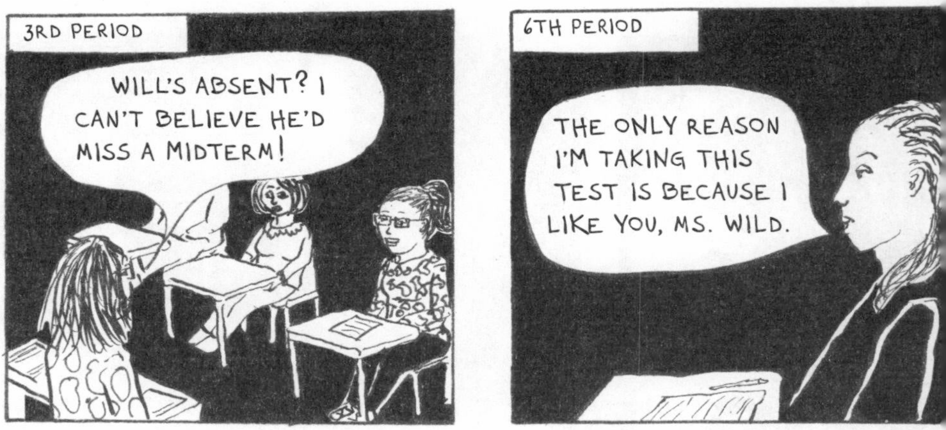
3RD PERIOD
WILL'S ABSENT? I CAN'T BELIEVE HE'D MISS A MIDTERM!
6TH PERIOD
THE ONLY REASON I'M TAKING THIS TEST IS BECAUSE I LIKE YOU, MS. WILD.

FOLLOWED BY GRADING...

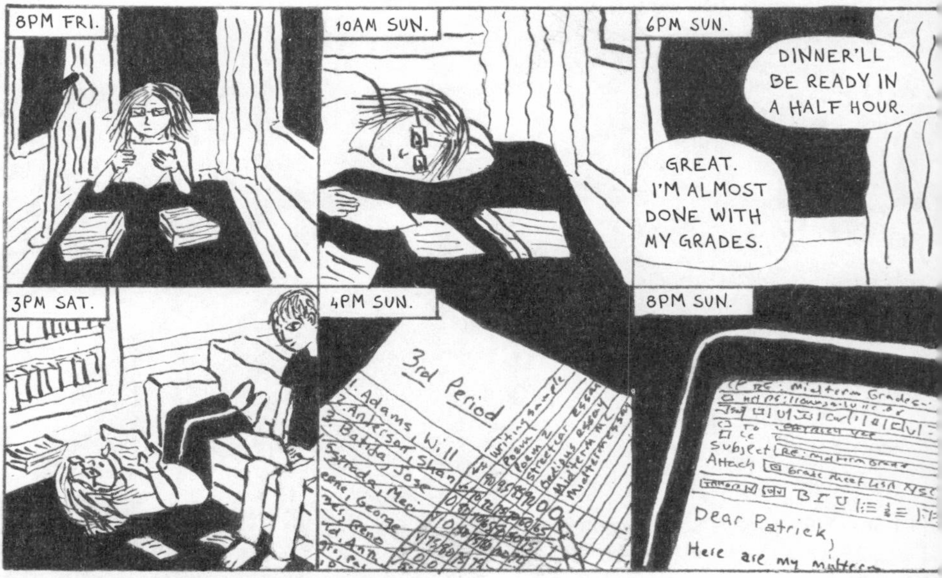
8PM FRI.
10AM SUN.
6PM SUN.
DINNER'LL BE READY IN A HALF HOUR.
GREAT. I'M ALMOST DONE WITH MY GRADES.
3PM SAT.
4PM SUN.
3rd Period
8PM SUN.
Dear Patrick,

FOLLOWED BY OPEN SCHOOL NIGHT.

AT OUR SCHOOL THIS IS WHEN MIDTERM PROGRESS REPORTS ARE GIVEN OUT AND PARENTS AND GUARDIANS ARE INVITED TO SPEAK TO THE TEACHERS.

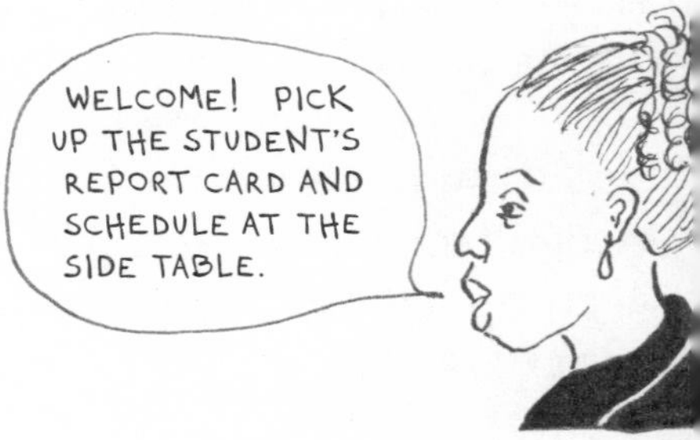
WELCOME! PICK UP THE STUDENT'S REPORT CARD AND SCHEDULE AT THE SIDE TABLE.

4:00

HI, MS. WILDE. I'M NATALIE'S MOM.

I'M HAPPY TO MEET YOU.

HAS SHE TOLD YOU SHE'S PREGNANT?

MOM!

I'M SORRY, SWEETIE, BUT...

I GOT PREGNANT WITH NATALIE AT 16. I JUST WANTED AN EASIER LIFE FOR HER.

MOM, IT'S GOING TO BE ALL RIGHT.

I KNOW...

5:30

HEY, WILD.

HI, LADIES! MAY I SEE YOUR REPORT CARDS?

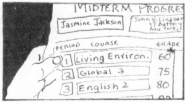

MIDTERM PROGRES

Jasmine Jackson

John V. Lindsay
17 Battery
New York, ℓ

PERIOD	COURSE	GRADE
1	Living Environ.	60 *
2	Global 3	75
3	English 2	80

* A 60 IS A FAILURE. IF JASMINE DOES NOT PASS ALL HER CLASSES AT THE END OF THE SEMESTER, SHE MAY AGE OUT BEFORE SHE CAN GRADUATE.

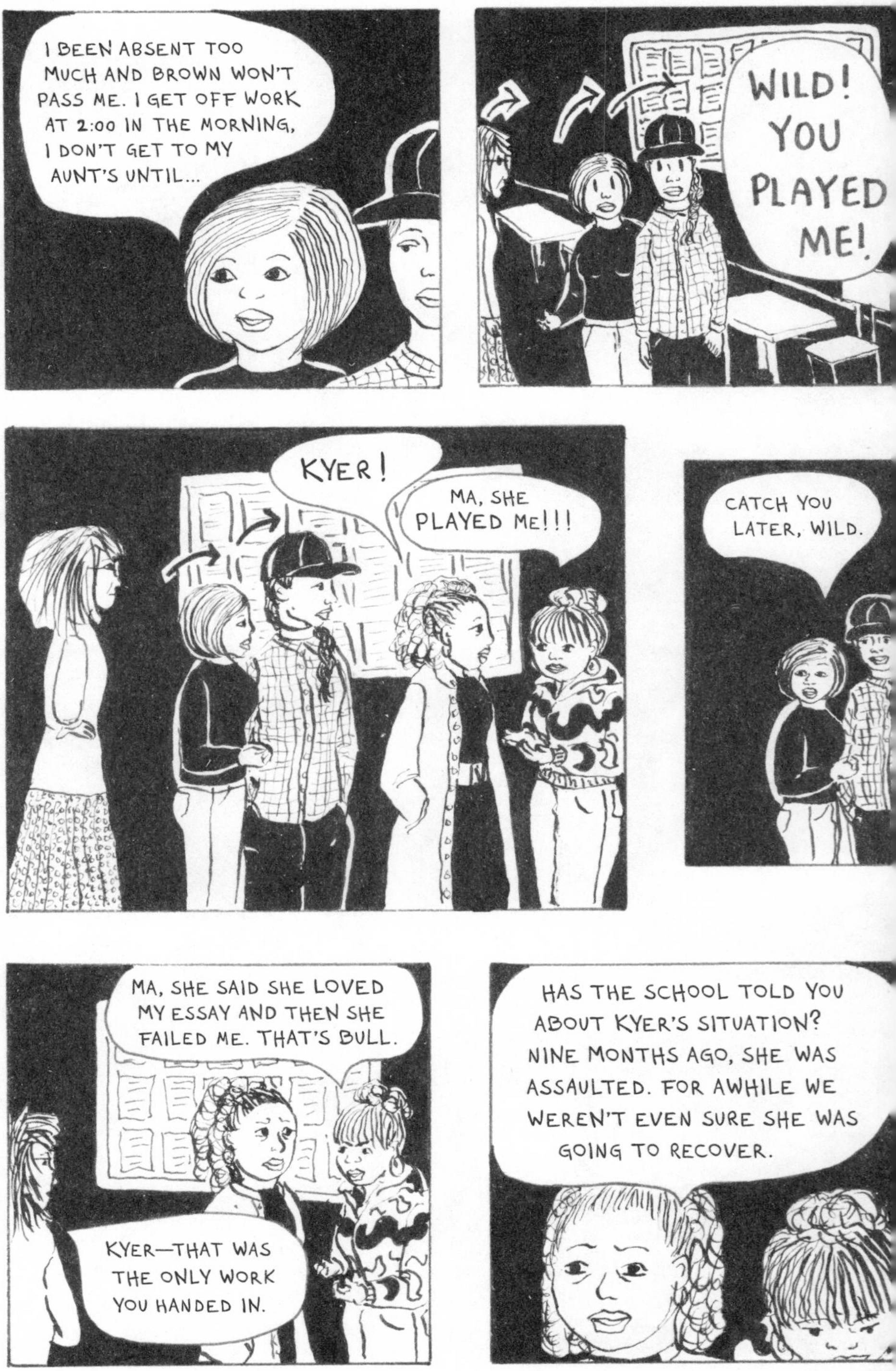
I BEEN ABSENT TOO MUCH AND BROWN WON'T PASS ME. I GET OFF WORK AT 2:00 IN THE MORNING, I DON'T GET TO MY AUNT'S UNTIL...
WILD! YOU PLAYED ME!
KYER!
MA, SHE PLAYED ME!!!
CATCH YOU LATER, WILD.
MA, SHE SAID SHE LOVED MY ESSAY AND THEN SHE FAILED ME. THAT'S BULL.
KYER—THAT WAS THE ONLY WORK YOU HANDED IN.
HAS THE SCHOOL TOLD YOU ABOUT KYER'S SITUATION? NINE MONTHS AGO, SHE WAS ASSAULTED. FOR AWHILE WE WEREN'T EVEN SURE SHE WAS GOING TO RECOVER.

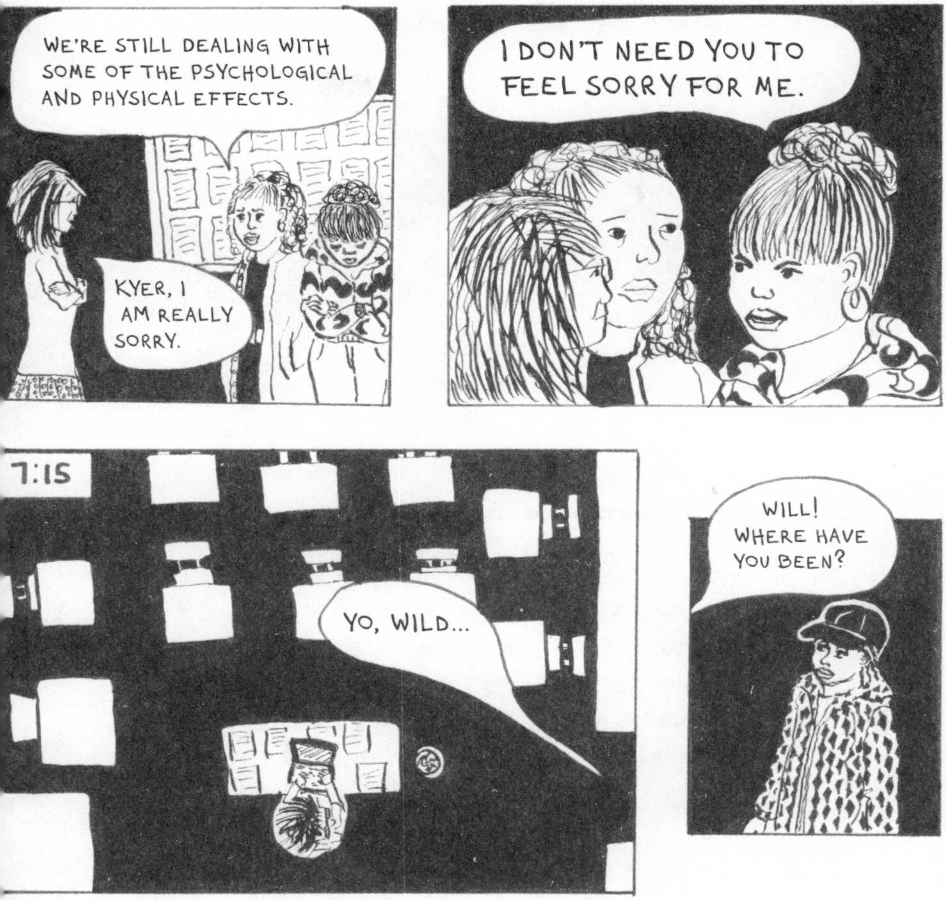

WE'RE STILL DEALING WITH SOME OF THE PSYCHOLOGICAL AND PHYSICAL EFFECTS.
KYER, I AM REALLY SORRY.
I DON'T NEED YOU TO FEEL SORRY FOR ME.
7:15
YO, WILD...
WILL! WHERE HAVE YOU BEEN?

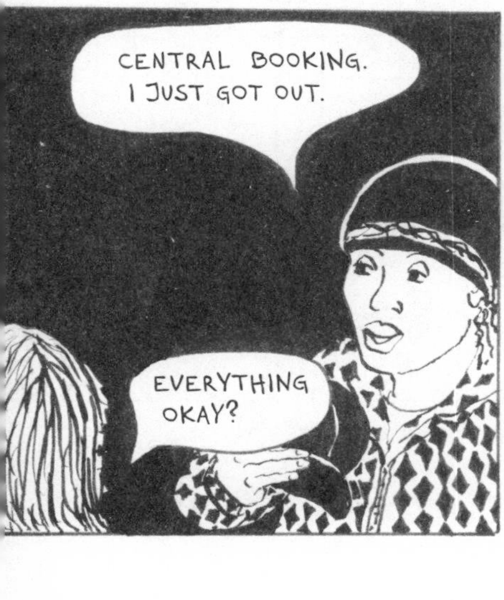

CENTRAL BOOKING. I JUST GOT OUT.
EVERYTHING OKAY?

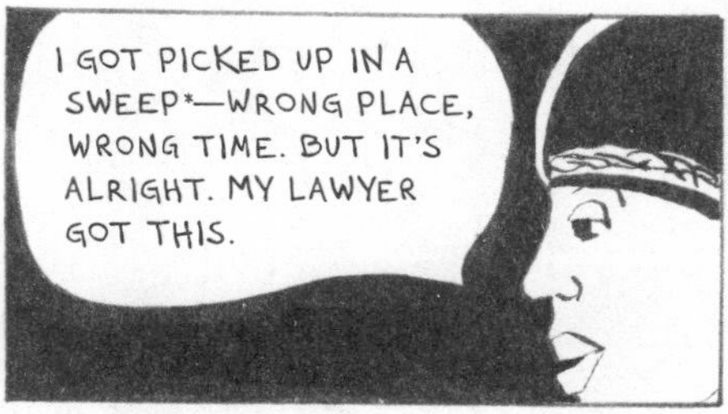

I GOT PICKED UP IN A SWEEP*—WRONG PLACE, WRONG TIME. BUT IT'S ALRIGHT. MY LAWYER GOT THIS.

* A SWEEP IS WHERE THE COPS LOCK DOWN AN AREA DIRECTLY AFTER A CRIME AND BRING EVERYONE ON THE STREET IN AS POSSIBLE SUSPECTS.

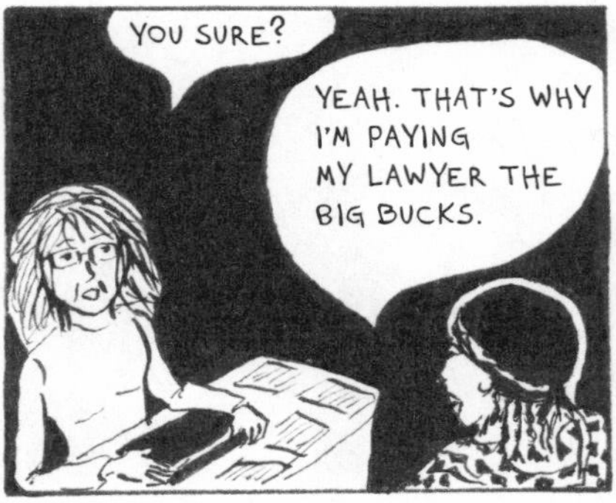
YOU SURE?
YEAH. THAT'S WHY I'M PAYING MY LAWYER THE BIG BUCKS.

IF THIS IS SEEN AS A VIOLATION OF WILL'S PROBATION, HE COULD BE IN BIG TROUBLE.

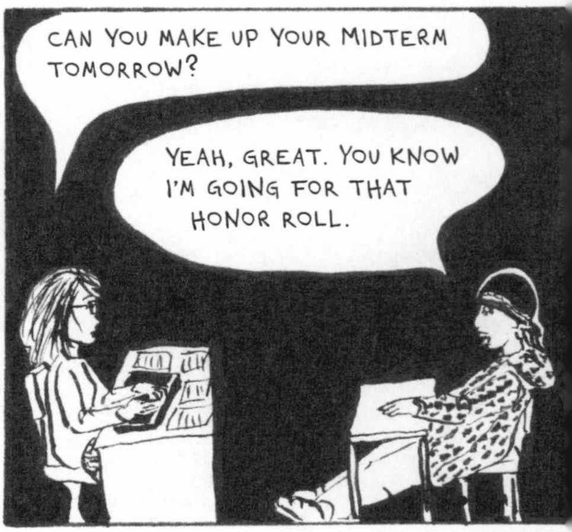
CAN YOU MAKE UP YOUR MIDTERM TOMORROW?
YEAH, GREAT. YOU KNOW I'M GOING FOR THAT HONOR ROLL.

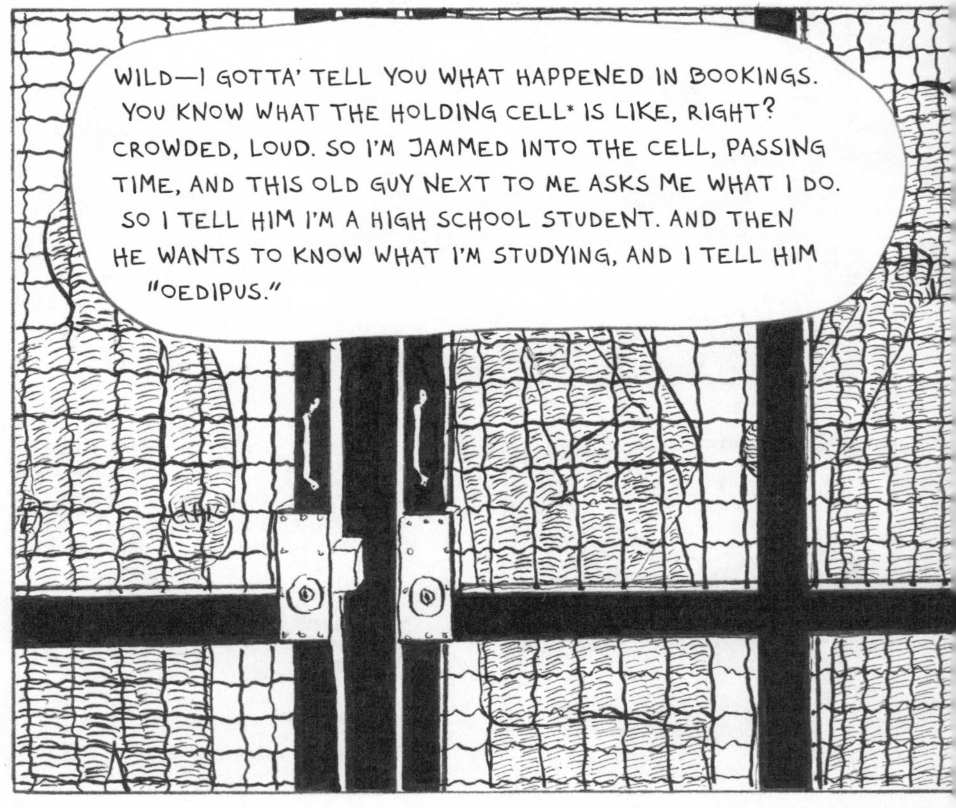
WILD—I GOTTA' TELL YOU WHAT HAPPENED IN BOOKINGS. YOU KNOW WHAT THE HOLDING CELL* IS LIKE, RIGHT? CROWDED, LOUD. SO I'M JAMMED INTO THE CELL, PASSING TIME, AND THIS OLD GUY NEXT TO ME ASKS ME WHAT I DO. SO I TELL HIM I'M A HIGH SCHOOL STUDENT. AND THEN HE WANTS TO KNOW WHAT I'M STUDYING, AND I TELL HIM "OEDIPUS."

* PEOPLE SUSPECTED OF A CRIME ARE BROUGHT TO THE COURTS BY THE COPS, WHERE THEY ARE LOCKED IN A HOLDING CELL UNTIL THEY SEE A JUDGE, WHO THEN DETERMINES IF THEY HAVE TO STAY, CAN GO FREE, OR MUST POST BAIL UNTIL TRIAL.

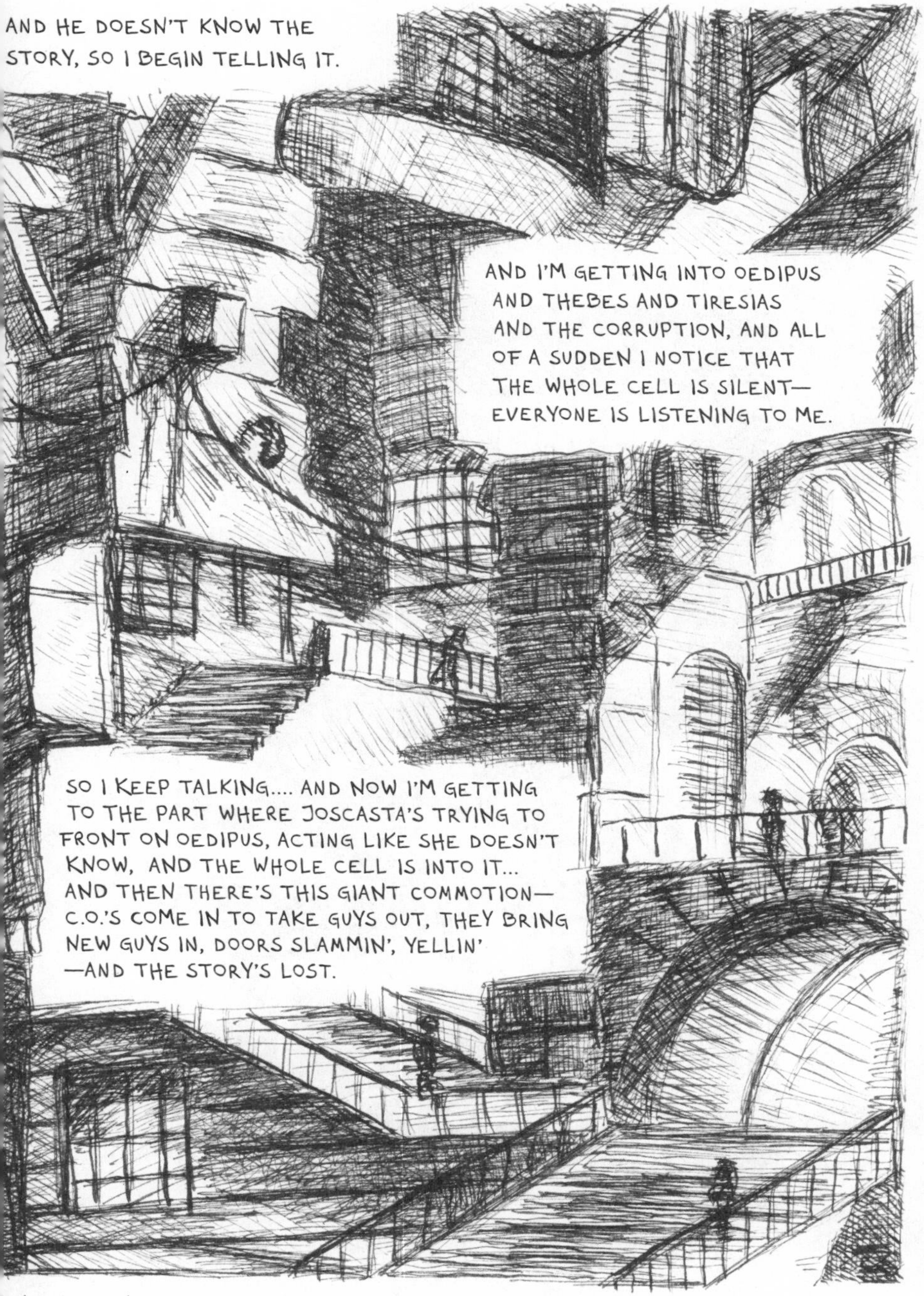
AND HE DOESN'T KNOW THE STORY, SO I BEGIN TELLING IT.
AND I'M GETTING INTO OEDIPUS AND THEBES AND TIRESIAS AND THE CORRUPTION, AND ALL OF A SUDDEN I NOTICE THAT THE WHOLE CELL IS SILENT— EVERYONE IS LISTENING TO ME.
SO I KEEP TALKING.... AND NOW I'M GETTING TO THE PART WHERE JOSCASTA'S TRYING TO FRONT ON OEDIPUS, ACTING LIKE SHE DOESN'T KNOW, AND THE WHOLE CELL IS INTO IT... AND THEN THERE'S THIS GIANT COMMOTION— C.O.'S COME IN TO TAKE GUYS OUT, THEY BRING NEW GUYS IN, DOORS SLAMMIN', YELLIN' —AND THE STORY'S LOST.

INALLY THINGS SETTLE DOWN, AND I'M THINKING MAYBE I'LL TRY TO GET A LITTLE LEEP. SO I'M MOVING TO THE BACK OF THE CELL TO SEE IF I CAN FIND A CORNER HERE I CAN SIT DOWN, AND THIS WHOLE GROUP OF GUYS TURNS TO ME. NOW I'M NOT TUPID, SO I'M WATCHING MY BACK. BUT THEN THEY SAY TO ME, ALMOST IN ONE VOICE:

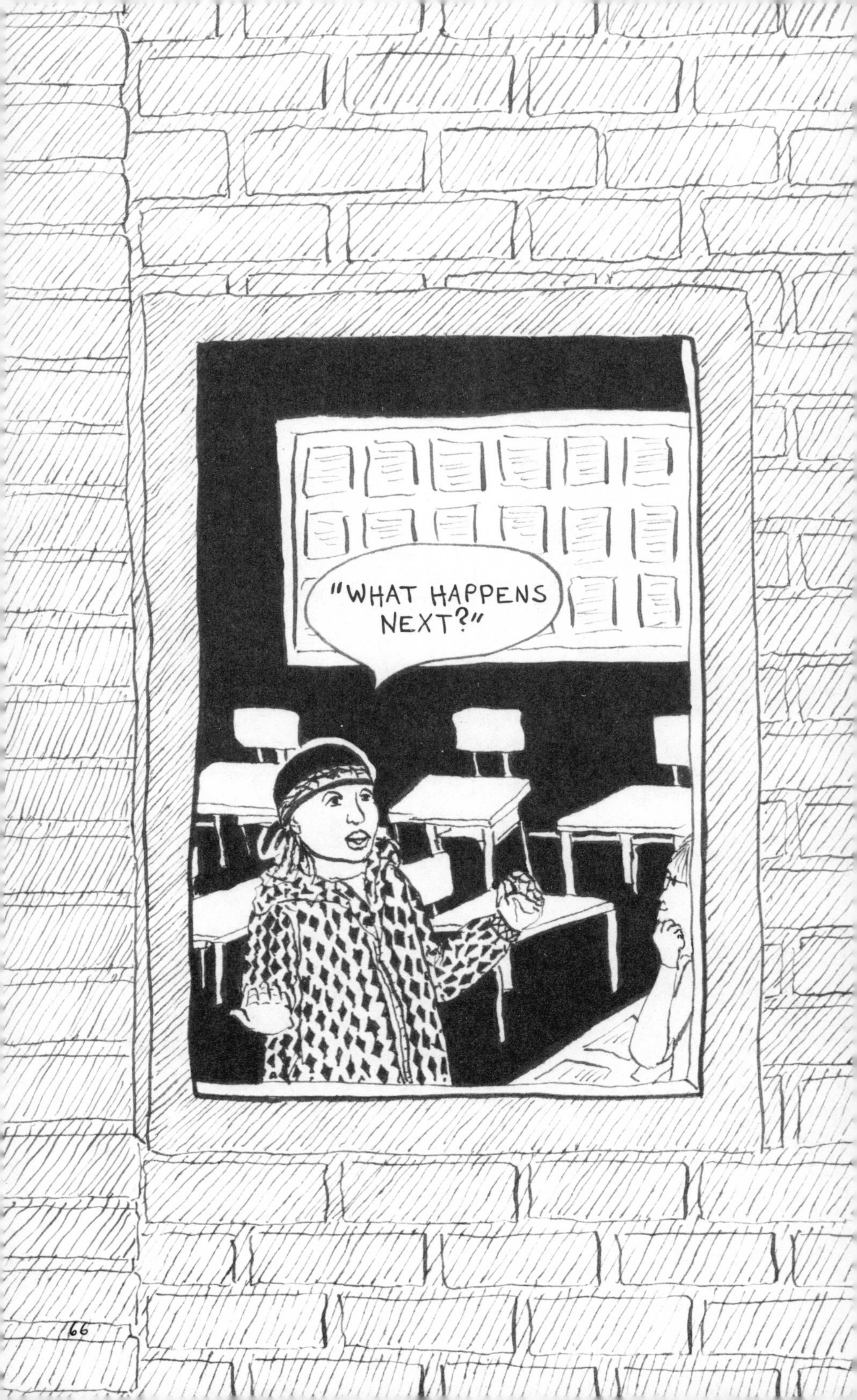
"WHAT HAPPENS NEXT?"

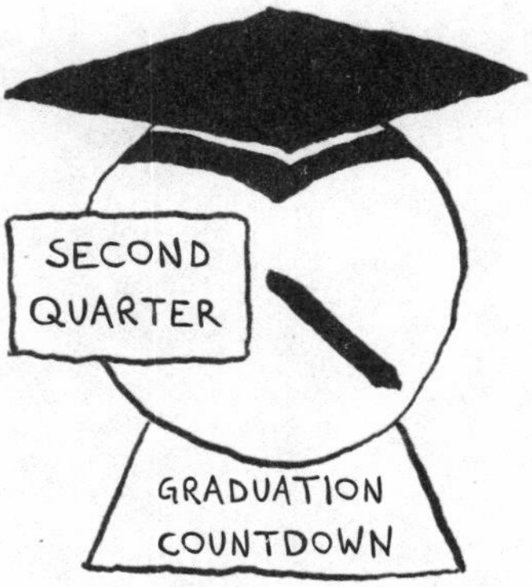
SECOND
QUARTER
GRADUATION
COUNTDOWN

CHAPTER FIVE

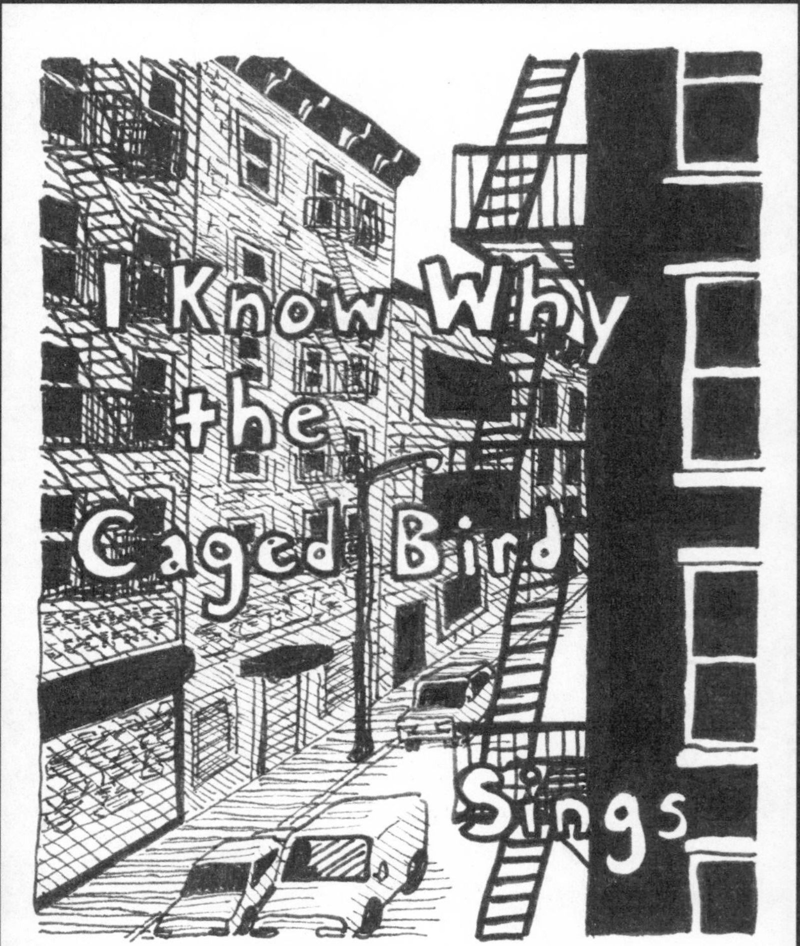
I Know Why the Caged Bird Sings

"ALL GREAT ACHIEVEMENTS REQUIRE TIME."
MAYA ANGELOU

DAY AFTER OPEN SCHOOL NIGHT

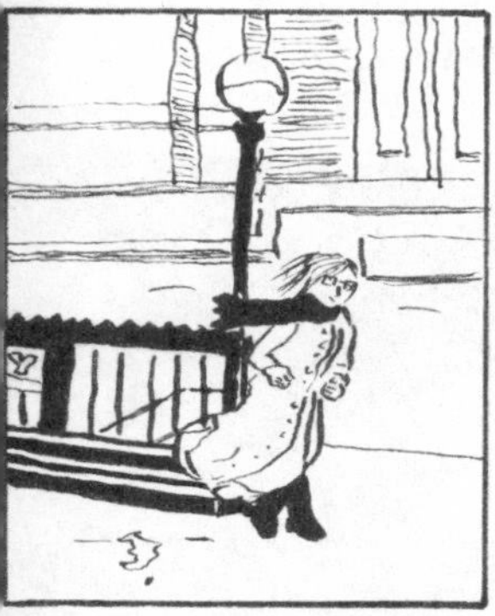

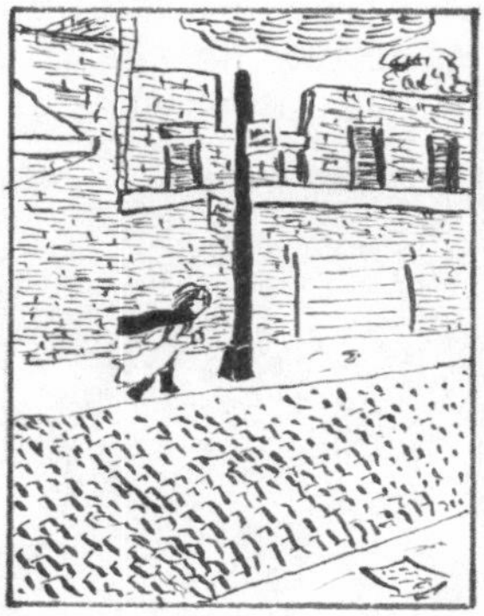

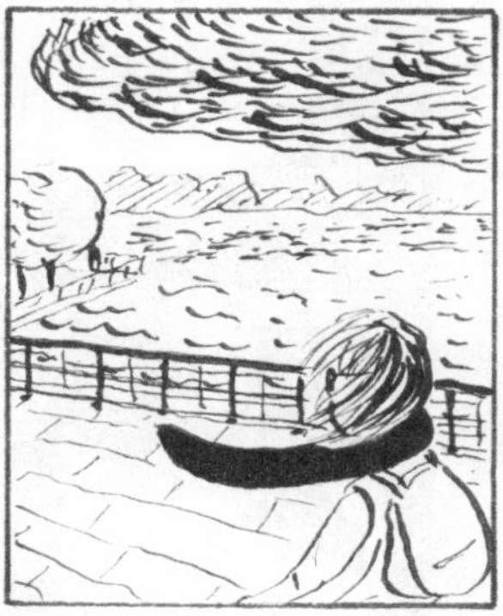

ON MY WAY TO WORK, I TAKE THE SUBWAY FIVE STOPS PAST THE STOP FOR WILDCAT. THEN I WALK BACK TO THE SCHOOL, GOING ALONG THE HUDSON RIVER.

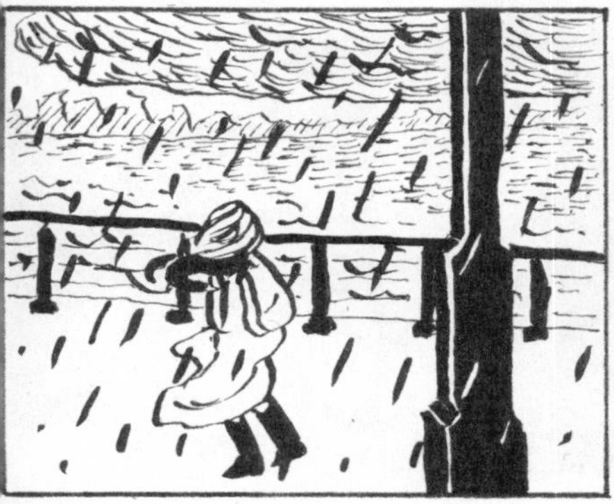

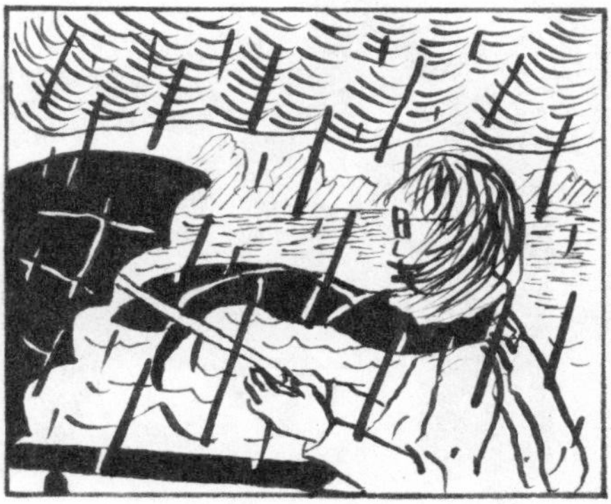

IT'S A WAY TO GET EXERCISE, BUT ALSO TO HAVE SOME TIME ALONE. I GET TO CLEAR MY HEAD OR WORK OUT PROBLEMS OR JUST THINK.

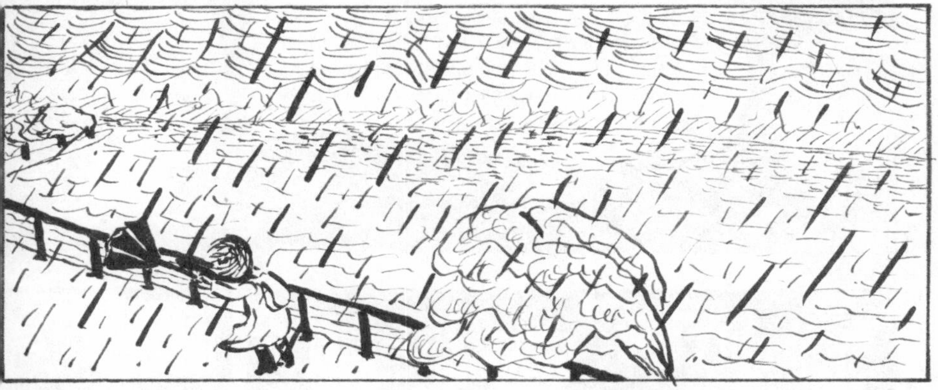

RIGHT NOW I'M THINKING ABOUT WHY I'M GOING BACK TO SCHOOL LESS THAN TWELVE HOURS AFTER I LEFT.

SO WILL'S BACK, BUT HOW COME JASMINE ISN'T HERE?

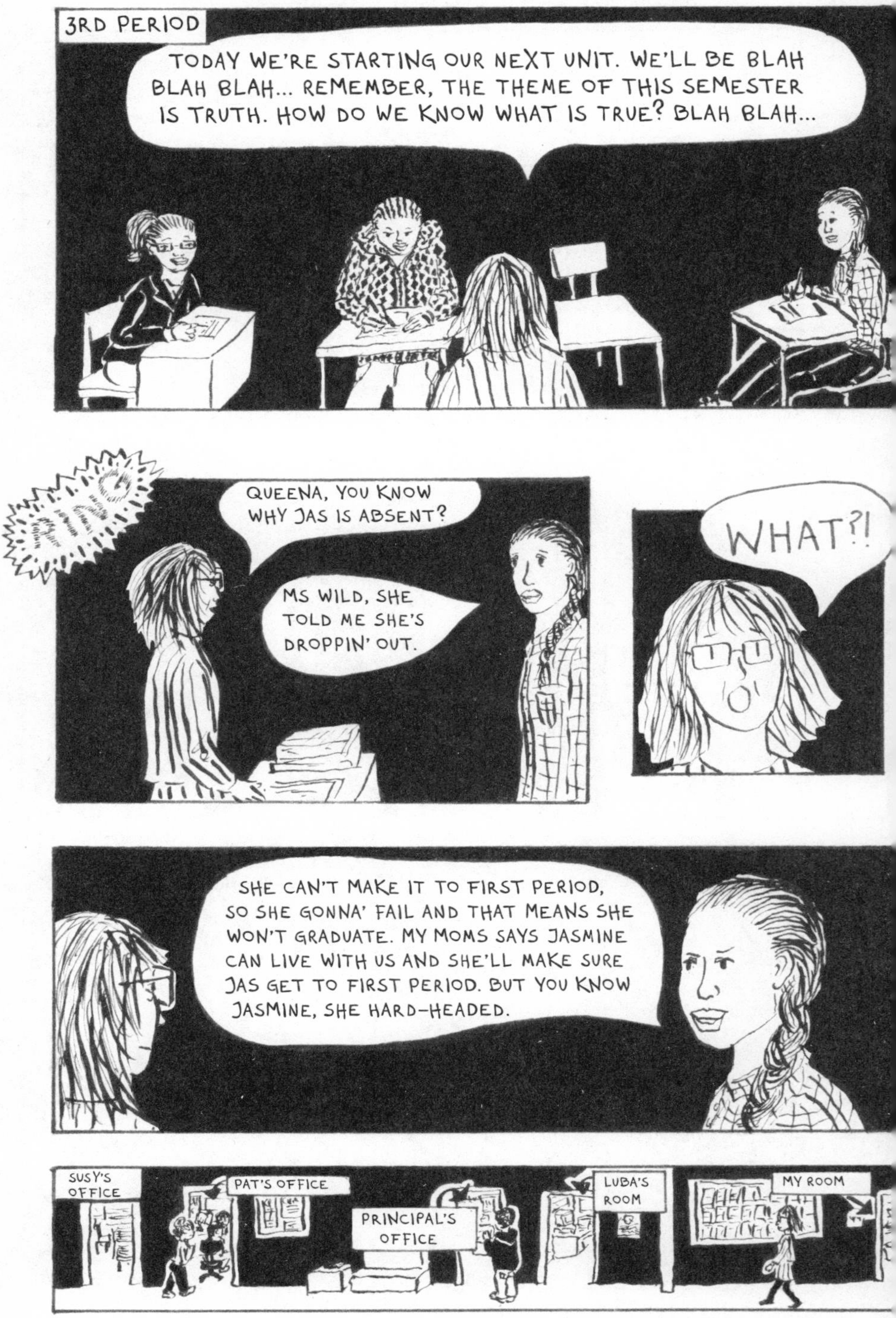
3RD PERIOD
TODAY WE'RE STARTING OUR NEXT UNIT. WE'LL BE BLAH BLAH BLAH... REMEMBER, THE THEME OF THIS SEMESTER IS TRUTH. HOW DO WE KNOW WHAT IS TRUE? BLAH BLAH...
QUEENA, YOU KNOW WHY JAS IS ABSENT?
MS WILD, SHE TOLD ME SHE'S DROPPIN' OUT.
WHAT?!
SHE CAN'T MAKE IT TO FIRST PERIOD, SO SHE GONNA' FAIL AND THAT MEANS SHE WON'T GRADUATE. MY MOMS SAYS JASMINE CAN LIVE WITH US AND SHE'LL MAKE SURE JAS GET TO FIRST PERIOD. BUT YOU KNOW JASMINE, SHE HARD-HEADED.
SUSY'S OFFICE
PAT'S OFFICE
PRINCIPAL'S OFFICE
LUBA'S ROOM
MY ROOM

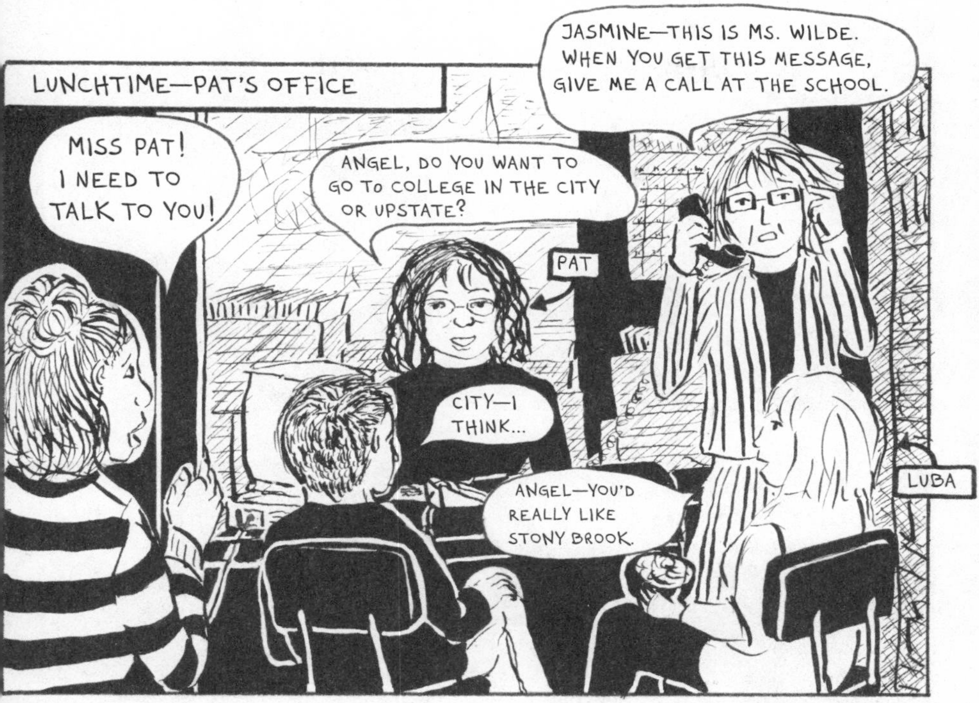
LUNCHTIME—PAT'S OFFICE
MISS PAT! I NEED TO TALK TO YOU!
ANGEL, DO YOU WANT TO GO TO COLLEGE IN THE CITY OR UPSTATE?
JASMINE—THIS IS MS. WILDE. WHEN YOU GET THIS MESSAGE, GIVE ME A CALL AT THE SCHOOL.
PAT
CITY—I THINK...
LUBA
ANGEL—YOU'D REALLY LIKE STONY BROOK.

I DECIDE I HAVE TO TRY TO GET AHOLD OF JASMINE BEFORE SHE DOES SOMETHING DRASTIC. PAT ALWAYS HAS ALL THE NUMBERS AND INFORMATION. SHE'S THE GUIDANCE COUNSELOR FOR SENIORS, AND SHE AND LUBA ARE MY BEST FRIENDS AT WILDCAT.

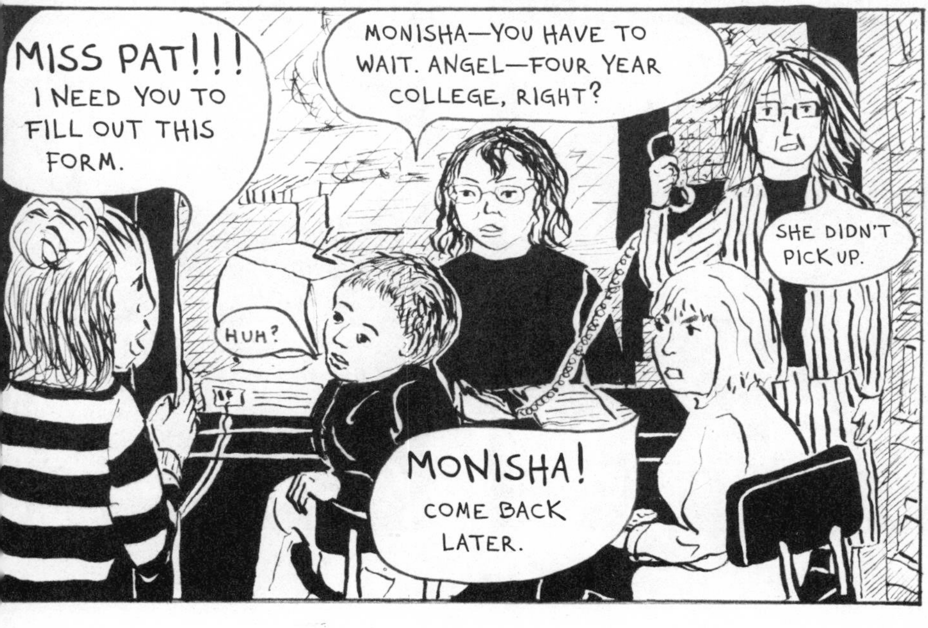
MISS PAT!!! I NEED YOU TO FILL OUT THIS FORM.
MONISHA—YOU HAVE TO WAIT. ANGEL—FOUR YEAR COLLEGE, RIGHT?
SHE DIDN'T PICK UP.
HUH?
MONISHA! COME BACK LATER.

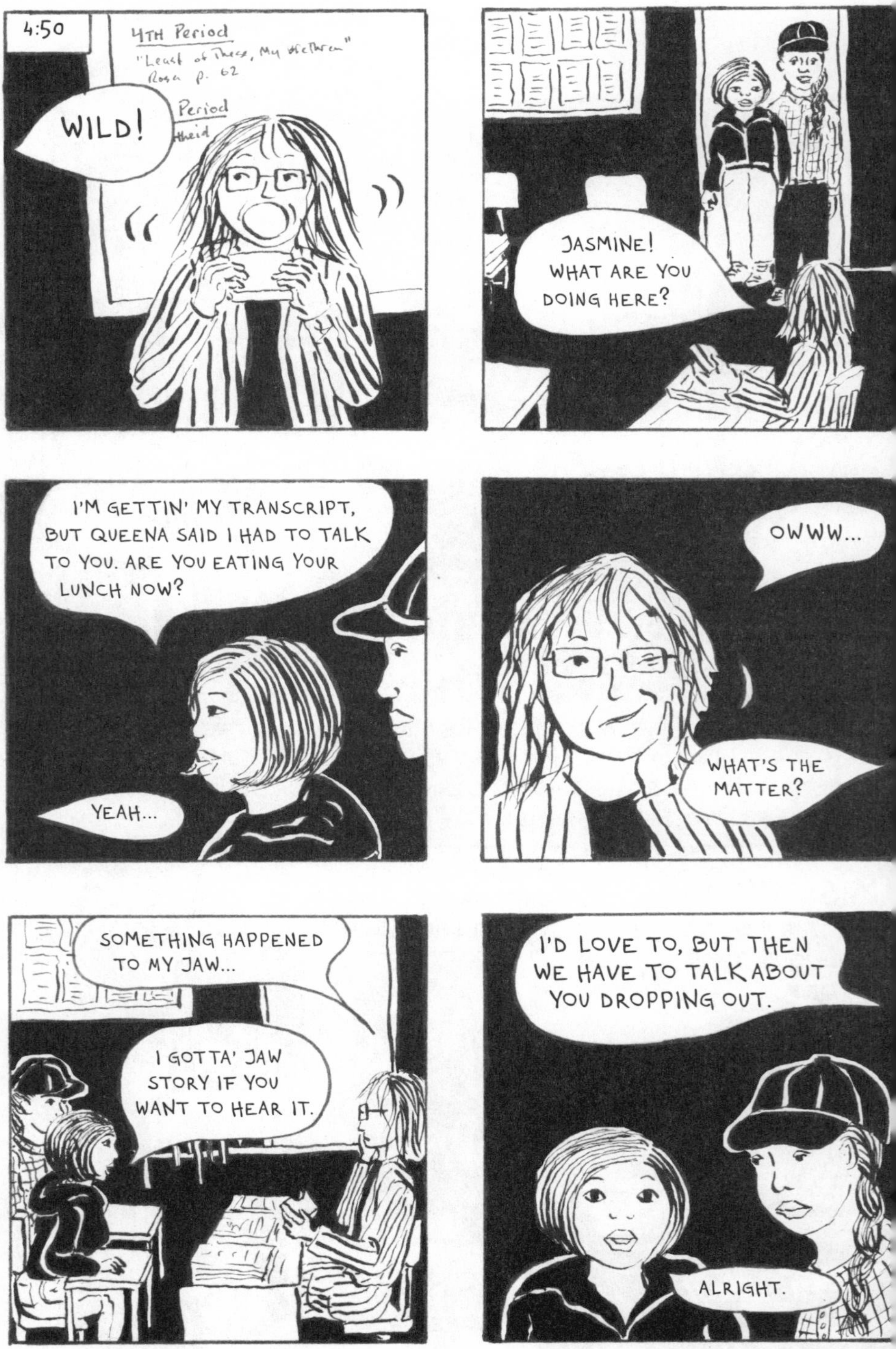
4:50
4TH Period
"Least of These, My Brethren"
Rosa p. 62
Period
WILD!
JASMINE! WHAT ARE YOU DOING HERE?
I'M GETTIN' MY TRANSCRIPT, BUT QUEENA SAID I HAD TO TALK TO YOU. ARE YOU EATING YOUR LUNCH NOW?
YEAH...
OWWW...
WHAT'S THE MATTER?
SOMETHING HAPPENED TO MY JAW...
I GOTTA' JAW STORY IF YOU WANT TO HEAR IT.
I'D LOVE TO, BUT THEN WE HAVE TO TALK ABOUT YOU DROPPING OUT.
ALRIGHT.

JASMINE'S JAW STORY

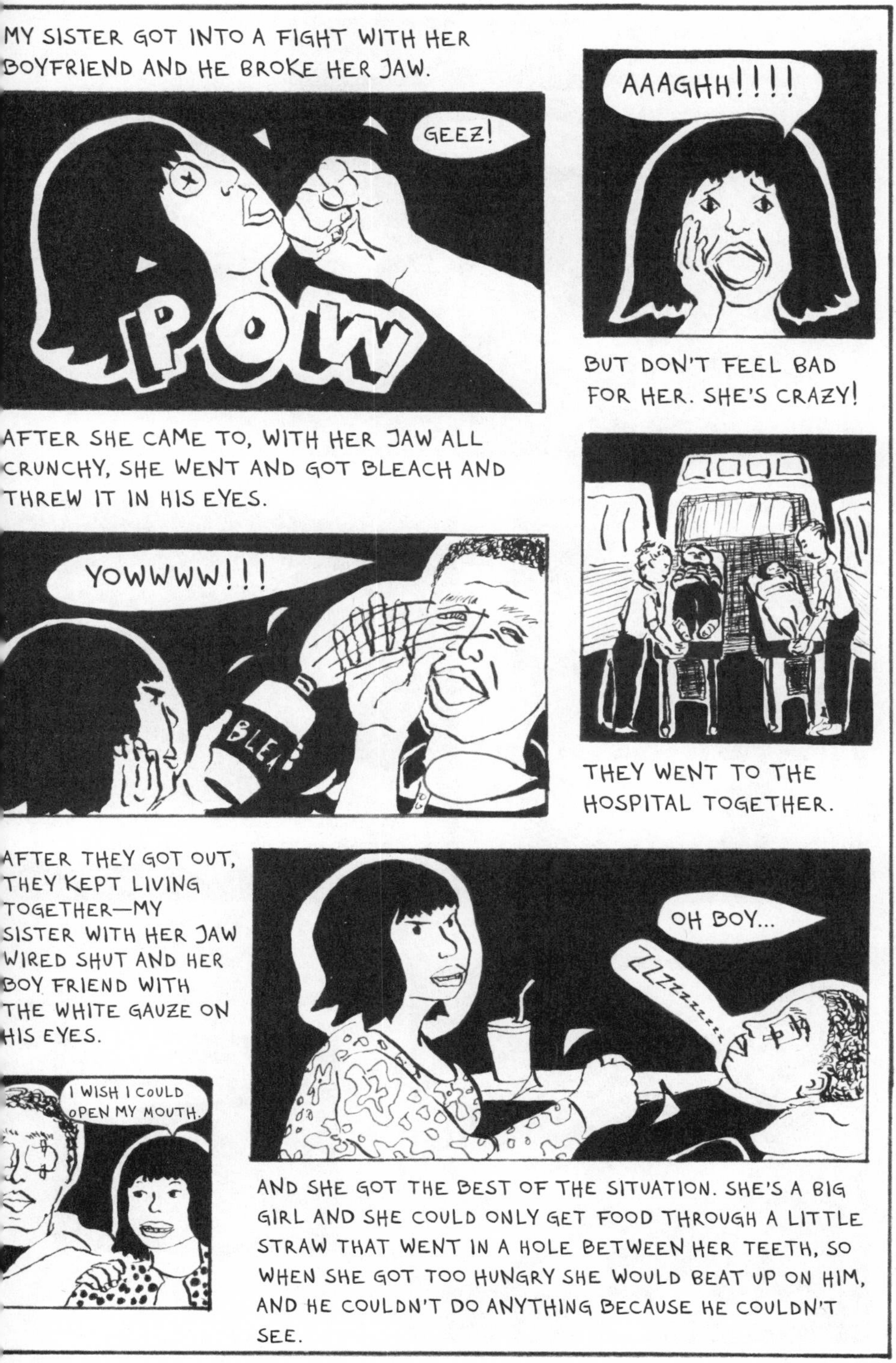

MY SISTER GOT INTO A FIGHT WITH HER BOYFRIEND AND HE BROKE HER JAW.
GEEZ!
POW
AAAGHH!!!!
BUT DON'T FEEL BAD FOR HER. SHE'S CRAZY!
AFTER SHE CAME TO, WITH HER JAW ALL CRUNCHY, SHE WENT AND GOT BLEACH AND THREW IT IN HIS EYES.
YOWWWW!!!
BLEA
THEY WENT TO THE HOSPITAL TOGETHER.
AFTER THEY GOT OUT, THEY KEPT LIVING TOGETHER—MY SISTER WITH HER JAW WIRED SHUT AND HER BOY FRIEND WITH THE WHITE GAUZE ON HIS EYES.
I WISH I COULD OPEN MY MOUTH.
OH BOY...
ZZZzzzzzzz
AND SHE GOT THE BEST OF THE SITUATION. SHE'S A BIG GIRL AND SHE COULD ONLY GET FOOD THROUGH A LITTLE STRAW THAT WENT IN A HOLE BETWEEN HER TEETH, SO WHEN SHE GOT TOO HUNGRY SHE WOULD BEAT UP ON HIM, AND HE COULDN'T DO ANYTHING BECAUSE HE COULDN'T SEE.

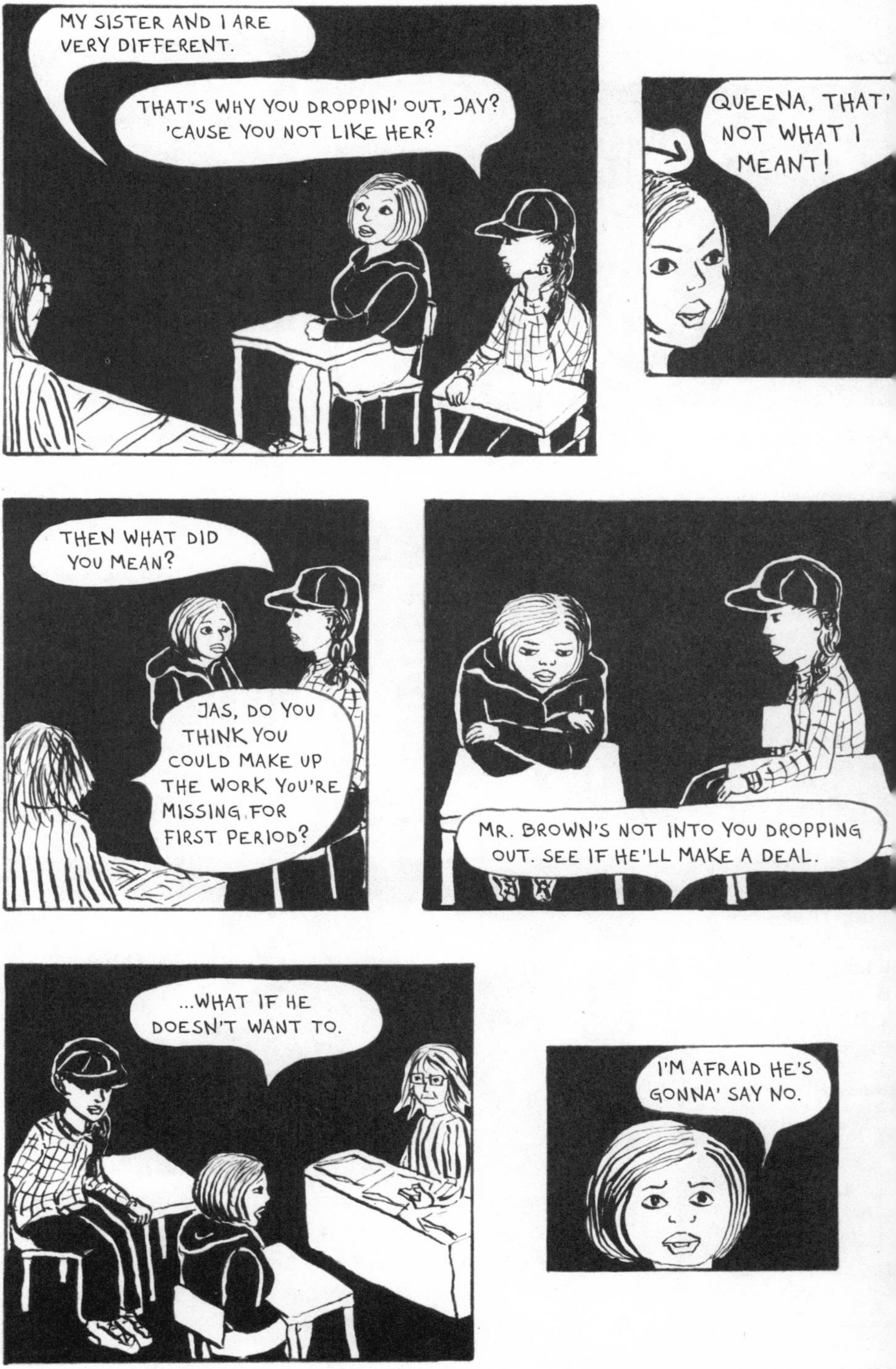
MY SISTER AND I ARE VERY DIFFERENT.
THAT'S WHY YOU DROPPIN' OUT, JAY? 'CAUSE YOU NOT LIKE HER?
QUEENA, THAT' NOT WHAT I MEANT!
THEN WHAT DID YOU MEAN?
JAS, DO YOU THINK YOU COULD MAKE UP THE WORK YOU'RE MISSING FOR FIRST PERIOD?
MR. BROWN'S NOT INTO YOU DROPPING OUT. SEE IF HE'LL MAKE A DEAL.
...WHAT IF HE DOESN'T WANT TO.
I'M AFRAID HE'S GONNA' SAY NO.

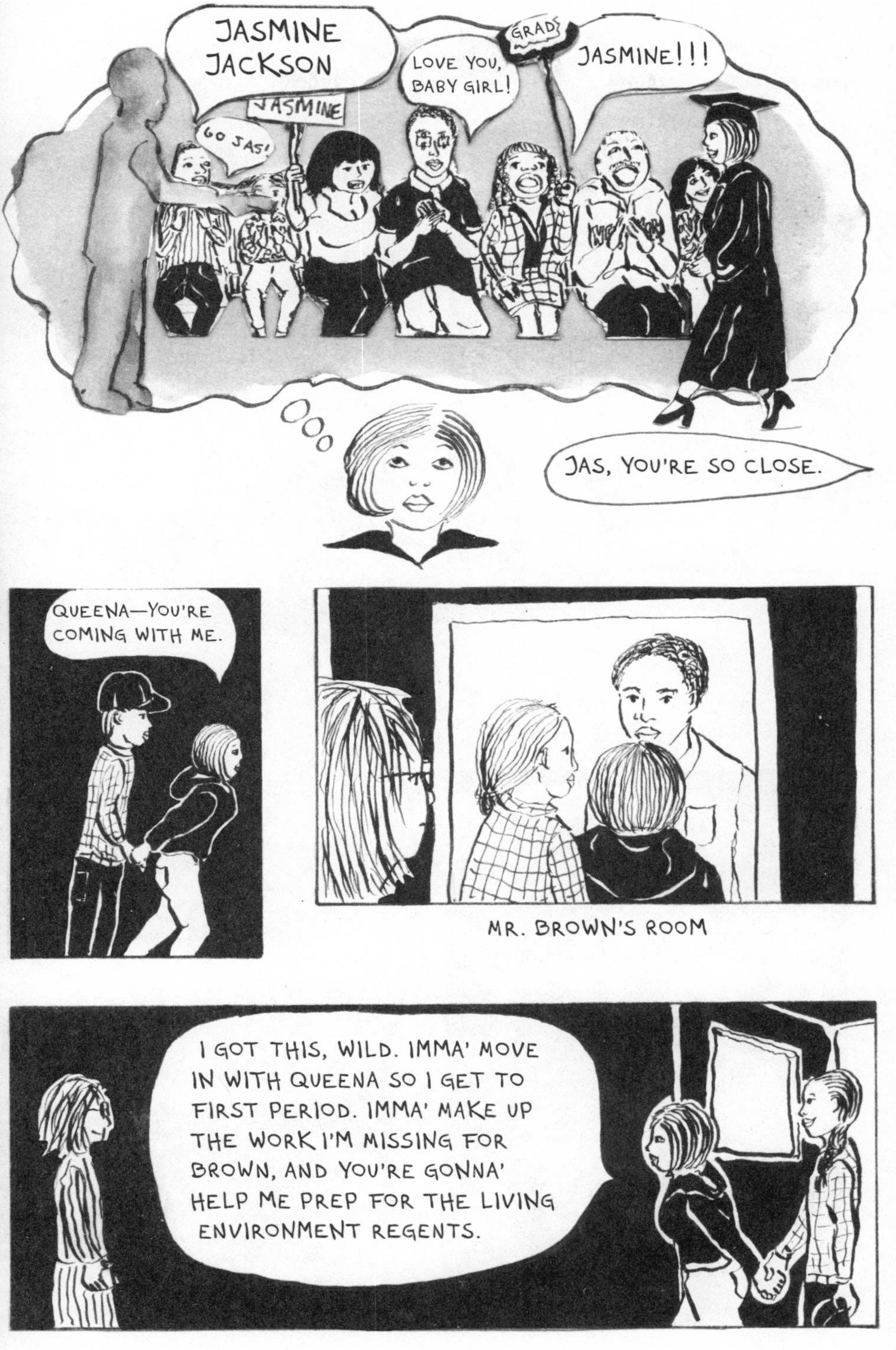
JASMINE JACKSON
GO JAS!
JASMINE
LOVE YOU, BABY GIRL!
GRADS
JASMINE!!!
JAS, YOU'RE SO CLOSE.
QUEENA—YOU'RE COMING WITH ME.
MR. BROWN'S ROOM
I GOT THIS, WILD. IMMA' MOVE IN WITH QUEENA SO I GET TO FIRST PERIOD. IMMA' MAKE UP THE WORK I'M MISSING FOR BROWN, AND YOU'RE GONNA' HELP ME PREP FOR THE LIVING ENVIRONMENT REGENTS.

WHETHER JASMINE DROPS OUT OR NOT, SCHOOL KEEPS GOING

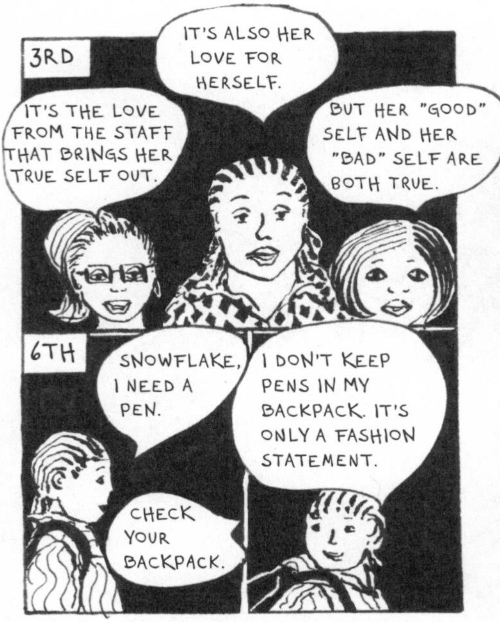
3RD
IT'S THE LOVE FROM THE STAFF THAT BRINGS HER TRUE SELF OUT.
IT'S ALSO HER LOVE FOR HERSELF.
BUT HER "GOOD" SELF AND HER "BAD" SELF ARE BOTH TRUE.
6TH
SNOWFLAKE, I NEED A PEN.
CHECK YOUR BACKPACK.
I DON'T KEEP PENS IN MY BACKPACK. IT'S ONLY A FASHION STATEMENT.

ONCE MIDTERMS ARE OVER, THE SEMESTER FEELS LIKE IT IS FLYING BY.

BEFORE YOU KNOW IT, THANKSGIVING'S ARRIVED.

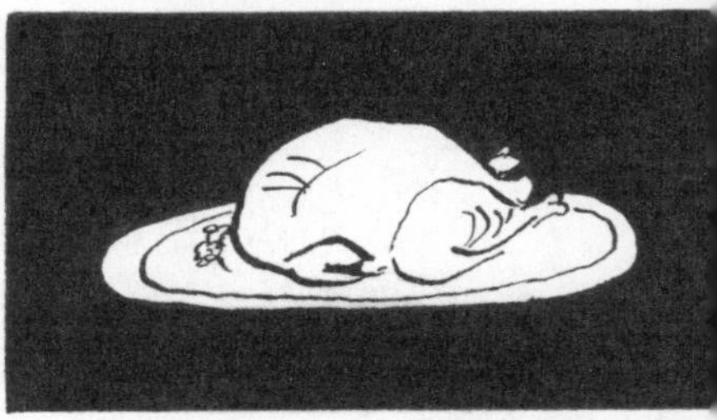

THEN A FEW MORE WEEKS OF SCHOOL BEFORE WINTER BREAK.

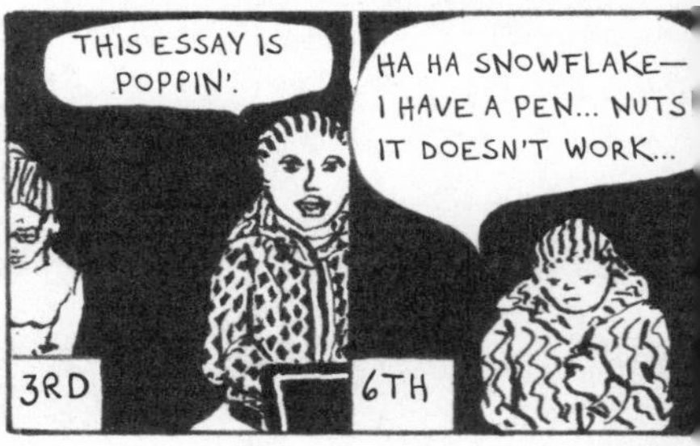
THIS ESSAY IS POPPIN'.
3RD
HA HA SNOWFLAKE— I HAVE A PEN... NUTS IT DOESN'T WORK...
6TH

THIS YEAR WE'RE HAVING A TALENT SHOW BEFORE THE HOLIDAYS

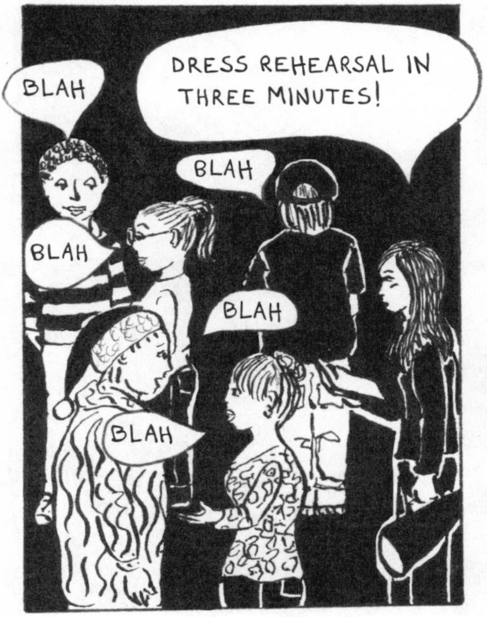
BLAH
DRESS REHEARSAL IN THREE MINUTES!
BLAH
BLAH
BLAH
BLAH

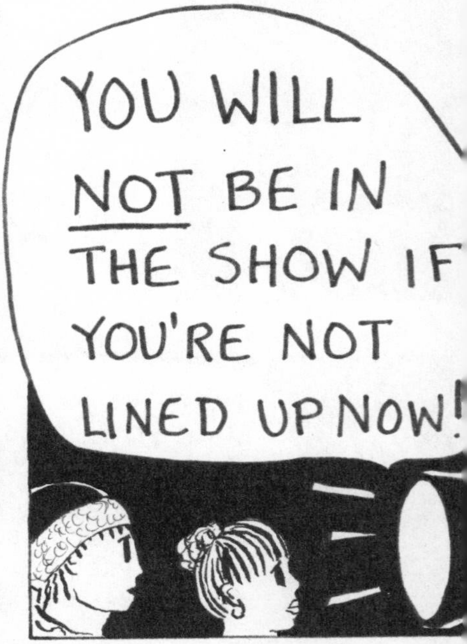
YOU WILL NOT BE IN THE SHOW IF YOU'RE NOT LINED UP NOW!

OUR C.F.O. CECILIA IS ORGANIZING IT.

SHE'S REALLY GOOD.

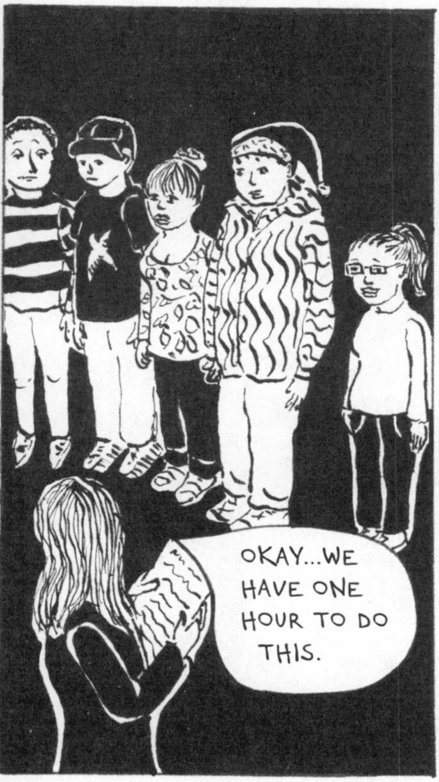
OKAY...WE HAVE ONE HOUR TO DO THIS.

THIS SHOW IS A WONDERFUL EXPERIENCE FOR THE STUDENTS.

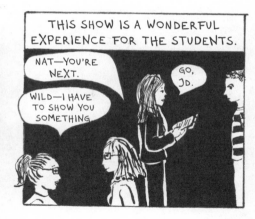

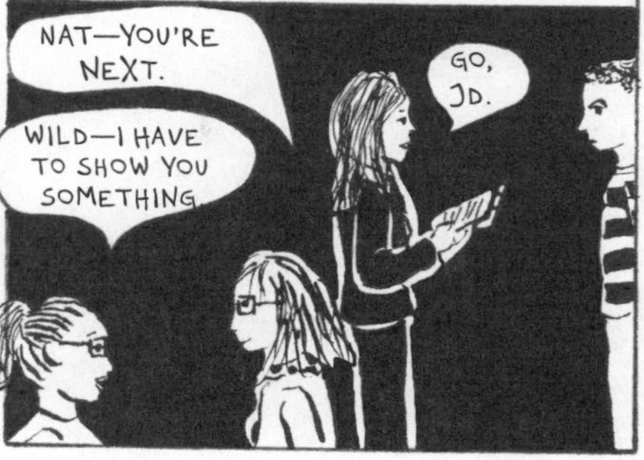
NAT—YOU'RE NEXT.
WILD—I HAVE TO SHOW YOU SOMETHING.
GO, JD.

THEY READ POEMS, DANCE, SING.

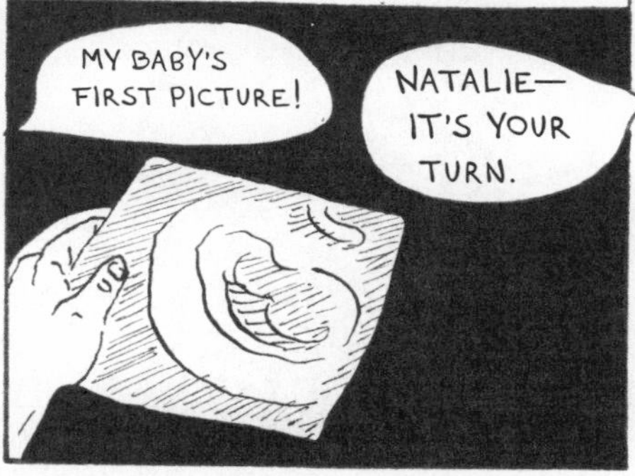
MY BABY'S FIRST PICTURE!
NATALIE—IT'S YOUR TURN.

PARENTS ATTEND, KIDS BRING THEIR LITTLE BROTHERS AND SISTERS...

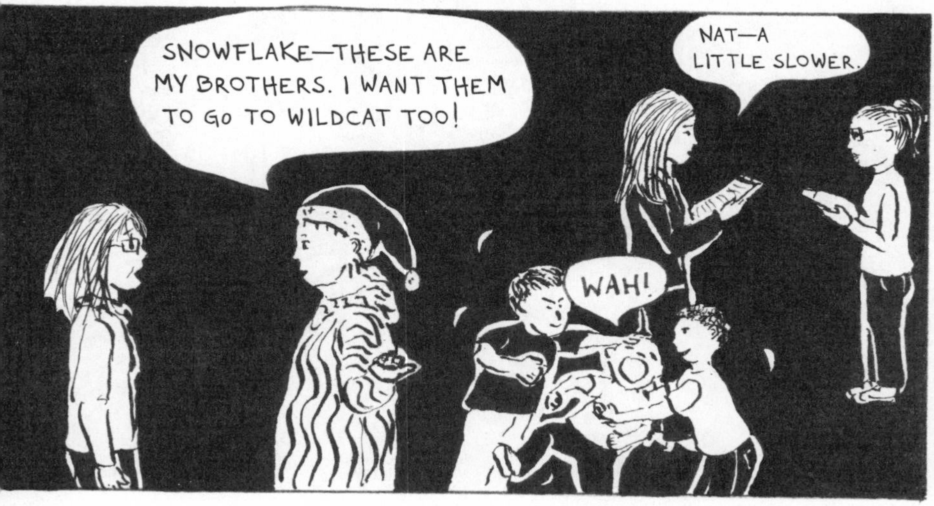
SNOWFLAKE—THESE ARE MY BROTHERS. I WANT THEM TO GO TO WILDCAT TOO!
NAT—A LITTLE SLOWER.
WAH!

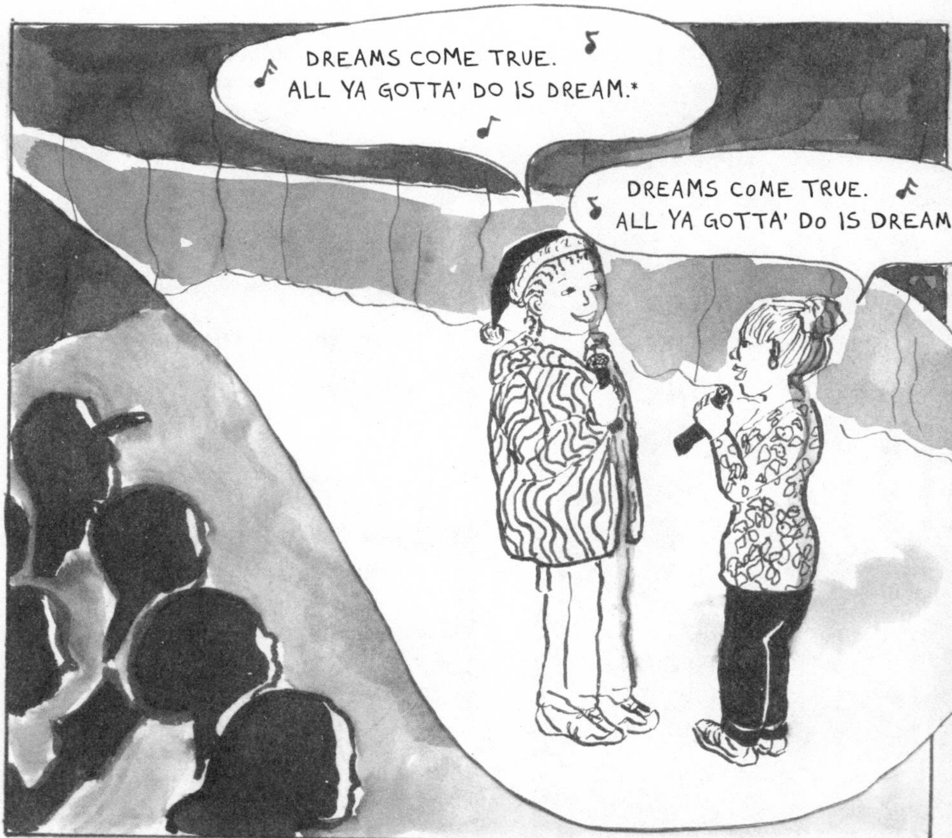
DREAMS COME TRUE. ALL YA GOTTA' DO IS DREAM.*
DREAMS COME TRUE. ALL YA GOTTA' DO IS DREAM.

AND IT'S BEAUTIFUL!

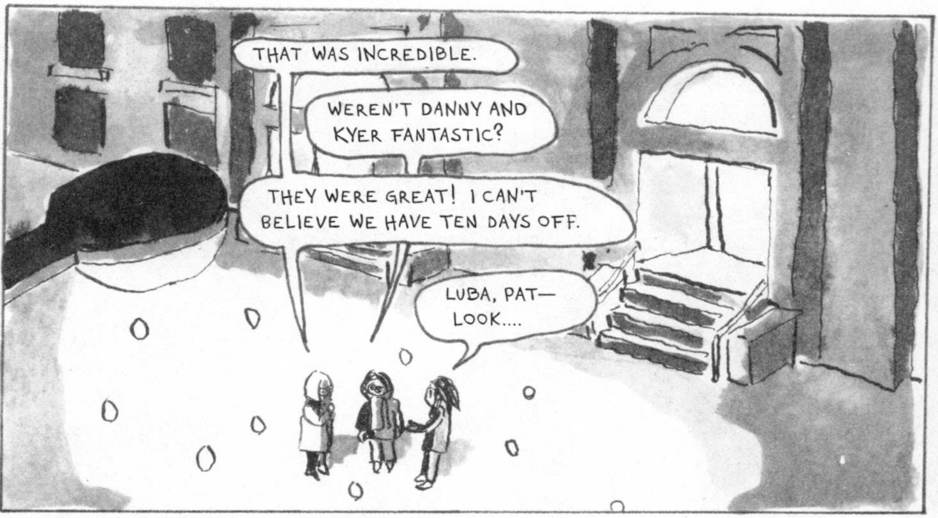
THAT WAS INCREDIBLE.
WEREN'T DANNY AND KYER FANTASTIC?
THEY WERE GREAT! I CAN'T BELIEVE WE HAVE TEN DAYS OFF.
LUBA, PAT— LOOK....

*FROM A SONG BY WILDCAT GRADUATE LUIS FLORES

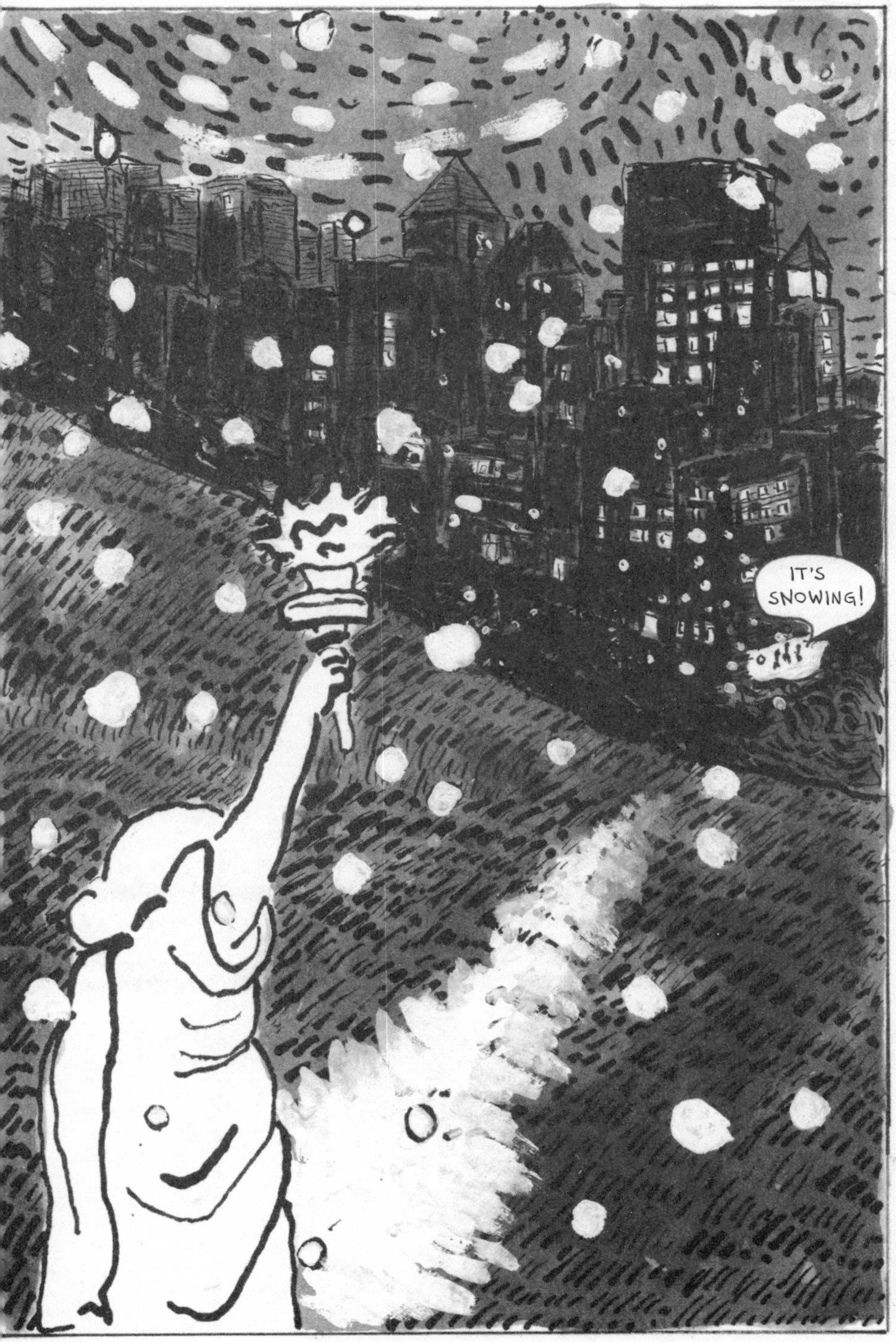
IT'S SNOWING!

AND NOW—WINTER BREAK!!!

VACATION ASSIGNMENT: WRITE A MONOLOGUE IN THE VOICE OF A CHARACTER WHO IS DESCRIBING HIS OR HER EXPERIENCES OVER WINTER BREAK. AUTOBIOGRAPHICAL OR FICTION.

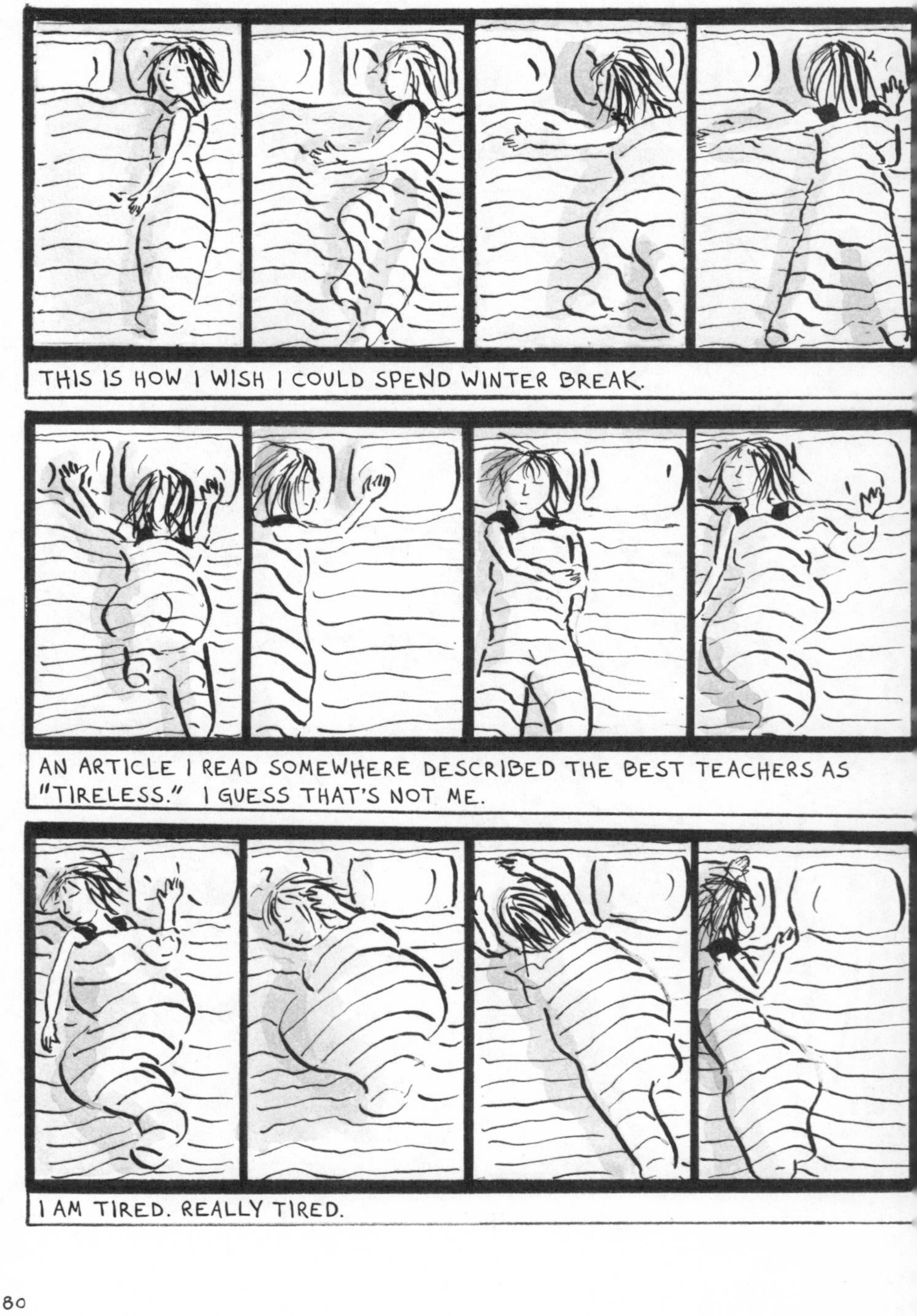
THIS IS HOW I WISH I COULD SPEND WINTER BREAK.
AN ARTICLE I READ SOMEWHERE DESCRIBED THE BEST TEACHERS AS "TIRELESS." I GUESS THAT'S NOT ME.
I AM TIRED. REALLY TIRED.

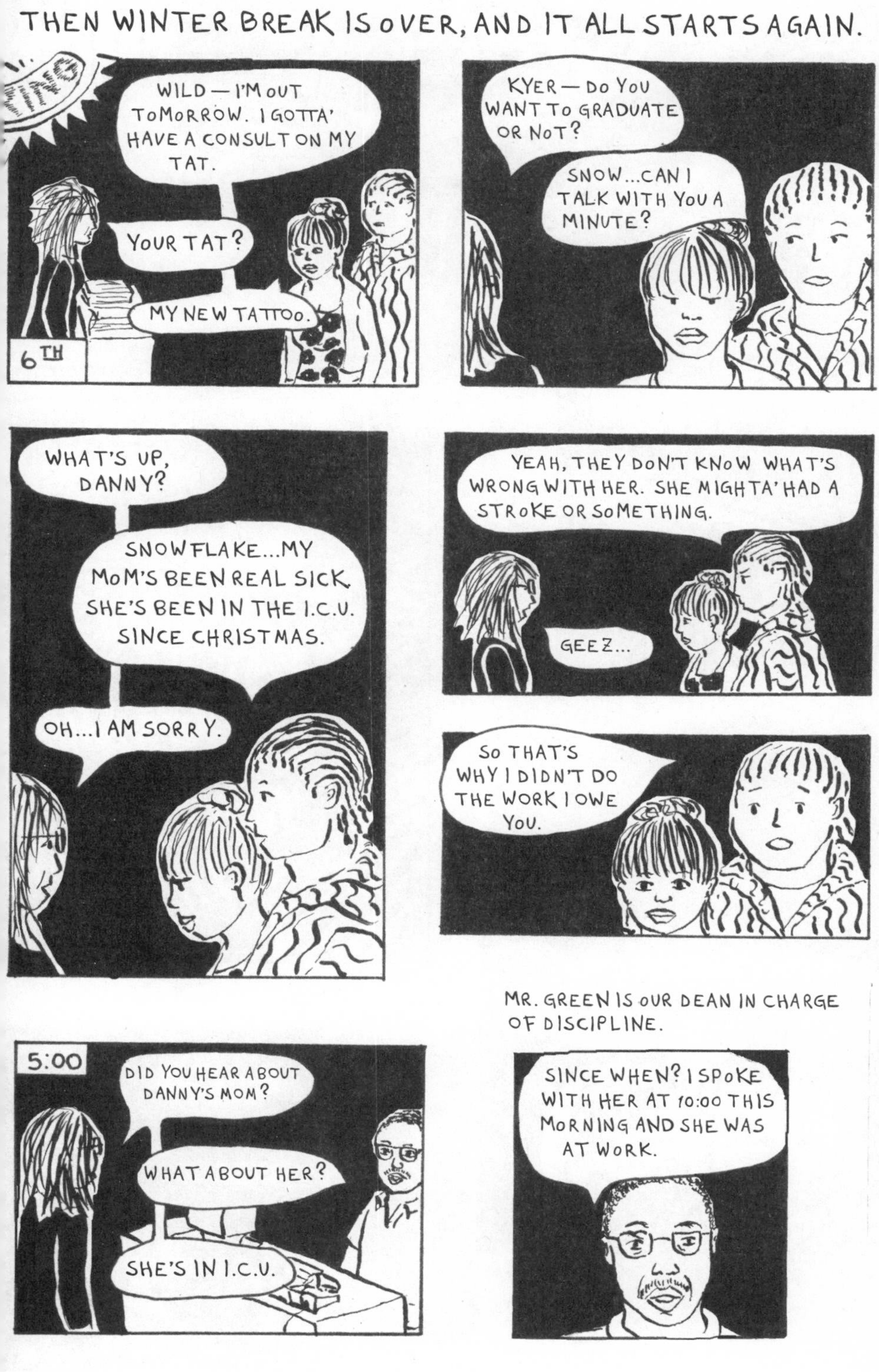
THEN WINTER BREAK IS OVER, AND IT ALL STARTS AGAIN.
6TH
WILD — I'M OUT TOMORROW. I GOTTA' HAVE A CONSULT ON MY TAT.
YOUR TAT?
MY NEW TATTOO.
KYER — DO YOU WANT TO GRADUATE OR NOT?
SNOW...CAN I TALK WITH YOU A MINUTE?
WHAT'S UP, DANNY?
SNOWFLAKE...MY MOM'S BEEN REAL SICK. SHE'S BEEN IN THE I.C.U. SINCE CHRISTMAS.
OH...I AM SORRY.
YEAH, THEY DON'T KNOW WHAT'S WRONG WITH HER. SHE MIGHTA' HAD A STROKE OR SOMETHING.
GEEZ...
SO THAT'S WHY I DIDN'T DO THE WORK I OWE YOU.
5:00
DID YOU HEAR ABOUT DANNY'S MOM?
WHAT ABOUT HER?
SHE'S IN I.C.U.
MR. GREEN IS OUR DEAN IN CHARGE OF DISCIPLINE.
SINCE WHEN? I SPOKE WITH HER AT 10:00 THIS MORNING AND SHE WAS AT WORK.

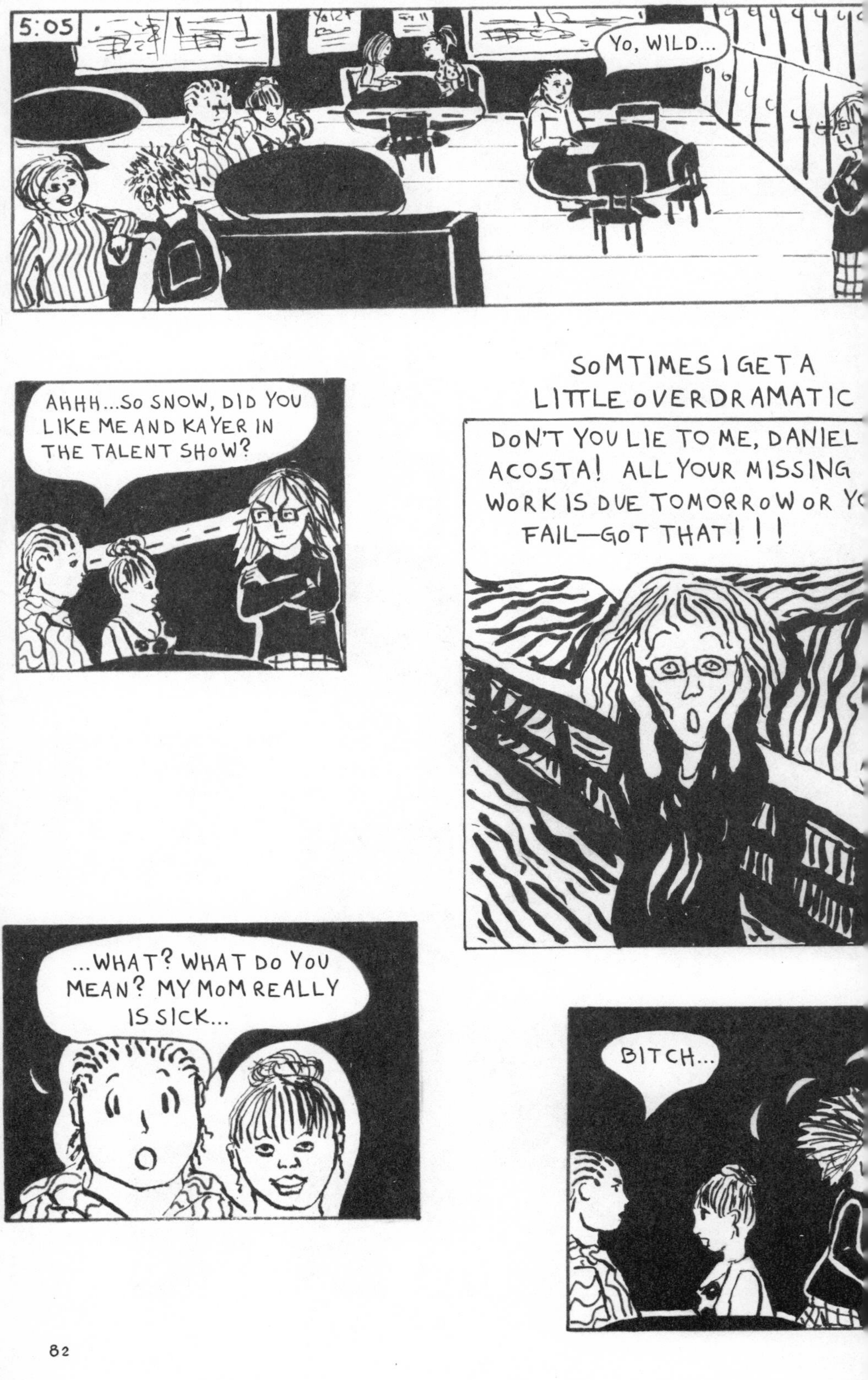
5:05
Yo, WILD...
AHHH...So SNOW, DID YOU LIKE ME AND KAYER IN THE TALENT SHoW?
SoMTIMES I GET A LITTLE oVERDRAMATIC
DoN'T YOU LIE TO ME, DANIEL ACOSTA! ALL YOUR MISSING WoRK IS DUE TOMORRoW oR Y
FAIL—GoT THAT!!!
...WHAT? WHAT Do YoU MEAN? MY MoM REALLY IS SICK...
BITCH...

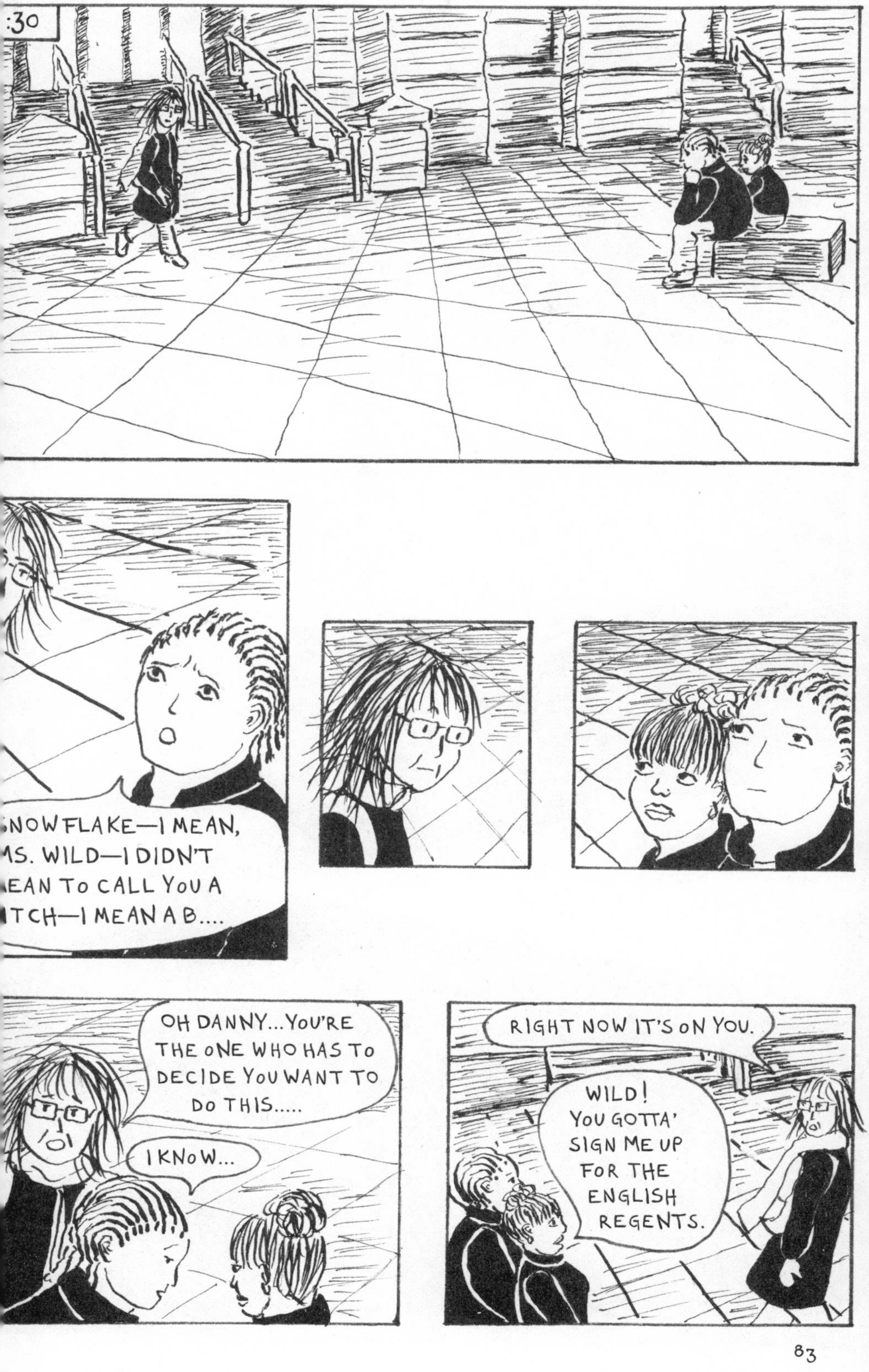
:30
SNOWFLAKE—I MEAN, MS. WILD—I DIDN'T EAN TO CALL YOU A TCH—I MEAN A B....
OH DANNY... YOU'RE THE ONE WHO HAS TO DECIDE YOU WANT TO DO THIS.....
I KNOW...
RIGHT NOW IT'S ON YOU.
WILD! YOU GOTTA' SIGN ME UP FOR THE ENGLISH REGENTS.

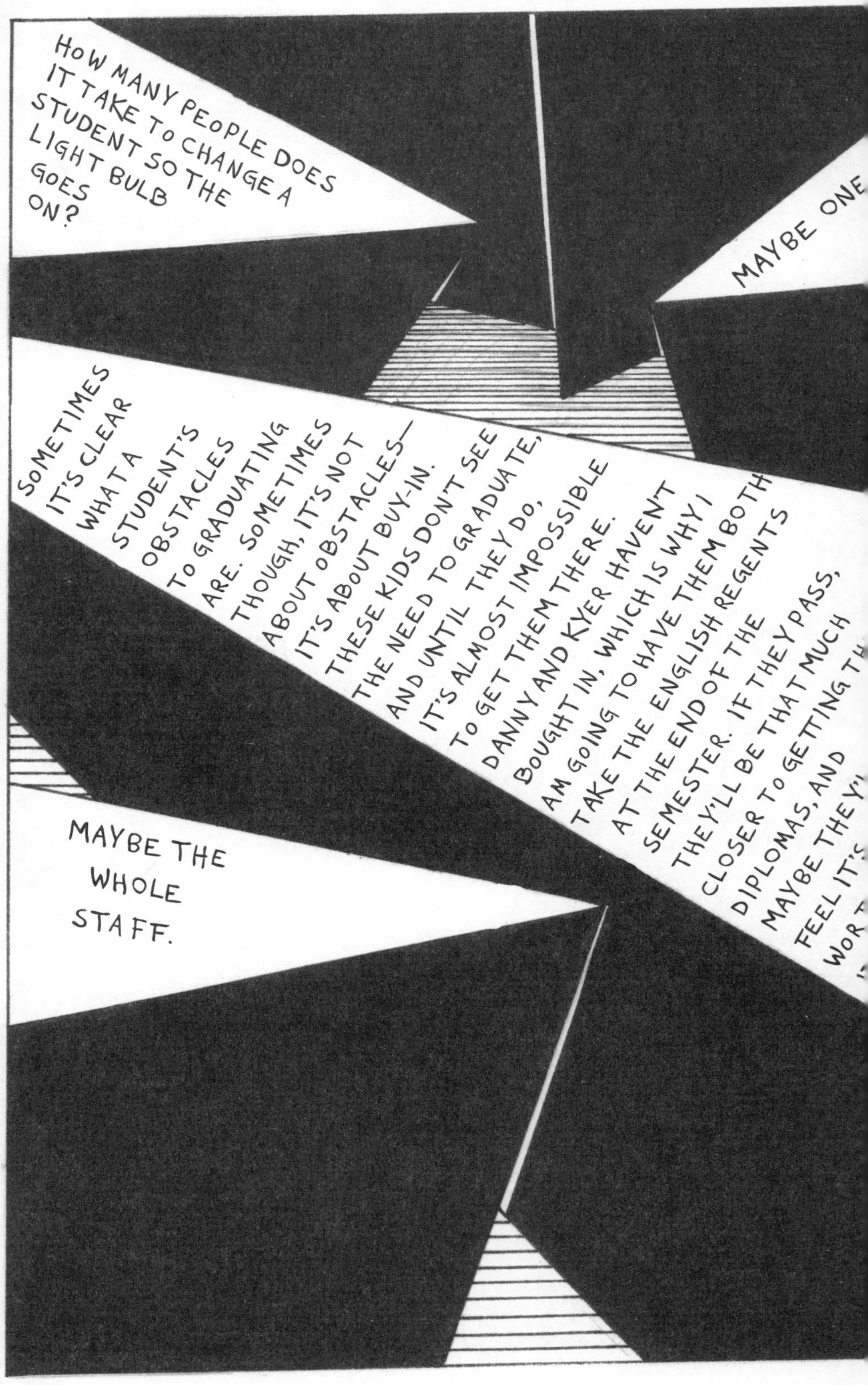

HOW MANY PEOPLE DOES IT TAKE TO CHANGE A STUDENT SO THE LIGHT BULB GOES ON?
MAYBE ONE
SOMETIMES IT'S CLEAR WHAT A STUDENT'S OBSTACLES TO GRADUATING ARE. SOMETIMES THOUGH, IT'S NOT ABOUT OBSTACLES— IT'S ABOUT BUY-IN. THESE KIDS DON'T SEE THE NEED TO GRADUATE, AND UNTIL THEY DO, IT'S ALMOST IMPOSSIBLE TO GET THEM THERE. DANNY AND KYER HAVEN'T BOUGHT IN, WHICH IS WHY I AM GOING TO HAVE THEM BOTH TAKE THE ENGLISH REGENTS AT THE END OF THE SEMESTER. IF THEY PASS, THEY'LL BE THAT MUCH CLOSER TO GETTING TH
DIPLOMAS, AND MAYBE THEY'
FEEL IT'S
WOR
MAYBE THE WHOLE STAFF.

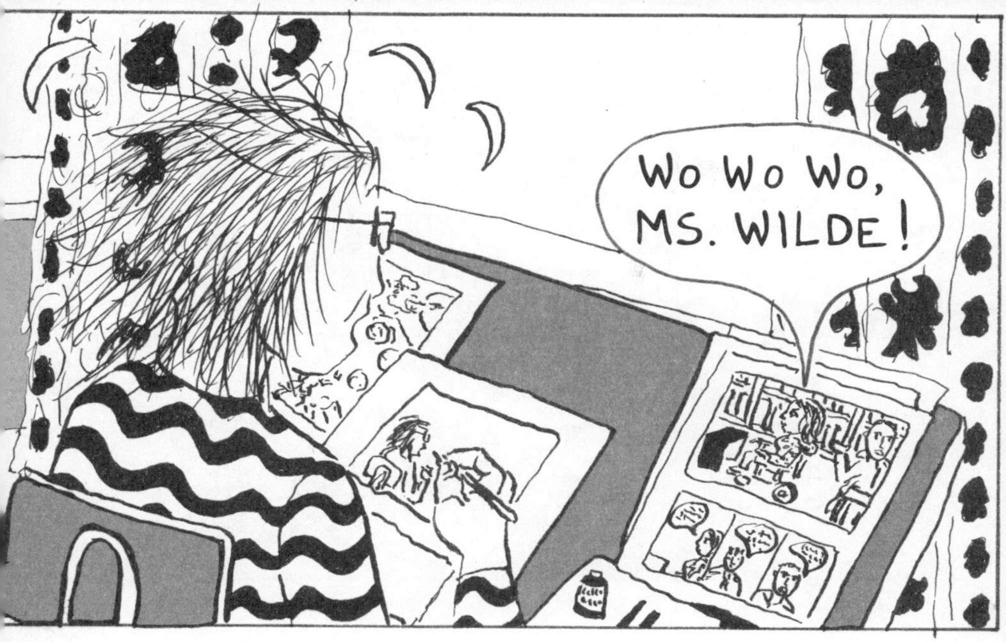
WO WO WO, MS. WILDE!

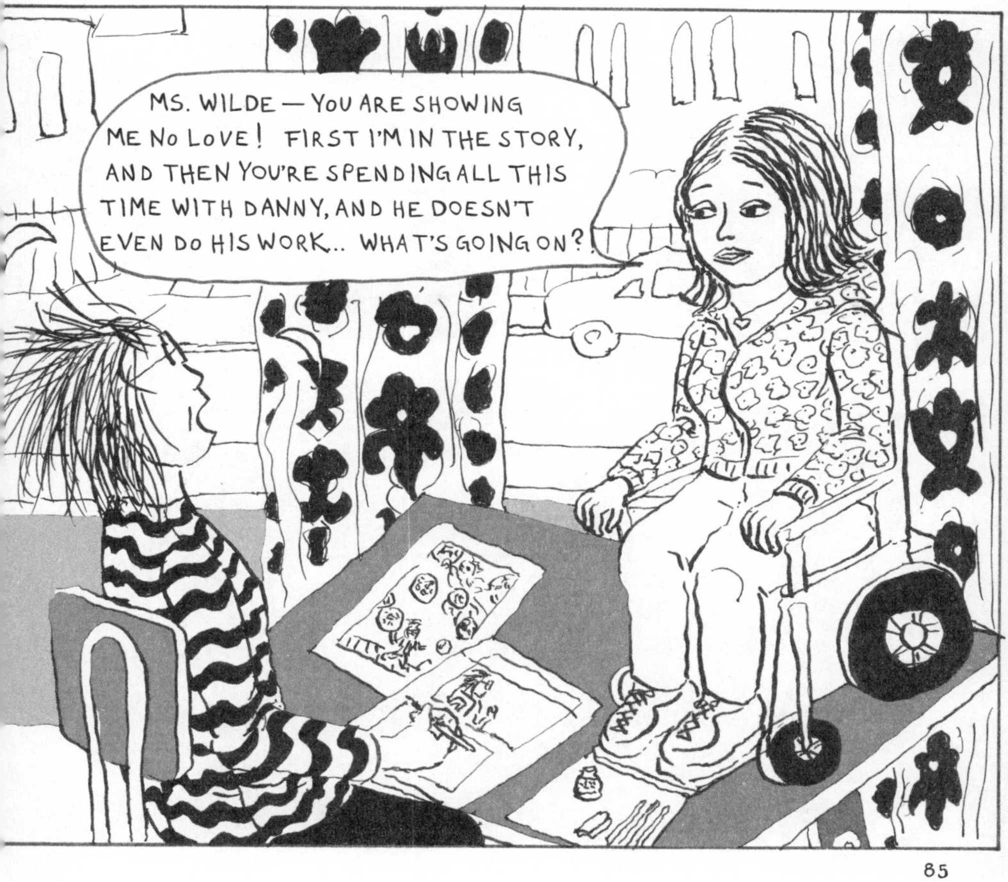
MS. WILDE — YOU ARE SHOWING ME NO LOVE! FIRST I'M IN THE STORY, AND THEN YOU'RE SPENDING ALL THIS TIME WITH DANNY, AND HE DOESN'T EVEN DO HIS WORK... WHAT'S GOING ON?

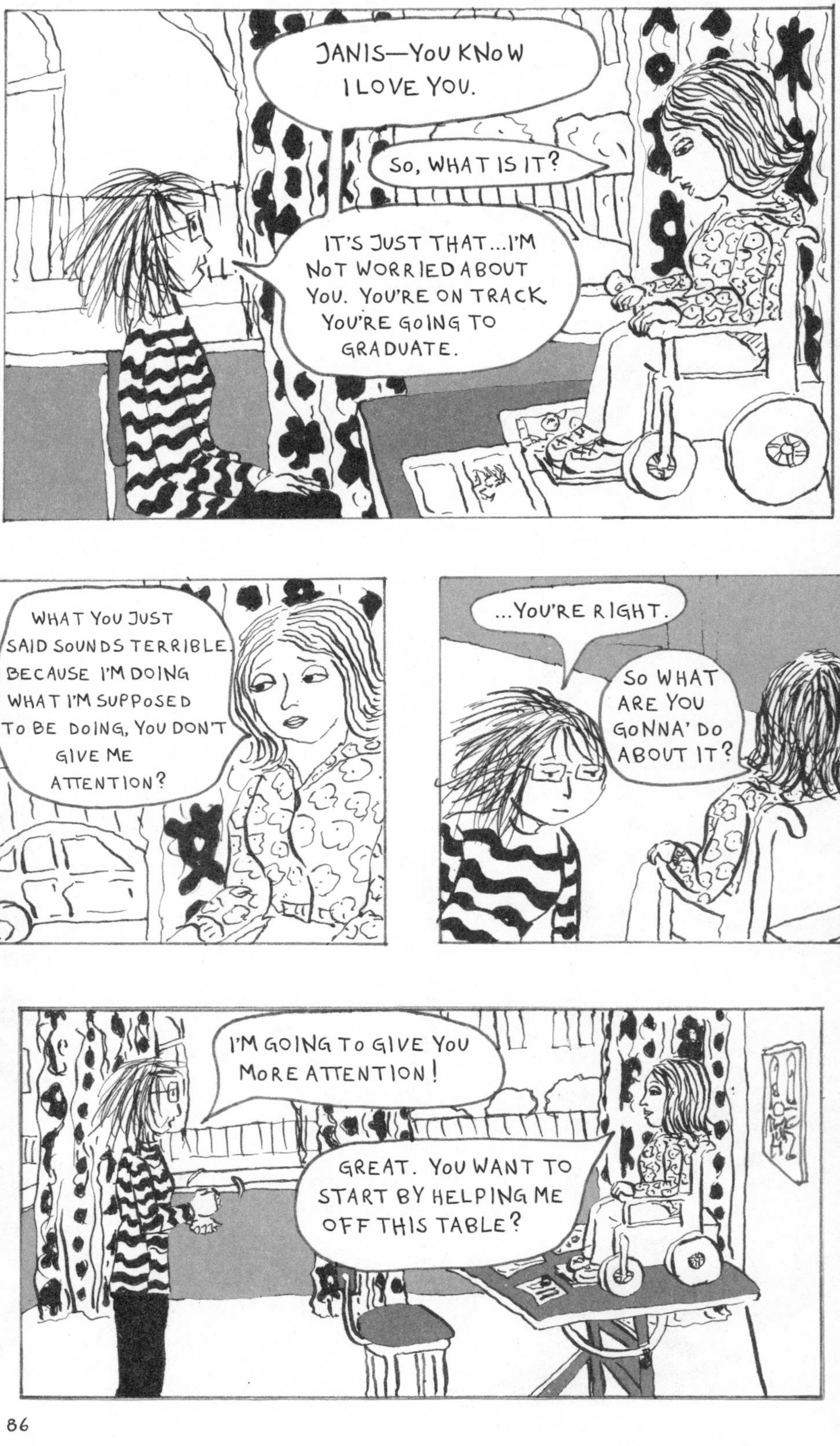

JANIS—YOU KNOW I LOVE YOU.
SO, WHAT IS IT?
IT'S JUST THAT...I'M NOT WORRIED ABOUT YOU. YOU'RE ON TRACK. YOU'RE GOING TO GRADUATE.
WHAT YOU JUST SAID SOUNDS TERRIBLE. BECAUSE I'M DOING WHAT I'M SUPPOSED TO BE DOING, YOU DON'T GIVE ME ATTENTION?
...YOU'RE RIGHT.
SO WHAT ARE YOU GONNA' DO ABOUT IT?
I'M GOING TO GIVE YOU MORE ATTENTION!
GREAT. YOU WANT TO START BY HELPING ME OFF THIS TABLE?

TEACHING ALWAYS INVOLVES JUGGLING

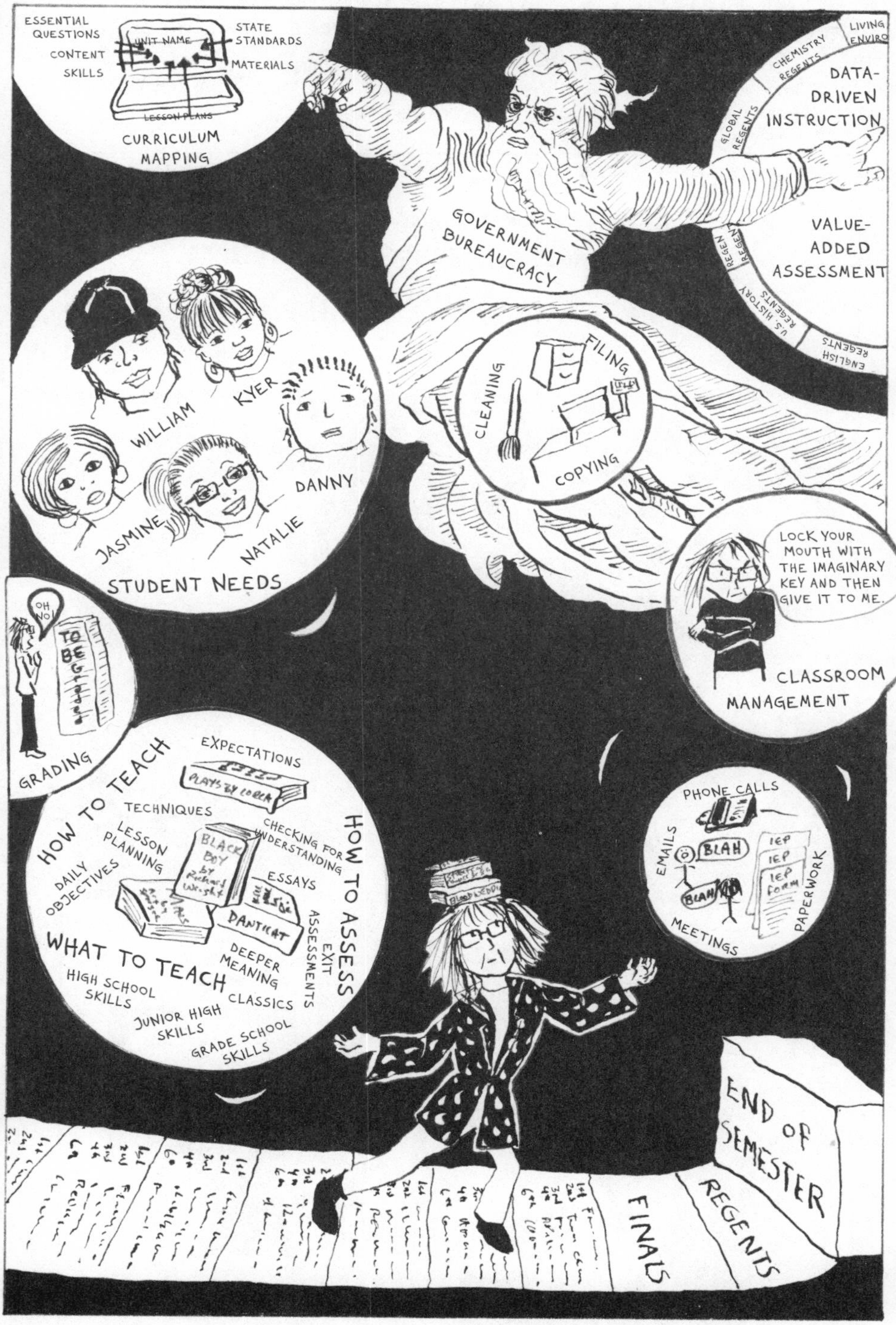

ESSENTIAL QUESTIONS
CONTENT
SKILLS
UNIT NAME
STATE STANDARDS
MATERIALS
LESSON PLANS
CURRICULUM MAPPING
GOVERNMENT BUREAUCRACY
LIVING ENVIRO
CHEMISTRY REGENTS
GLOBAL REGENTS
DATA-DRIVEN INSTRUCTION
VALUE-ADDED ASSESSMENT
REGEN
REGENTS
U.S. HISTORY REGENTS
ENGLISH REGENTS
WILLIAM
KYER
DANNY
JASMINE
NATALIE
STUDENT NEEDS
CLEANING
FILING
COPYING
LOCK YOUR MOUTH WITH THE IMAGINARY KEY AND THEN GIVE IT TO ME.
CLASSROOM MANAGEMENT
OH NO!
TO BE GRADED
GRADING
HOW TO TEACH
EXPECTATIONS
PLAYS BY LORCA
TECHNIQUES
LESSON PLANNING
DAILY OBJECTIVES
CHECKING FOR UNDERSTANDING
BLACK BOY by Richard Wright
ESSAYS
DANTICAT
HOW TO ASSESS
EXIT ASSESSMENTS
DEEPER MEANING
WHAT TO TEACH
HIGH SCHOOL SKILLS
JUNIOR HIGH SKILLS
CLASSICS
GRADE SCHOOL SKILLS
PHONE CALLS
EMAILS
BLAH
BLAH
IEP
IEP
IEP FORM
PAPERWORK
MEETINGS
FINALS
REGENTS
END OF SEMESTER

SPEAKING OF JUGGLING, IT'S TIME FOR THE REGENTS, THOSE MANDATORY NEW YORK STATE TESTS. WHY IS THIS ABOUT JUGGLING? BECAUSE TEST SCORES MATTER — IN TERMS OF OUR SCHOOL'S SUCCESS AND MY EVALUATION. WHAT'S THE BEST WAY TO GET HIGH TEST SCOES? TEST PREP. JUST ASK PRINCETON REVIEW AND KAPLAN. BUT TEST PREP IS JUST THAT, AND IT'S NOT EDUCATION. WHAT'S A TEACHER TO DO?

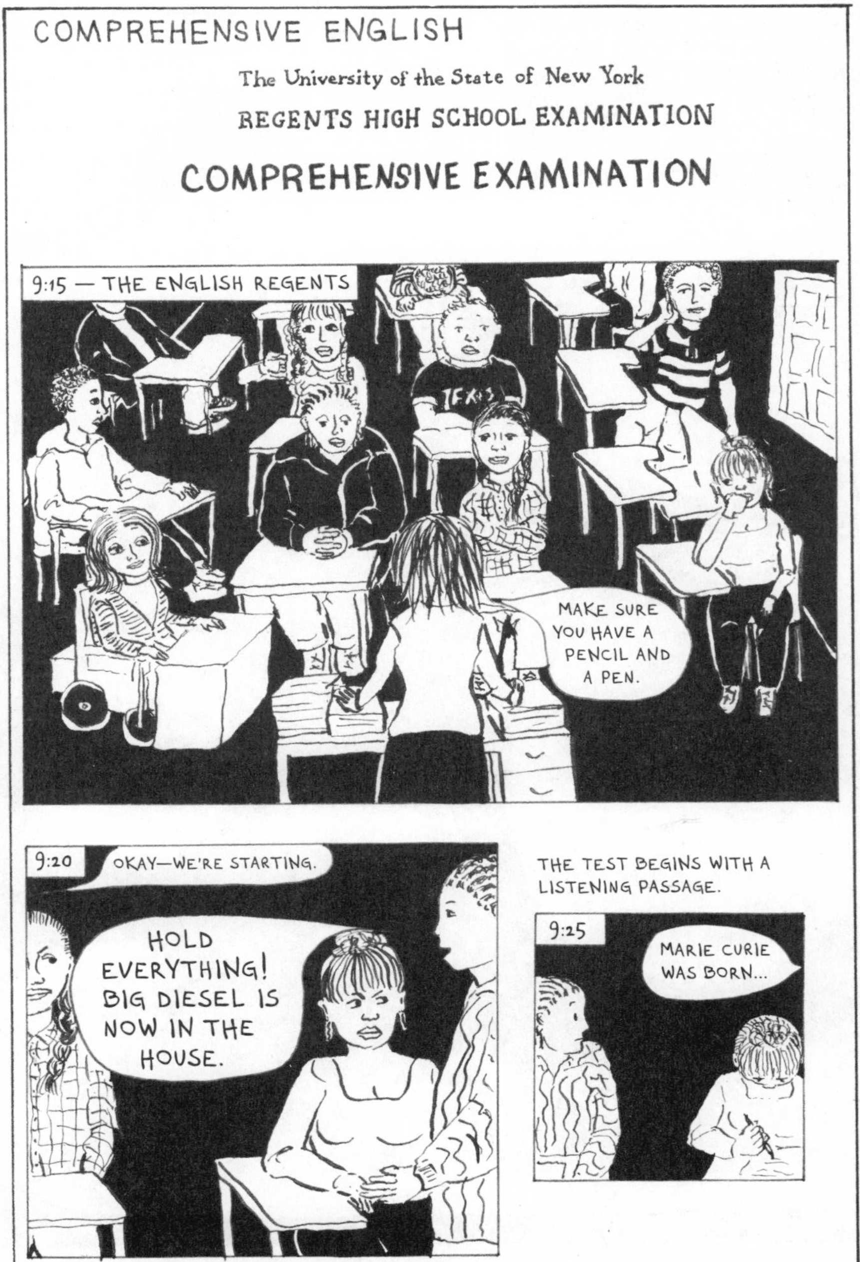

COMPREHENSIVE ENGLISH
The University of the State of New York
REGENTS HIGH SCHOOL EXAMINATION
COMPREHENSIVE EXAMINATION
9:15 — THE ENGLISH REGENTS
MAKE SURE YOU HAVE A PENCIL AND A PEN.
9:20
OKAY—WE'RE STARTING.
HOLD EVERYTHING! BIG DIESEL IS NOW IN THE HOUSE.
THE TEST BEGINS WITH A LISTENING PASSAGE.
9:25
MARIE CURIE WAS BORN...
DO NOT OPEN THIS EXAMINATION BOOKLET UNTIL THE SIGNAL IS GIVEN.

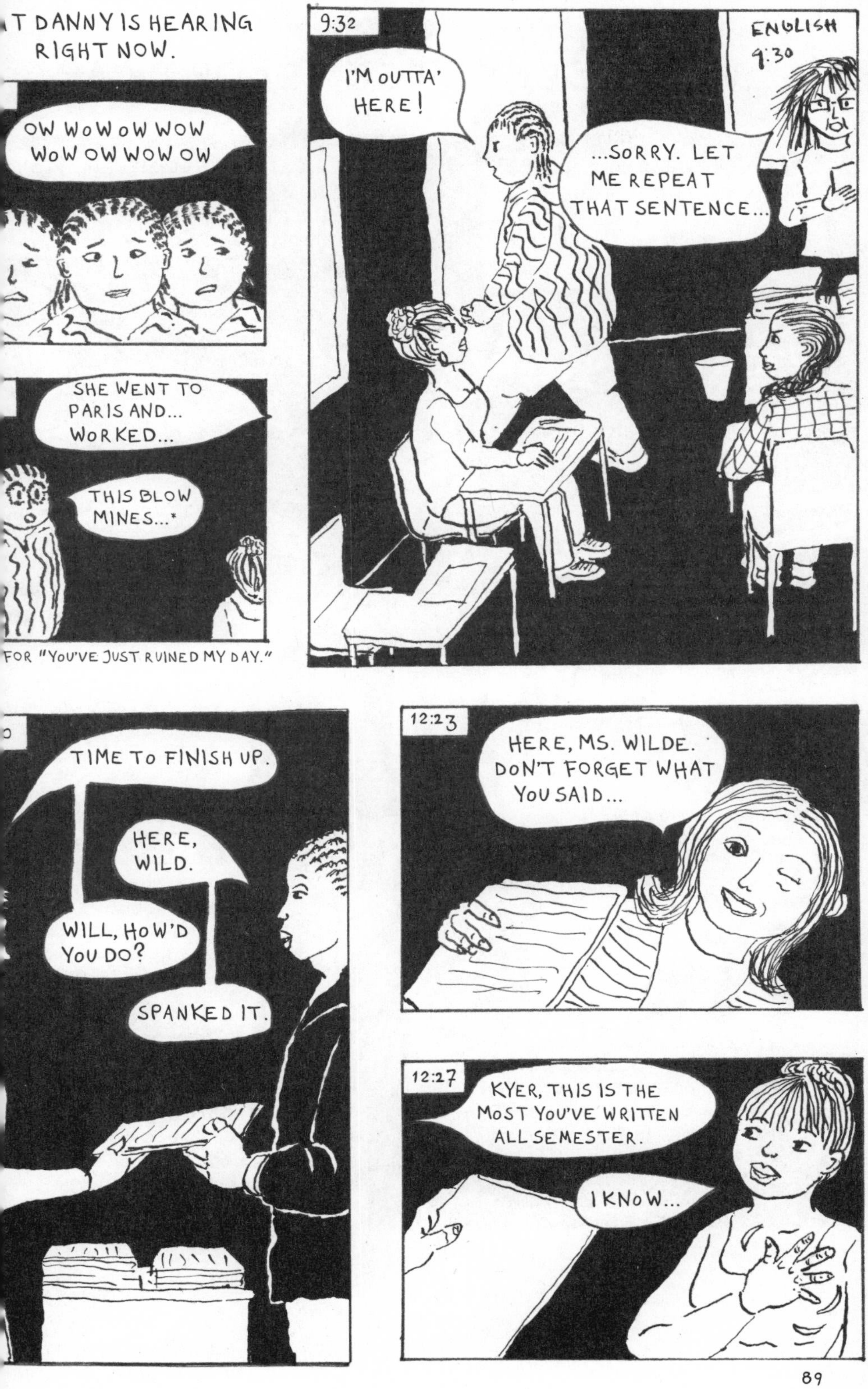
T DANNY IS HEARING RIGHT NOW.
OW WOW OW WOW WOW OW WOW OW
SHE WENT TO PARIS AND... WORKED...
THIS BLOW MINES...*
FOR "YOU'VE JUST RUINED MY DAY."
9:32
ENGLISH 9:30
I'M OUTTA' HERE!
...SORRY. LET ME REPEAT THAT SENTENCE...
TIME TO FINISH UP.
HERE, WILD.
WILL, HOW'D YOU DO?
SPANKED IT.
12:23
HERE, MS. WILDE. DON'T FORGET WHAT YOU SAID...
12:27
KYER, THIS IS THE MOST YOU'VE WRITTEN ALL SEMESTER.
I KNOW...

FIRST SEMESTER REPORT CARD

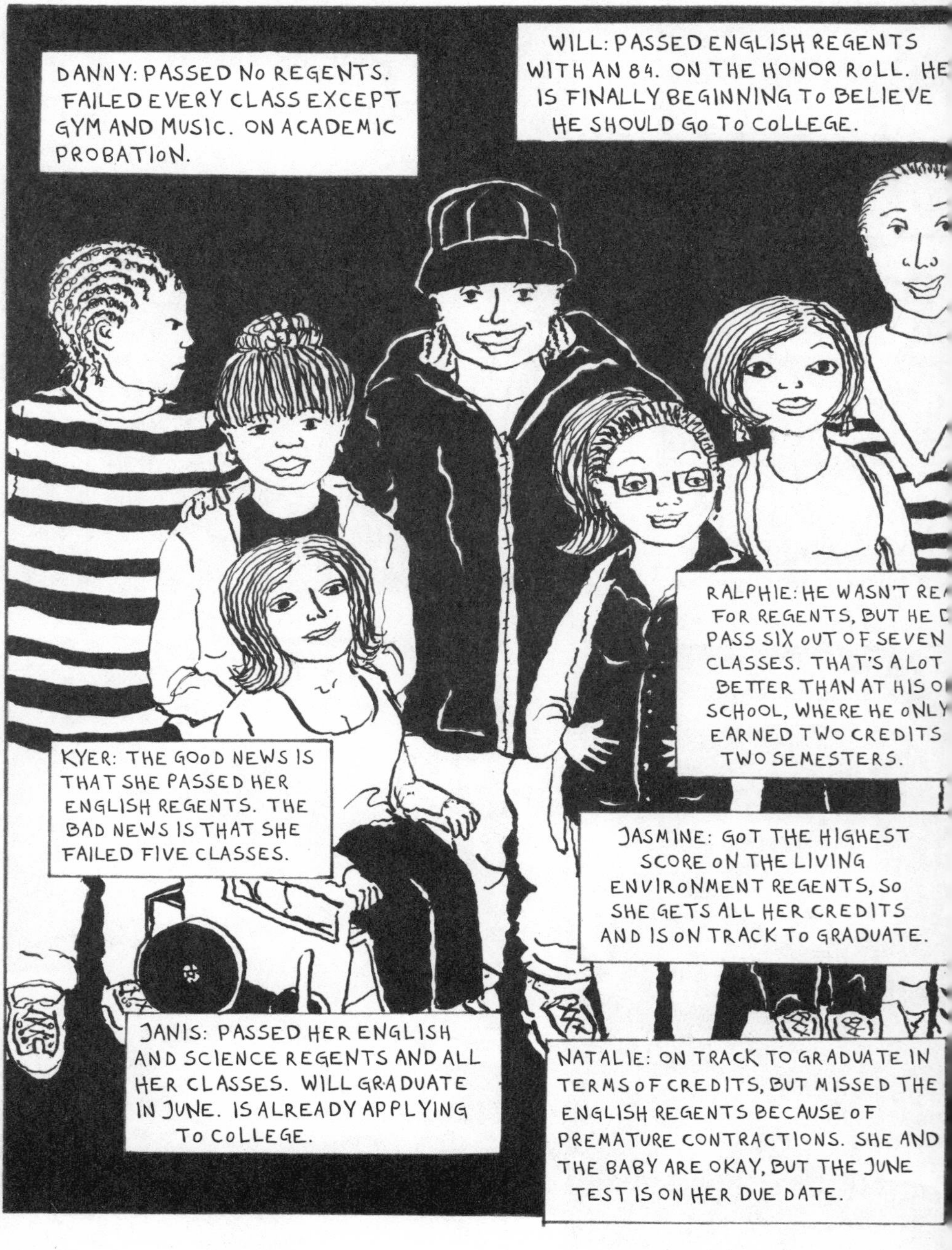
DANNY: PASSED NO REGENTS. FAILED EVERY CLASS EXCEPT GYM AND MUSIC. ON ACADEMIC PROBATION.
WILL: PASSED ENGLISH REGENTS WITH AN 84. ON THE HONOR ROLL. HE IS FINALLY BEGINNING TO BELIEVE HE SHOULD GO TO COLLEGE.
RALPHIE: HE WASN'T RE FOR REGENTS, BUT HE D PASS SIX OUT OF SEVEN CLASSES. THAT'S A LOT BETTER THAN AT HIS O SCHOOL, WHERE HE ONLY EARNED TWO CREDITS TWO SEMESTERS.
KYER: THE GOOD NEWS IS THAT SHE PASSED HER ENGLISH REGENTS. THE BAD NEWS IS THAT SHE FAILED FIVE CLASSES.
JASMINE: GOT THE HIGHEST SCORE ON THE LIVING ENVIRONMENT REGENTS, SO SHE GETS ALL HER CREDITS AND IS ON TRACK TO GRADUATE.
JANIS: PASSED HER ENGLISH AND SCIENCE REGENTS AND ALL HER CLASSES. WILL GRADUATE IN JUNE. IS ALREADY APPLYING TO COLLEGE.
NATALIE: ON TRACK TO GRADUATE IN TERMS OF CREDITS, BUT MISSED THE ENGLISH REGENTS BECAUSE OF PREMATURE CONTRACTIONS. SHE AND THE BABY ARE OKAY, BUT THE JUNE TEST IS ON HER DUE DATE.

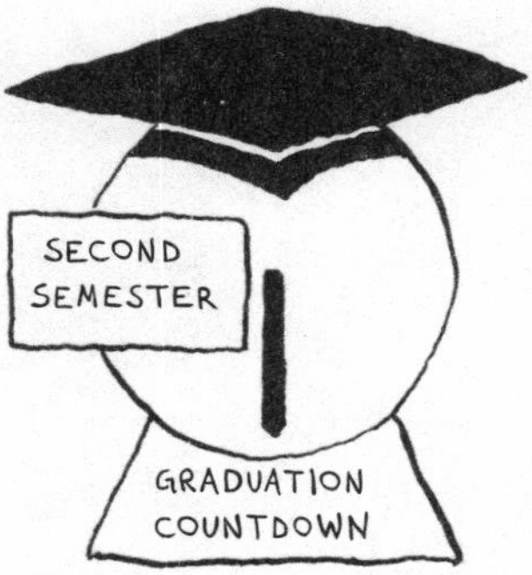
SECOND SEMESTER
GRADUATION COUNTDOWN

CHAPTER SIX

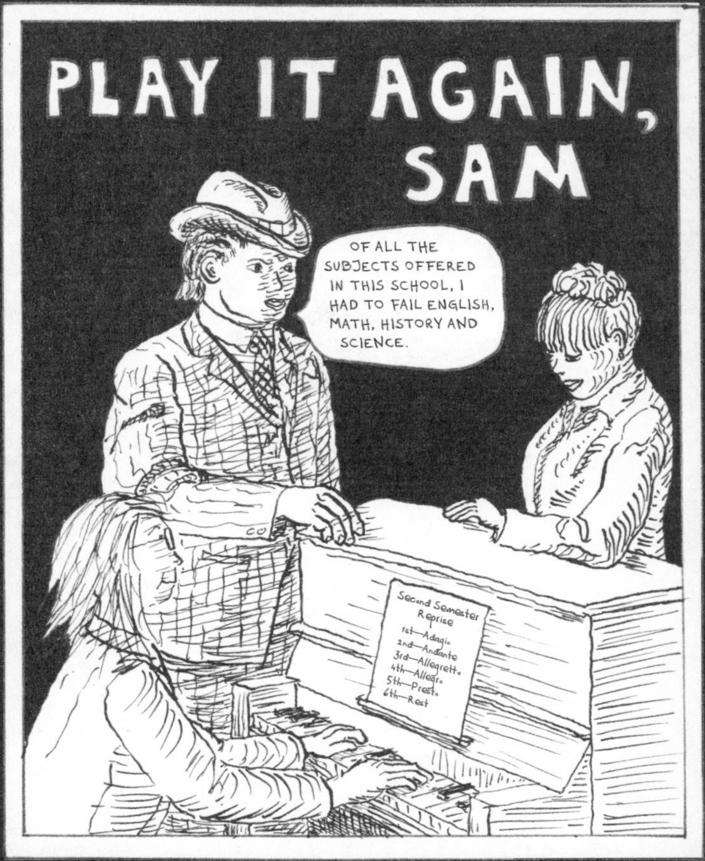
PLAY IT AGAIN, SAM
OF ALL THE SUBJECTS OFFERED IN THIS SCHOOL, I HAD TO FAIL ENGLISH, MATH, HISTORY AND SCIENCE.
Second Semester Reprise
1st—Adagio
2nd—Andante
3rd—Allegretto
4th—Allegro
5th—Presto
6th—Rest

"I THINK THIS IS THE BEGINNING OF A BEAUTIFUL FRIENDSHIP."

RICK IN "CASABLANCA"

I USED TO DREAM THAT I DIDN'T HAVE A PLACE TO LIVE.

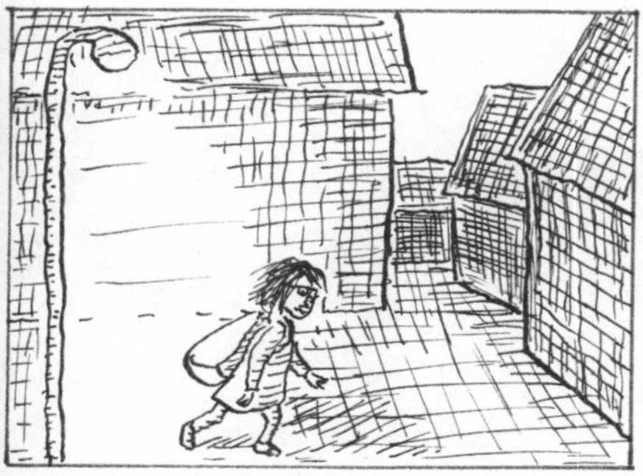

THEN MY DREAMS CHANGED AND I HAD A PLACE TO LIVE, BUT IT WAS NEVER VERY SECURE.

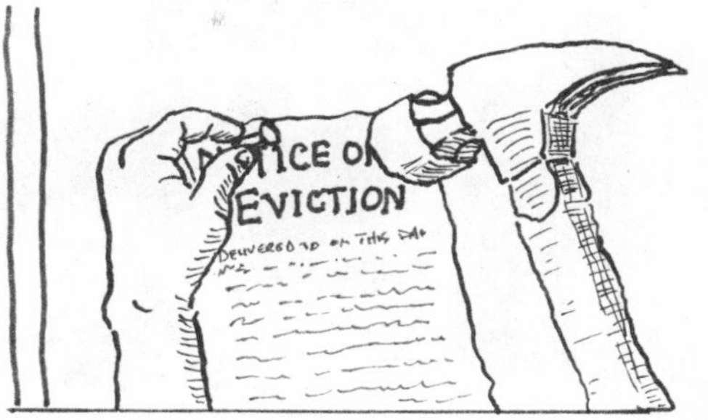

EVICTION

RECENTLY, IN MY DREAMS I AM LIVING IN A PLACE THAT'S MINE, BUT —LIKE PENELOPE AND HER SUITORS, THERE ARE TOO MANY PEOPLE HANGING OUT AND EATING MY FOOD WHO WON'T LEAVE.

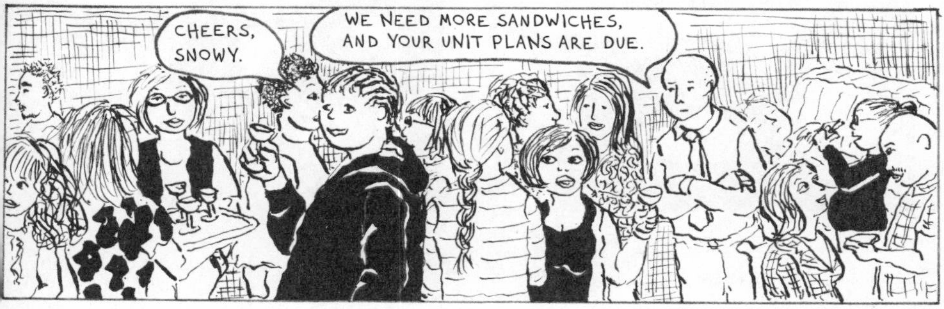

CHEERS, SNOWY.
WE NEED MORE SANDWICHES, AND YOUR UNIT PLANS ARE DUE.

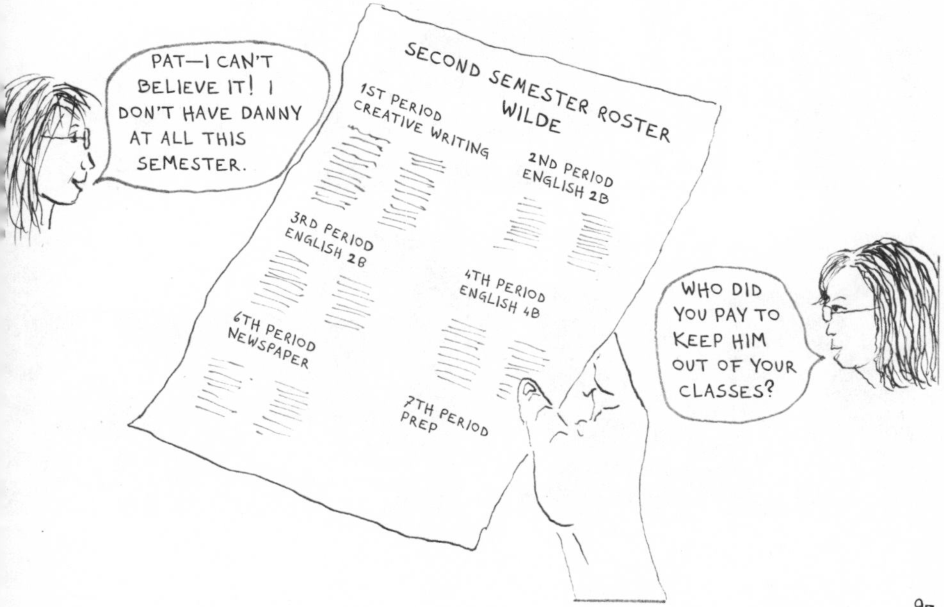

PAT—I CAN'T BELIEVE IT! I DON'T HAVE DANNY AT ALL THIS SEMESTER.
SECOND SEMESTER ROSTER
WILDE
1ST PERIOD CREATIVE WRITING
2ND PERIOD ENGLISH 2B
3RD PERIOD ENGLISH 2B
4TH PERIOD ENGLISH 4B
6TH PERIOD NEWSPAPER
7TH PERIOD PREP
WHO DID YOU PAY TO KEEP HIM OUT OF YOUR CLASSES?

SECOND SEMESTER: NEW CLASSES, BUT MOST OF THE SAME STUDENTS. BECAUSE EIGHT ENGLISH CREDITS ARE NEEDED FOR GRADUATION, MR. STEINER AND I END UP SEEING MANY OF THE SAME KIDS FOR TWO OR MORE SEMESTERS.

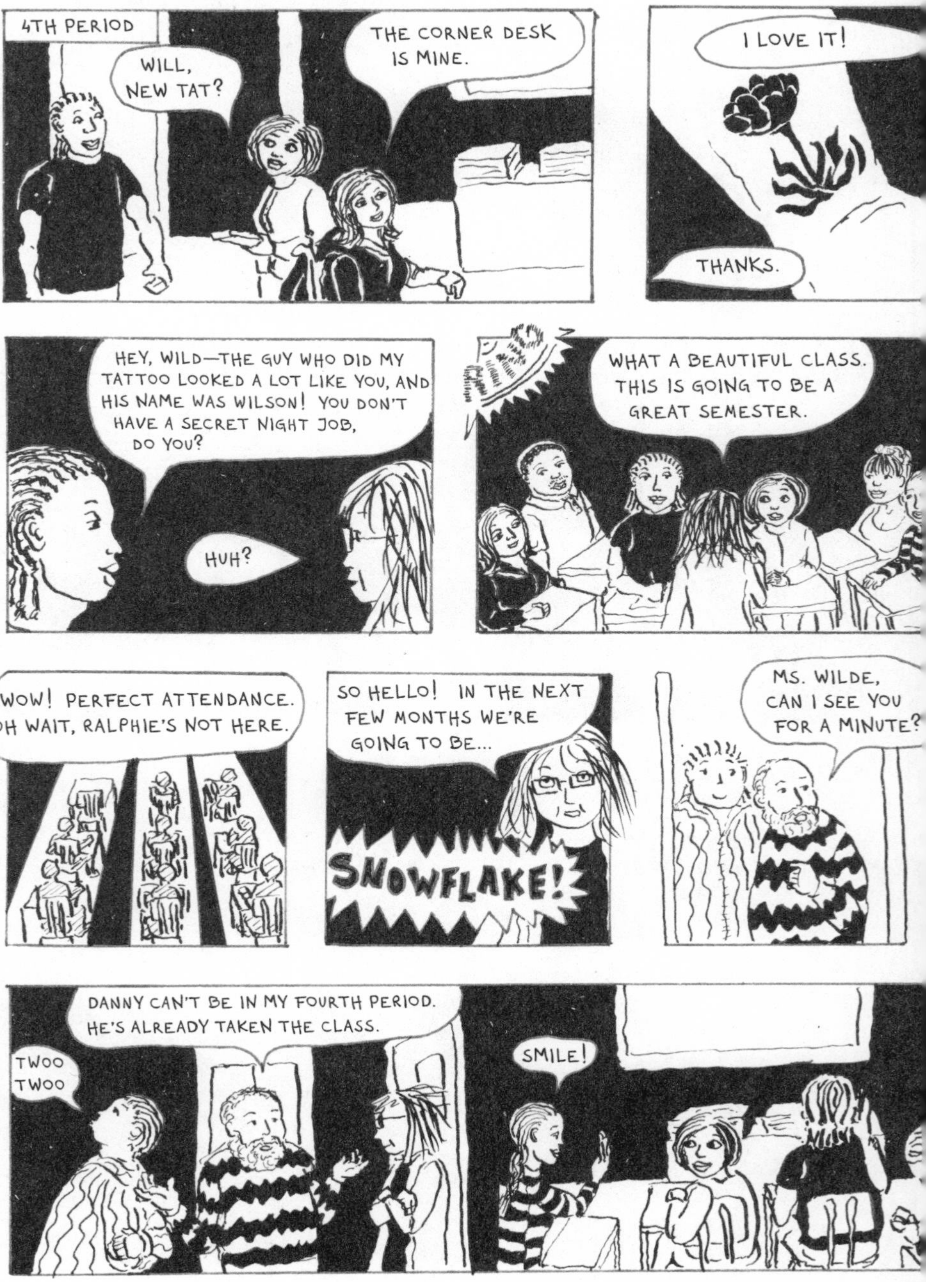

4TH PERIOD
WILL, NEW TAT?
THE CORNER DESK IS MINE.
I LOVE IT!
THANKS.
HEY, WILD—THE GUY WHO DID MY TATTOO LOOKED A LOT LIKE YOU, AND HIS NAME WAS WILSON! YOU DON'T HAVE A SECRET NIGHT JOB, DO YOU?
HUH?
WHAT A BEAUTIFUL CLASS. THIS IS GOING TO BE A GREAT SEMESTER.
WOW! PERFECT ATTENDANCE. OH WAIT, RALPHIE'S NOT HERE.
SO HELLO! IN THE NEXT FEW MONTHS WE'RE GOING TO BE...
SNOWFLAKE!
MS. WILDE, CAN I SEE YOU FOR A MINUTE?
DANNY CAN'T BE IN MY FOURTH PERIOD. HE'S ALREADY TAKEN THE CLASS.
TWOO TWOO
SMILE!

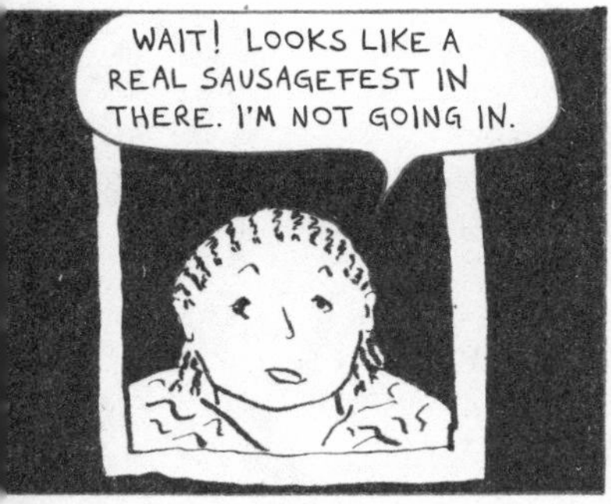
WAIT! LOOKS LIKE A REAL SAUSAGEFEST IN THERE. I'M NOT GOING IN.

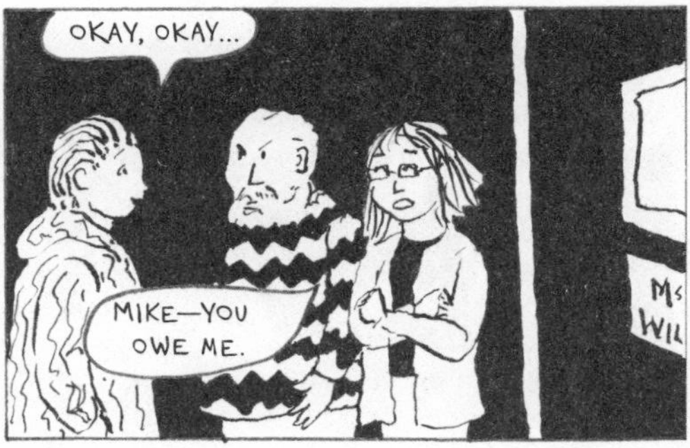
OKAY, OKAY...
MIKE—YOU OWE ME.

FIRST STAFF MEETING OF SECOND SEMESTER—

ON FRIDAY AFTERNOONS THE STUDENTS ARE LET OUT EARLY SO THAT TEACHERS, SUPPORT STAFF, AND ADMINISTRATORS CAN MEET. WE LOOK AT DATA, GO OVER BUREAUCRATIC RESPONSIBILITIES, HAVE EDUCATIONAL WORKSHOPS, AND DISCUSS STUDENTS.

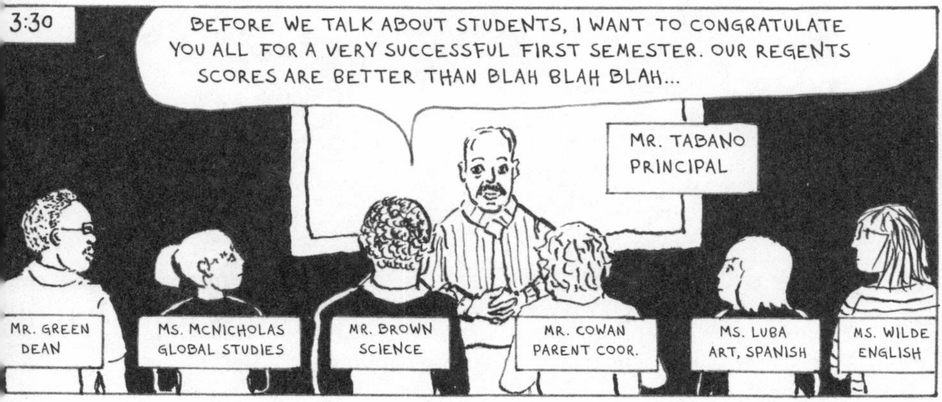
3:30
BEFORE WE TALK ABOUT STUDENTS, I WANT TO CONGRATULATE YOU ALL FOR A VERY SUCCESSFUL FIRST SEMESTER. OUR REGENTS SCORES ARE BETTER THAN BLAH BLAH BLAH...
MR. TABANO PRINCIPAL
MR. GREEN DEAN
MS. MCNICHOLAS GLOBAL STUDIES
MR. BROWN SCIENCE
MR. COWAN PARENT COOR.
MS. LUBA ART, SPANISH
MS. WILDE ENGLISH

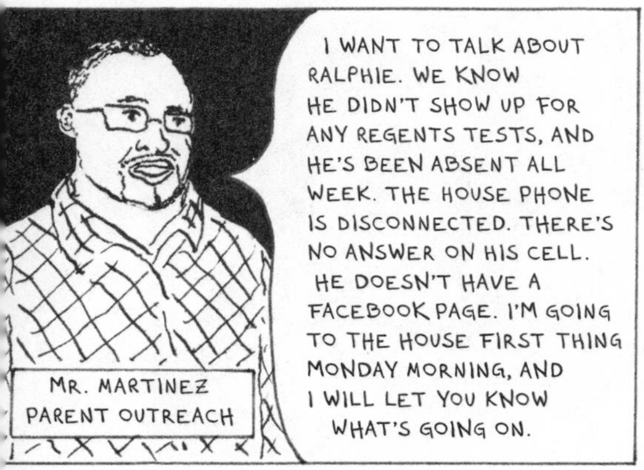
I WANT TO TALK ABOUT RALPHIE. WE KNOW HE DIDN'T SHOW UP FOR ANY REGENTS TESTS, AND HE'S BEEN ABSENT ALL WEEK. THE HOUSE PHONE IS DISCONNECTED. THERE'S NO ANSWER ON HIS CELL. HE DOESN'T HAVE A FACEBOOK PAGE. I'M GOING TO THE HOUSE FIRST THING MONDAY MORNING, AND I WILL LET YOU KNOW WHAT'S GOING ON.
MR. MARTINEZ PARENT OUTREACH

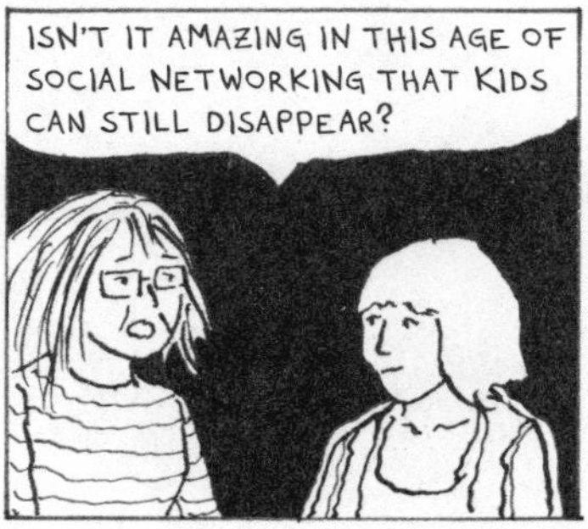
ISN'T IT AMAZING IN THIS AGE OF SOCIAL NETWORKING THAT KIDS CAN STILL DISAPPEAR?

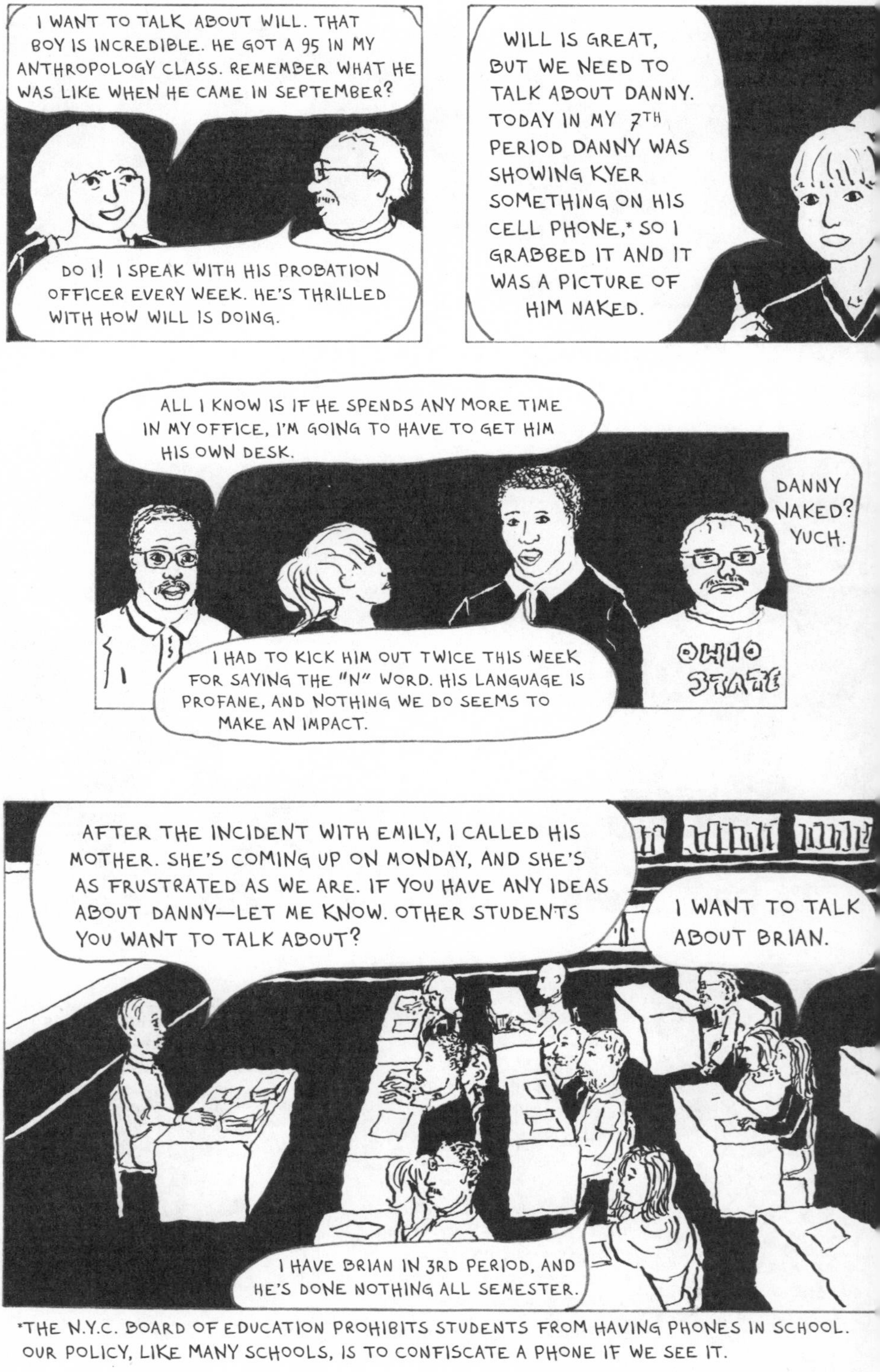
I WANT TO TALK ABOUT WILL. THAT BOY IS INCREDIBLE. HE GOT A 95 IN MY ANTHROPOLOGY CLASS. REMEMBER WHAT HE WAS LIKE WHEN HE CAME IN SEPTEMBER?
DO I! I SPEAK WITH HIS PROBATION OFFICER EVERY WEEK. HE'S THRILLED WITH HOW WILL IS DOING.
WILL IS GREAT, BUT WE NEED TO TALK ABOUT DANNY. TODAY IN MY 7TH PERIOD DANNY WAS SHOWING KYER SOMETHING ON HIS CELL PHONE,* SO I GRABBED IT AND IT WAS A PICTURE OF HIM NAKED.
ALL I KNOW IS IF HE SPENDS ANY MORE TIME IN MY OFFICE, I'M GOING TO HAVE TO GET HIM HIS OWN DESK.
DANNY NAKED? YUCH.
I HAD TO KICK HIM OUT TWICE THIS WEEK FOR SAYING THE "N" WORD. HIS LANGUAGE IS PROFANE, AND NOTHING WE DO SEEMS TO MAKE AN IMPACT.
OHIO STATE
AFTER THE INCIDENT WITH EMILY, I CALLED HIS MOTHER. SHE'S COMING UP ON MONDAY, AND SHE'S AS FRUSTRATED AS WE ARE. IF YOU HAVE ANY IDEAS ABOUT DANNY—LET ME KNOW. OTHER STUDENTS YOU WANT TO TALK ABOUT?
I WANT TO TALK ABOUT BRIAN.
I HAVE BRIAN IN 3RD PERIOD, AND HE'S DONE NOTHING ALL SEMESTER.

*THE N.Y.C. BOARD OF EDUCATION PROHIBITS STUDENTS FROM HAVING PHONES IN SCHOOL. OUR POLICY, LIKE MANY SCHOOLS, IS TO CONFISCATE A PHONE IF WE SEE IT.

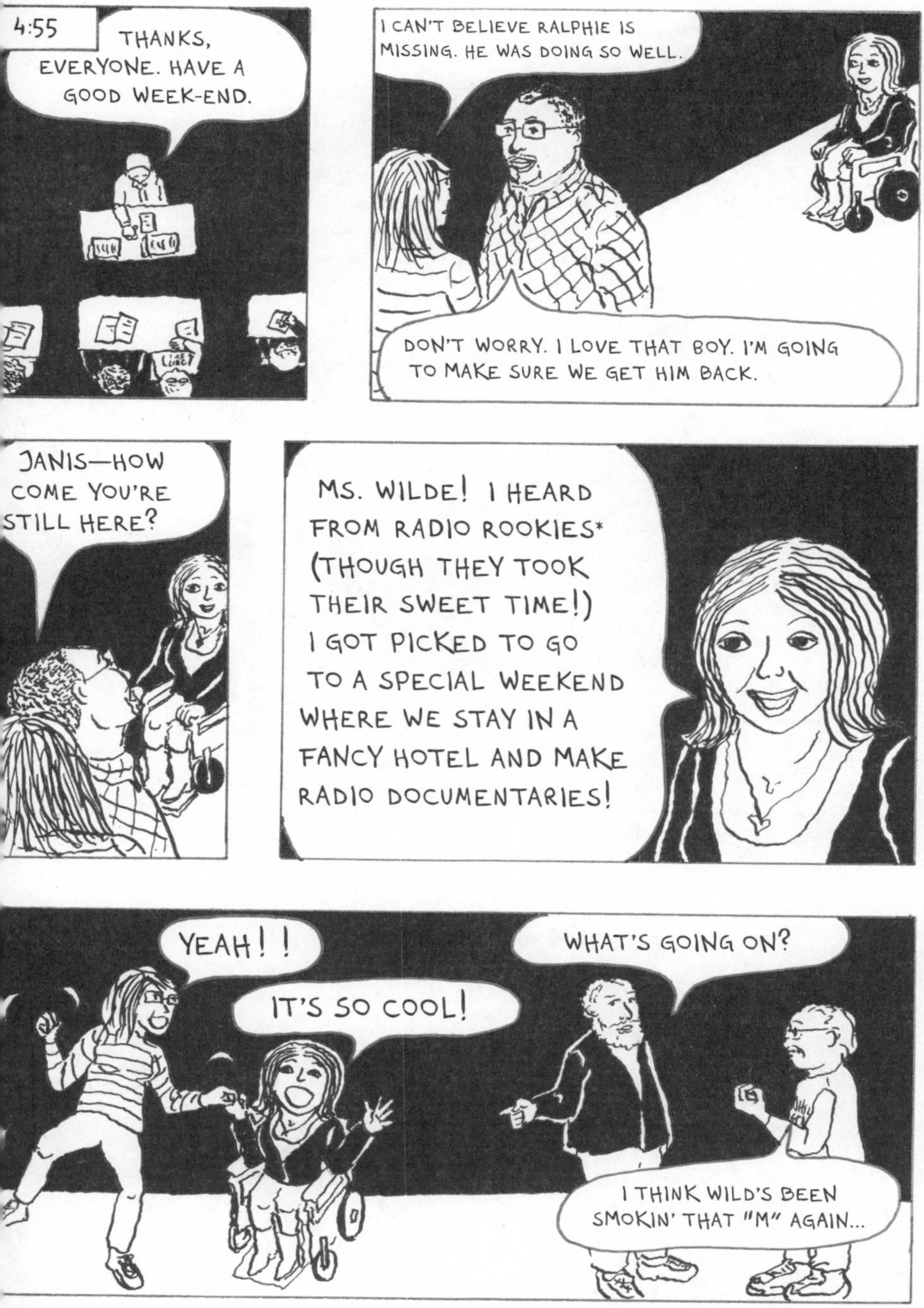
4:55
THANKS, EVERYONE. HAVE A GOOD WEEK-END.
I CAN'T BELIEVE RALPHIE IS MISSING. HE WAS DOING SO WELL.
DON'T WORRY. I LOVE THAT BOY. I'M GOING TO MAKE SURE WE GET HIM BACK.
JANIS—HOW COME YOU'RE STILL HERE?
MS. WILDE! I HEARD FROM RADIO ROOKIES* (THOUGH THEY TOOK THEIR SWEET TIME!) I GOT PICKED TO GO TO A SPECIAL WEEKEND WHERE WE STAY IN A FANCY HOTEL AND MAKE RADIO DOCUMENTARIES!
YEAH!!
IT'S SO COOL!
WHAT'S GOING ON?
I THINK WILD'S BEEN SMOKIN' THAT "M" AGAIN...

RADIO ROOKIES IS THE PROGRAM JANIS APPLIED TO IN THE FALL. SPONSORED Y PUBLIC RADIO, IT GIVES TEENS EXPERIENCE PRODUCING THEIR OWN RADIO OCUMENTARIES.

JANIS'S RADIO ROOKIE WEEKEND

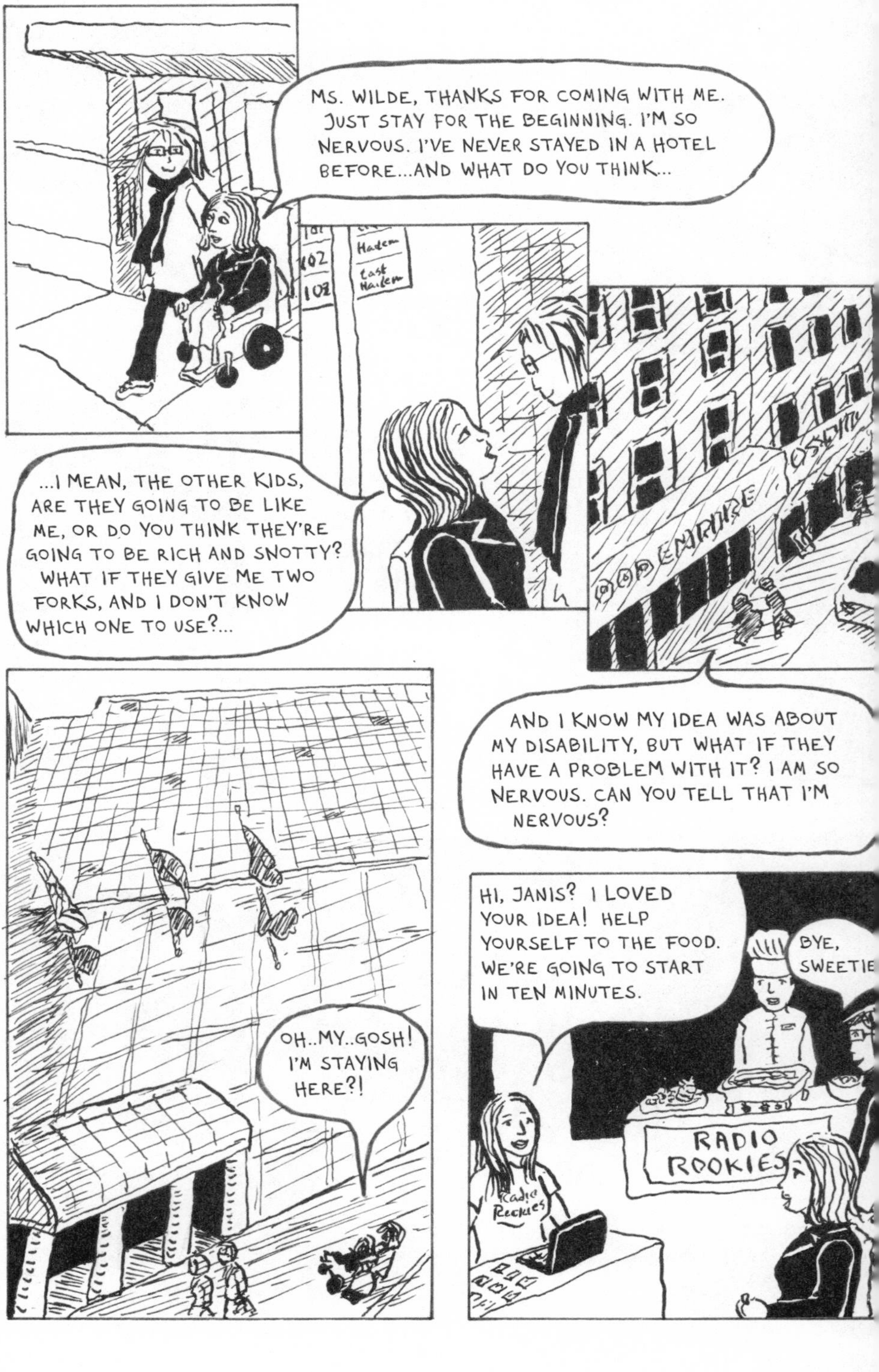
MS. WILDE, THANKS FOR COMING WITH ME. JUST STAY FOR THE BEGINNING. I'M SO NERVOUS. I'VE NEVER STAYED IN A HOTEL BEFORE...AND WHAT DO YOU THINK...
...I MEAN, THE OTHER KIDS, ARE THEY GOING TO BE LIKE ME, OR DO YOU THINK THEY'RE GOING TO BE RICH AND SNOTTY? WHAT IF THEY GIVE ME TWO FORKS, AND I DON'T KNOW WHICH ONE TO USE?...
AND I KNOW MY IDEA WAS ABOUT MY DISABILITY, BUT WHAT IF THEY HAVE A PROBLEM WITH IT? I AM SO NERVOUS. CAN YOU TELL THAT I'M NERVOUS?
OH..MY..GOSH! I'M STAYING HERE?!
HI, JANIS? I LOVED YOUR IDEA! HELP YOURSELF TO THE FOOD. WE'RE GOING TO START IN TEN MINUTES.
BYE, SWEETIE
RADIO ROOKIES
Radio Rookies

A DAY IN MY WHEELS
BY JANIS DIAZ

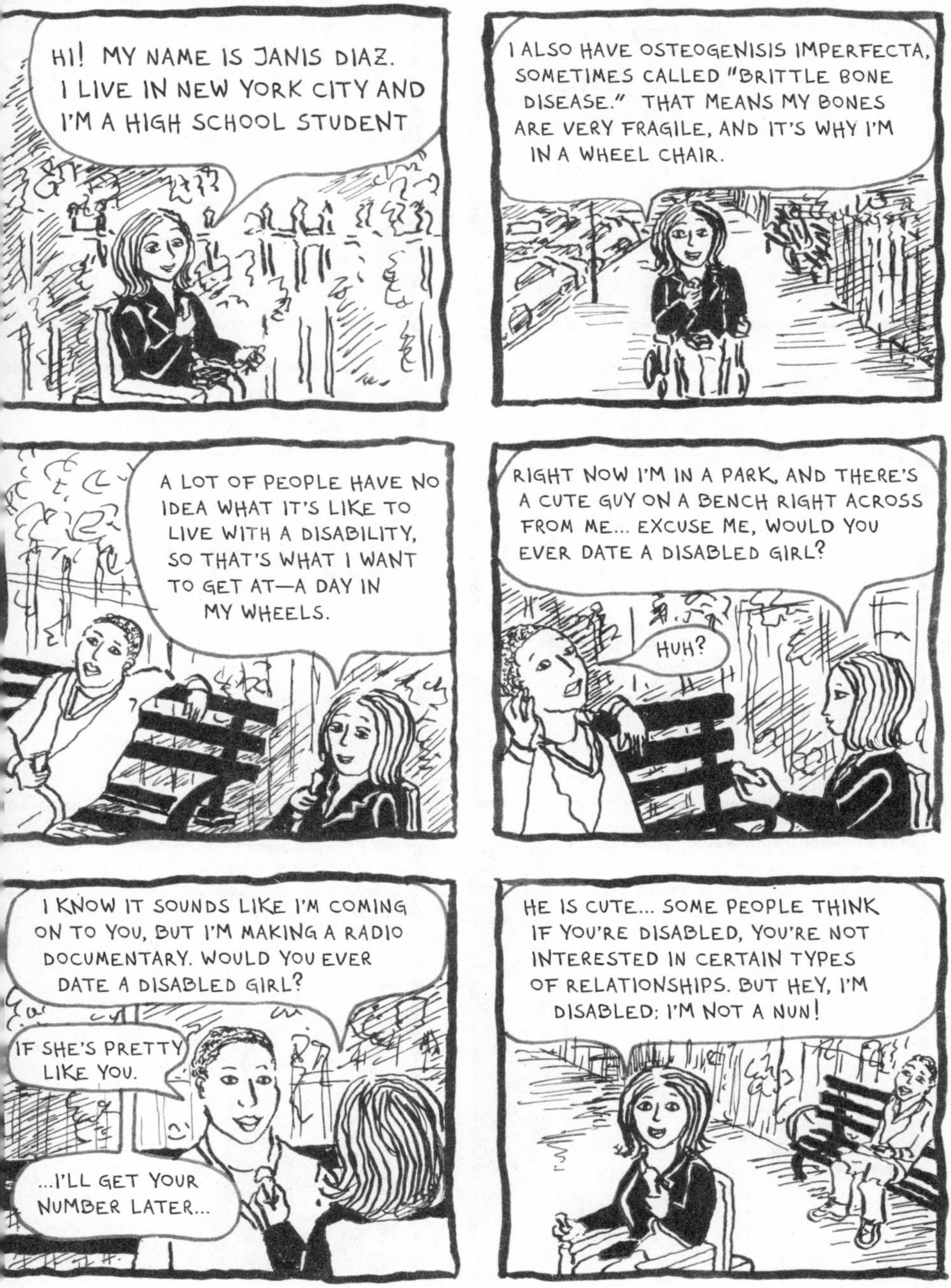
HI! MY NAME IS JANIS DIAZ. I LIVE IN NEW YORK CITY AND I'M A HIGH SCHOOL STUDENT
I ALSO HAVE OSTEOGENISIS IMPERFECTA, SOMETIMES CALLED "BRITTLE BONE DISEASE." THAT MEANS MY BONES ARE VERY FRAGILE, AND IT'S WHY I'M IN A WHEEL CHAIR.
A LOT OF PEOPLE HAVE NO IDEA WHAT IT'S LIKE TO LIVE WITH A DISABILITY, SO THAT'S WHAT I WANT TO GET AT—A DAY IN MY WHEELS.
RIGHT NOW I'M IN A PARK, AND THERE'S A CUTE GUY ON A BENCH RIGHT ACROSS FROM ME... EXCUSE ME, WOULD YOU EVER DATE A DISABLED GIRL?
HUH?
I KNOW IT SOUNDS LIKE I'M COMING ON TO YOU, BUT I'M MAKING A RADIO DOCUMENTARY. WOULD YOU EVER DATE A DISABLED GIRL?
IF SHE'S PRETTY LIKE YOU.
...I'LL GET YOUR NUMBER LATER...
HE IS CUTE... SOME PEOPLE THINK IF YOU'RE DISABLED, YOU'RE NOT INTERESTED IN CERTAIN TYPES OF RELATIONSHIPS. BUT HEY, I'M DISABLED; I'M NOT A NUN!

GETTING PLACES CAN BE DIFFICULT WHEN YOU'RE DISABLED, BUT IN NEW YORK CITY THE BUS IS USUALLY A GOOD WAY TO GET AROUND.

THAT IS, IF THEY STOP! SOME BUS DRIVERS DON'T LIKE PICKING UP DISABLED PEOPLE BECAUSE THEY FEEL LIKE IT'S TOO MUCH WORK TO HELP US GET ON THE BUS. AND SOMETIMES WHEN THEY DO STOP, PEOPLE ACT LIKE WE SHOULDN'T BE RIDING THE BUS BECAUSE IT TAKES US LONGER TO BOARD.

IF YOU'RE DISABLED, YOU CAN'T LEAVE YOUR HOUSE WITHOUT ENCOUNTERING OBSTACLES—LIKE ATTITUDES...OR STAIRS. LET'S JUST ROLL HOME.

THE ONLY THING THAT'S WORSE THAN THE PEOPLE ON THE BUS WHO ONLY SEE MY CHAIR, IS PEOPLE WHO THINK —BECAUSE I'M IN A CHAIR, I MUST BE INCAPABLE OR DIFFERENT FROM THEM

BUT WHY WOULD BEING IN A CHAIR MEAN YOU'RE NOT SMART OR TALENTED? IT IS TRUE THAT SOMETIMES WE NEED ADAPTATIONS. FOR EXAMPLE, THIS STRING HELPS ME CLOSE THE DOOR.

BUT IT'S NO BIG DEAL. THERE'S A BOY I KNOW WHO'S DISABLED, AND HE HAS SCARS FROM HIS SURGERIES. I TOLD HIM THAT HIS SCARS SHOW HE'S BEEN THROUGH WAR, AND THAT HE'S BRAVE AND STRONG. I HAVE SCARS TOO—THEY'RE A PART OF WHO I AM, AND I THINK MY EXPERIENCES HAVE GIVEN ME A REAL APPRECIATION FOR WHAT IS IMPORTANT IN LIFE. I WOULDN'T TRADE MY DISABILITY TO BE LIKE OTHER PEOPLE. IT'S WHO I AM. THIS IS JANIS DIAZ

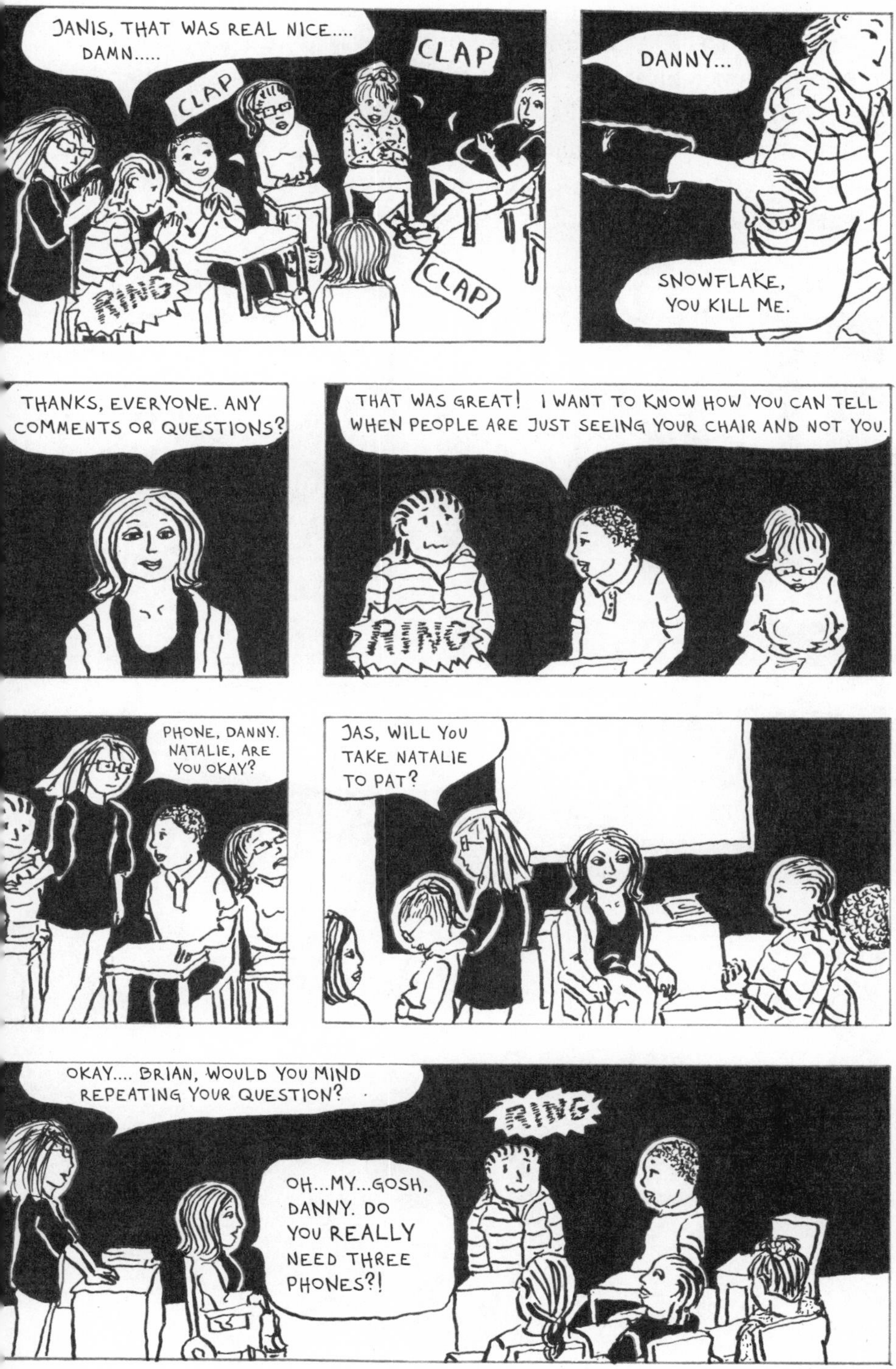
JANIS, THAT WAS REAL NICE.... DAMN.....
CLAP
CLAP
CLAP
RING
DANNY...
SNOWFLAKE, YOU KILL ME.
THANKS, EVERYONE. ANY COMMENTS OR QUESTIONS?
THAT WAS GREAT! I WANT TO KNOW HOW YOU CAN TELL WHEN PEOPLE ARE JUST SEEING YOUR CHAIR AND NOT YOU.
RING
PHONE, DANNY. NATALIE, ARE YOU OKAY?
JAS, WILL YOU TAKE NATALIE TO PAT?
OKAY.... BRIAN, WOULD YOU MIND REPEATING YOUR QUESTION?
RING
OH...MY...GOSH, DANNY. DO YOU REALLY NEED THREE PHONES?!

DANNY IS STILL ATTENDING WILDCAT, EVEN AFTER THE NAKED CELL PHONE PHOTO INCIDENT. THAT'S THE THING ABOUT A SECOND CHANCE SCHOOL—WE GIVE KIDS SECOND CHANCES, BECAUSE CHANGE DOESN'T NECESSARILY HAPPEN QUICKLY OR EASILY. WOULD OUR SCHOOL HAVE BETTER DATA IF WE "ENCOURAGED" KIDS LIKE DANNY TO TRANSFER SOMEWHERE ELSE? ABSOLUTELY. BUT WOULD THAT HELP DANNY?

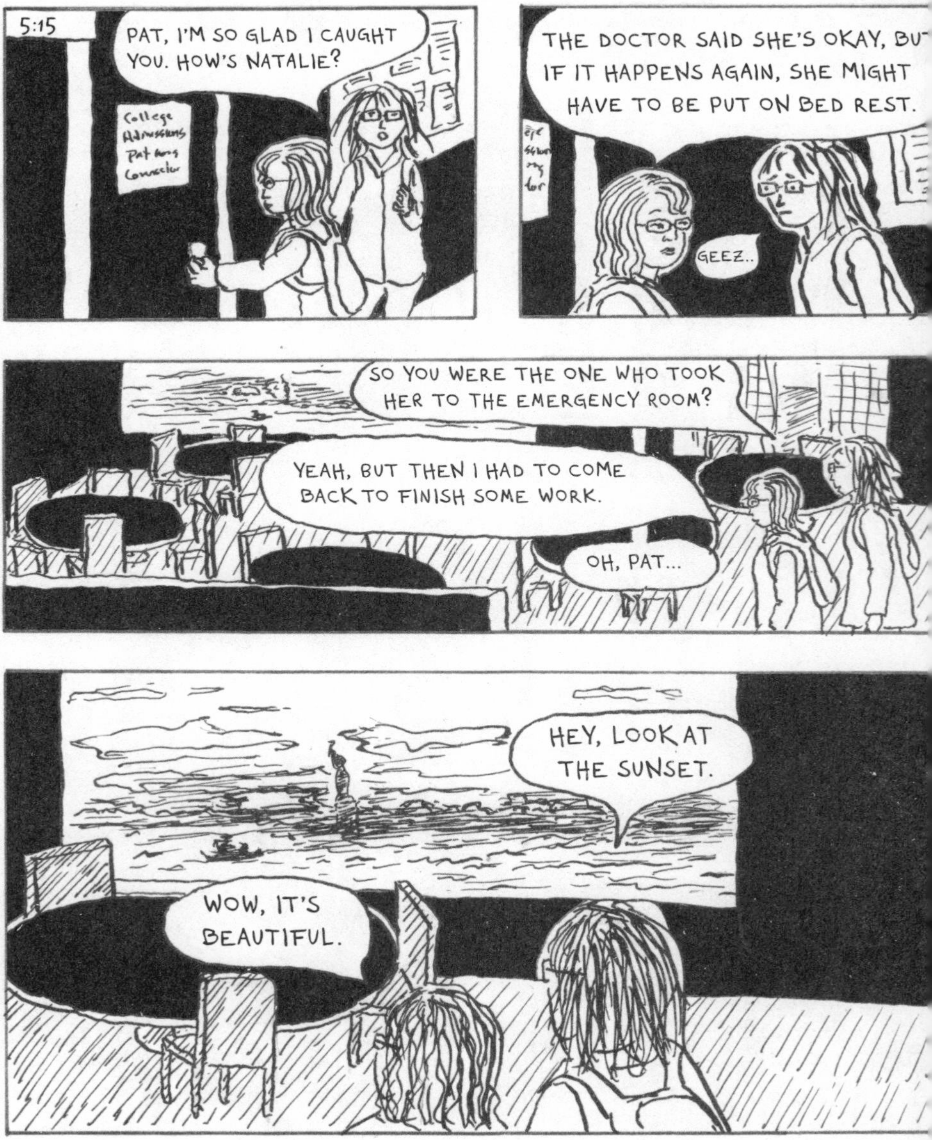

5:15
PAT, I'M SO GLAD I CAUGHT YOU. HOW'S NATALIE?
THE DOCTOR SAID SHE'S OKAY, BU
IF IT HAPPENS AGAIN, SHE MIGHT HAVE TO BE PUT ON BED REST.
GEEZ..
SO YOU WERE THE ONE WHO TOOK HER TO THE EMERGENCY ROOM?
YEAH, BUT THEN I HAD TO COME BACK TO FINISH SOME WORK.
OH, PAT...
HEY, LOOK AT THE SUNSET.
WOW, IT'S BEAUTIFUL.

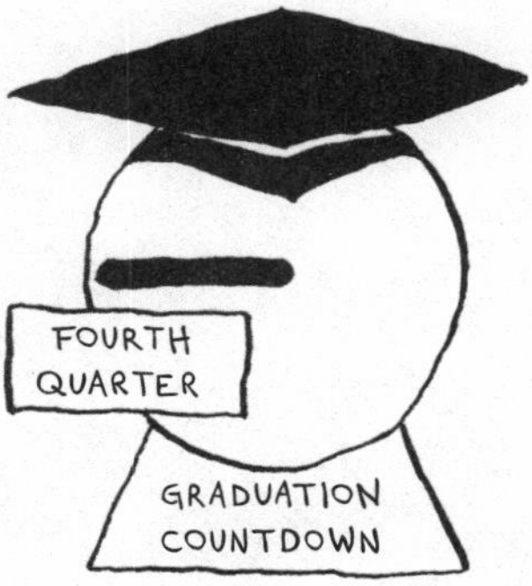
FOURTH
QUARTER
GRADUATION
COUNTDOWN

CHAPTER SEVEN

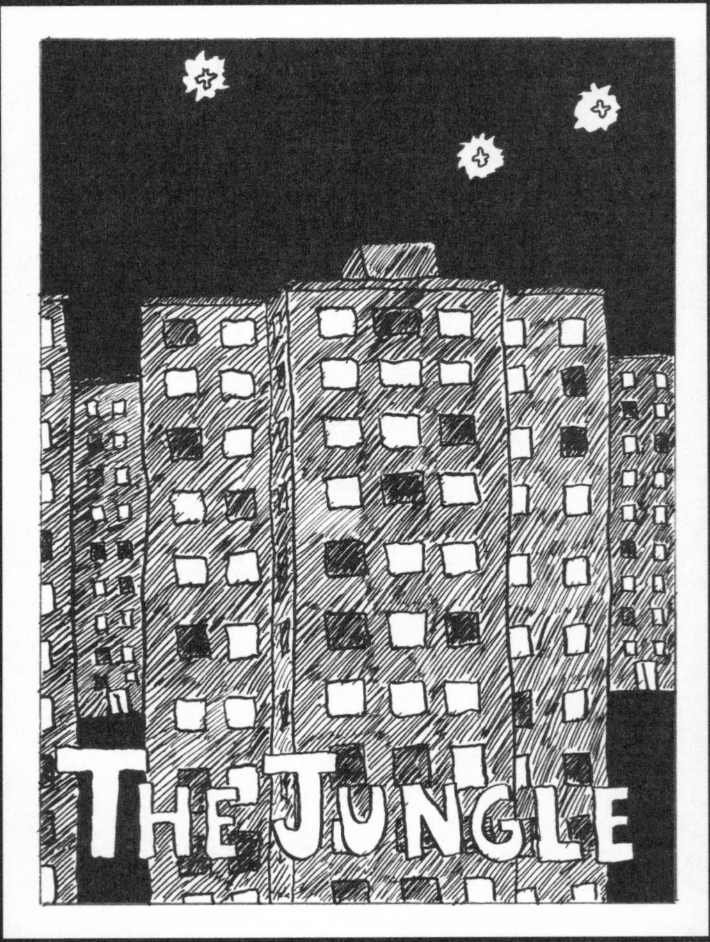
THE JUNGLE

"THERE IS NO WILDERNESS WHERE I CAN HIDE FROM THESE THINGS, AND THERE IS NO HAVEN WHERE I CAN ESCAPE THEM."

UPTON SINCLAIR

IN 4TH PERIOD WE'RE WORKING ON A UNIT BASED AROUND THE IDEA OF JUSTICE. TODAY THE STUDENTS ARE LOOKING AT THE SIXTH AMENDMENT—INTERPRETING THE CONCEPTS AND CONNECTING THEM TO JUSTICE OR INJUSTICE.

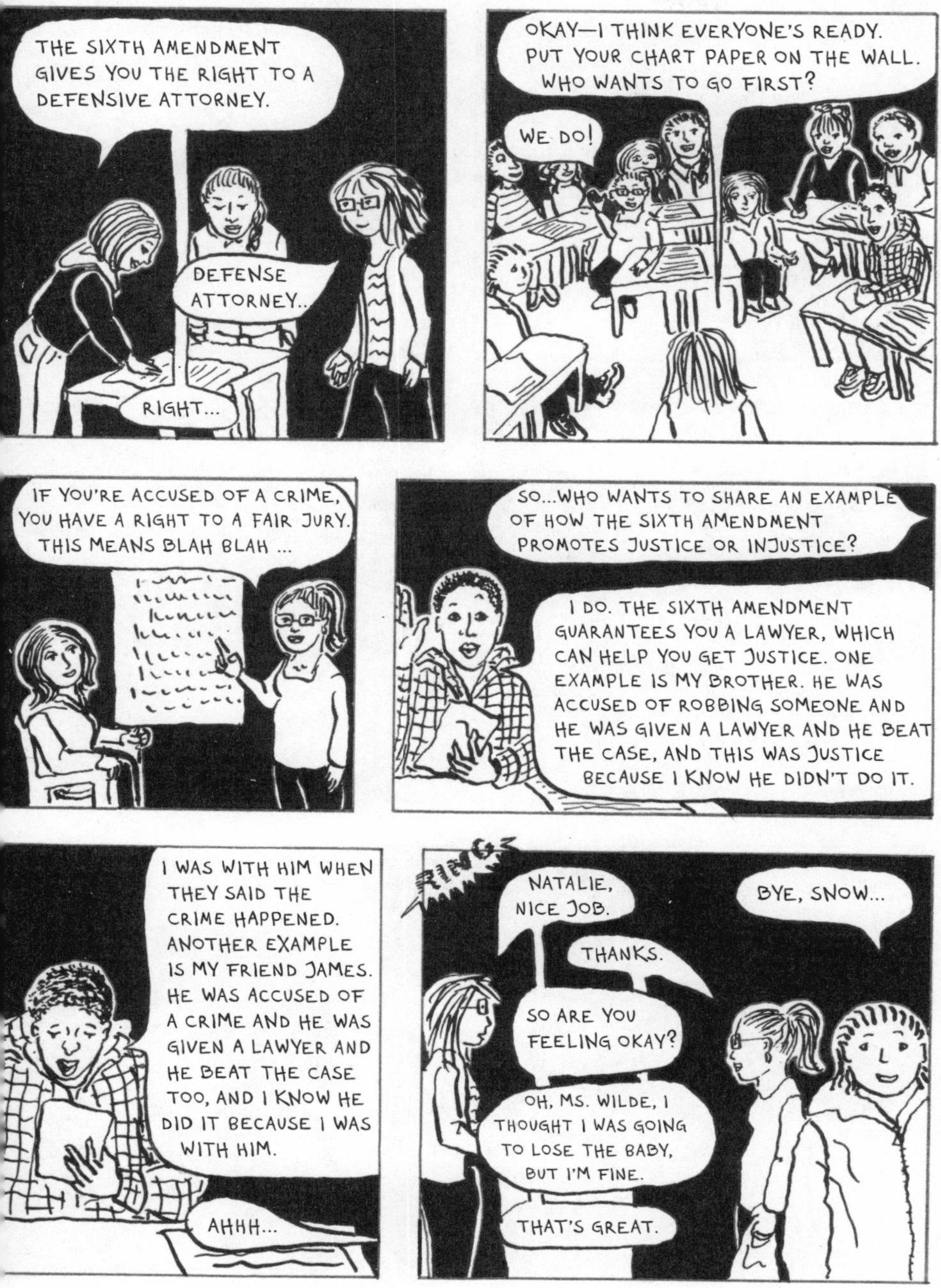

THE SIXTH AMENDMENT GIVES YOU THE RIGHT TO A DEFENSIVE ATTORNEY.
DEFENSE ATTORNEY...
RIGHT...
OKAY—I THINK EVERYONE'S READY. PUT YOUR CHART PAPER ON THE WALL. WHO WANTS TO GO FIRST?
WE DO!
IF YOU'RE ACCUSED OF A CRIME, YOU HAVE A RIGHT TO A FAIR JURY. THIS MEANS BLAH BLAH ...
SO...WHO WANTS TO SHARE AN EXAMPLE OF HOW THE SIXTH AMENDMENT PROMOTES JUSTICE OR INJUSTICE?
I DO. THE SIXTH AMENDMENT GUARANTEES YOU A LAWYER, WHICH CAN HELP YOU GET JUSTICE. ONE EXAMPLE IS MY BROTHER. HE WAS ACCUSED OF ROBBING SOMEONE AND HE WAS GIVEN A LAWYER AND HE BEAT THE CASE, AND THIS WAS JUSTICE BECAUSE I KNOW HE DIDN'T DO IT.
I WAS WITH HIM WHEN THEY SAID THE CRIME HAPPENED. ANOTHER EXAMPLE IS MY FRIEND JAMES. HE WAS ACCUSED OF A CRIME AND HE WAS GIVEN A LAWYER AND HE BEAT THE CASE TOO, AND I KNOW HE DID IT BECAUSE I WAS WITH HIM.
AHHH...
RING
NATALIE, NICE JOB.
BYE, SNOW...
THANKS.
SO ARE YOU FEELING OKAY?
OH, MS. WILDE, I THOUGHT I WAS GOING TO LOSE THE BABY, BUT I'M FINE.
THAT'S GREAT.

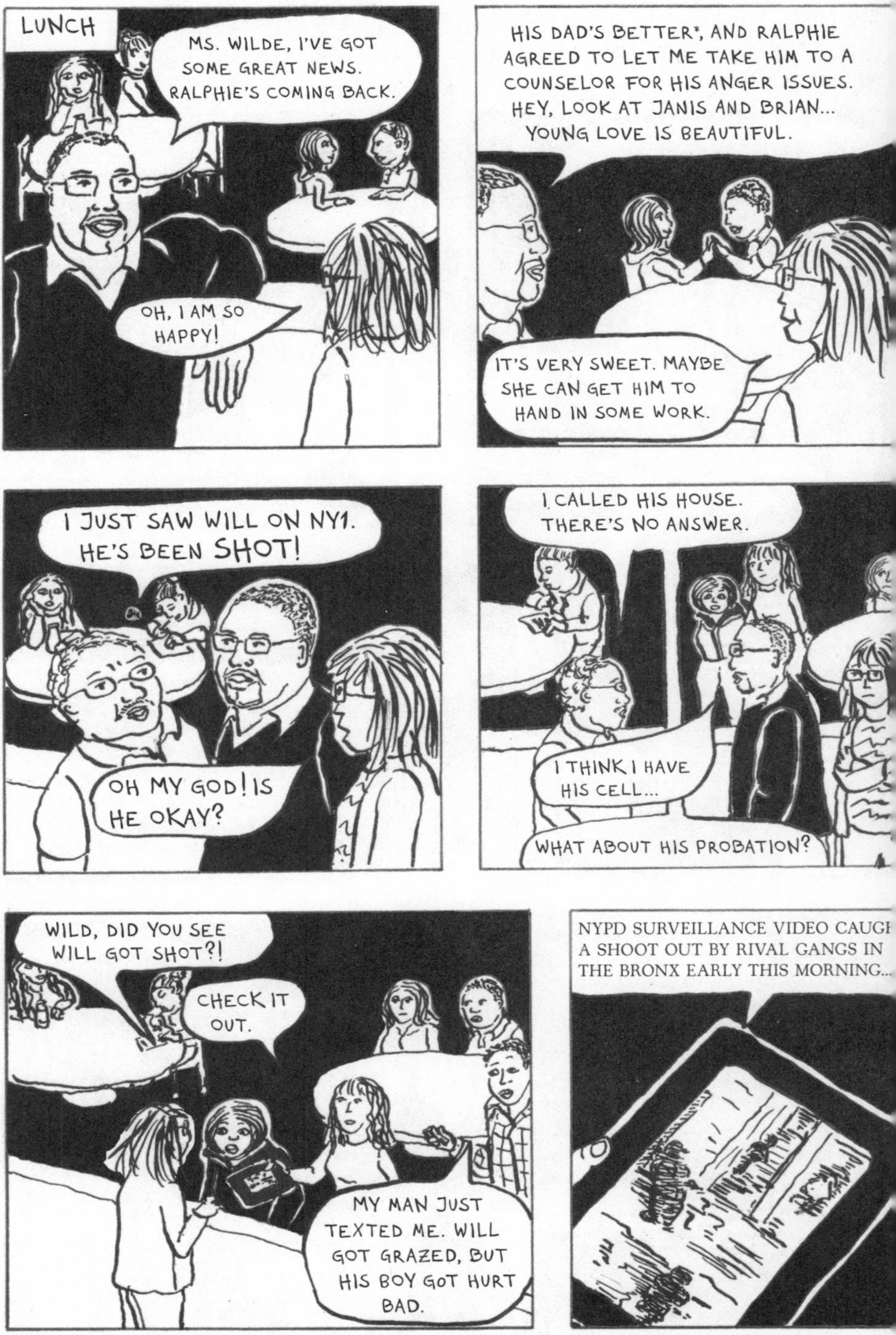
LUNCH
MS. WILDE, I'VE GOT SOME GREAT NEWS. RALPHIE'S COMING BACK.
OH, I AM SO HAPPY!
HIS DAD'S BETTER*, AND RALPHIE AGREED TO LET ME TAKE HIM TO A COUNSELOR FOR HIS ANGER ISSUES. HEY, LOOK AT JANIS AND BRIAN... YOUNG LOVE IS BEAUTIFUL.
IT'S VERY SWEET. MAYBE SHE CAN GET HIM TO HAND IN SOME WORK.
I JUST SAW WILL ON NY1. HE'S BEEN SHOT!
OH MY GOD! IS HE OKAY?
I CALLED HIS HOUSE. THERE'S NO ANSWER.
I THINK I HAVE HIS CELL...
WHAT ABOUT HIS PROBATION?
WILD, DID YOU SEE WILL GOT SHOT?!
CHECK IT OUT.
MY MAN JUST TEXTED ME. WILL GOT GRAZED, BUT HIS BOY GOT HURT BAD.
NYPD SURVEILLANCE VIDEO CAUGH
A SHOOT OUT BY RIVAL GANGS IN
THE BRONX EARLY THIS MORNING...

*RALPHIE'S DAD HAD SURGERY, SO RALPHIE HAD TO TAKE OVER HIS DAD'S WORK AS A BUILDING SUPER.

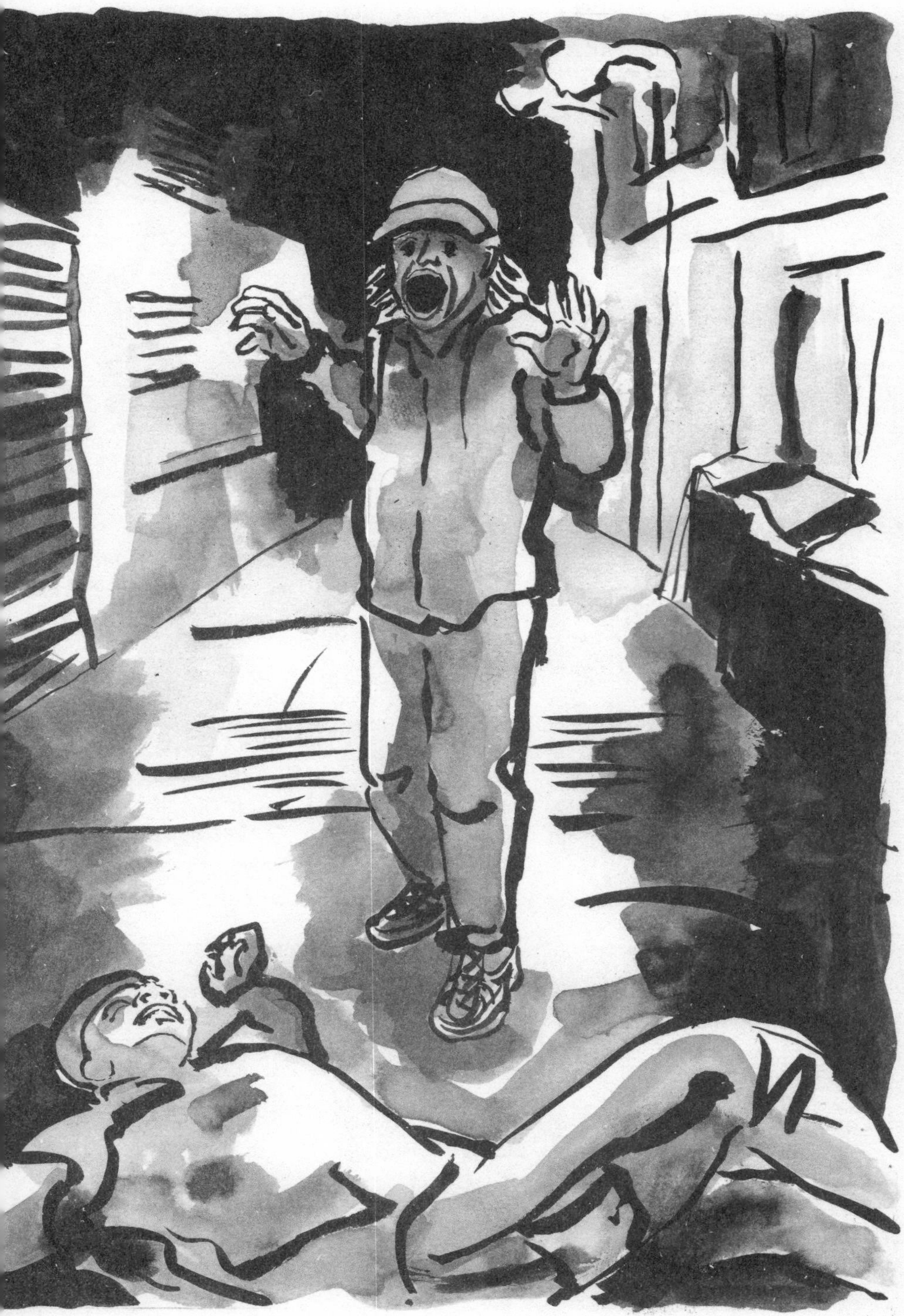

A WEEK LATER, WILL IS BACK AT SCHOOL. LIKE TYRONE SAID, HE'LL RECOVER FROM HIS PHYSICAL WOUNDS. THE OTHER CONSEQUENCES AREN'T CLEAR.

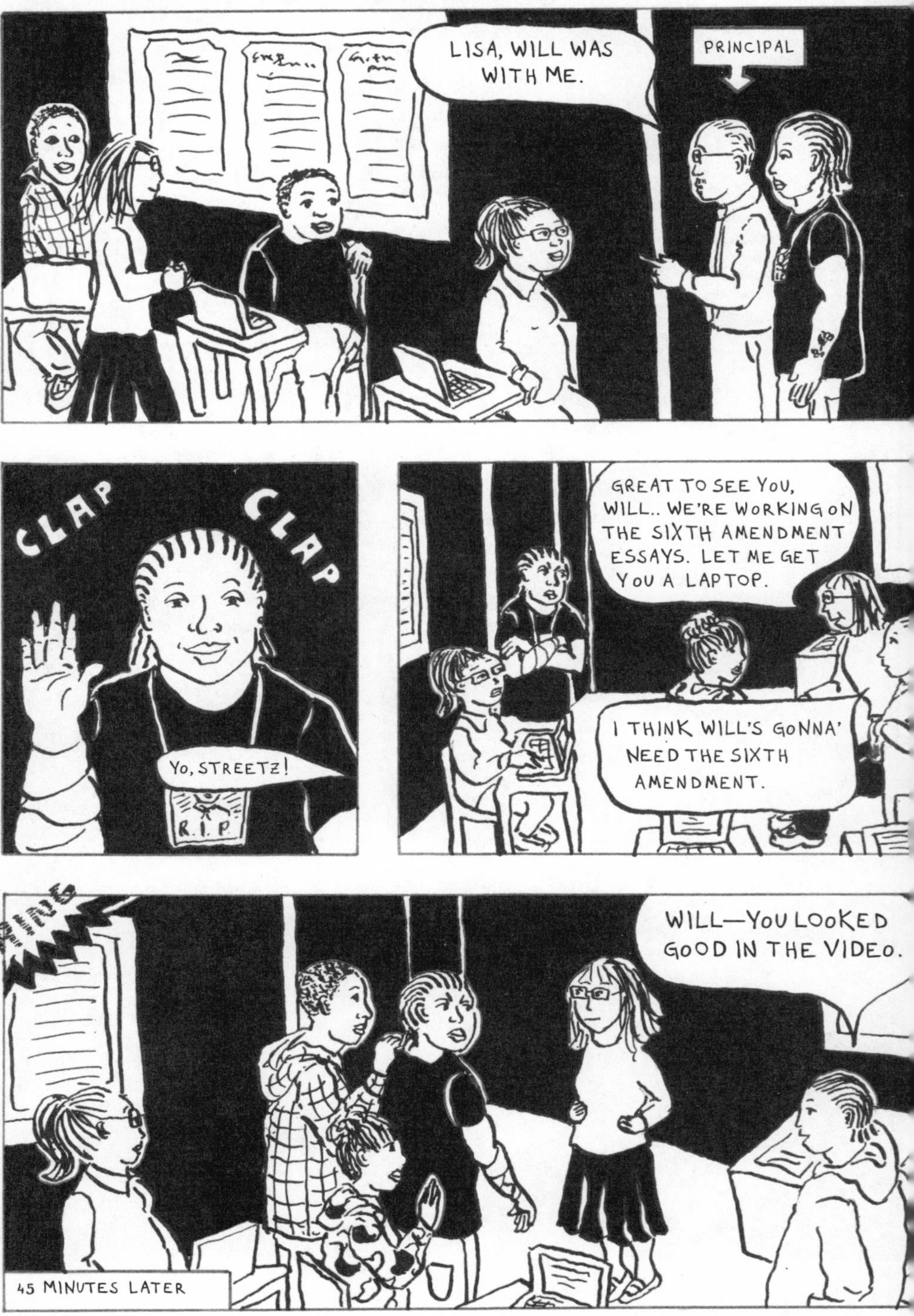

LISA, WILL WAS WITH ME.
PRINCIPAL
CLAP CLAP
YO, STREETZ!
R.I.P.
GREAT TO SEE YOU, WILL.. WE'RE WORKING ON THE SIXTH AMENDMENT ESSAYS. LET ME GET YOU A LAPTOP.
I THINK WILL'S GONNA' NEED THE SIXTH AMENDMENT.
WILL—YOU LOOKED GOOD IN THE VIDEO.
45 MINUTES LATER

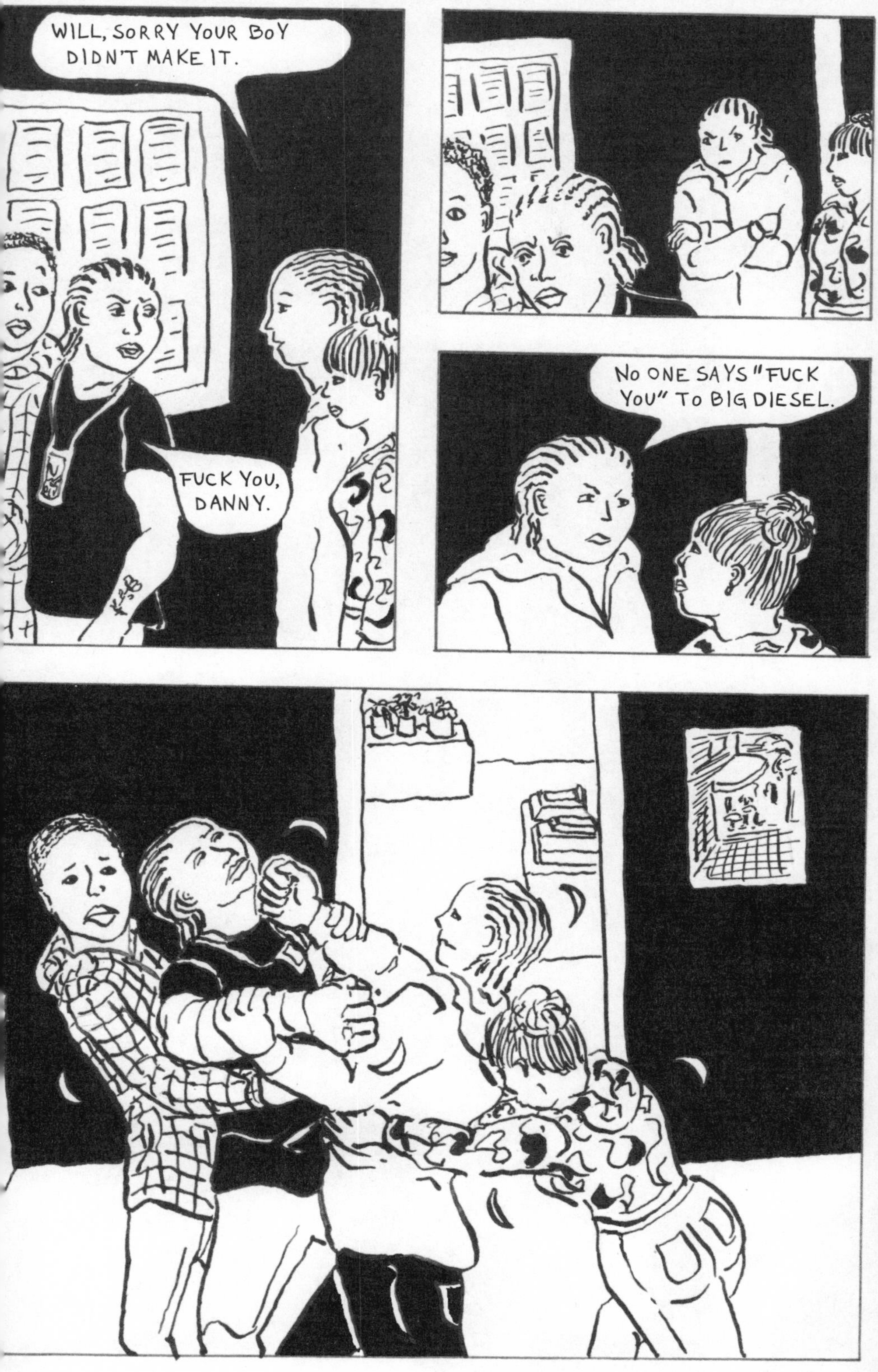
WILL, SORRY YOUR BOY DIDN'T MAKE IT.
FUCK YOU, DANNY.
No ONE SAYS "FUCK YOU" TO BIG DIESEL.

FIGHTS ARE EXTREMELY RARE AT WILDCAT, BUT EVERY NOW AND THE
THEY HAPPEN. LIKE ALL SCHOOLS, WE HAVE A SAFETY PLAN IN PLACE.

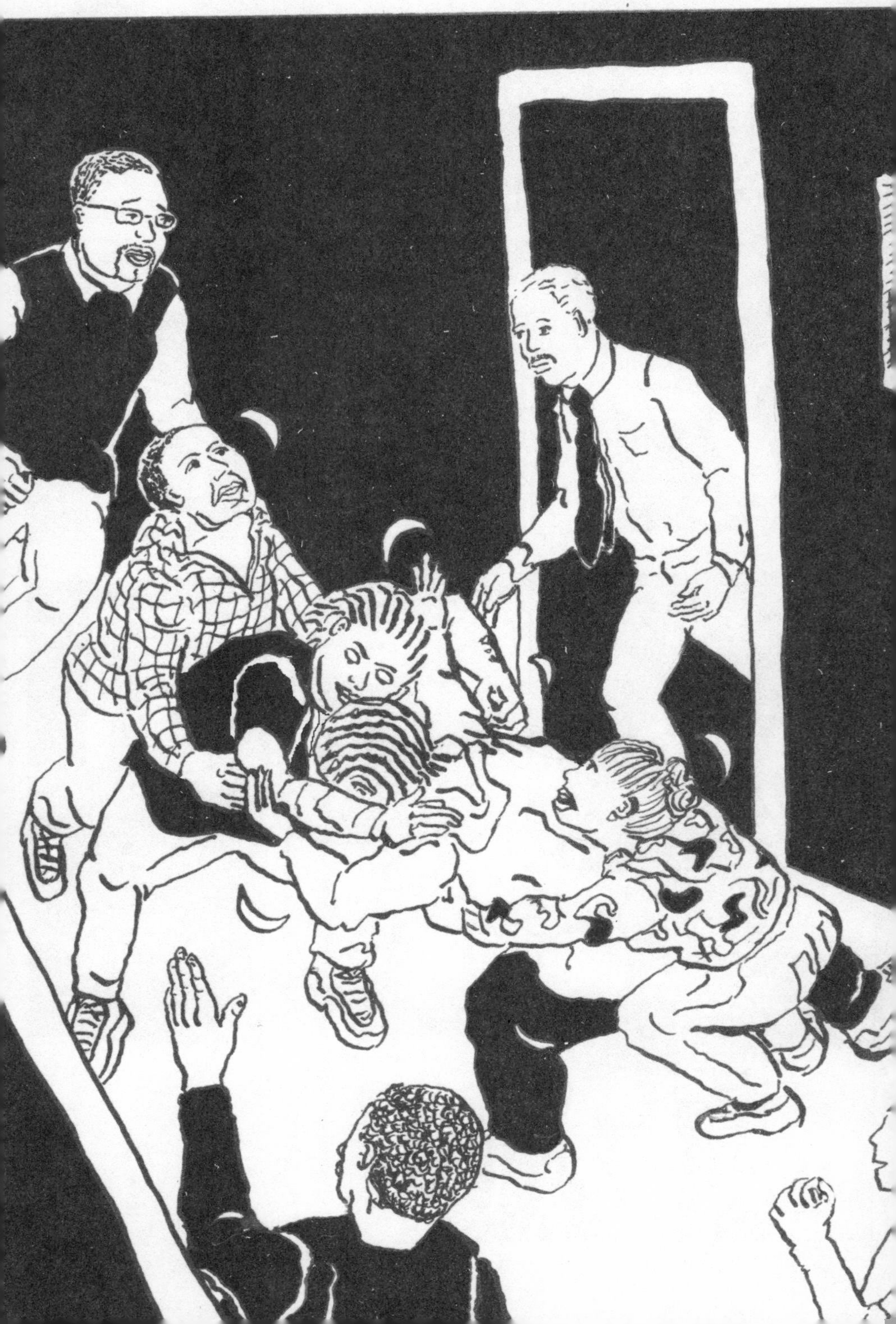

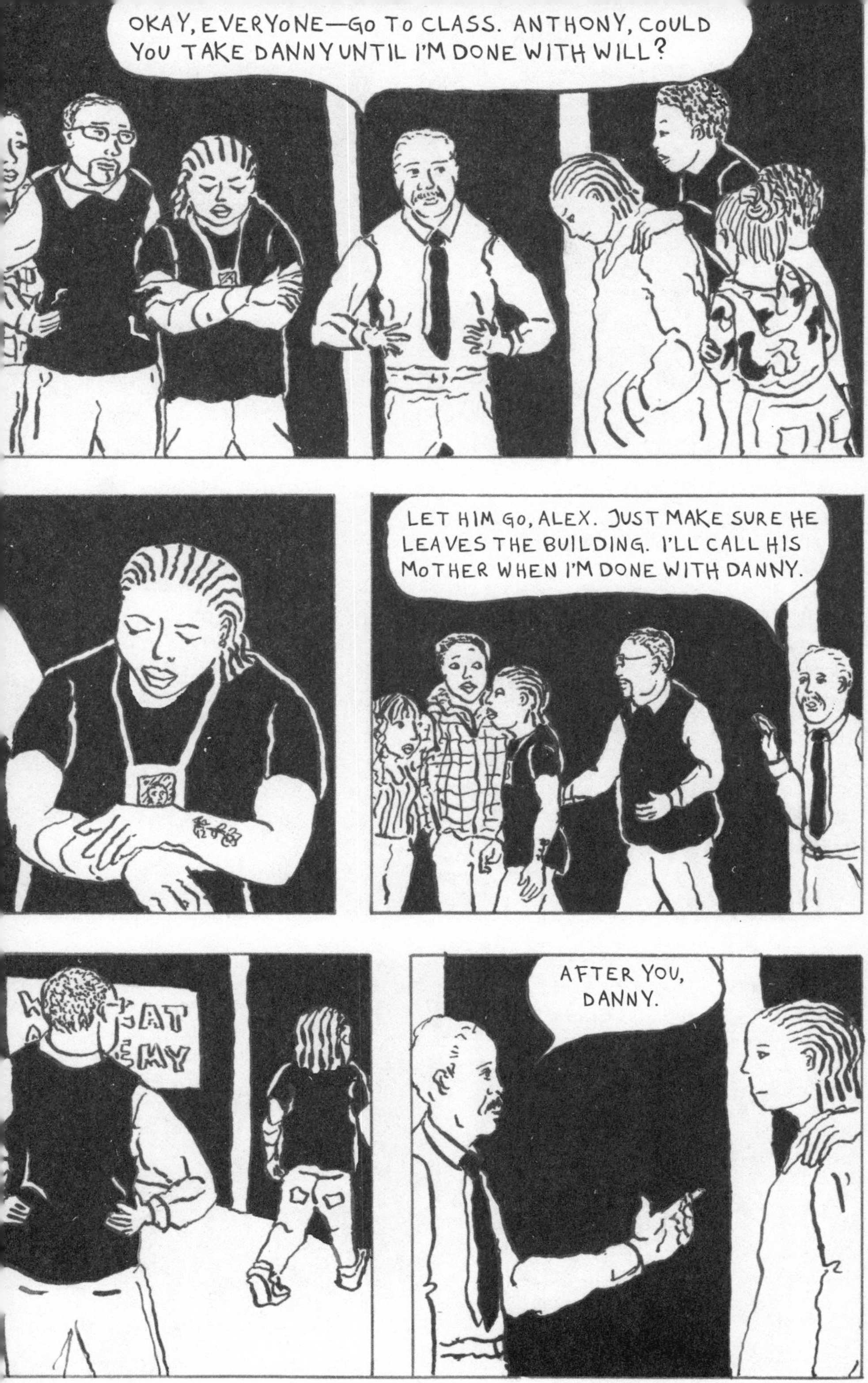
OKAY, EVERYONE—GO TO CLASS. ANTHONY, COULD YOU TAKE DANNY UNTIL I'M DONE WITH WILL?
LET HIM GO, ALEX. JUST MAKE SURE HE LEAVES THE BUILDING. I'LL CALL HIS MOTHER WHEN I'M DONE WITH DANNY.
AFTER YOU, DANNY.

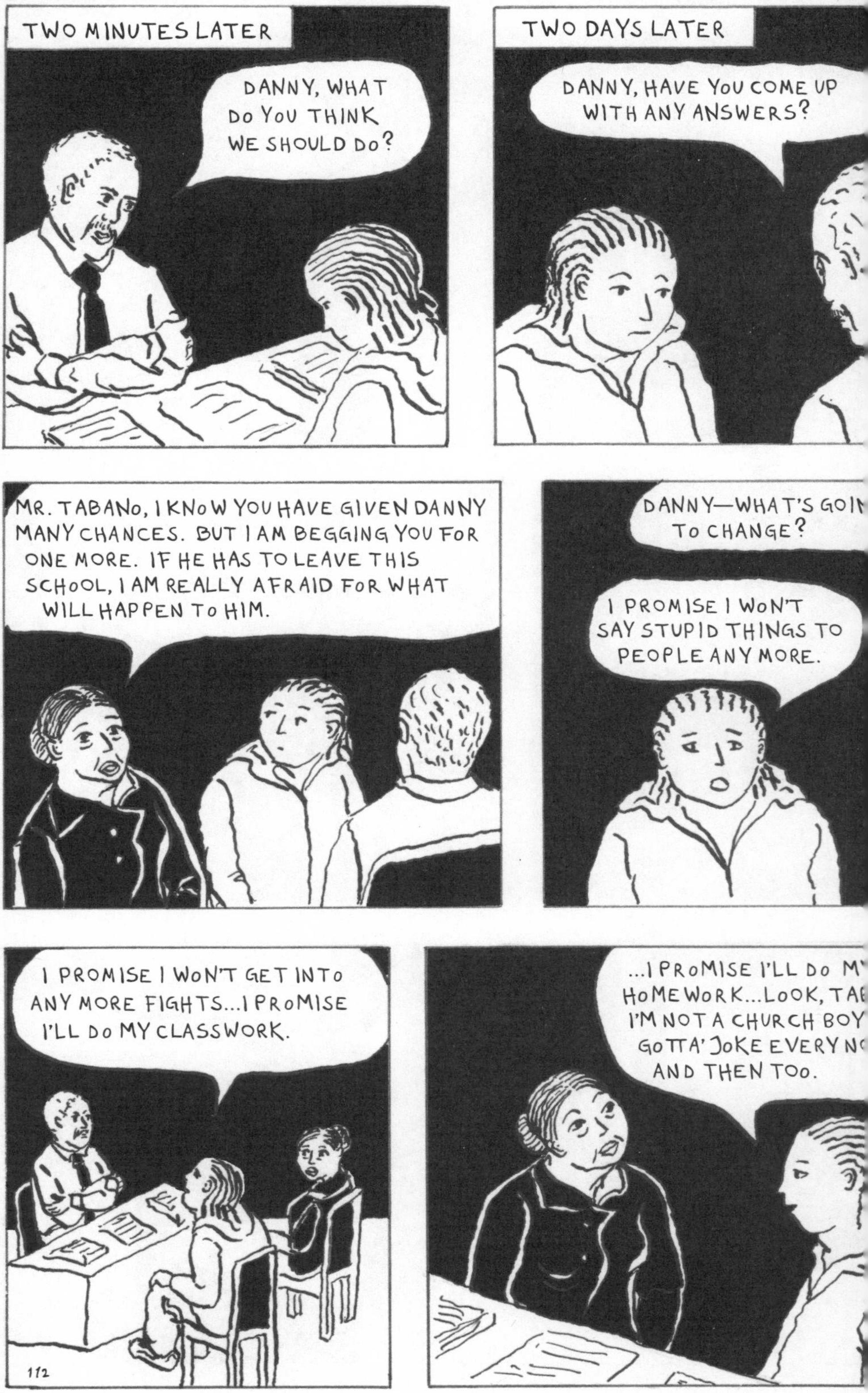
TWO MINUTES LATER
DANNY, WHAT DO YOU THINK WE SHOULD DO?
TWO DAYS LATER
DANNY, HAVE YOU COME UP WITH ANY ANSWERS?
MR. TABANO, I KNOW YOU HAVE GIVEN DANNY MANY CHANCES. BUT I AM BEGGING YOU FOR ONE MORE. IF HE HAS TO LEAVE THIS SCHOOL, I AM REALLY AFRAID FOR WHAT WILL HAPPEN TO HIM.
DANNY—WHAT'S GOIN TO CHANGE?
I PROMISE I WON'T SAY STUPID THINGS TO PEOPLE ANY MORE.
I PROMISE I WON'T GET INTO ANY MORE FIGHTS...I PROMISE I'LL DO MY CLASSWORK.
...I PROMISE I'LL DO M HOMEWORK...LOOK, TA I'M NOT A CHURCH BOY GOTTA' JOKE EVERY N AND THEN TOO.

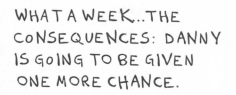

WHAT A WEEK...THE CONSEQUENCES: DANNY IS GOING TO BE GIVEN ONE MORE CHANCE.

THIS TIME I THINK IT REALLY IS HIS LAST CHANCE. AND WILL? I HAVE A FEELING HE WON'T BE BACK FOR AWHILE. I DON'T KNOW WHAT THE SHOOTING MEANS FOR HIS PROBATION.

WHAT I DO KNOW IS THAT I HAVE TO GRADE ALL THESE ESSAYS BY MONDAY.

BUT I AM REALLY WORRIED ABOUT WILL.

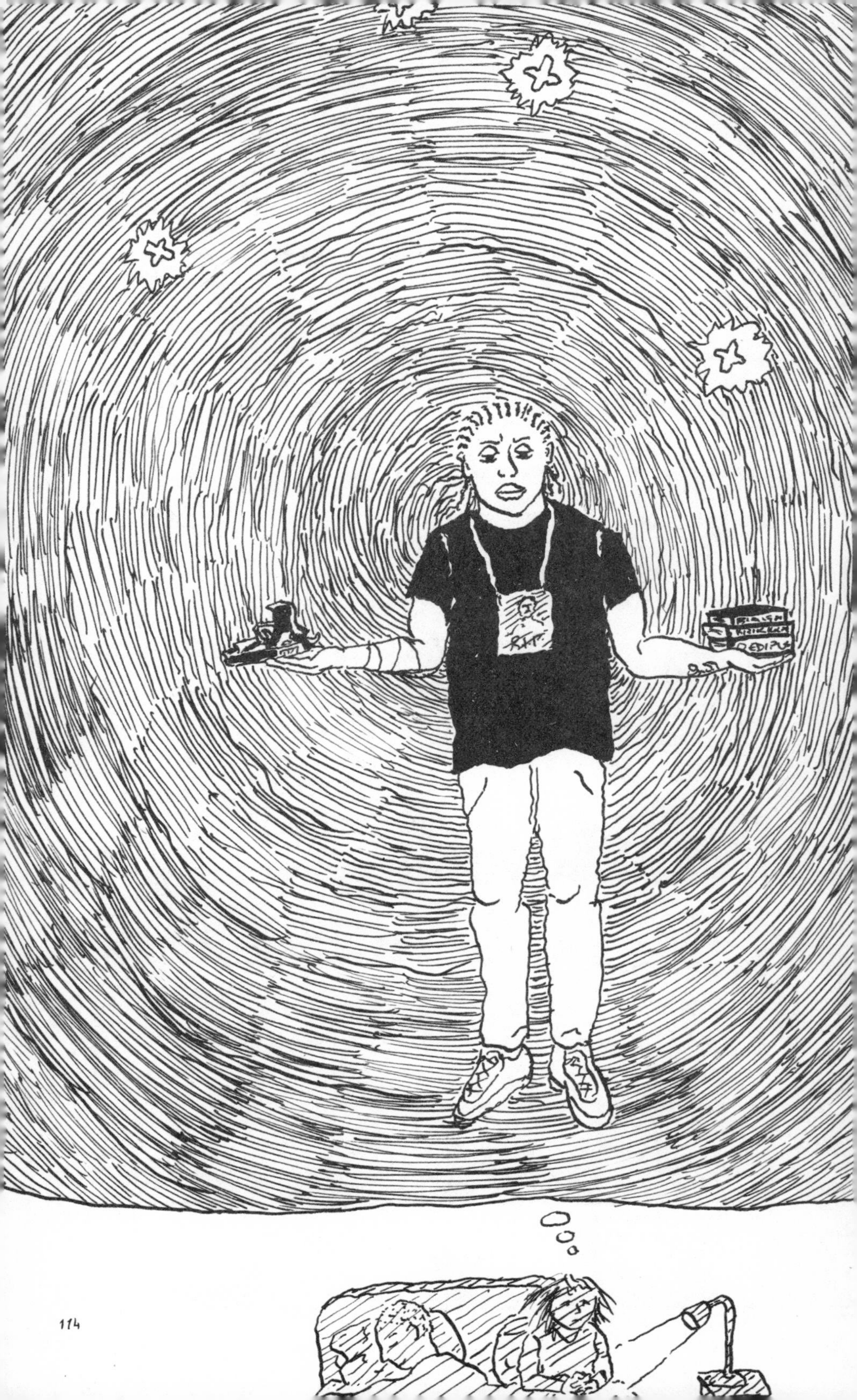
OEDIPUS

ELEVENTH HOUR

GRADUATION COUNTDOWN

CHAPTER EIGHT

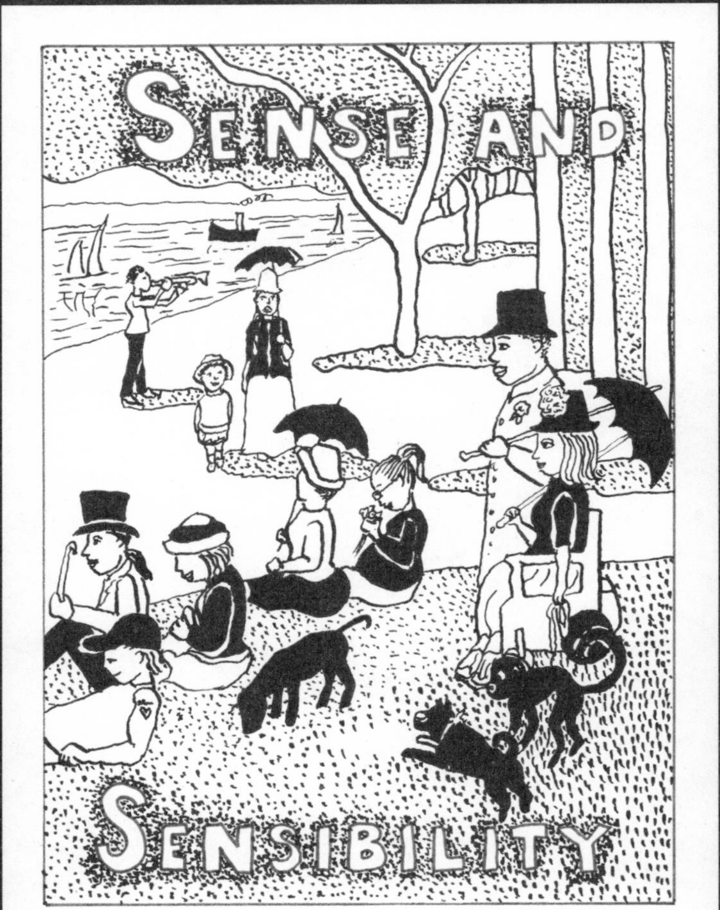
SENSE AND
SENSIBILITY

"IF THINGS ARE GOING UNTOWARDLY ONE MONTH, THEY ARE SURE TO MEND THE NEXT."

JANE AUSTEN

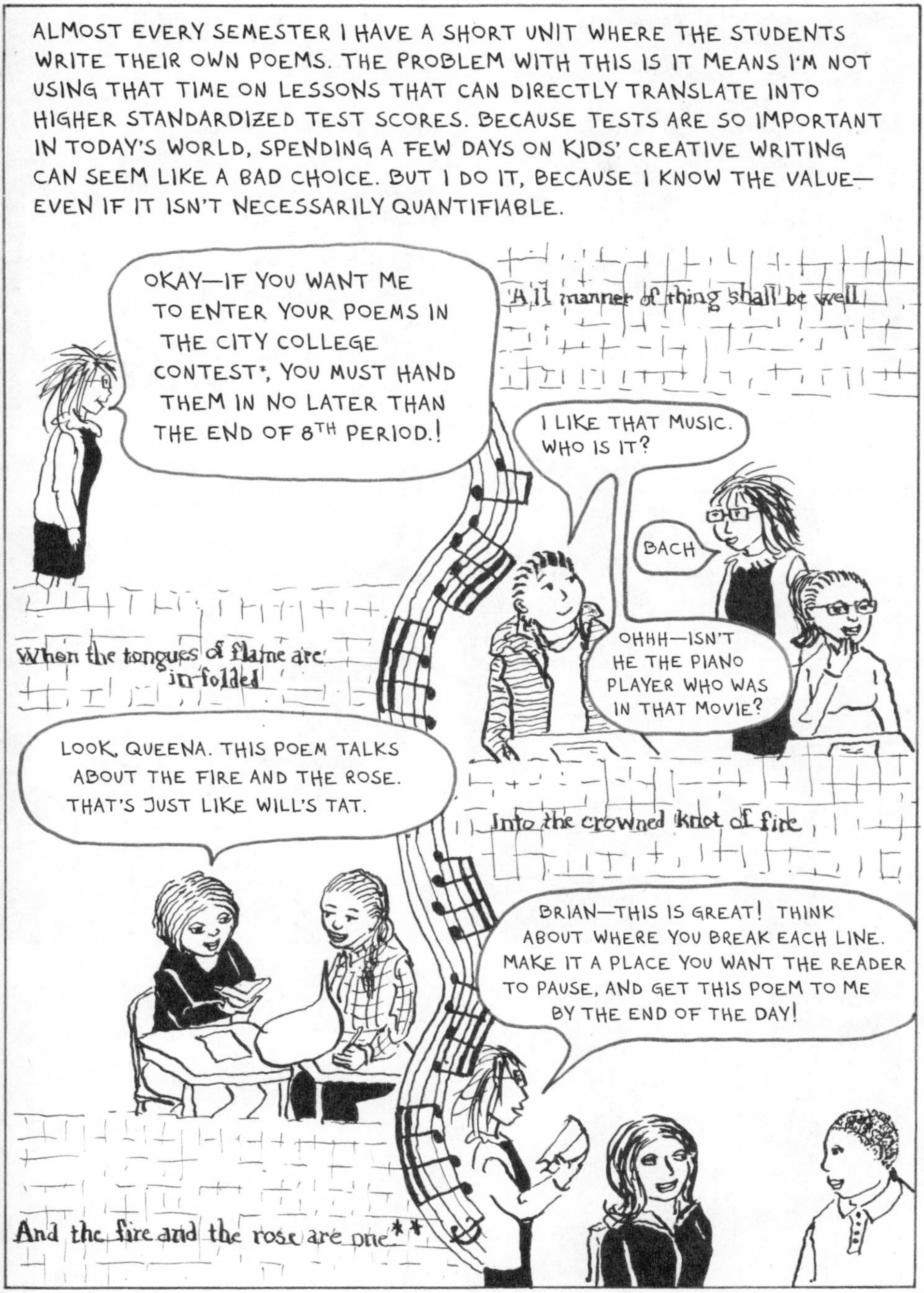
ALMOST EVERY SEMESTER I HAVE A SHORT UNIT WHERE THE STUDENTS WRITE THEIR OWN POEMS. THE PROBLEM WITH THIS IS IT MEANS I'M NOT USING THAT TIME ON LESSONS THAT CAN DIRECTLY TRANSLATE INTO HIGHER STANDARDIZED TEST SCORES. BECAUSE TESTS ARE SO IMPORTANT IN TODAY'S WORLD, SPENDING A FEW DAYS ON KIDS' CREATIVE WRITING CAN SEEM LIKE A BAD CHOICE. BUT I DO IT, BECAUSE I KNOW THE VALUE—EVEN IF IT ISN'T NECESSARILY QUANTIFIABLE.
OKAY—IF YOU WANT ME TO ENTER YOUR POEMS IN THE CITY COLLEGE CONTEST*, YOU MUST HAND THEM IN NO LATER THAN THE END OF 8TH PERIOD.!
All manner of thing shall be well
I LIKE THAT MUSIC. WHO IS IT?
BACH
OHHH—ISN'T HE THE PIANO PLAYER WHO WAS IN THAT MOVIE?
When the tongues of flame are in-folded
LOOK, QUEENA. THIS POEM TALKS ABOUT THE FIRE AND THE ROSE. THAT'S JUST LIKE WILL'S TAT.
Into the crowned knot of fire
BRIAN—THIS IS GREAT! THINK ABOUT WHERE YOU BREAK EACH LINE. MAKE IT A PLACE YOU WANT THE READER TO PAUSE, AND GET THIS POEM TO ME BY THE END OF THE DAY!
And the fire and the rose are one**

*CITY COLLEGE HAS AN ANNUAL POETRY COMPETITION FOR N.Y.C. PUBLIC HIGH SCHOOL STUDENTS

** FROM "FOUR QUARTETS" BY T.S. ELIOT

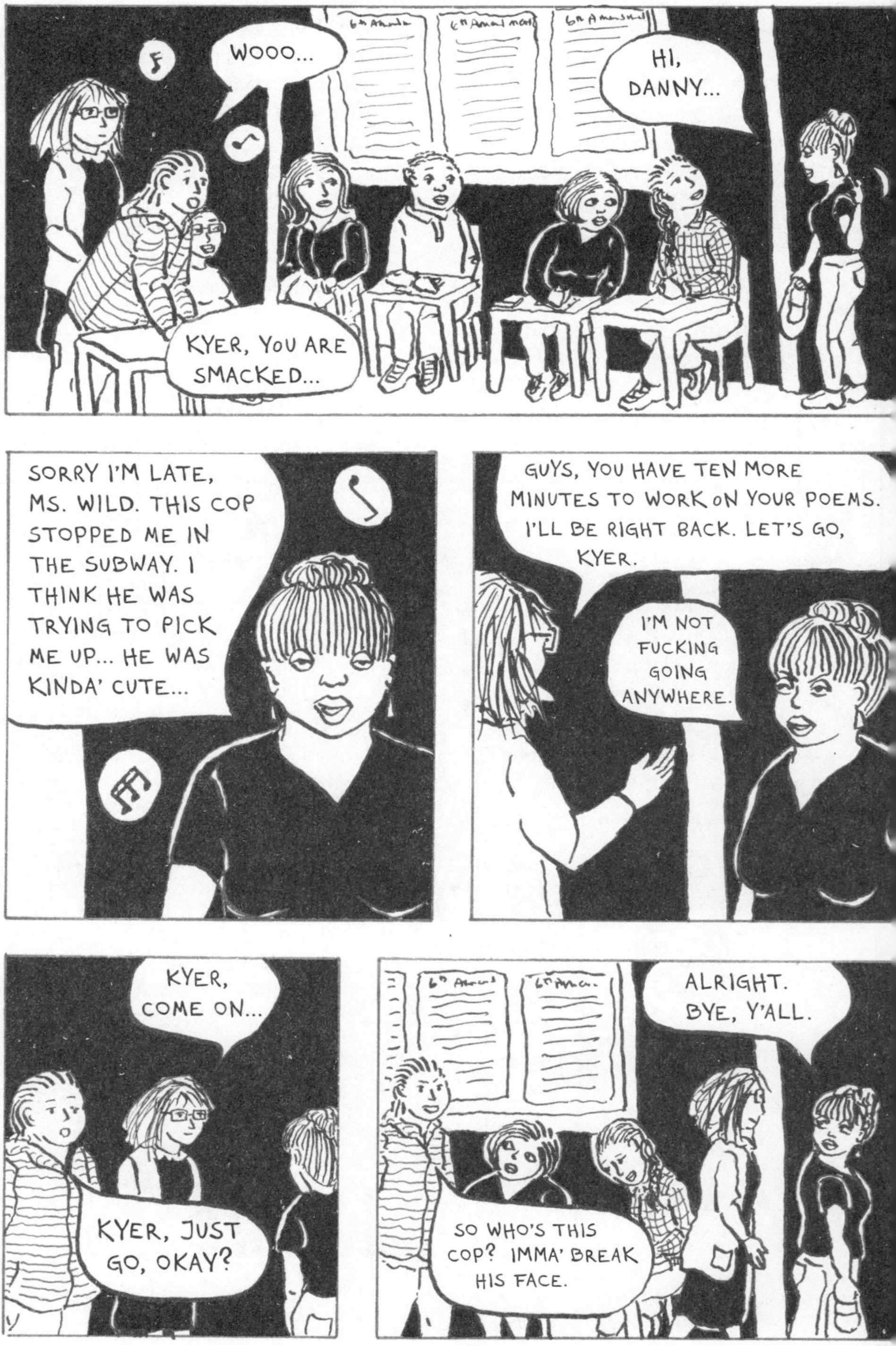
WOOO...
KYER, YOU ARE SMACKED...
HI, DANNY...
SORRY I'M LATE, MS. WILD. THIS COP STOPPED ME IN THE SUBWAY. I THINK HE WAS TRYING TO PICK ME UP... HE WAS KINDA' CUTE...
GUYS, YOU HAVE TEN MORE MINUTES TO WORK ON YOUR POEMS. I'LL BE RIGHT BACK. LET'S GO, KYER.
I'M NOT FUCKING GOING ANYWHERE.
KYER, COME ON...
KYER, JUST GO, OKAY?
ALRIGHT. BYE, Y'ALL.
SO WHO'S THIS COP? IMMA' BREAK HIS FACE.

FTER SCHOOL

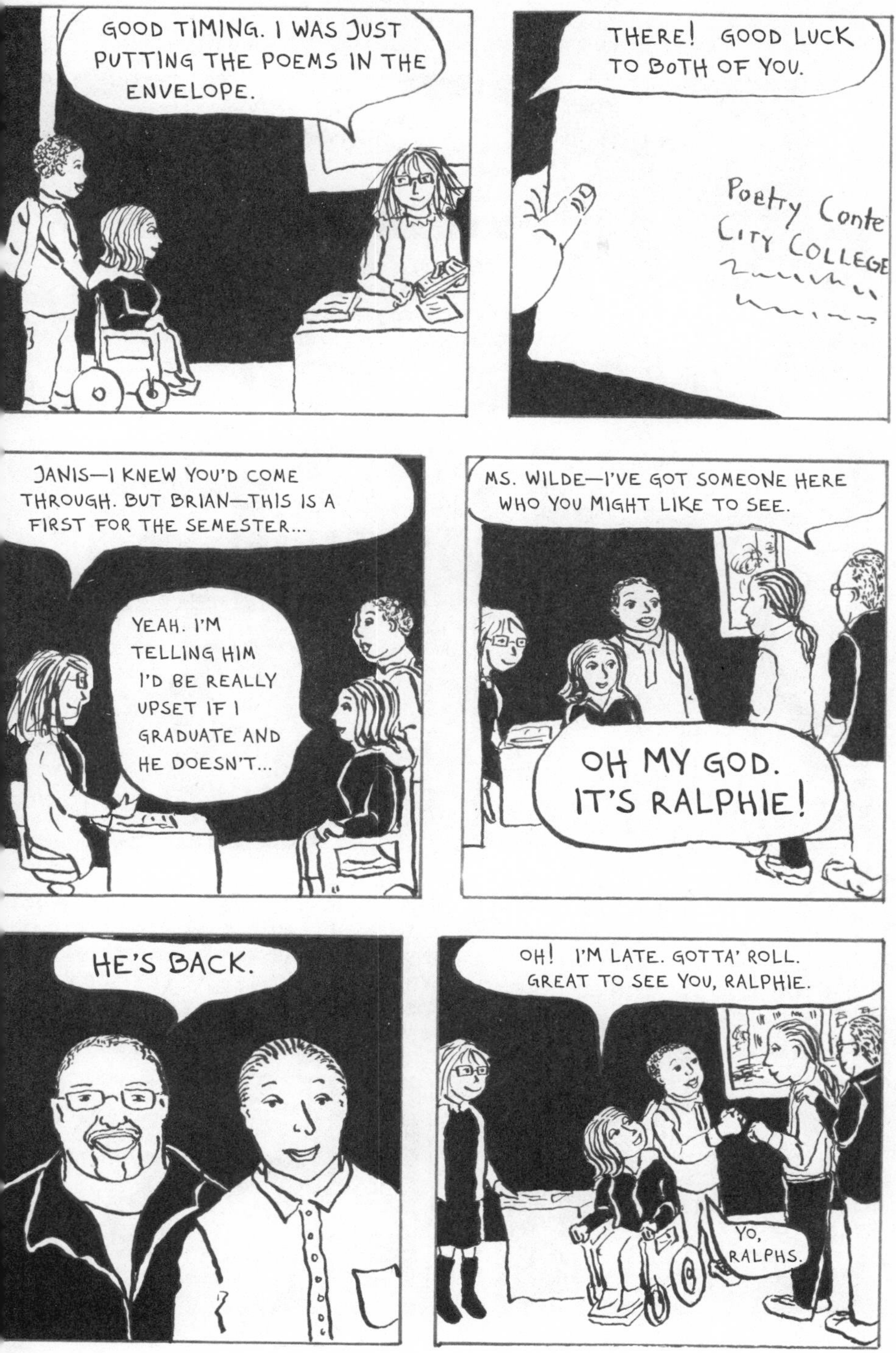
GOOD TIMING. I WAS JUST PUTTING THE POEMS IN THE ENVELOPE.
THERE! GOOD LUCK TO BOTH OF YOU.
Poetry Conte
CITY COLLEGE
JANIS—I KNEW YOU'D COME THROUGH. BUT BRIAN—THIS IS A FIRST FOR THE SEMESTER...
YEAH. I'M TELLING HIM I'D BE REALLY UPSET IF I GRADUATE AND HE DOESN'T...
MS. WILDE—I'VE GOT SOMEONE HERE WHO YOU MIGHT LIKE TO SEE.
OH MY GOD. IT'S RALPHIE!
HE'S BACK.
OH! I'M LATE. GOTTA' ROLL. GREAT TO SEE YOU, RALPHIE.
YO, RALPHS.

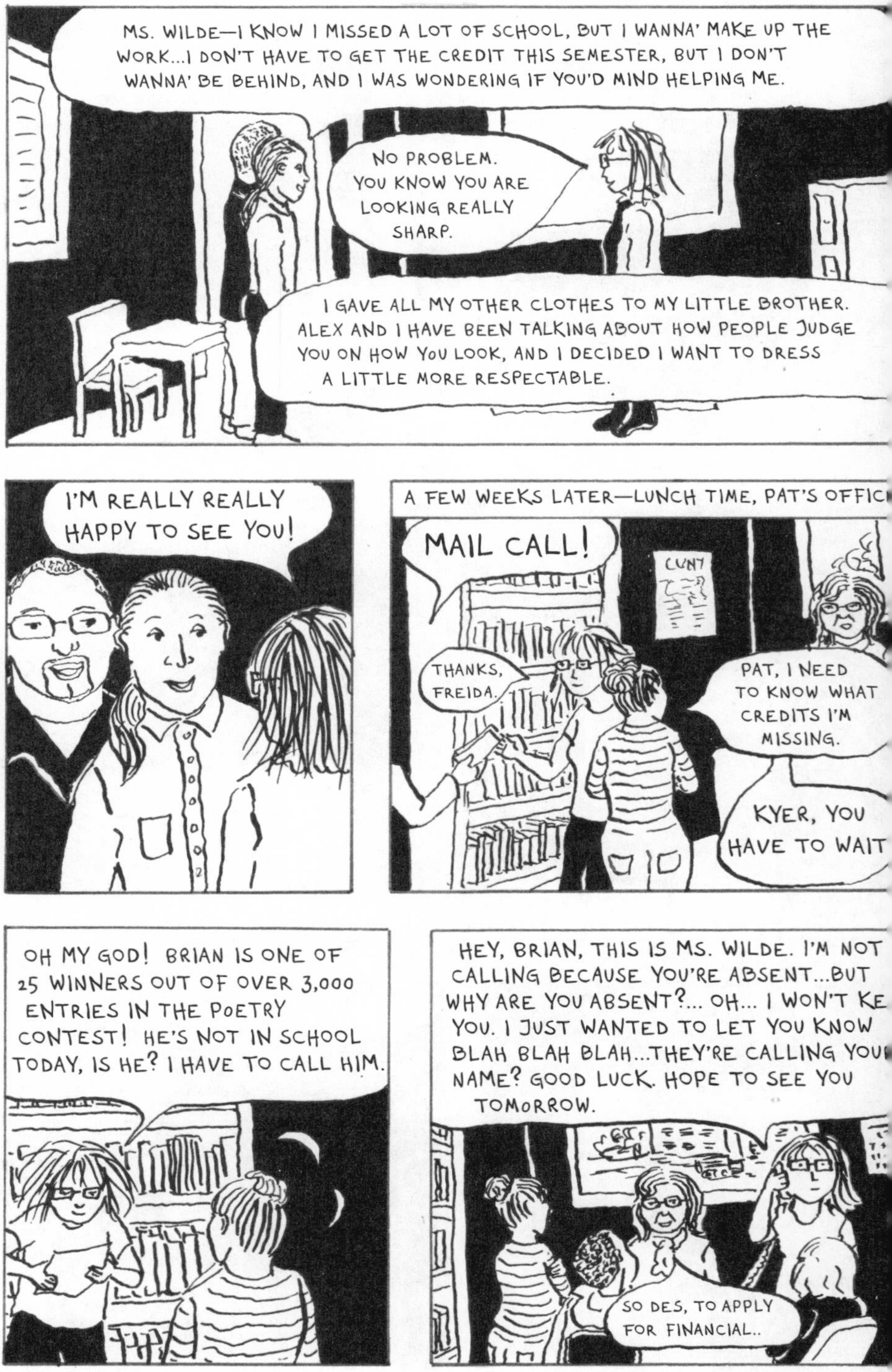
MS. WILDE—I KNOW I MISSED A LOT OF SCHOOL, BUT I WANNA' MAKE UP THE WORK...I DON'T HAVE TO GET THE CREDIT THIS SEMESTER, BUT I DON'T WANNA' BE BEHIND, AND I WAS WONDERING IF YOU'D MIND HELPING ME.
NO PROBLEM. YOU KNOW YOU ARE LOOKING REALLY SHARP.
I GAVE ALL MY OTHER CLOTHES TO MY LITTLE BROTHER. ALEX AND I HAVE BEEN TALKING ABOUT HOW PEOPLE JUDGE YOU ON HOW YOU LOOK, AND I DECIDED I WANT TO DRESS A LITTLE MORE RESPECTABLE.
I'M REALLY REALLY HAPPY TO SEE YOU!
A FEW WEEKS LATER—LUNCH TIME, PAT'S OFFIC
MAIL CALL!
CUNY
THANKS, FREIDA.
PAT, I NEED TO KNOW WHAT CREDITS I'M MISSING.
KYER, YOU HAVE TO WAIT
OH MY GOD! BRIAN IS ONE OF 25 WINNERS OUT OF OVER 3,000 ENTRIES IN THE POETRY CONTEST! HE'S NOT IN SCHOOL TODAY, IS HE? I HAVE TO CALL HIM.
HEY, BRIAN, THIS IS MS. WILDE. I'M NOT CALLING BECAUSE YOU'RE ABSENT...BUT WHY ARE YOU ABSENT?... OH... I WON'T KE YOU. I JUST WANTED TO LET YOU KNOW BLAH BLAH BLAH...THEY'RE CALLING YOU NAME? GOOD LUCK. HOPE TO SEE YOU TOMORROW.
SO DES, TO APPLY FOR FINANCIAL..

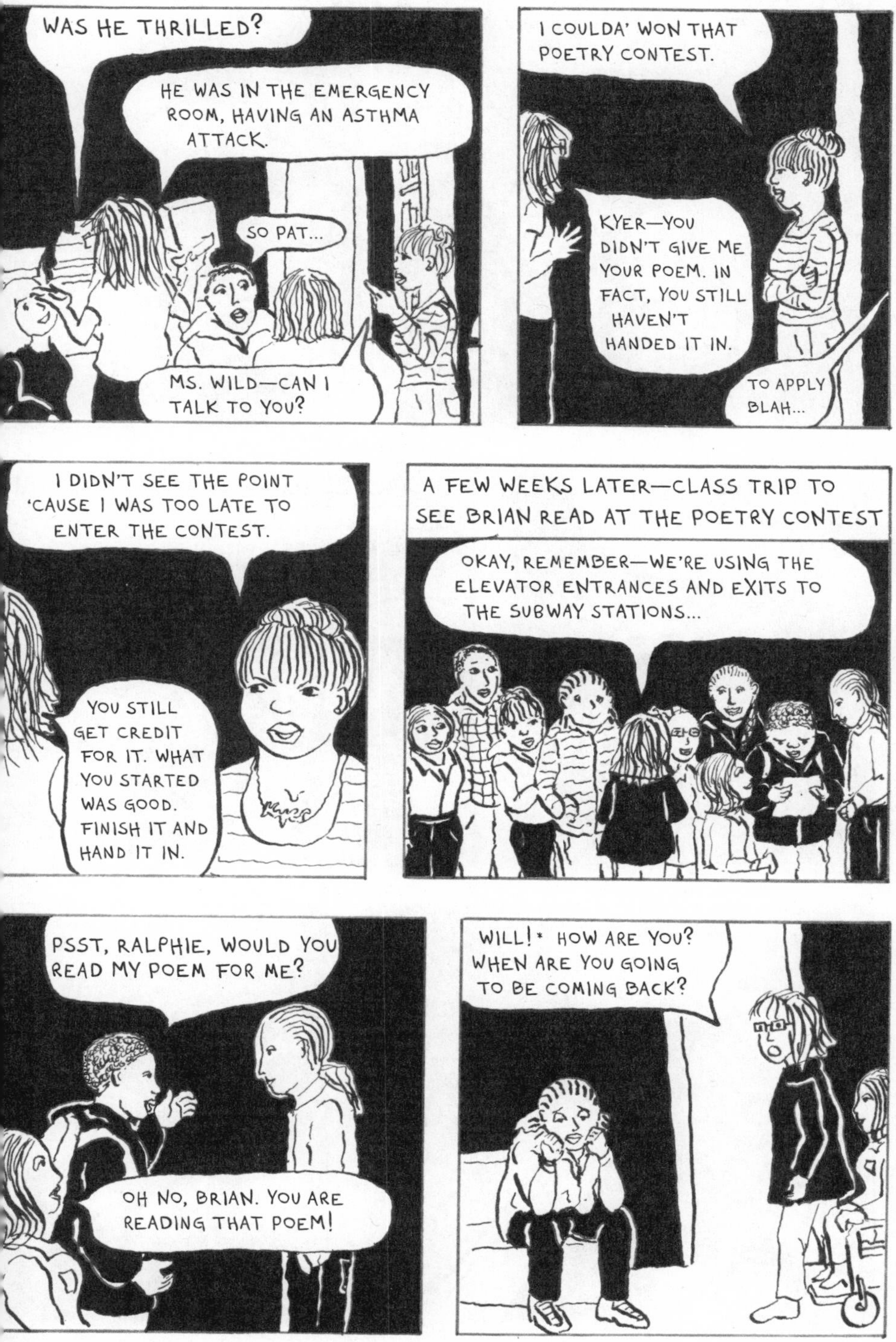
WAS HE THRILLED?
HE WAS IN THE EMERGENCY ROOM, HAVING AN ASTHMA ATTACK.
SO PAT...
MS. WILD—CAN I TALK TO YOU?
I COULDA' WON THAT POETRY CONTEST.
KYER—YOU DIDN'T GIVE ME YOUR POEM. IN FACT, YOU STILL HAVEN'T HANDED IT IN.
TO APPLY BLAH...
I DIDN'T SEE THE POINT 'CAUSE I WAS TOO LATE TO ENTER THE CONTEST.
YOU STILL GET CREDIT FOR IT. WHAT YOU STARTED WAS GOOD. FINISH IT AND HAND IT IN.
A FEW WEEKS LATER—CLASS TRIP TO SEE BRIAN READ AT THE POETRY CONTEST
OKAY, REMEMBER—WE'RE USING THE ELEVATOR ENTRANCES AND EXITS TO THE SUBWAY STATIONS...
PSST, RALPHIE, WOULD YOU READ MY POEM FOR ME?
OH NO, BRIAN. YOU ARE READING THAT POEM!
WILL!* HOW ARE YOU? WHEN ARE YOU GOING TO BE COMING BACK?

*WILL HAS BEEN OUT FOR THE PAST MONTH AS HE SORTS OUT HIS LEGAL SITUATION.

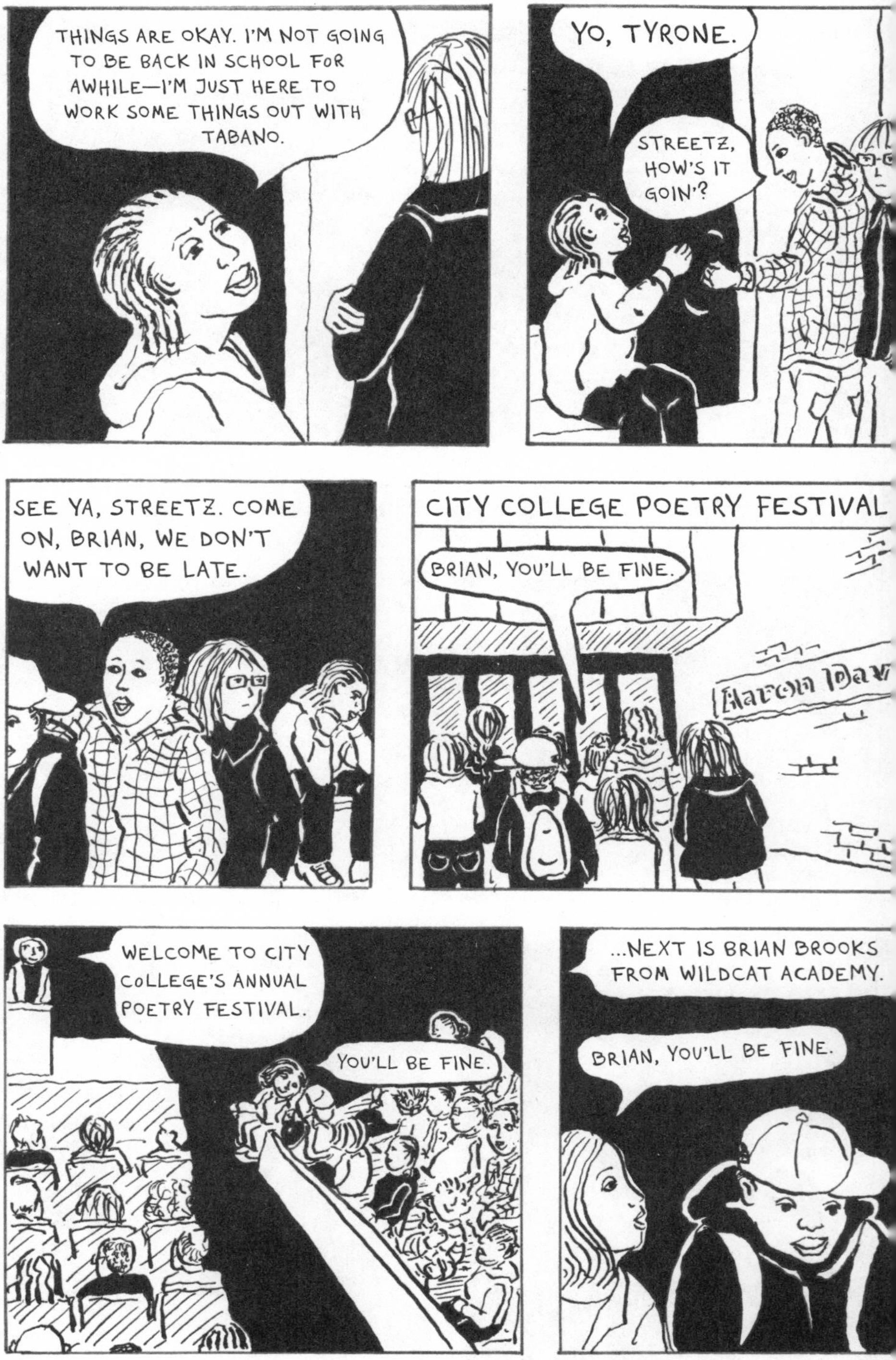
THINGS ARE OKAY. I'M NOT GOING TO BE BACK IN SCHOOL FOR AWHILE—I'M JUST HERE TO WORK SOME THINGS OUT WITH TABANO.
YO, TYRONE.
STREETZ, HOW'S IT GOIN'?
SEE YA, STREETZ. COME ON, BRIAN, WE DON'T WANT TO BE LATE.
CITY COLLEGE POETRY FESTIVAL
BRIAN, YOU'LL BE FINE.
WELCOME TO CITY COLLEGE'S ANNUAL POETRY FESTIVAL.
YOU'LL BE FINE.
...NEXT IS BRIAN BROOKS FROM WILDCAT ACADEMY.
BRIAN, YOU'LL BE FINE.

"IMMATURITY IS"*

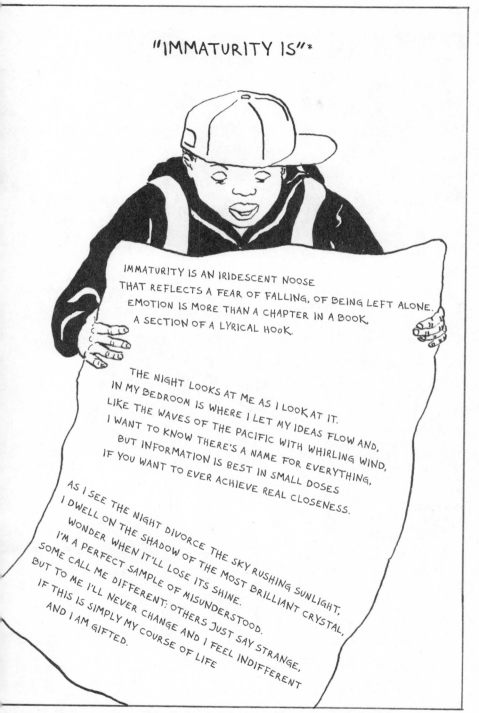

IMMATURITY IS AN IRIDESCENT NOOSE
THAT REFLECTS A FEAR OF FALLING, OF BEING LEFT ALONE.
EMOTION IS MORE THAN A CHAPTER IN A BOOK,
A SECTION OF A LYRICAL HOOK.

THE NIGHT LOOKS AT ME AS I LOOK AT IT.
IN MY BEDROOM IS WHERE I LET MY IDEAS FLOW AND,
LIKE THE WAVES OF THE PACIFIC WITH WHIRLING WIND,
I WANT TO KNOW THERE'S A NAME FOR EVERYTHING,
BUT INFORMATION IS BEST IN SMALL DOSES
IF YOU WANT TO EVER ACHIEVE REAL CLOSENESS.

AS I SEE THE NIGHT DIVORCE THE SKY RUSHING SUNLIGHT,
I DWELL ON THE SHADOW OF THE MOST BRILLIANT CRYSTAL,
WONDER WHEN IT'LL LOSE ITS SHINE.
I'M A PERFECT SAMPLE OF MISUNDERSTOOD.
SOME CALL ME DIFFERENT; OTHERS JUST SAY STRANGE,
BUT TO ME I'LL NEVER CHANGE AND I FEEL INDIFFERENT
IF THIS IS SIMPLY MY COURSE OF LIFE
AND I AM GIFTED.

*POEM BY WILDCAT GRADUATE ANDRES VELEZ. USED WITH PERMISSION.

OUTSIDE AFTER THE POETRY READING

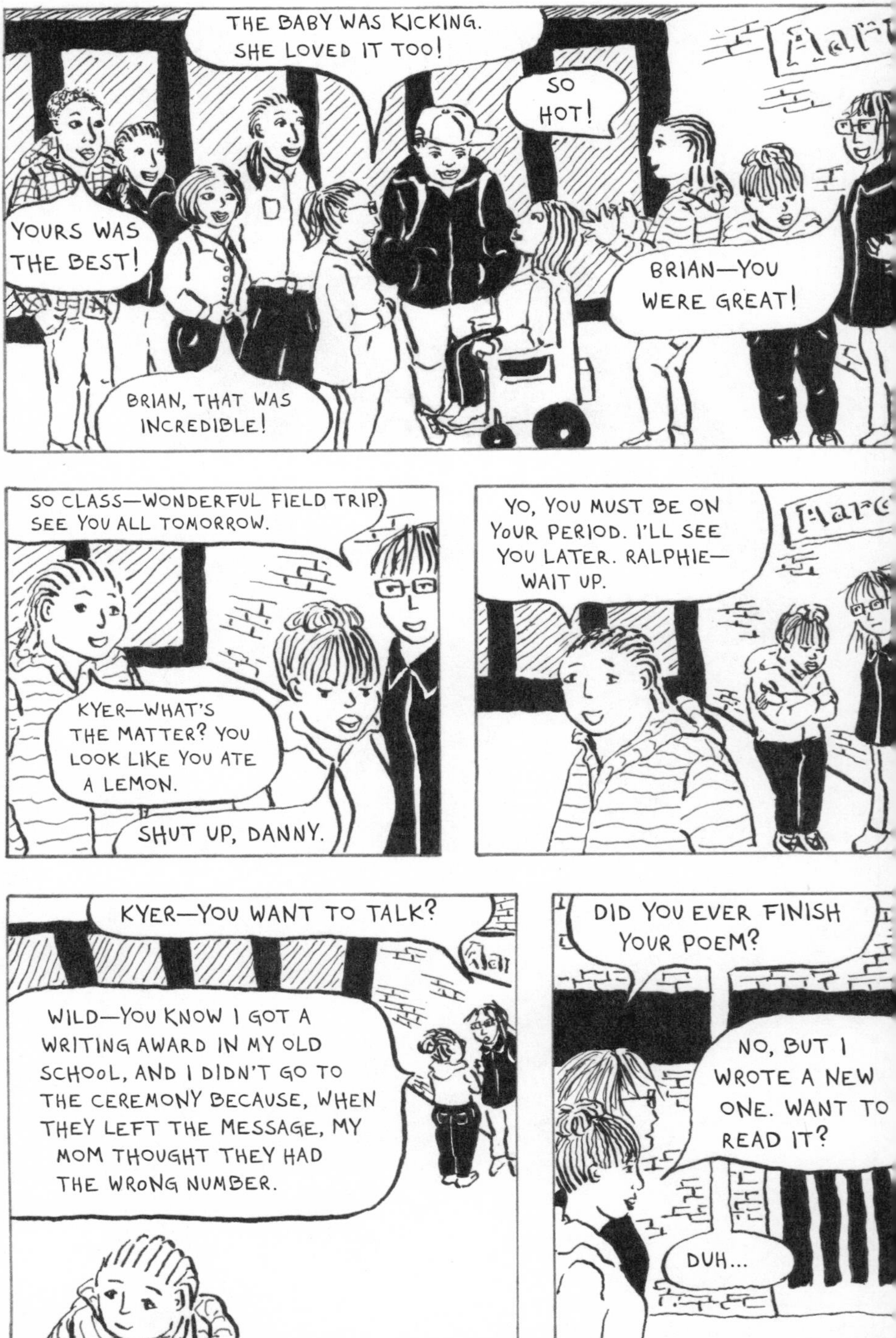
THE BABY WAS KICKING. SHE LOVED IT TOO!
SO HOT!
YOURS WAS THE BEST!
BRIAN—YOU WERE GREAT!
BRIAN, THAT WAS INCREDIBLE!
SO CLASS—WONDERFUL FIELD TRIP. SEE YOU ALL TOMORROW.
KYER—WHAT'S THE MATTER? YOU LOOK LIKE YOU ATE A LEMON.
SHUT UP, DANNY.
YO, YOU MUST BE ON YOUR PERIOD. I'LL SEE YOU LATER. RALPHIE—WAIT UP.
KYER—YOU WANT TO TALK?
WILD—YOU KNOW I GOT A WRITING AWARD IN MY OLD SCHOOL, AND I DIDN'T GO TO THE CEREMONY BECAUSE, WHEN THEY LEFT THE MESSAGE, MY MOM THOUGHT THEY HAD THE WRONG NUMBER.
DID YOU EVER FINISH YOUR POEM?
NO, BUT I WROTE A NEW ONE. WANT TO READ IT?
DUH...

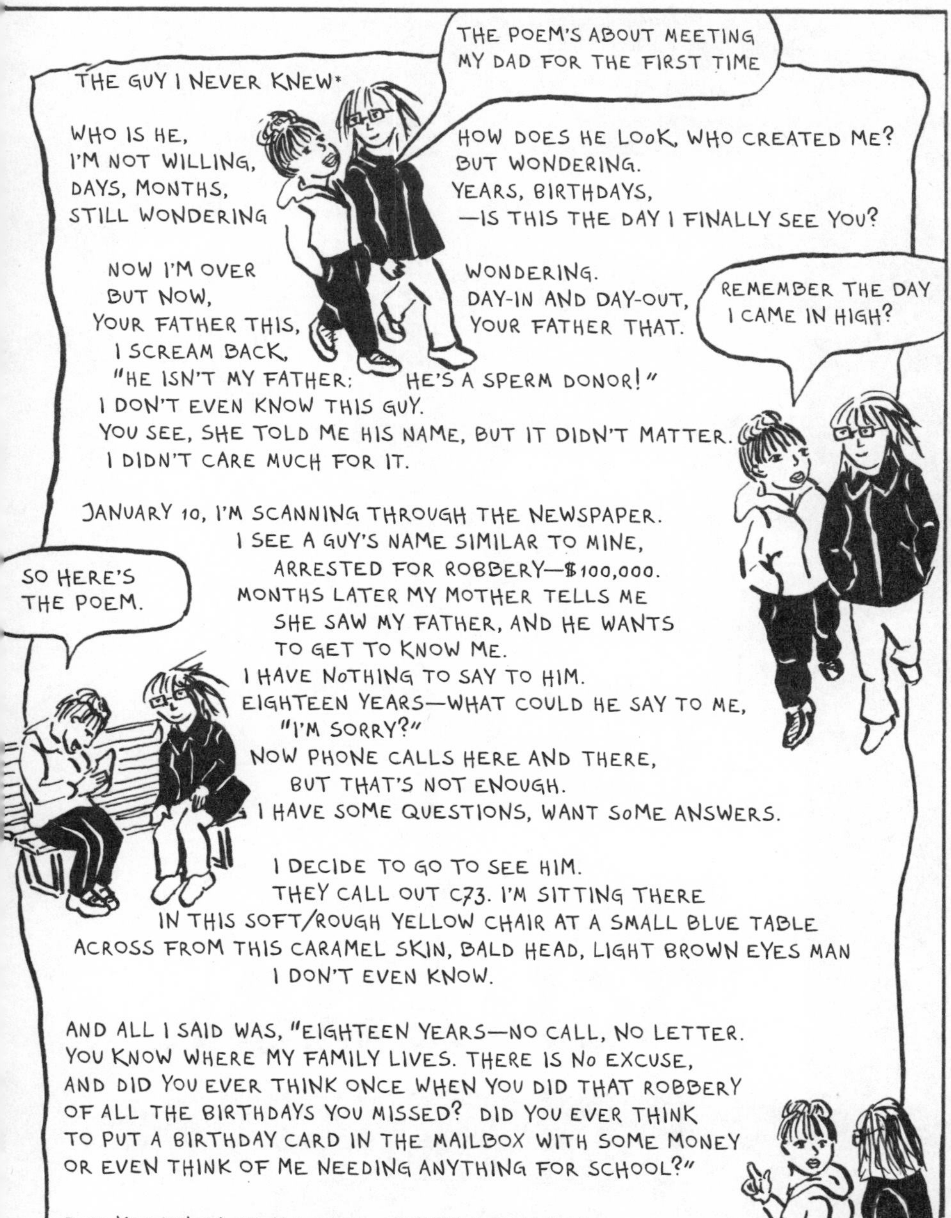
THE POEM'S ABOUT MEETING MY DAD FOR THE FIRST TIME
SO HERE'S THE POEM.
THE GUY I NEVER KNEW*
WHO IS HE, HOW DOES HE LOOK, WHO CREATED ME?
I'M NOT WILLING, BUT WONDERING.
DAYS, MONTHS, YEARS, BIRTHDAYS,
STILL WONDERING —IS THIS THE DAY I FINALLY SEE YOU?
NOW I'M OVER WONDERING.
BUT NOW, DAY-IN AND DAY-OUT,
YOUR FATHER THIS, YOUR FATHER THAT.
I SCREAM BACK,
"HE ISN'T MY FATHER: HE'S A SPERM DONOR!"
I DON'T EVEN KNOW THIS GUY.
YOU SEE, SHE TOLD ME HIS NAME, BUT IT DIDN'T MATTER.
I DIDN'T CARE MUCH FOR IT.
JANUARY 10, I'M SCANNING THROUGH THE NEWSPAPER.
I SEE A GUY'S NAME SIMILAR TO MINE,
ARRESTED FOR ROBBERY—$100,000.
MONTHS LATER MY MOTHER TELLS ME
SHE SAW MY FATHER, AND HE WANTS
TO GET TO KNOW ME.
I HAVE NOTHING TO SAY TO HIM.
EIGHTEEN YEARS—WHAT COULD HE SAY TO ME,
"I'M SORRY?"
NOW PHONE CALLS HERE AND THERE,
BUT THAT'S NOT ENOUGH.
I HAVE SOME QUESTIONS, WANT SOME ANSWERS.
I DECIDE TO GO TO SEE HIM.
THEY CALL OUT C73. I'M SITTING THERE
IN THIS SOFT/ROUGH YELLOW CHAIR AT A SMALL BLUE TABLE
ACROSS FROM THIS CARAMEL SKIN, BALD HEAD, LIGHT BROWN EYES MAN
I DON'T EVEN KNOW.
AND ALL I SAID WAS, "EIGHTEEN YEARS—NO CALL, NO LETTER.
YOU KNOW WHERE MY FAMILY LIVES. THERE IS NO EXCUSE,
AND DID YOU EVER THINK ONCE WHEN YOU DID THAT ROBBERY
OF ALL THE BIRTHDAYS YOU MISSED? DID YOU EVER THINK
TO PUT A BIRTHDAY CARD IN THE MAILBOX WITH SOME MONEY
OR EVEN THINK OF ME NEEDING ANYTHING FOR SCHOOL?"
BUT YOU KNOW, IT ALL GOOD. THIS IS A NEW YEAR,
WE CAN PUT THIS BEHIND US
AND NOW YOU CAN BECOME
MY FATHER.
REMEMBER THE DAY I CAME IN HIGH?
THAT WAS THE DAY I WAS SUPPOSED TO MEET HIM, AND I JUST COULDN'T HANDLE IT.

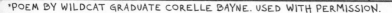

*POEM BY WILDCAT GRADUATE CORELLE BAYNE. USED WITH PERMISSION.

CHAPTER NINE

PYGMALION

"REMEMBER YOU ARE A HUMAN BEING WITH
A SOUL AND THE DIVINE GIFT OF ARTICULATE
SPEECH."

GEORGE BERNARD SHAW

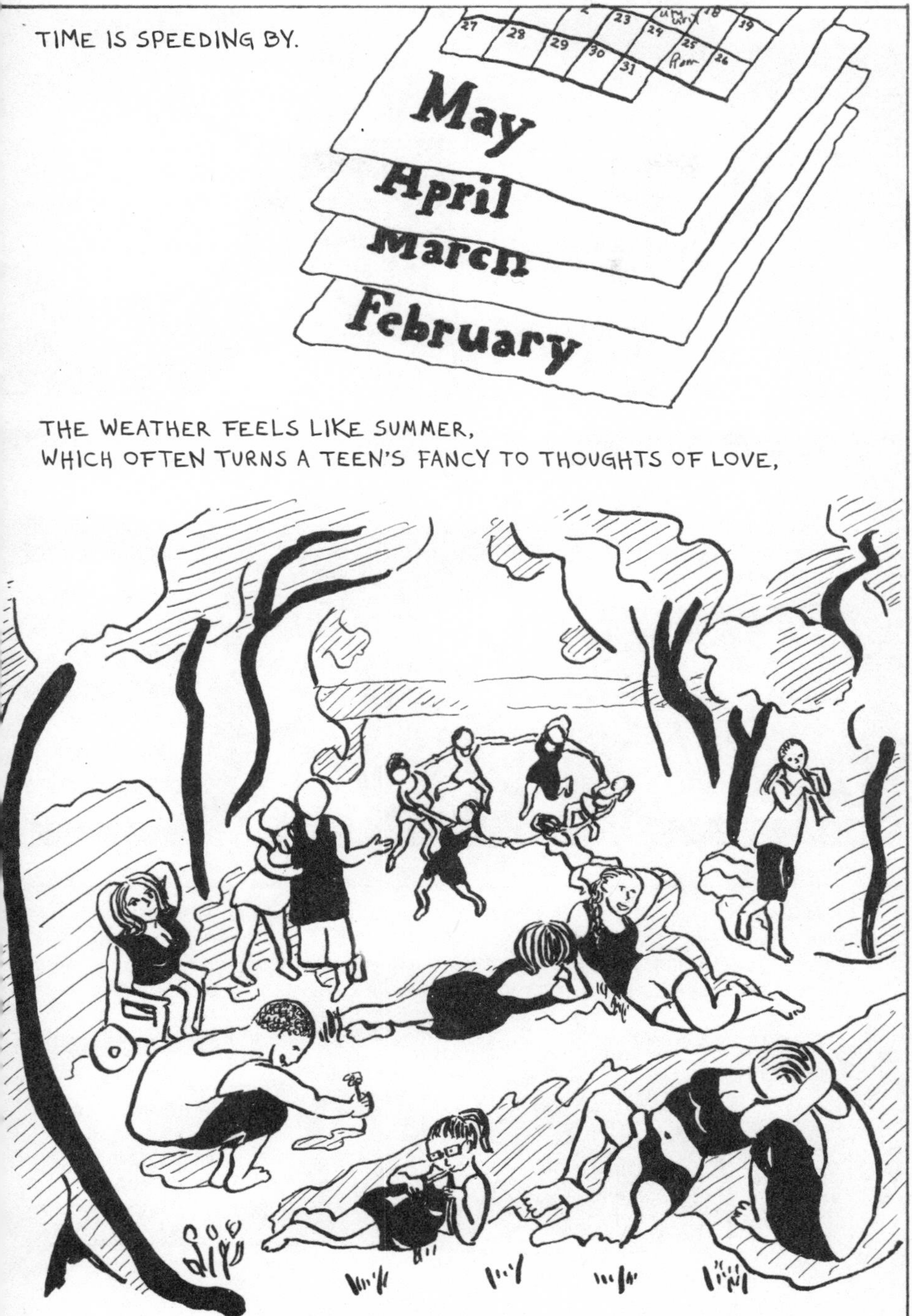
TIME IS SPEEDING BY.
May
April
March
February
THE WEATHER FEELS LIKE SUMMER,
WHICH OFTEN TURNS A TEEN'S FANCY TO THOUGHTS OF LOVE,
AND OFTEN TURNS AN ADMINISTRATOR'S FANCY TO THOUGHTS OF...

DRESS CODE.

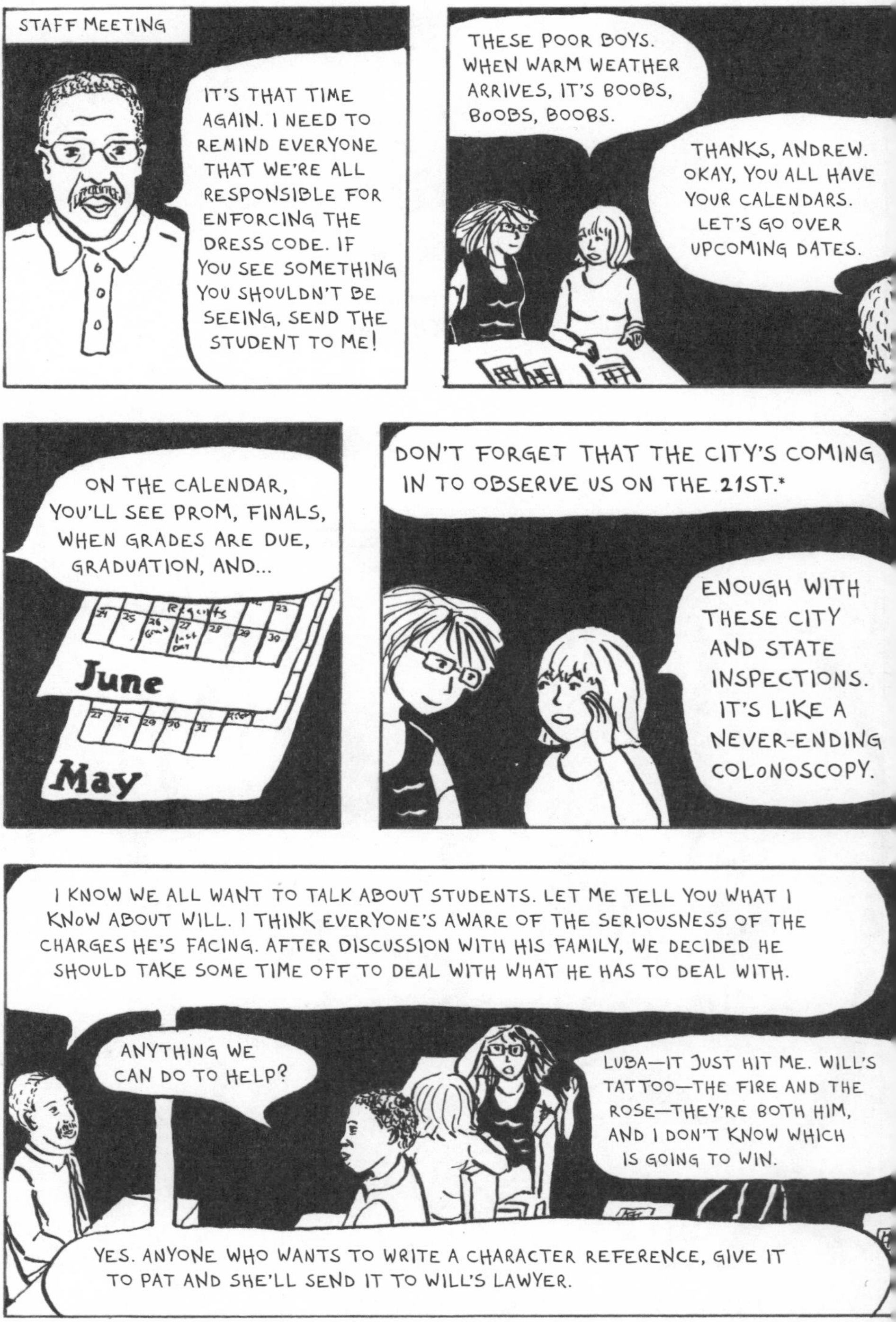
STAFF MEETING
IT'S THAT TIME AGAIN. I NEED TO REMIND EVERYONE THAT WE'RE ALL RESPONSIBLE FOR ENFORCING THE DRESS CODE. IF YOU SEE SOMETHING YOU SHOULDN'T BE SEEING, SEND THE STUDENT TO ME!
THESE POOR BOYS. WHEN WARM WEATHER ARRIVES, IT'S BOOBS, BOOBS, BOOBS.
THANKS, ANDREW. OKAY, YOU ALL HAVE YOUR CALENDARS. LET'S GO OVER UPCOMING DATES.
ON THE CALENDAR, YOU'LL SEE PROM, FINALS, WHEN GRADES ARE DUE, GRADUATION, AND...
June
May
DON'T FORGET THAT THE CITY'S COMING IN TO OBSERVE US ON THE 21ST.*
ENOUGH WITH THESE CITY AND STATE INSPECTIONS. IT'S LIKE A NEVER-ENDING COLONOSCOPY.
I KNOW WE ALL WANT TO TALK ABOUT STUDENTS. LET ME TELL YOU WHAT I KNOW ABOUT WILL. I THINK EVERYONE'S AWARE OF THE SERIOUSNESS OF THE CHARGES HE'S FACING. AFTER DISCUSSION WITH HIS FAMILY, WE DECIDED HE SHOULD TAKE SOME TIME OFF TO DEAL WITH WHAT HE HAS TO DEAL WITH.
ANYTHING WE CAN DO TO HELP?
LUBA—IT JUST HIT ME. WILL'S TATTOO—THE FIRE AND THE ROSE—THEY'RE BOTH HIM, AND I DON'T KNOW WHICH IS GOING TO WIN.
YES. ANYONE WHO WANTS TO WRITE A CHARACTER REFERENCE, GIVE IT TO PAT AND SHE'LL SEND IT TO WILL'S LAWYER.

*THE CITY AND STATE USUALLY COME INTO SCHOOLS AT LEAST ONCE A YEAR AS PART OF THEIR EVALUATION PROCE

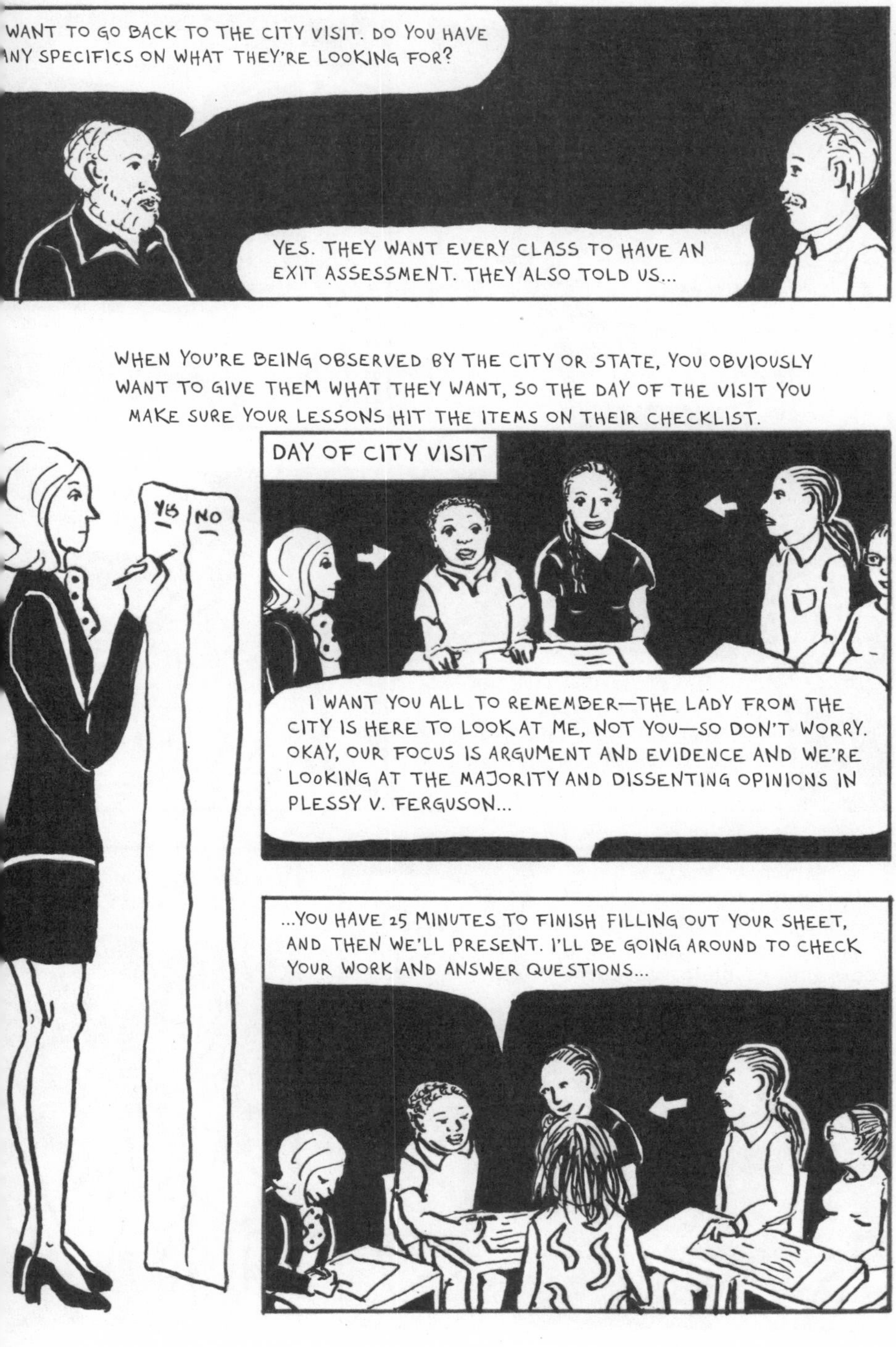
WANT TO GO BACK TO THE CITY VISIT. DO YOU HAVE NY SPECIFICS ON WHAT THEY'RE LOOKING FOR?
YES. THEY WANT EVERY CLASS TO HAVE AN EXIT ASSESSMENT. THEY ALSO TOLD US...
WHEN YOU'RE BEING OBSERVED BY THE CITY OR STATE, YOU OBVIOUSLY WANT TO GIVE THEM WHAT THEY WANT, SO THE DAY OF THE VISIT YOU MAKE SURE YOUR LESSONS HIT THE ITEMS ON THEIR CHECKLIST.
YES
NO
DAY OF CITY VISIT
I WANT YOU ALL TO REMEMBER—THE LADY FROM THE CITY IS HERE TO LOOK AT ME, NOT YOU—SO DON'T WORRY. OKAY, OUR FOCUS IS ARGUMENT AND EVIDENCE AND WE'RE LOOKING AT THE MAJORITY AND DISSENTING OPINIONS IN PLESSY V. FERGUSON...
...YOU HAVE 25 MINUTES TO FINISH FILLING OUT YOUR SHEET, AND THEN WE'LL PRESENT. I'LL BE GOING AROUND TO CHECK YOUR WORK AND ANSWER QUESTIONS...

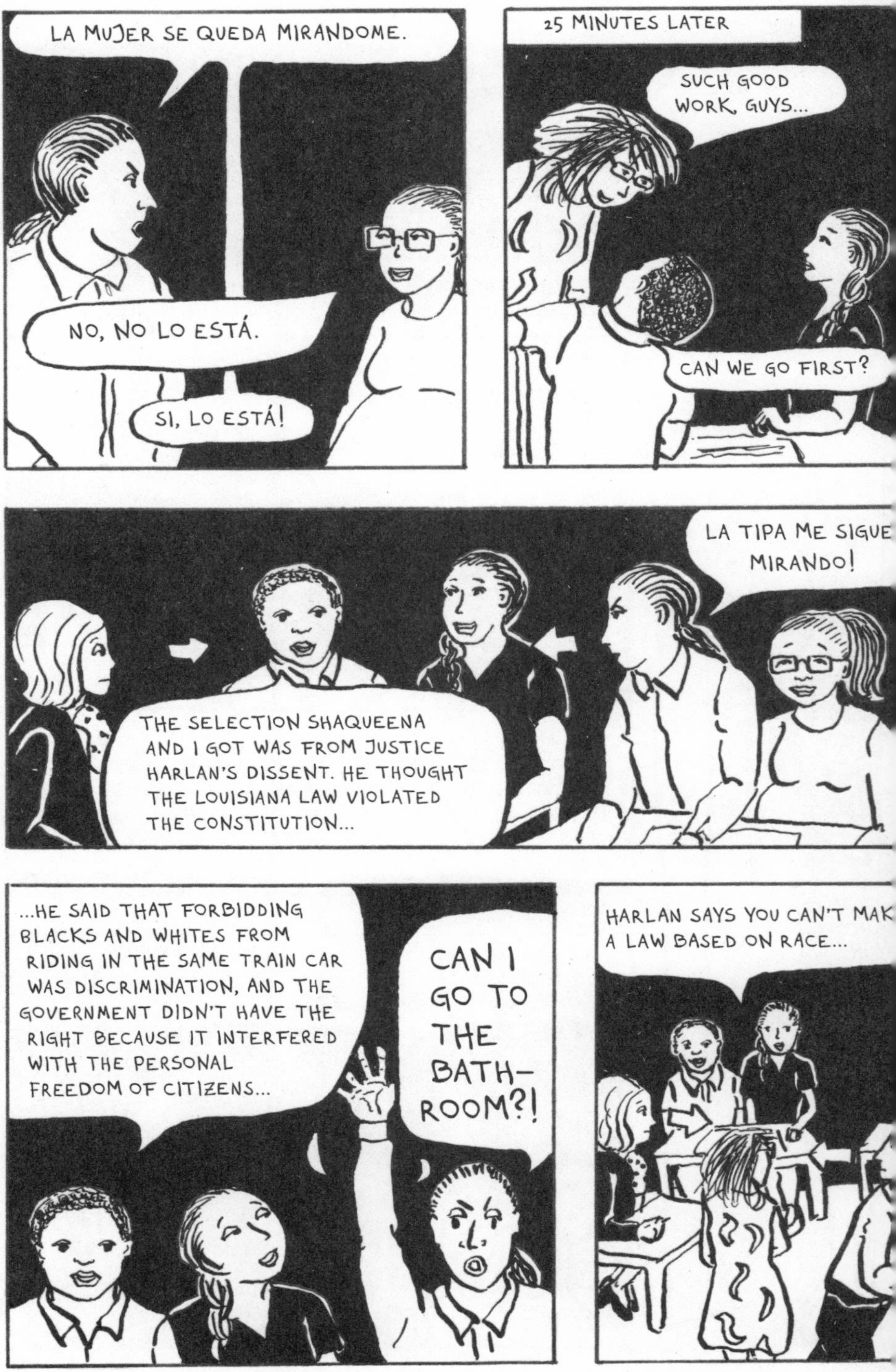
LA MUJER SE QUEDA MIRANDOME.
NO, NO LO ESTÁ.
SI, LO ESTÁ!
25 MINUTES LATER
SUCH GOOD WORK, GUYS...
CAN WE GO FIRST?
LA TIPA ME SIGUE MIRANDO!
THE SELECTION SHAQUEENA AND I GOT WAS FROM JUSTICE HARLAN'S DISSENT. HE THOUGHT THE LOUISIANA LAW VIOLATED THE CONSTITUTION...
...HE SAID THAT FORBIDDING BLACKS AND WHITES FROM RIDING IN THE SAME TRAIN CAR WAS DISCRIMINATION, AND THE GOVERNMENT DIDN'T HAVE THE RIGHT BECAUSE IT INTERFERED WITH THE PERSONAL FREEDOM OF CITIZENS...
CAN I GO TO THE BATH-ROOM?!
HARLAN SAYS YOU CAN'T MAK
A LAW BASED ON RACE...

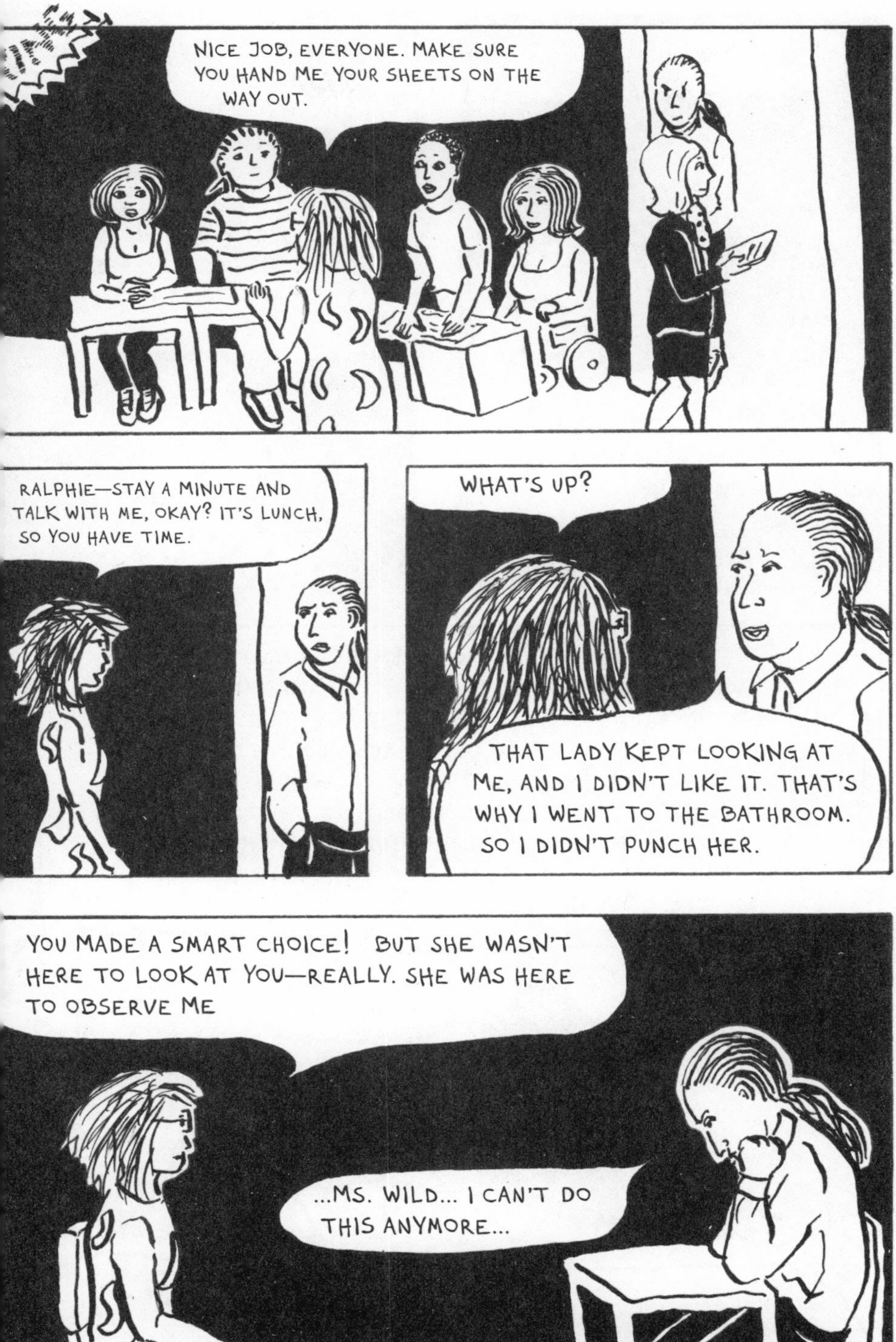
NICE JOB, EVERYONE. MAKE SURE YOU HAND ME YOUR SHEETS ON THE WAY OUT.
RALPHIE—STAY A MINUTE AND TALK WITH ME, OKAY? IT'S LUNCH, SO YOU HAVE TIME.
WHAT'S UP?
THAT LADY KEPT LOOKING AT ME, AND I DIDN'T LIKE IT. THAT'S WHY I WENT TO THE BATHROOM. SO I DIDN'T PUNCH HER.
YOU MADE A SMART CHOICE! BUT SHE WASN'T HERE TO LOOK AT YOU—REALLY. SHE WAS HERE TO OBSERVE ME
...MS. WILD... I CAN'T DO THIS ANYMORE...

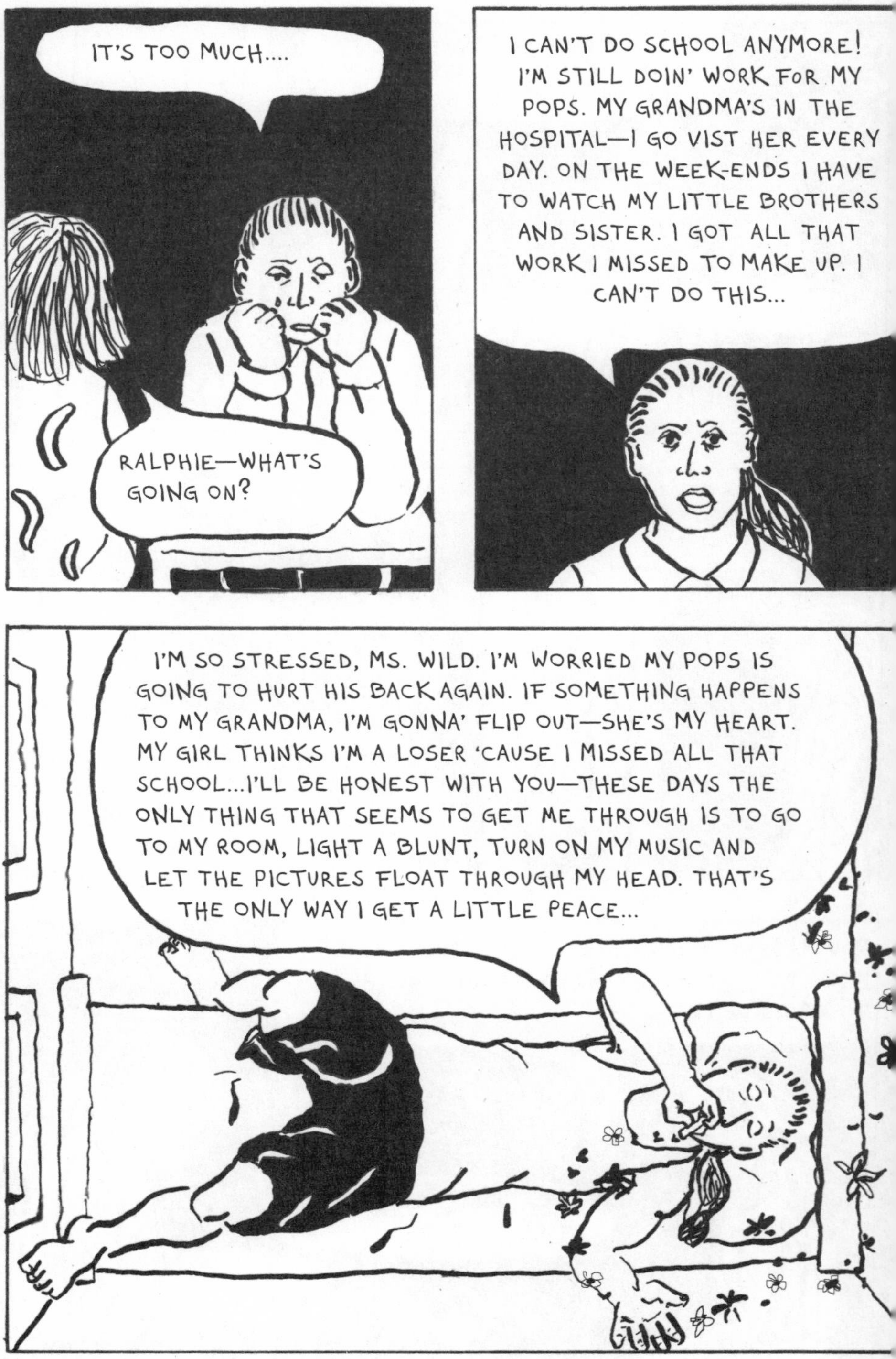
IT'S TOO MUCH....
RALPHIE—WHAT'S GOING ON?
I CAN'T DO SCHOOL ANYMORE! I'M STILL DOIN' WORK FOR MY POPS. MY GRANDMA'S IN THE HOSPITAL—I GO VIST HER EVERY DAY. ON THE WEEK-ENDS I HAVE TO WATCH MY LITTLE BROTHERS AND SISTER. I GOT ALL THAT WORK I MISSED TO MAKE UP. I CAN'T DO THIS...
I'M SO STRESSED, MS. WILD. I'M WORRIED MY POPS IS GOING TO HURT HIS BACK AGAIN. IF SOMETHING HAPPENS TO MY GRANDMA, I'M GONNA' FLIP OUT—SHE'S MY HEART. MY GIRL THINKS I'M A LOSER 'CAUSE I MISSED ALL THAT SCHOOL...I'LL BE HONEST WITH YOU—THESE DAYS THE ONLY THING THAT SEEMS TO GET ME THROUGH IS TO GO TO MY ROOM, LIGHT A BLUNT, TURN ON MY MUSIC AND LET THE PICTURES FLOAT THROUGH MY HEAD. THAT'S THE ONLY WAY I GET A LITTLE PEACE...

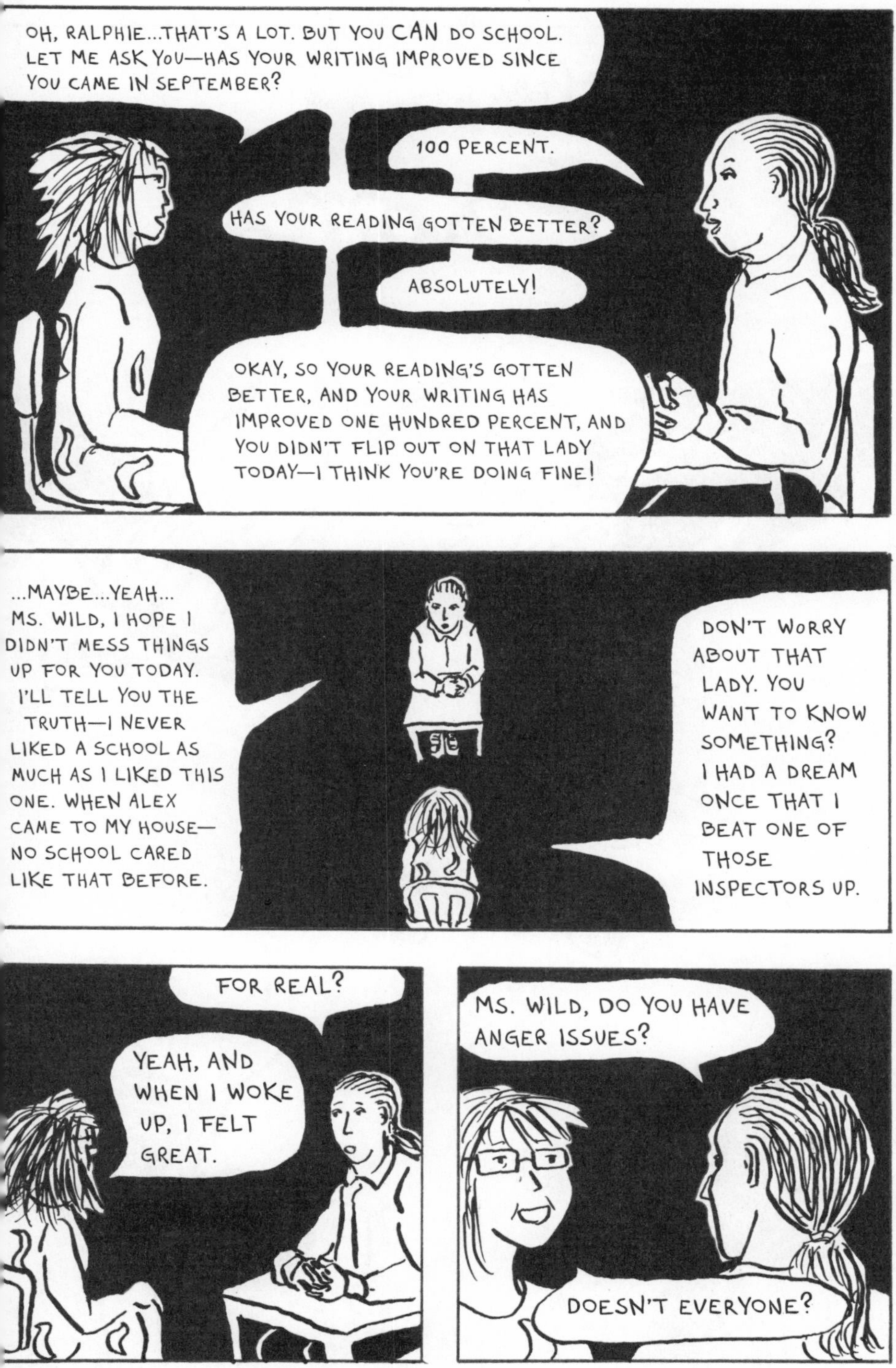
OH, RALPHIE...THAT'S A LOT. BUT YOU CAN DO SCHOOL. LET ME ASK YOU—HAS YOUR WRITING IMPROVED SINCE YOU CAME IN SEPTEMBER?
100 PERCENT.
HAS YOUR READING GOTTEN BETTER?
ABSOLUTELY!
OKAY, SO YOUR READING'S GOTTEN BETTER, AND YOUR WRITING HAS IMPROVED ONE HUNDRED PERCENT, AND YOU DIDN'T FLIP OUT ON THAT LADY TODAY—I THINK YOU'RE DOING FINE!
...MAYBE...YEAH... MS. WILD, I HOPE I DIDN'T MESS THINGS UP FOR YOU TODAY. I'LL TELL YOU THE TRUTH—I NEVER LIKED A SCHOOL AS MUCH AS I LIKED THIS ONE. WHEN ALEX CAME TO MY HOUSE—NO SCHOOL CARED LIKE THAT BEFORE.
DON'T WORRY ABOUT THAT LADY. YOU WANT TO KNOW SOMETHING? I HAD A DREAM ONCE THAT I BEAT ONE OF THOSE INSPECTORS UP.
FOR REAL?
YEAH, AND WHEN I WOKE UP, I FELT GREAT.
MS. WILD, DO YOU HAVE ANGER ISSUES?
DOESN'T EVERYONE?

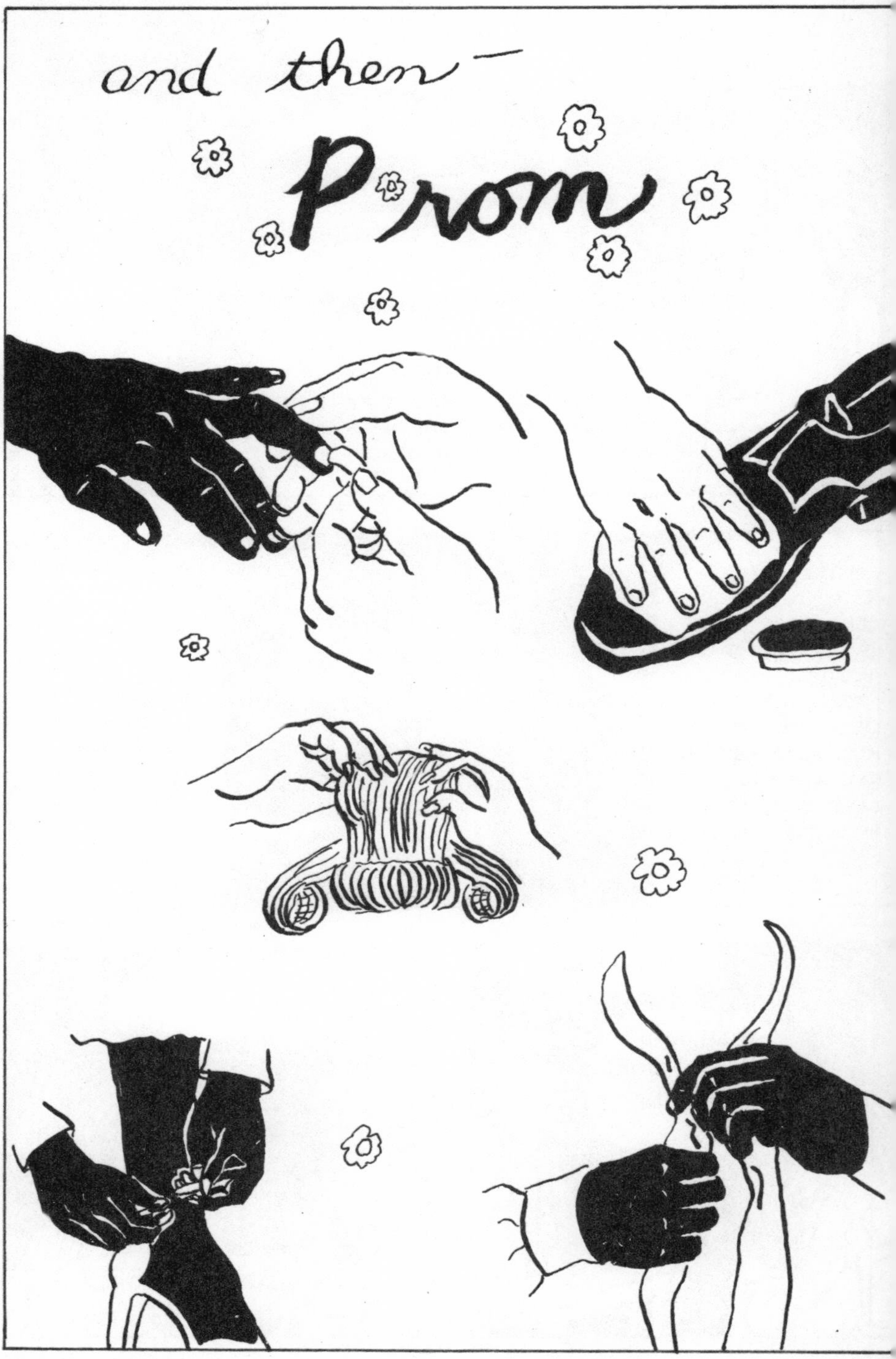
and then –
Prom

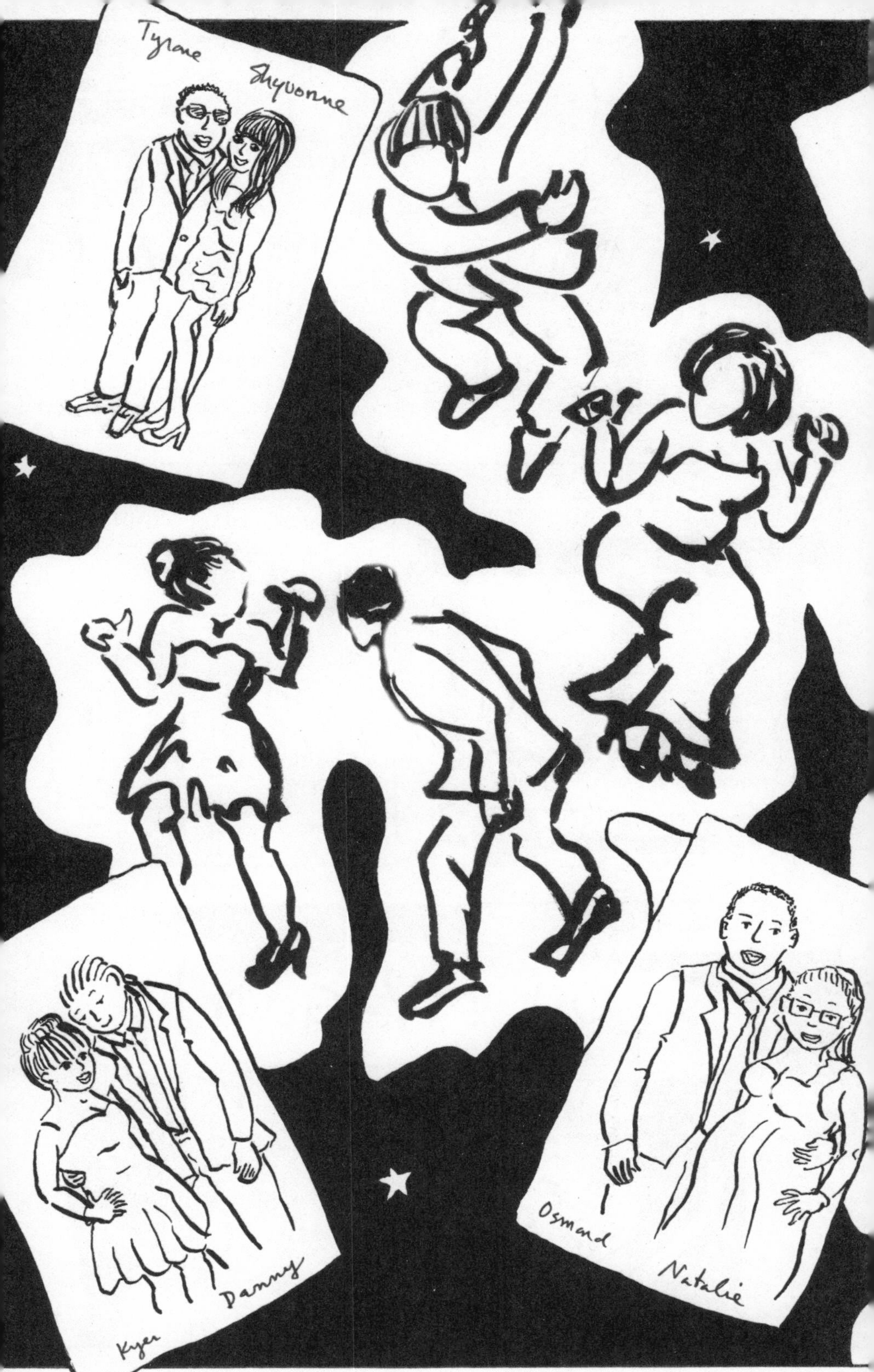

Tyrone
Shyvonne
Danny
Kyer
Osmand
Natalie

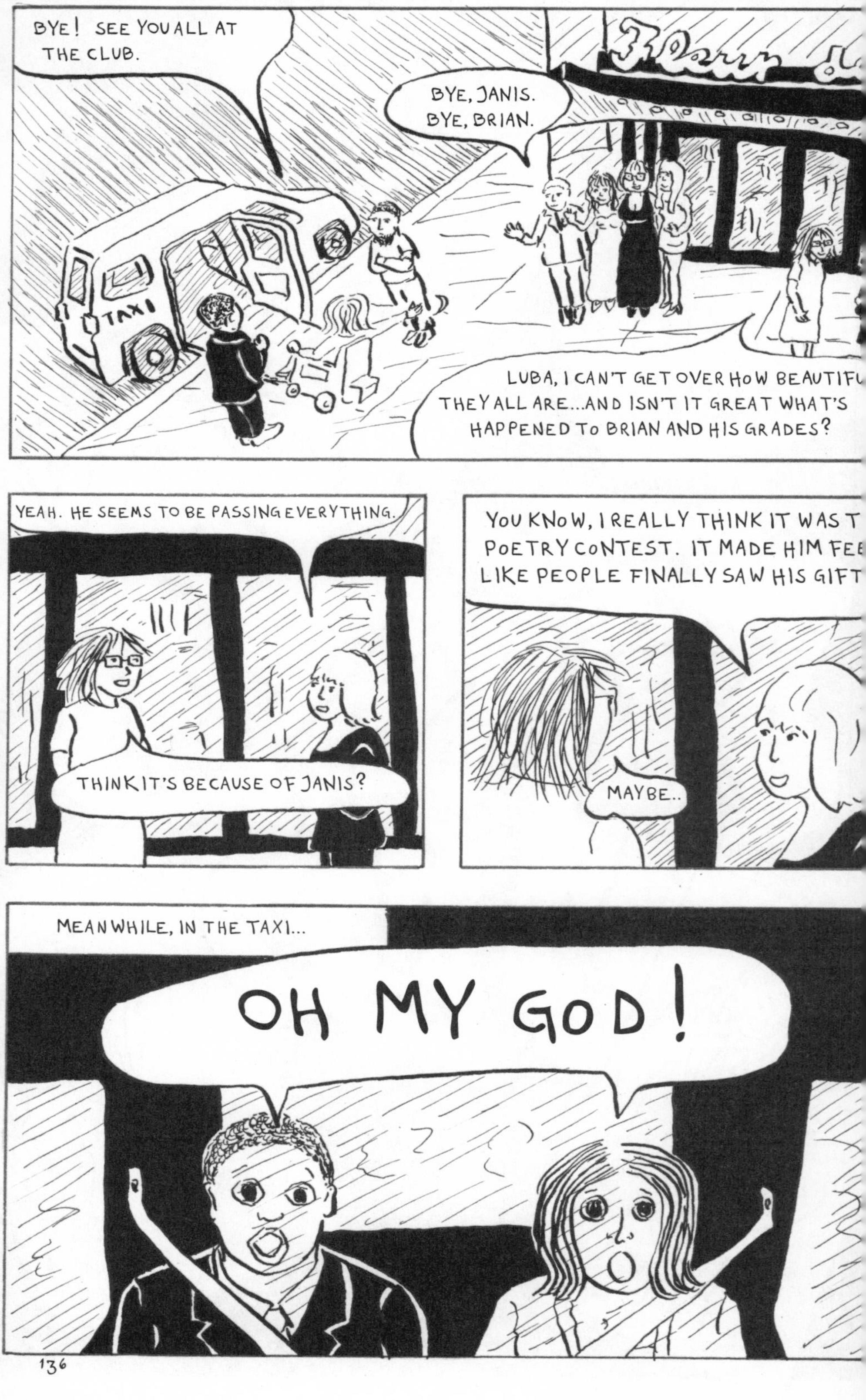
BYE! SEE YOU ALL AT THE CLUB.
BYE, JANIS. BYE, BRIAN.
TAXI
LUBA, I CAN'T GET OVER HOW BEAUTIFU THEY ALL ARE...AND ISN'T IT GREAT WHAT'S HAPPENED TO BRIAN AND HIS GRADES?
YEAH. HE SEEMS TO BE PASSING EVERYTHING.
THINK IT'S BECAUSE OF JANIS?
YOU KNOW, I REALLY THINK IT WAS T POETRY CONTEST. IT MADE HIM FEE LIKE PEOPLE FINALLY SAW HIS GIFT
MAYBE..
MEANWHILE, IN THE TAXI...
OH MY GOD!

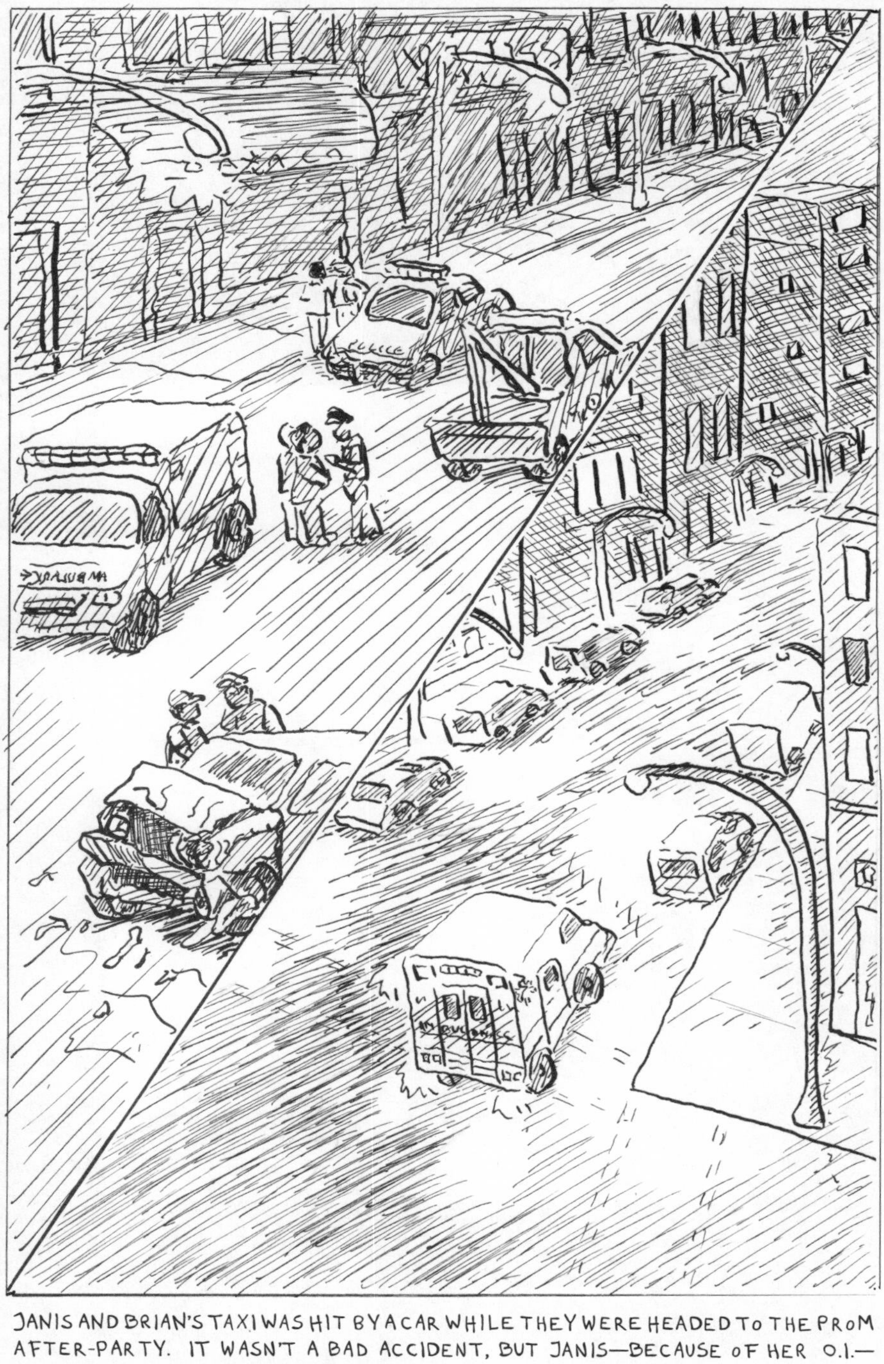

JANIS AND BRIAN'S TAXI WAS HIT BY A CAR WHILE THEY WERE HEADED TO THE PROM AFTER-PARTY. IT WASN'T A BAD ACCIDENT, BUT JANIS—BECAUSE OF HER O.I.—COULD BE IN THE HOSPITAL FOR MONTHS...

"WHAT HAPPENS NEXT?" IS AN INCREDIBLY RESONANT QUESTION FOR OUR STUDENTS. FOR MOST MIDDLE CLASS KIDS, THE NARRATIVE IS DEFINED—GET YOUR HIGH SCHOOL DIPLOMA AND GO TO COLLEGE. BUT OUR STUDENTS' NARRATIVES ARE OFTEN NOT FIXED. PROBLEMS OR TRAGEDIES, WHICH CAN HAPPEN TO ANYONE, ARE NEARLY ALWAYS AMPLIFIED BY POVERTY.

CHAPTER TEN

Go Tell it on the Mountain

"NOT EVERYTHING THAT IS FACED CAN BE
CHANGED, BUT NOTHING CAN BE CHANGED UNTIL
IT IS FACED."

JAMES BALDWIN

THIS IS WHERE IT ALL SHAKES DOWN—WHO'S GOING TO GET THE CREDITS THEY NEED, WHO'S GOING TO PASS THE REGENTS, WHO'S GOING TO WALK ACROSS THE TAGE IN JUNE AND GET A DIPLOMA. THERE'S SO MUCH TO DO, AND SO LITTLE TIME. ALWAYS FEEL I AM BARELY KEEPING UP WITH THE TEACHING, THE GRADING, THE TEST PREP, AND THE TRIAGE.

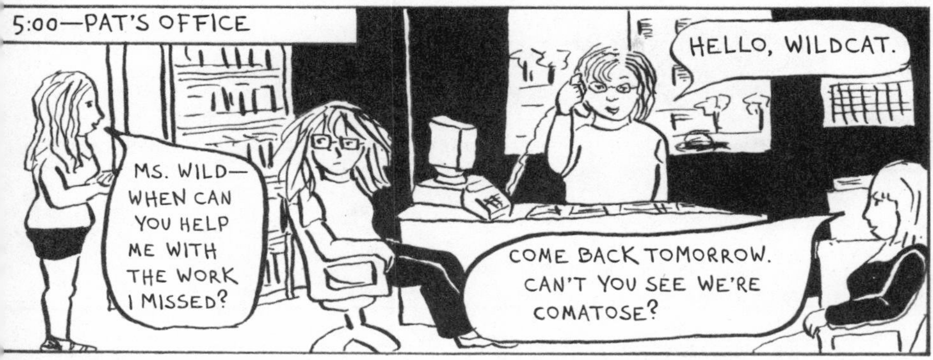
5:00—PAT'S OFFICE
HELLO, WILDCAT.
MS. WILD—WHEN CAN YOU HELP ME WITH THE WORK I MISSED?
COME BACK TOMORROW. CAN'T YOU SEE WE'RE COMATOSE?

AND THEN LIFE GIVES ME A REMINDER THAT PUTS IT ALL IN PERSPECTIVE.

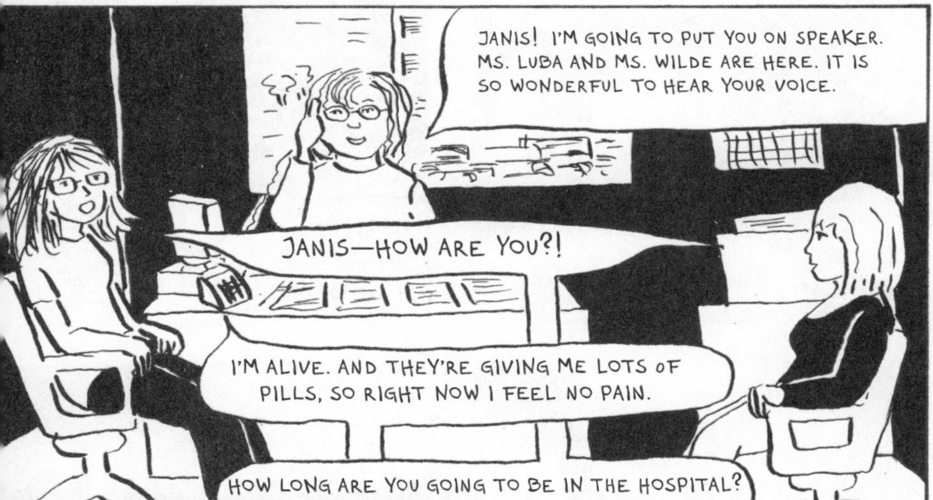
JANIS! I'M GOING TO PUT YOU ON SPEAKER. MS. LUBA AND MS. WILDE ARE HERE. IT IS SO WONDERFUL TO HEAR YOUR VOICE.
JANIS—HOW ARE YOU?!
I'M ALIVE. AND THEY'RE GIVING ME LOTS OF PILLS, SO RIGHT NOW I FEEL NO PAIN.
HOW LONG ARE YOU GOING TO BE IN THE HOSPITAL?

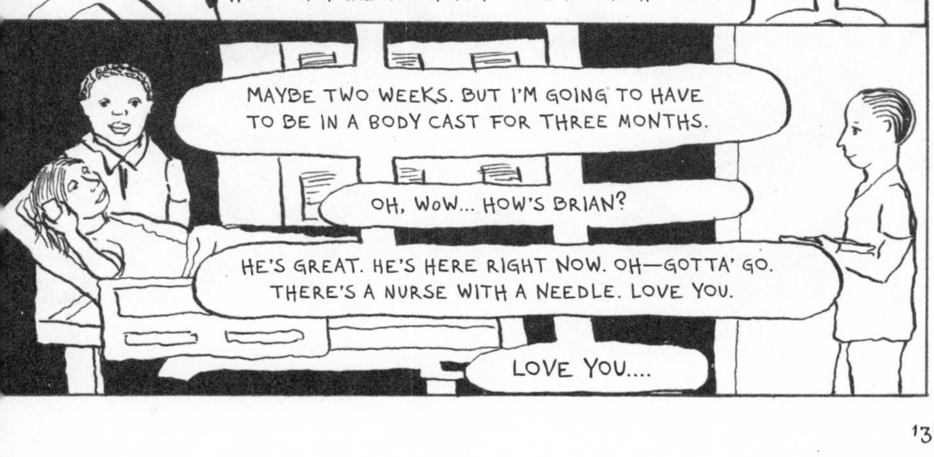
MAYBE TWO WEEKS. BUT I'M GOING TO HAVE TO BE IN A BODY CAST FOR THREE MONTHS.
OH, WOW... HOW'S BRIAN?
HE'S GREAT. HE'S HERE RIGHT NOW. OH—GOTTA' GO. THERE'S A NURSE WITH A NEEDLE. LOVE YOU.
LOVE YOU....

SO JANIS WILL NOT BE GRADUATING IN JUNE. SHE'LL PROBABLY BE AB TO FINISH HER INCOMPLETES OVER THE SUMMER, BUT SHE WILL HAVE TAKE HER FINAL REGENTS NEXT JANUARY. HOWEVER, SHE WILL BE ABLE GRADUATE, AND THAT'S WHAT COUNTS.

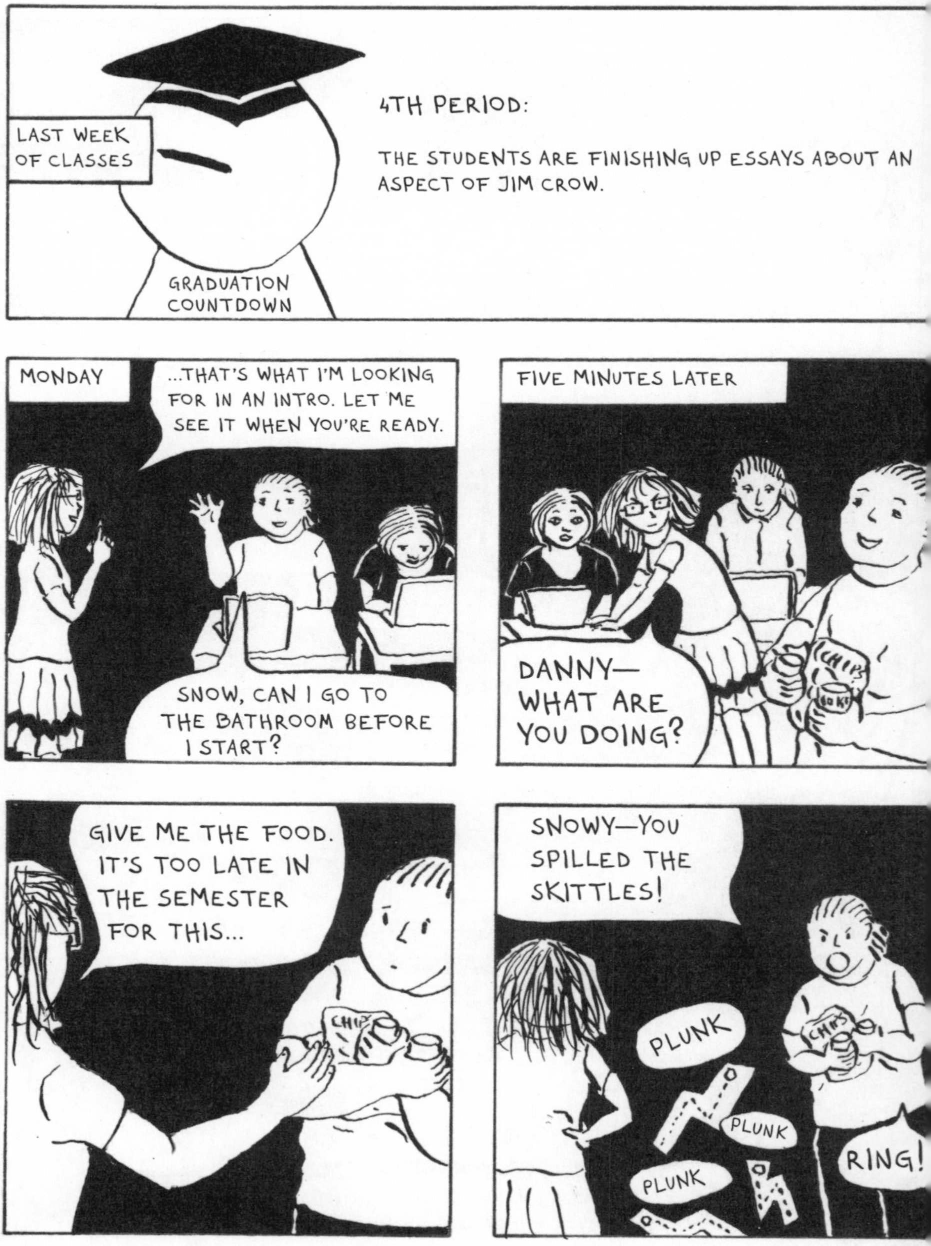
LAST WEEK OF CLASSES
GRADUATION COUNTDOWN
4TH PERIOD:
THE STUDENTS ARE FINISHING UP ESSAYS ABOUT AN ASPECT OF JIM CROW.
MONDAY
...THAT'S WHAT I'M LOOKING FOR IN AN INTRO. LET ME SEE IT WHEN YOU'RE READY.
SNOW, CAN I GO TO THE BATHROOM BEFORE I START?
FIVE MINUTES LATER
DANNY— WHAT ARE YOU DOING?
CHIPS
SODA
GIVE ME THE FOOD. IT'S TOO LATE IN THE SEMESTER FOR THIS...
CHIPS
SNOWY—YOU SPILLED THE SKITTLES!
PLUNK
PLUNK
PLUNK
CHIPS
RING!

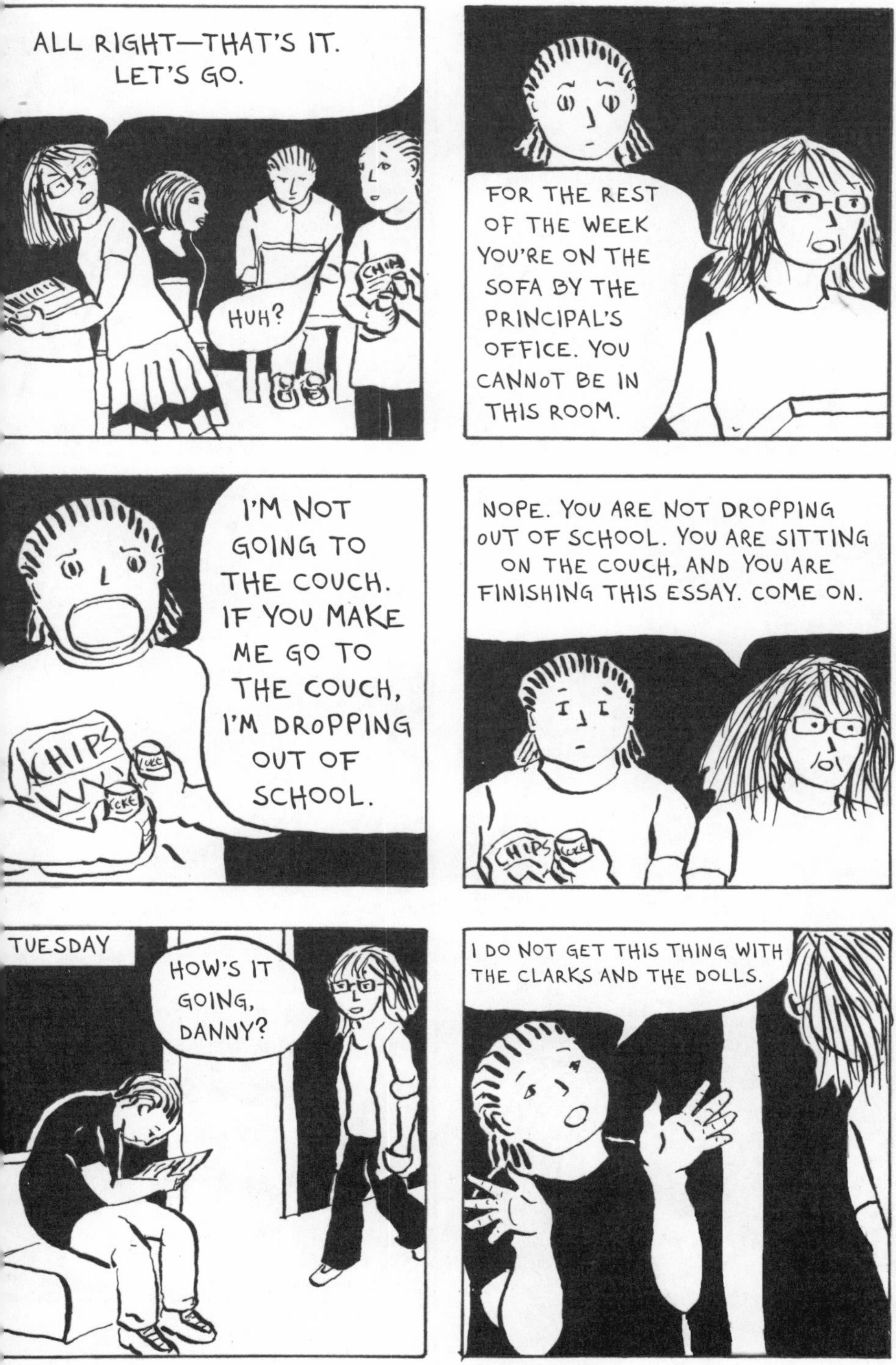
ALL RIGHT—THAT'S IT. LET'S GO.
HUH?
CHIPS
FOR THE REST OF THE WEEK YOU'RE ON THE SOFA BY THE PRINCIPAL'S OFFICE. YOU CANNOT BE IN THIS ROOM.
I'M NOT GOING TO THE COUCH. IF YOU MAKE ME GO TO THE COUCH, I'M DROPPING OUT OF SCHOOL.
CHIPS
COKE
NOPE. YOU ARE NOT DROPPING OUT OF SCHOOL. YOU ARE SITTING ON THE COUCH, AND YOU ARE FINISHING THIS ESSAY. COME ON.
CHIPS
TUESDAY
HOW'S IT GOING, DANNY?
I DO NOT GET THIS THING WITH THE CLARKS AND THE DOLLS.

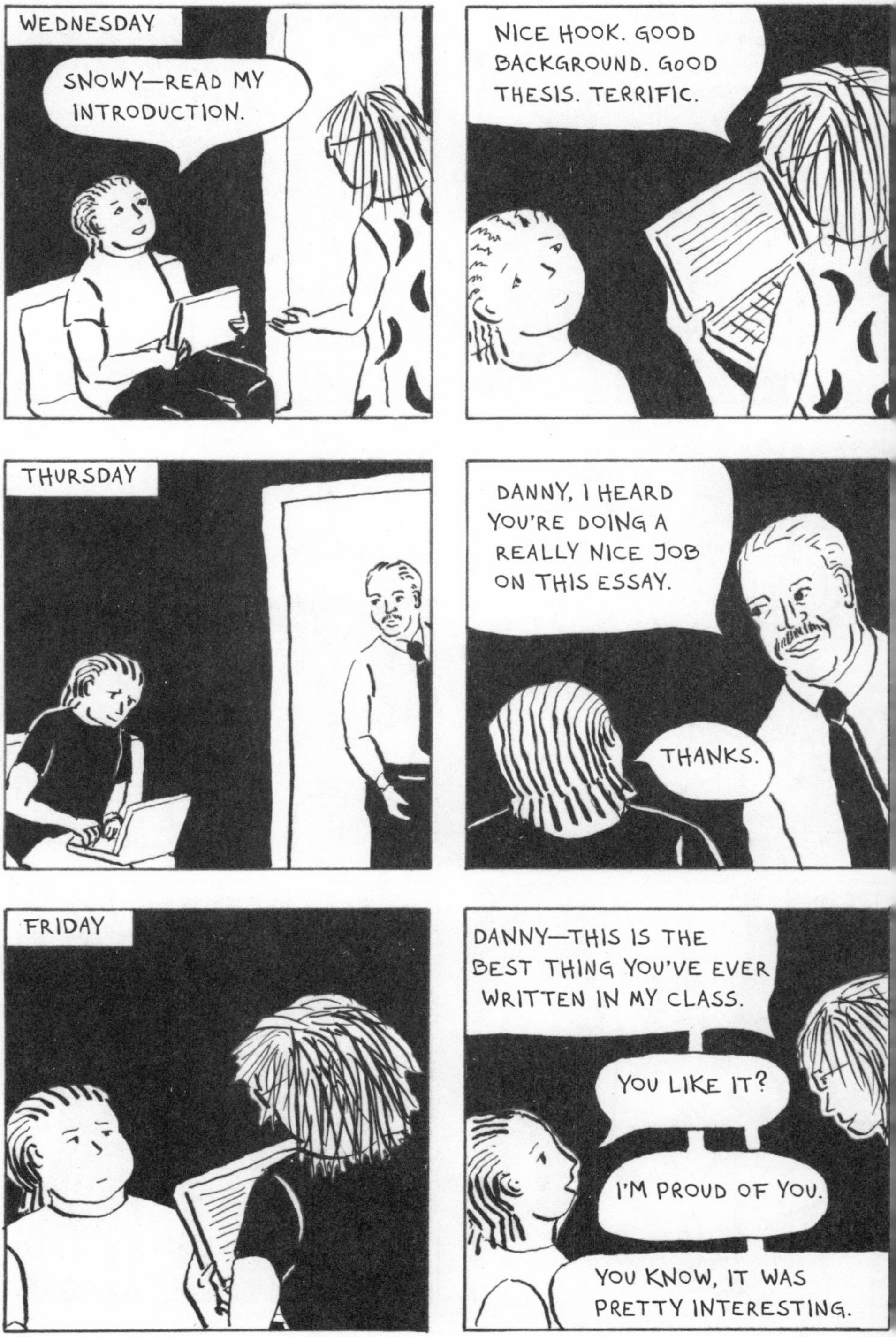
WEDNESDAY
SNOWY—READ MY INTRODUCTION.
NICE HOOK. GOOD BACKGROUND. GOOD THESIS. TERRIFIC.
THURSDAY
DANNY, I HEARD YOU'RE DOING A REALLY NICE JOB ON THIS ESSAY.
THANKS.
FRIDAY
DANNY—THIS IS THE BEST THING YOU'VE EVER WRITTEN IN MY CLASS.
YOU LIKE IT?
I'M PROUD OF YOU.
YOU KNOW, IT WAS PRETTY INTERESTING.

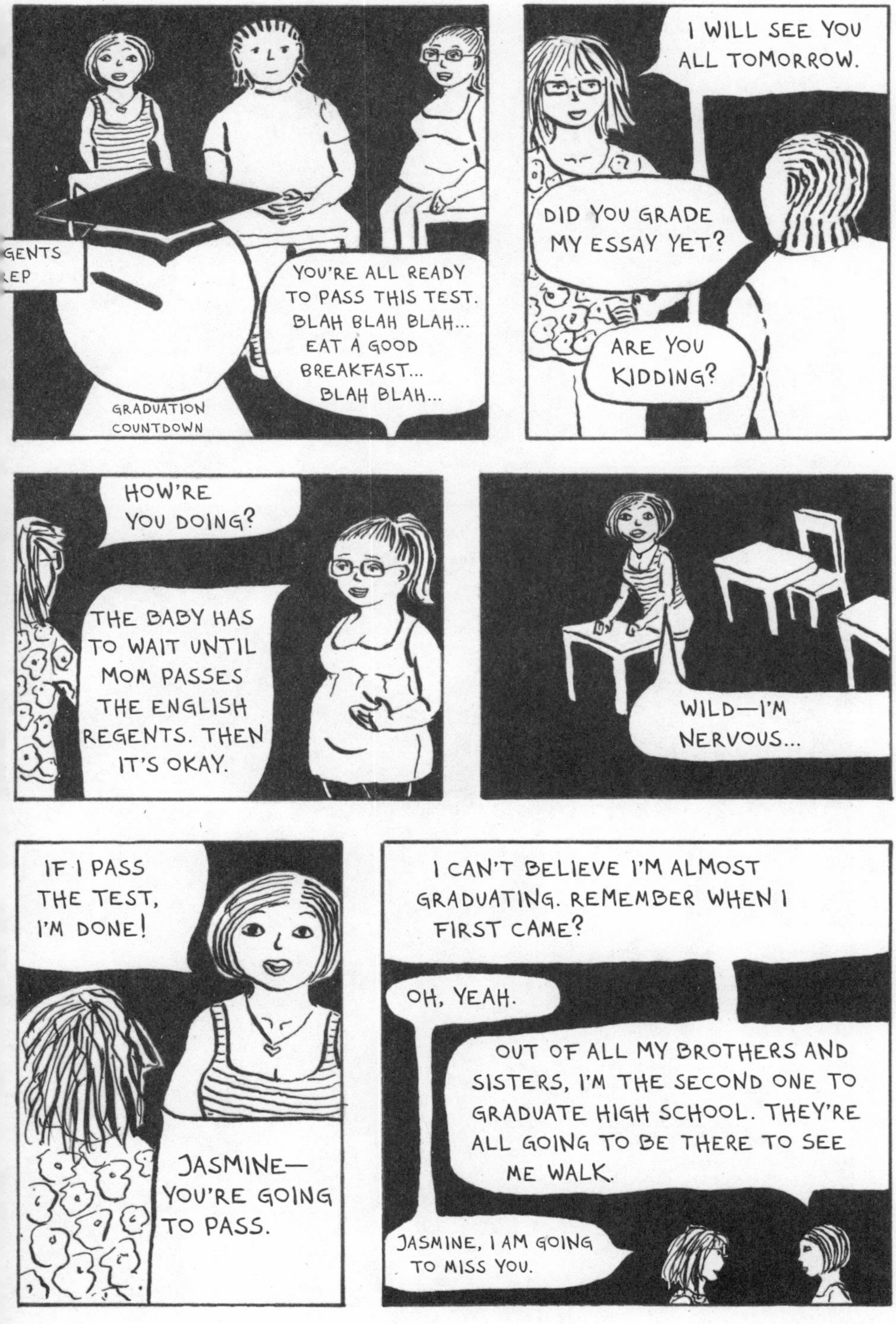
GENTS
EP
GRADUATION COUNTDOWN
YOU'RE ALL READY TO PASS THIS TEST. BLAH BLAH BLAH... EAT A GOOD BREAKFAST... BLAH BLAH...
I WILL SEE YOU ALL TOMORROW.
DID YOU GRADE MY ESSAY YET?
ARE YOU KIDDING?
HOW'RE YOU DOING?
THE BABY HAS TO WAIT UNTIL MOM PASSES THE ENGLISH REGENTS. THEN IT'S OKAY.
WILD—I'M NERVOUS...
IF I PASS THE TEST, I'M DONE!
JASMINE—YOU'RE GOING TO PASS.
I CAN'T BELIEVE I'M ALMOST GRADUATING. REMEMBER WHEN I FIRST CAME?
OH, YEAH.
OUT OF ALL MY BROTHERS AND SISTERS, I'M THE SECOND ONE TO GRADUATE HIGH SCHOOL. THEY'RE ALL GOING TO BE THERE TO SEE ME WALK.
JASMINE, I AM GOING TO MISS YOU.

9:15 - MORNING OF THE ENGLISH REGENTS

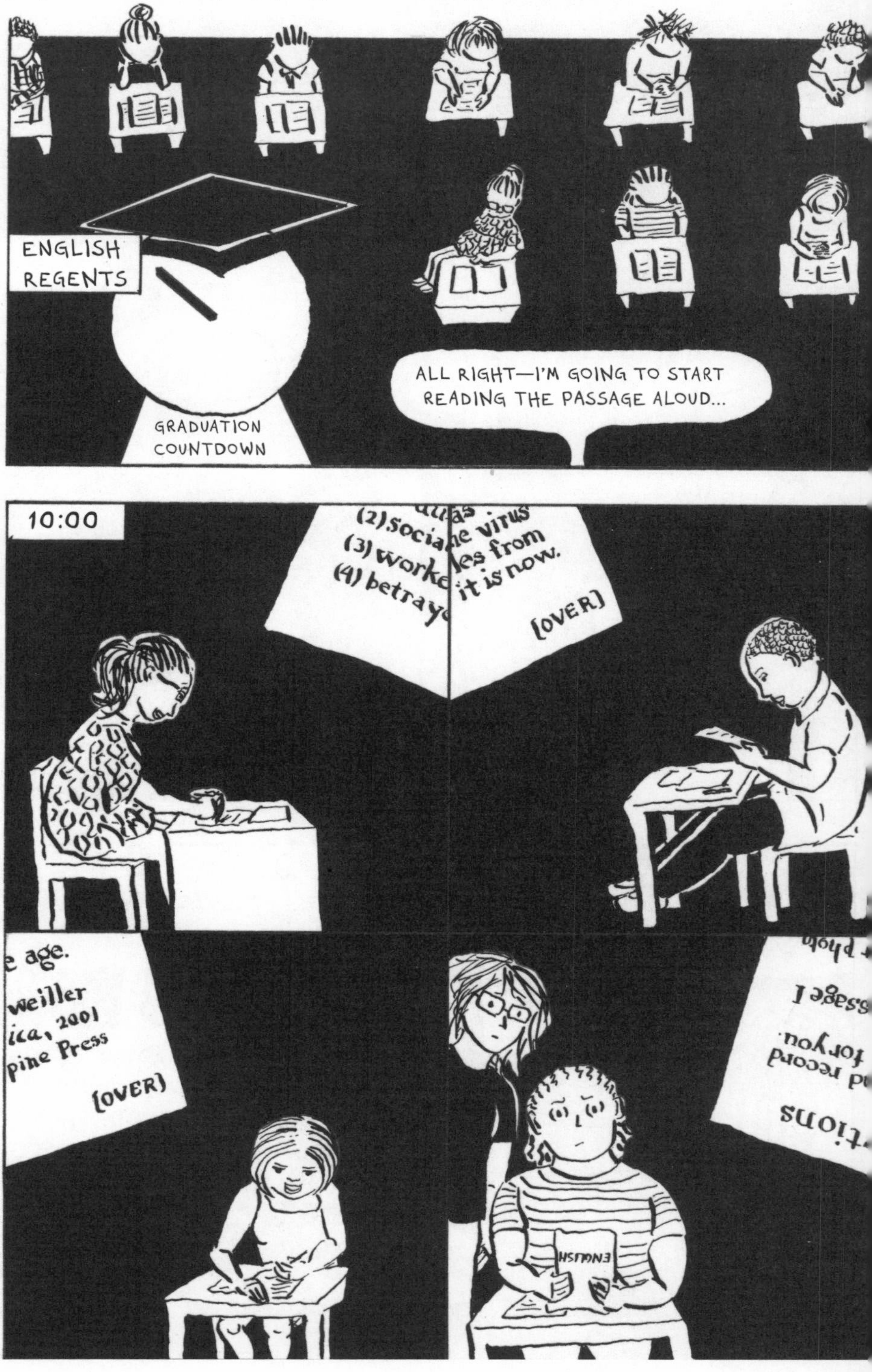
ENGLISH REGENTS
GRADUATION COUNTDOWN
ALL RIGHT—I'M GOING TO START READING THE PASSAGE ALOUD...
10:00
(2) socia
(3) worke
(4) betray
e virus
les from
it is now.
[OVER]
e age.
weiller
ica, 2001
pine Press
[OVER]

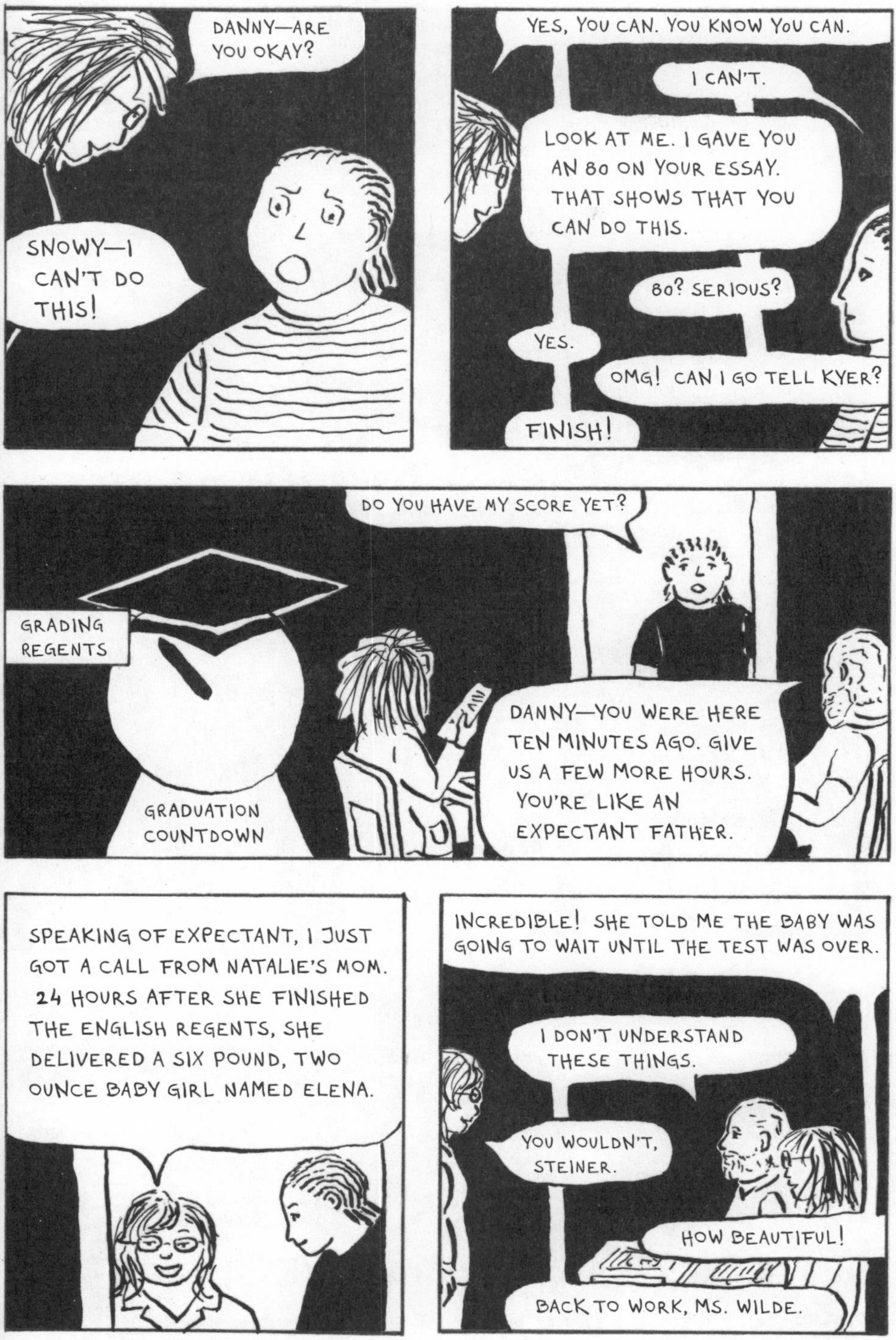
DANNY—ARE YOU OKAY?
SNOWY—I CAN'T DO THIS!
YES, YOU CAN. YOU KNOW YOU CAN.
I CAN'T.
LOOK AT ME. I GAVE YOU AN 80 ON YOUR ESSAY. THAT SHOWS THAT YOU CAN DO THIS.
80? SERIOUS?
YES.
OMG! CAN I GO TELL KYER?
FINISH!
GRADING REGENTS
GRADUATION COUNTDOWN
DO YOU HAVE MY SCORE YET?
DANNY—YOU WERE HERE TEN MINUTES AGO. GIVE US A FEW MORE HOURS. YOU'RE LIKE AN EXPECTANT FATHER.
SPEAKING OF EXPECTANT, I JUST GOT A CALL FROM NATALIE'S MOM. 24 HOURS AFTER SHE FINISHED THE ENGLISH REGENTS, SHE DELIVERED A SIX POUND, TWO OUNCE BABY GIRL NAMED ELENA.
INCREDIBLE! SHE TOLD ME THE BABY WAS GOING TO WAIT UNTIL THE TEST WAS OVER.
I DON'T UNDERSTAND THESE THINGS.
YOU WOULDN'T, STEINER.
HOW BEAUTIFUL!
BACK TO WORK, MS. WILDE.

IN A FILM, THE NEXT PANEL WOULD BE A FREEZE FRAME AS WE FIND OUT WHO WIL GRADUATE. IN A FAIRY TALE OR A STORY TOLD TO FULFILL THE DESIRES OF THE CITY, STAT AND FEDERAL BUREAUCRACIES, ALL THE CHARACTERS WOULD BE GETTING THAT PIECE PAPER IN A WEEK. BUT THIS IS NOT THAT STORY. EVEN THOUGH DANNY SEEMS AFFECTED DIVINE INTERVENTION (OR A BIT OF MATURITY), HE DOESN'T HAVE ENOUGH CREDITS TO DONE IN JUNE. IT IS ALSO CLEAR THAT WILL IS NOT GOING TO BE GRADUATING NOW, IF EVE

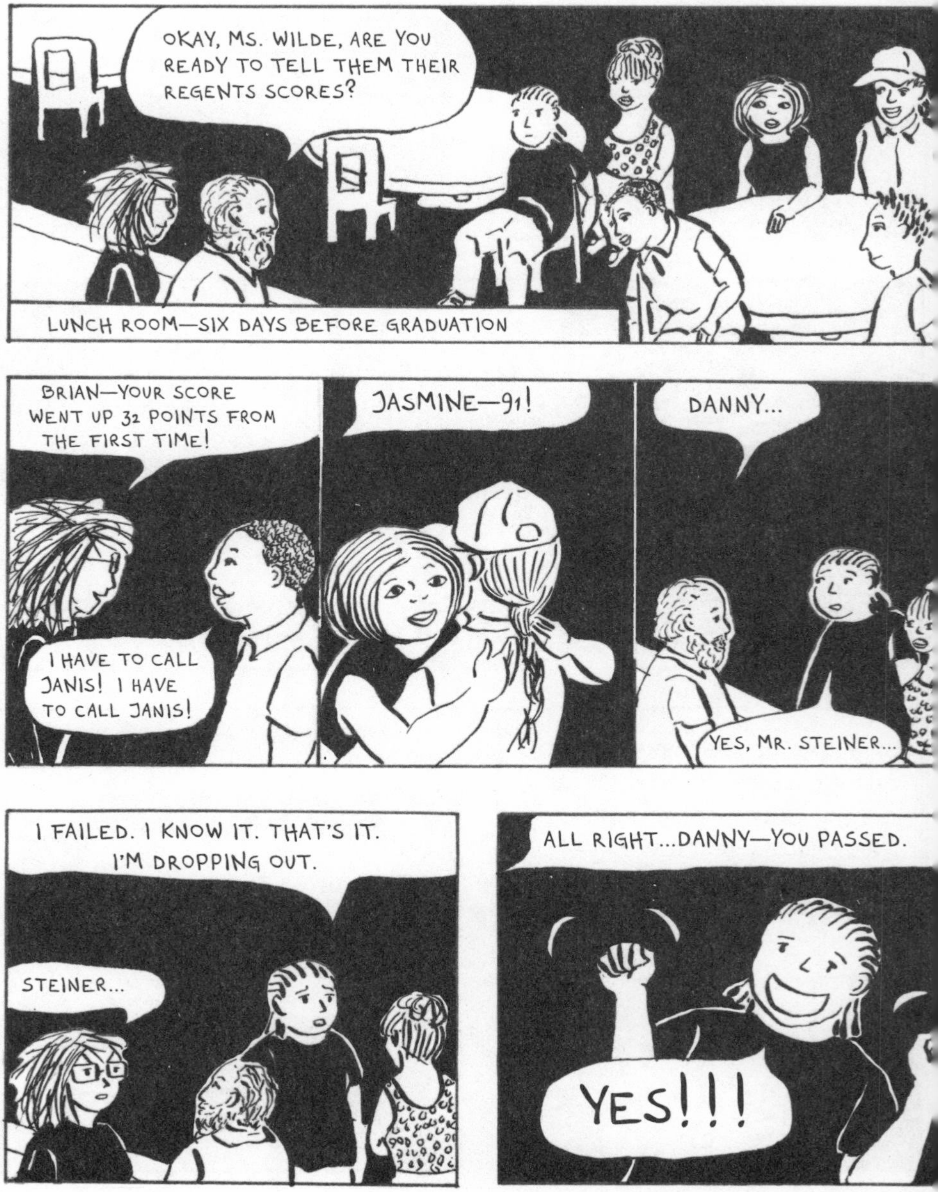

OKAY, MS. WILDE, ARE YOU READY TO TELL THEM THEIR REGENTS SCORES?
LUNCH ROOM—SIX DAYS BEFORE GRADUATION
BRIAN—YOUR SCORE WENT UP 32 POINTS FROM THE FIRST TIME!
I HAVE TO CALL JANIS! I HAVE TO CALL JANIS!
JASMINE—91!
DANNY...
YES, MR. STEINER...
I FAILED. I KNOW IT. THAT'S IT. I'M DROPPING OUT.
STEINER...
ALL RIGHT...DANNY—YOU PASSED.
YES!!!

ALTERNATIVE YEARBOOK

written and photographed by Wildcat Yearbook Staff

Jasmine Jones

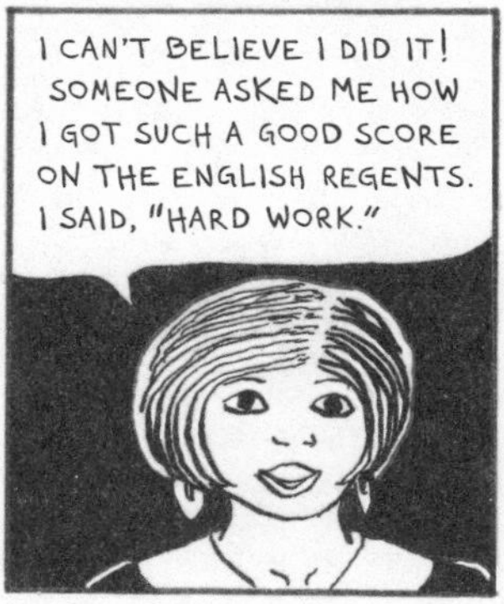
I CAN'T BELIEVE I DID IT! SOMEONE ASKED ME HOW I GOT SUCH A GOOD SCORE ON THE ENGLISH REGENTS. I SAID, "HARD WORK."

Graduating for Jasmine means accomplishing a goal she has set for her life. It wasn't easy for her to get to this point because she had a number of obstacles to overcome, but she didn't give up and now she will be attending college in the fall—the first person in her family to go. Congratulations, Jasmine.

Daniel Acosta

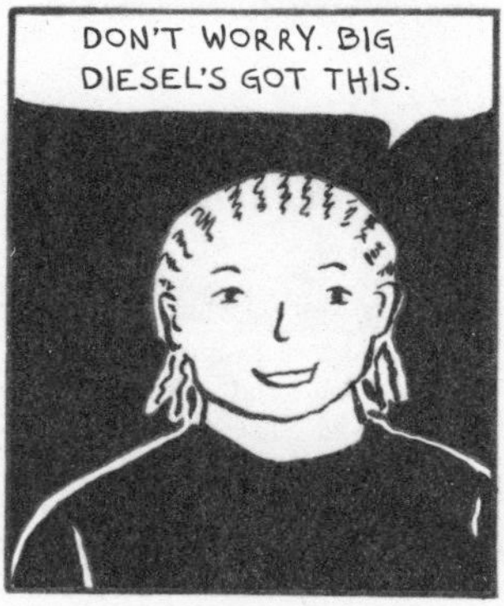
DON'T WORRY. BIG DIESEL'S GOT THIS.

Danny ended the semester in a great way— passing seven classes and getting a 72 on the English Regents. All Danny needs to graduate are twelve more credits and the U.S. History Regents, so expect him to be wearing a cap and gown next June.

Ralphie Gonzalez

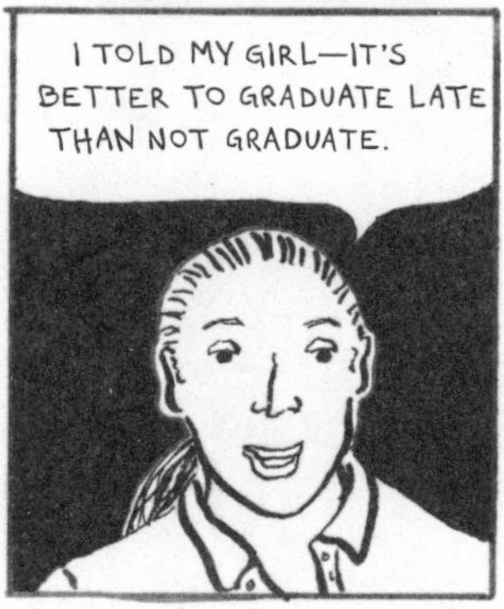
I TOLD MY GIRL—IT'S BETTER TO GRADUATE LATE THAN NOT GRADUATE.

Ralphie had to stop coming to school at the beginning of the semester because he had to work for his dad, but now he's back and he's better than ever. Ralphie plans on graduating next year, and then getting an apprenticehip in carpentry or electrical work.

Kyer Spencer

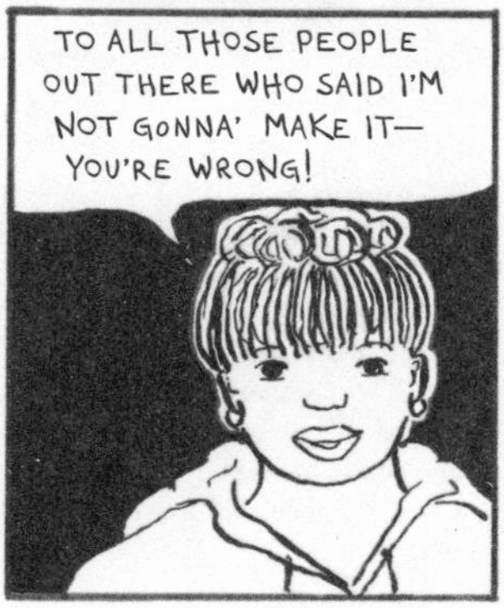
TO ALL THOSE PEOPLE OUT THERE WHO SAID I'M NOT GONNA' MAKE IT— YOU'RE WRONG!

Since she's been at Wildcat, Kyer has come a long way. She's already passed all her Regents, and this semester she passed every class. She hopes to graduate next spring and then go to college to achieve her dream of being a poet.

Brian Brooks

IT'S PRETTY COOL TO BE GRADUATING. JANIS— HANG IN THERE.

Brian is very excited to be graduating and moving on with his life. Once Brian decided to focus, graduating was not that difficult. Brian will be attending a CUNY school this fall to study computer graphic design. Good work, Brian.

Janis Diaz

BROKEN BONES ARE NOT GOING TO STOP ME FROM ACHIEVING MY DREAMS.

Janis is not letting her accident hold her back. She's going to graduate in January, and because of her *Radio Rookies* experience, she is going to go to college to become a disability rights advocate. Janis will be the first person in her family to graduate from high school.

Will Smith

I CAN'T DEAL WITH SCHOOL RIGHT NOW.

Will was on the Honor Roll first semester, but had to take a leave of absence second semester to take care of some personal business. Once things get more settled in his life, Will hopes to be back in school and finish his degree.

Natalie Maldonado

I AM SO PROUD OF EVERYONE WHO IS GRADUATING TODAY...

JOHN V. LINDSAY

WILDCAT ACADEMY

Natalie had a few rough moments this semester, being that she was pregnant, but it all worked out and now she is the proud mother of Elena. Natalie will take a year to stay home with her baby, but then it will be college and pursuing her dream of beoming a journalist. Great job, Natalie!

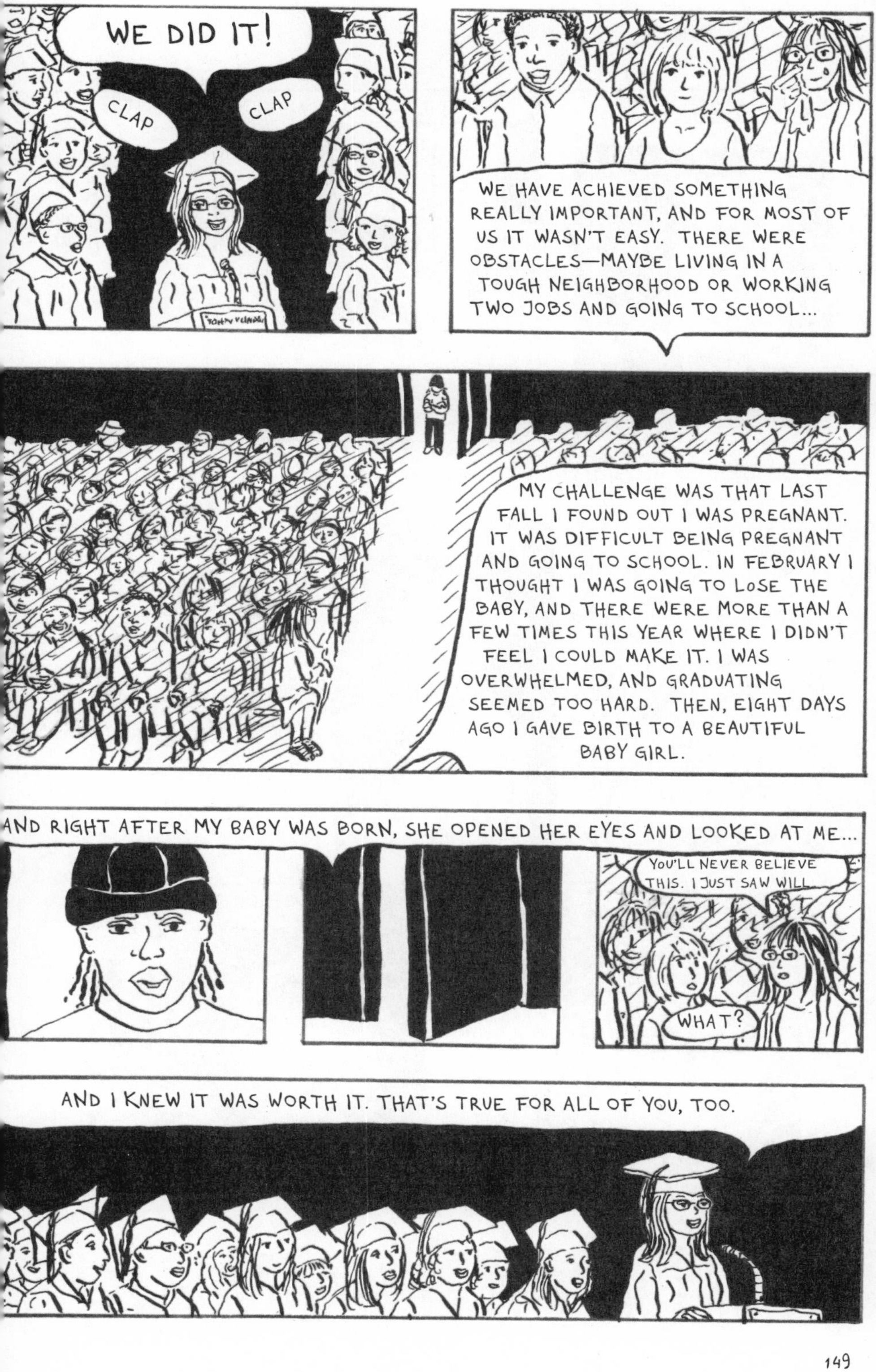
WE DID IT!
CLAP
CLAP
WE HAVE ACHIEVED SOMETHING REALLY IMPORTANT, AND FOR MOST OF US IT WASN'T EASY. THERE WERE OBSTACLES—MAYBE LIVING IN A TOUGH NEIGHBORHOOD OR WORKING TWO JOBS AND GOING TO SCHOOL...
MY CHALLENGE WAS THAT LAST FALL I FOUND OUT I WAS PREGNANT. IT WAS DIFFICULT BEING PREGNANT AND GOING TO SCHOOL. IN FEBRUARY I THOUGHT I WAS GOING TO LOSE THE BABY, AND THERE WERE MORE THAN A FEW TIMES THIS YEAR WHERE I DIDN'T FEEL I COULD MAKE IT. I WAS OVERWHELMED, AND GRADUATING SEEMED TOO HARD. THEN, EIGHT DAYS AGO I GAVE BIRTH TO A BEAUTIFUL BABY GIRL.
AND RIGHT AFTER MY BABY WAS BORN, SHE OPENED HER EYES AND LOOKED AT ME...
YOU'LL NEVER BELIEVE THIS. I JUST SAW WILL.
WHAT?
AND I KNEW IT WAS WORTH IT. THAT'S TRUE FOR ALL OF YOU, TOO.

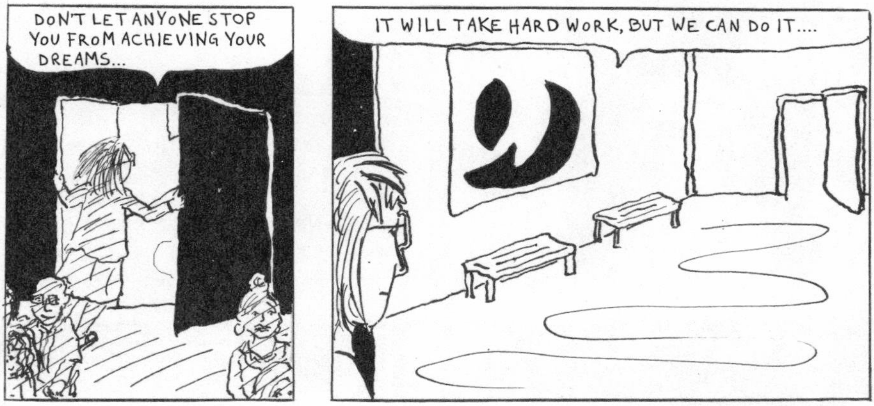
DON'T LET ANYONE STOP YOU FROM ACHIEVING YOUR DREAMS...
IT WILL TAKE HARD WORK, BUT WE CAN DO IT....

BACK INSIDE THE AUDITORIUM

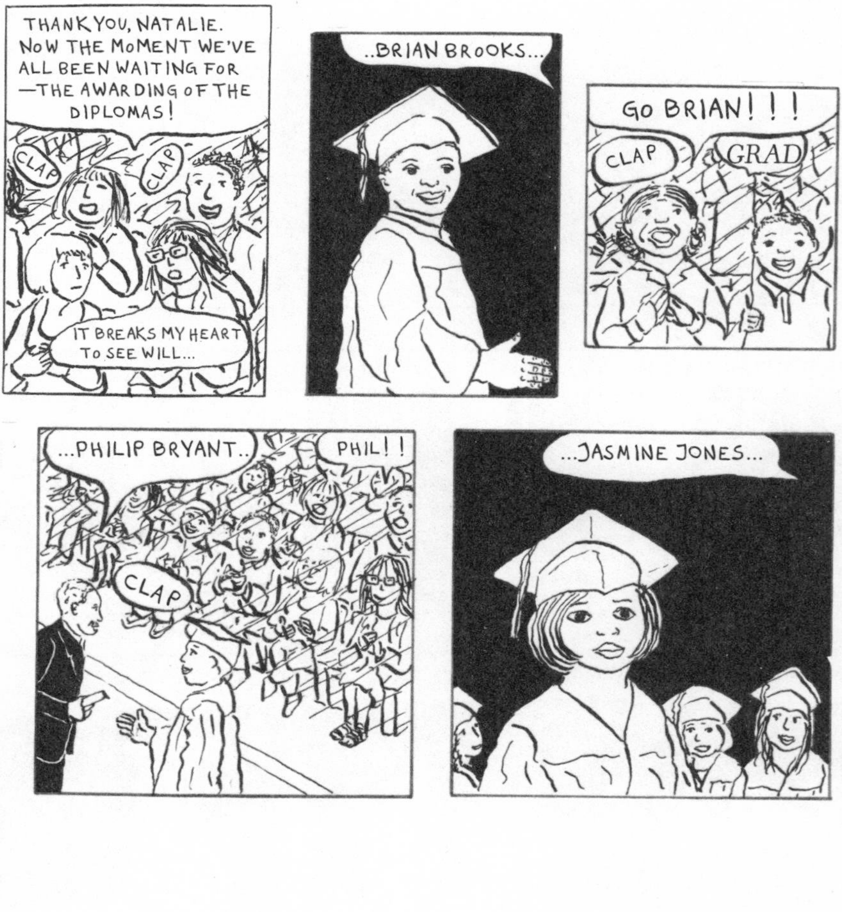
THANK YOU, NATALIE. NOW THE MOMENT WE'VE ALL BEEN WAITING FOR —THE AWARDING OF THE DIPLOMAS!
CLAP
CLAP
IT BREAKS MY HEART TO SEE WILL...
..BRIAN BROOKS...
GO BRIAN!!!
CLAP
GRAD
...PHILIP BRYANT..
PHIL!!
CLAP
...JASMINE JONES...

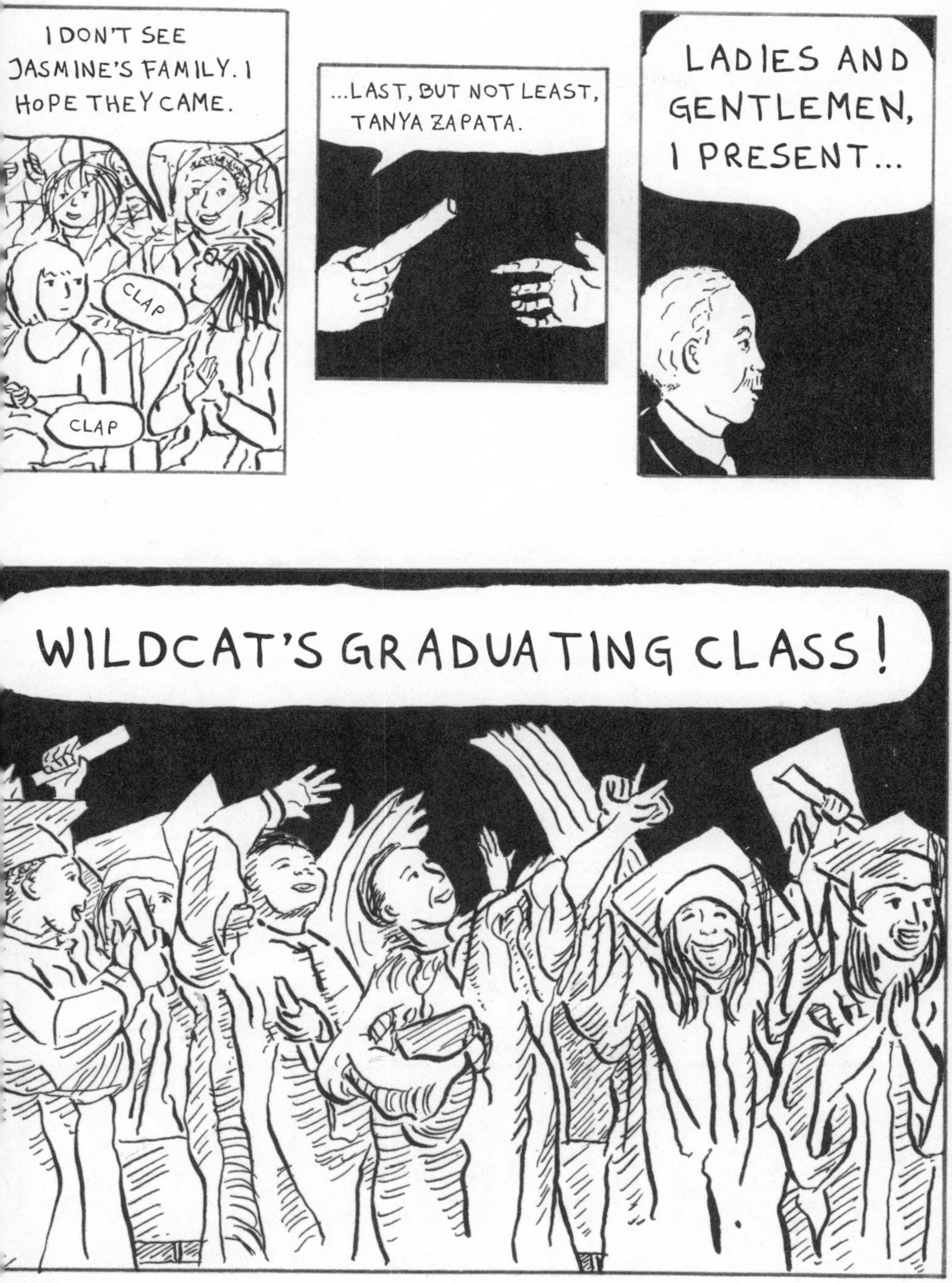
I DON'T SEE JASMINE'S FAMILY. I HOPE THEY CAME.
CLAP
CLAP
...LAST, BUT NOT LEAST, TANYA ZAPATA.
LADIES AND GENTLEMEN, I PRESENT...
WILDCAT'S GRADUATING CLASS!

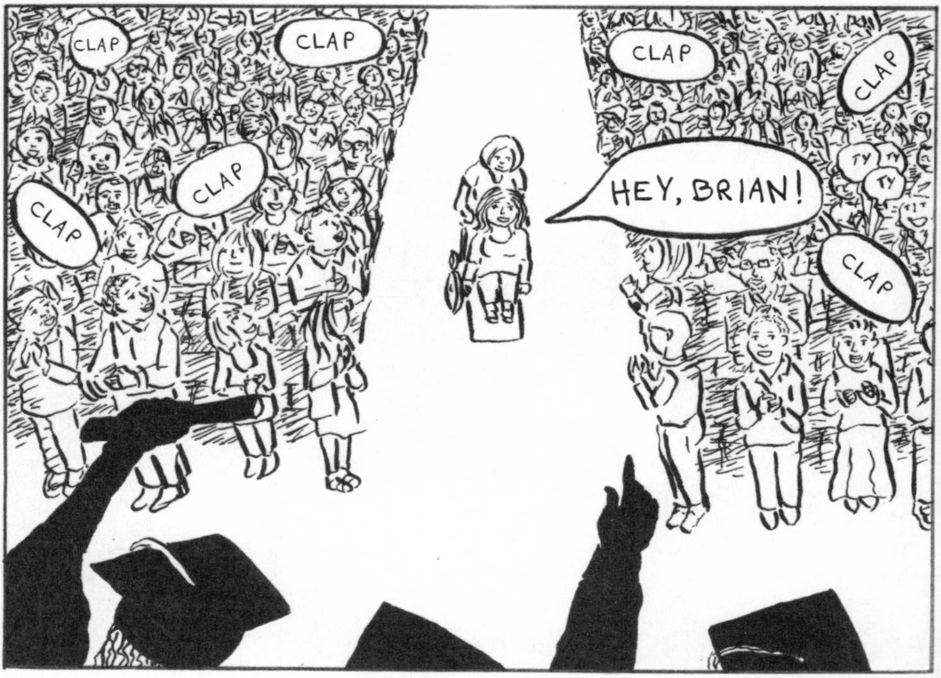
CLAP
CLAP
CLAP
CLAP
CLAP
HEY, BRIAN!
TY
TY
TY
CLAP
CLAP

AFTER THE CEREMONY

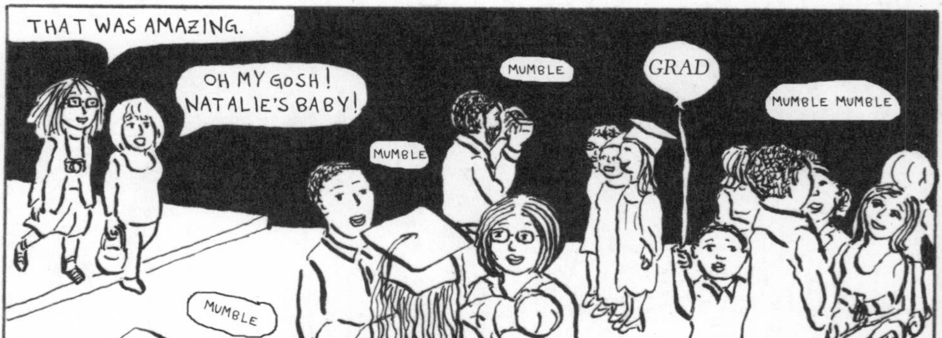
THAT WAS AMAZING.
OH MY GOSH! NATALIE'S BABY!
MUMBLE
GRAD
MUMBLE MUMBLE
MUMBLE
MUMBLE

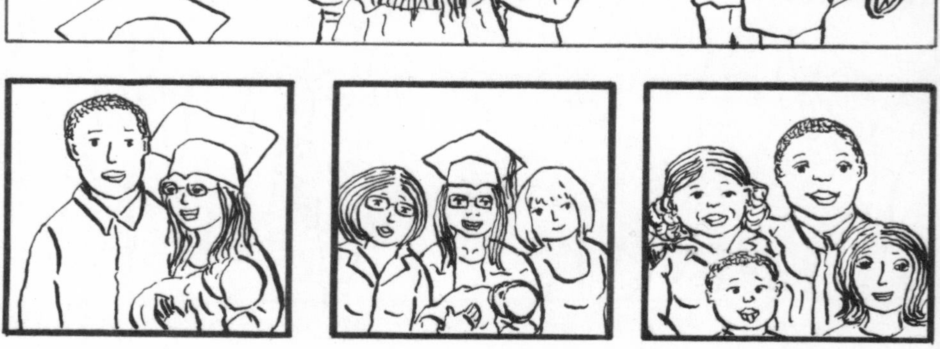

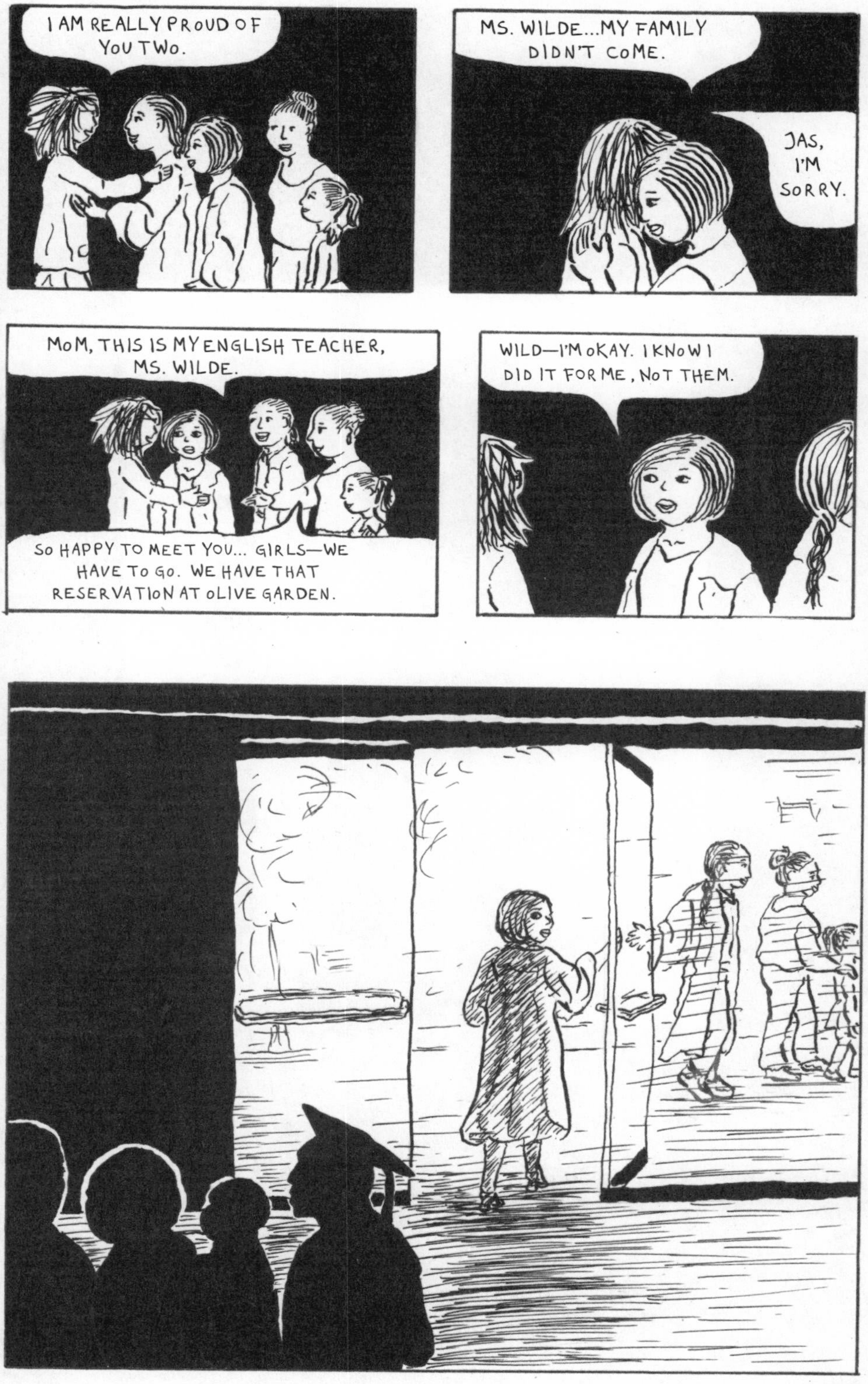
I AM REALLY PROUD OF YOU TWO.
MS. WILDE...MY FAMILY DIDN'T COME.
JAS, I'M SORRY.
MOM, THIS IS MY ENGLISH TEACHER, MS. WILDE.
SO HAPPY TO MEET YOU... GIRLS—WE HAVE TO GO. WE HAVE THAT RESERVATION AT OLIVE GARDEN.
WILD—I'M OKAY. I KNOW I DID IT FOR ME, NOT THEM.

EPILOGUE

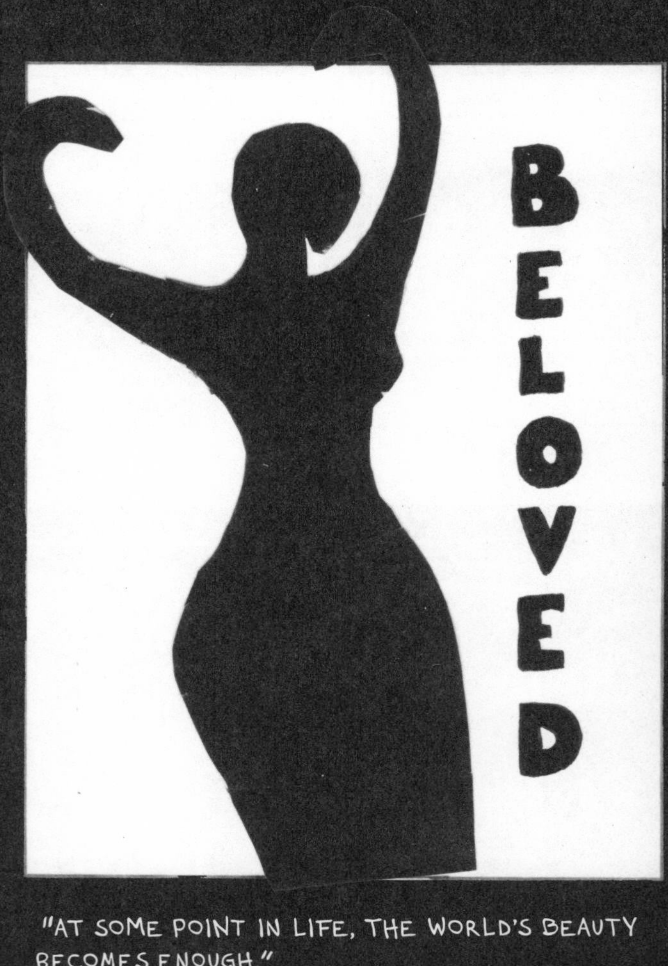
BELOVED

"AT SOME POINT IN LIFE, THE WORLD'S BEAUTY BECOMES ENOUGH."

TONI MORRISON

LEAVING GRADUATION

ALL I CAN SAY IS "WOW!"

BETWEEN NATALIE'S SPEECH AND JANIS'S APPEARANCE, IT WAS A THREE HANKIE GRADUATION. YOU LADIES READY TO GET ON THE TRAIN?

I'M GOING BACK TO SCHOOL. THERE ARE SOME BOOKS I FORGOT, AND I JUST WANT TO WALK A BIT.

BYE. I'LL MISS YOU BOTH.

STAY IN TOUCH.

A FEW NIGHTS AGO I HAD A DREAM WHERE I WAS SWIMMING IN A RIVER, AND MY FAMILY WAS THERE, ALONG WITH SOME STUDENTS.

ON BOTH SIDES OF THE RIVER WAS A CITY, BUT THE WATER WAS CLEAN. EVERYTHING WAS BEAUTIFUL AND THE MOOD WAS PEACEFUL.

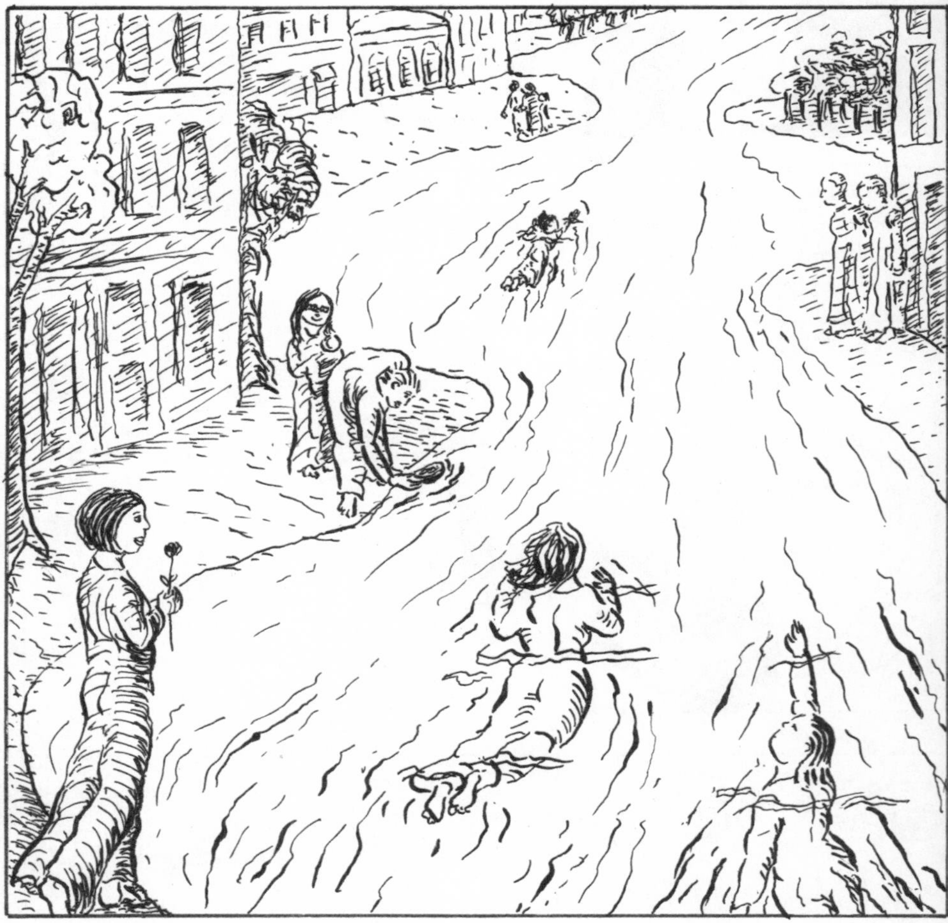

WHEN I WOKE UP, I REALIZED THE IMAGE WAS LIKE A DRAWING, BY WILLIAM BLAKE, CALLED "THE RIVER OF LIFE." AND I THOUGHT, YES—THIS IS WHAT I WANT FOR ALL OF US—A LITTLE HAPPINESS IN THIS BEAUTIFUL RIVER CALLED LIFE.

...AND I ALSO REALIZED THAT I REALLY NEEDED SUMMER BREAK, AND THAT WAS WHAT WOULD ALLOW ME TO DIVE BACK IN WITH THESE KIDS IN FALL.

BACK AT SCHOOL

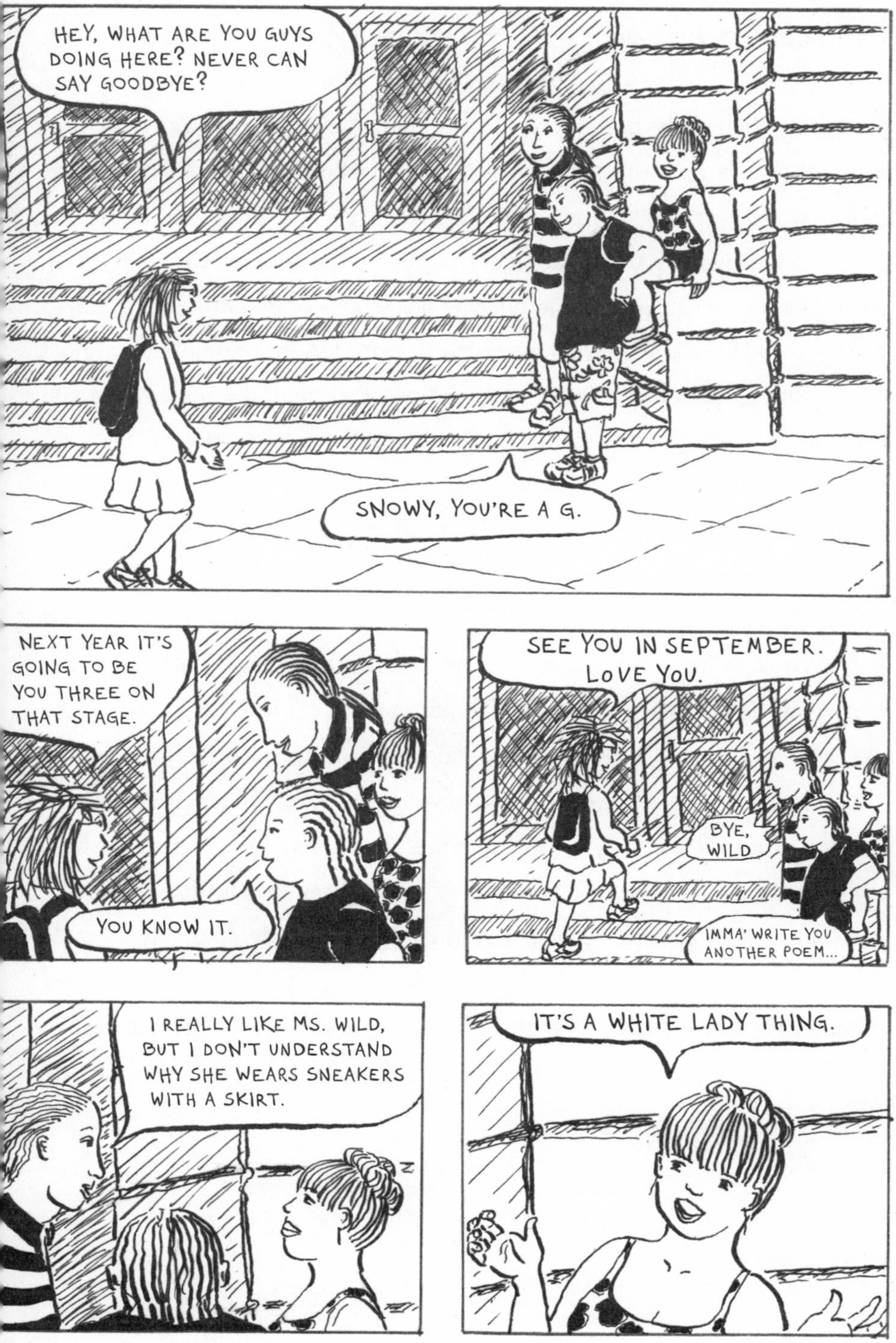
HEY, WHAT ARE YOU GUYS DOING HERE? NEVER CAN SAY GOODBYE?
SNOWY, YOU'RE A G.
NEXT YEAR IT'S GOING TO BE YOU THREE ON THAT STAGE.
YOU KNOW IT.
SEE YOU IN SEPTEMBER. LOVE YOU.
BYE, WILD
IMMA' WRITE YOU ANOTHER POEM...
I REALLY LIKE MS. WILD, BUT I DON'T UNDERSTAND WHY SHE WEARS SNEAKERS WITH A SKIRT.
IT'S A WHITE LADY THING.

AFTERWORD

I have been teaching since 1997, and during that time period I have seen many positive changes in public education. The kids who come to our school are definitely better prepared academically than in the past, and some of that is directly attributable to higher standards enforced through standardized testing.

However, in this brave new world of trying to verify everything with data, it is critical to value what is not so easily quantifiable, but also what we—as humans—know has worth. Creativity, for example, is almost impossible to evaluate using a standardized test, and the increase in the amount of standardized testing and its significance to the survival of public schools has lead—in many schools—to dropping creative, imaginative assignments and course options in favor of ones that help raise a student's test score.

One of the biggest challenges for public education going forward is how to enforce (and measure) academic skill success, while fostering what may be unmeasurable. This is particularly critical for students like the ones at Wildcat, where many of the kids are, as Jack Kerouac wrote, "The ones who see things differently," students who often have gifts that are not captured through multiple-choice questions. These are also kids whose access to resources outside of school is limited, and for whom the consequences of graduating or not graduating can be life changing.

Ultimately, we need public schools that policy makers would feel comfortable sending their own children to. As a society, we need to realize that these children—all of them—are our children.

Lisa Wilde
Brooklyn, NY
Nov. 30, 2104

ACKNOWLEDGEMENTS

This book has been supported by many people. To paraphrase Rachel Naomi Remen, may your kindness come back to you a hundredfold.

Huge thanks to Wildcat students, staff and administration. The students' and school's success speaks for itself. Great thanks to Ron Tabano, Pat Wong, Luba Koziolkowski, Anthony Brown, Alex Martinez, Michael Steiner, and DFaye Anderson. Many of you appeared in these pages (thank you!) and have provided incredible support for my teaching and this project. Also, wonderful Wildcat graduates Jessica De La Rosa, Tyrell Bramble, Andres Vélez, Corelle Bayne, Infinite Cubia and Matthew Shields provided their work, gave me their time, and gave much inspiration.

Big thanks to Joe Biel and Microcosm Publishing for having the belief in this project, and their vision of a "bookish" future. Deep thanks to Joanna Herman who was there at the conception of Yo, Miss. This project would not have existed without her unfailing guidance in every way—artistic and personal. Much thanks to Myra Goldberg, who had the faith that I could teach a workshop to graduate students.

Unlimited thanks to Anne DeMarinis, talented and smart designer that she is, who spent hours and hours with me helping my analogue brain switch ever-so-slightly to digital requirements of making a graphic novel. In addition, she designed my incredibly good looking website.

Loving thanks to my siblings Wallis Wilde-Menozzi, Hal Wilde and Alex Wilde, who show their belief in their little sister in so many ways, which helped and moved me.

Profound thanks to my husband's family including Holly Wolfe and Susan Murray. I can't imagine having any better in-laws than the Hellermann clan. Many, many thanks to friends Sarah Marques, Phyllis Trout, Mary Dore, Margot Edman for your friendship, feedback and support.

Unlimited thanks to everyone else who read, commented, gave me advice and all other forms of assistance. Unquantifiable thanks to Mark and Noah for being who they are.

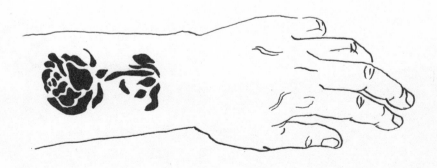

SUBSCRIBE TO EVERYTHING

Do you love what Microcosm publishes?

Do you want us to publish more great stuff?

Would you like to receive each new title as it's published?

Subscribe as a BFF to our new titles and we'll mail them all to you as they are released!

$10-30/mo, pay what you can afford. Include your t-shirt size and month/date of birthday for a possible surprise! Subscription begins the month after it is purchased.

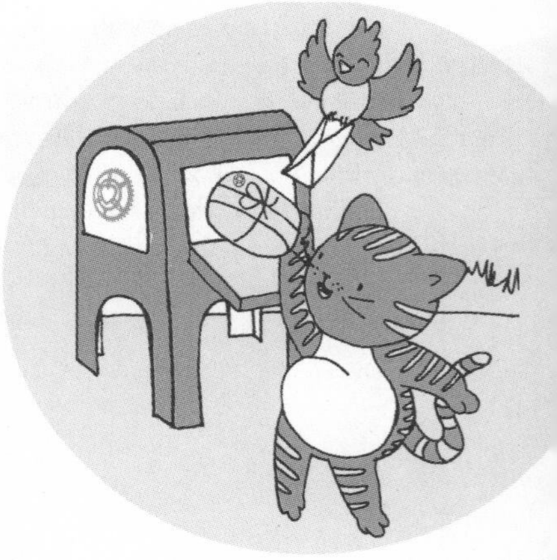

microcosmpublishing.com/bff

...AND HELP US GROW YOUR SMALL WORLD!